Religious Ethics

Religious Ethics

Meaning and Method

William Schweiker and David A. Clairmont

WILEY Blackwell

This edition first published 2020
© 2020 William Schweiker and David A. Clairmont

The right of William Schweiker and David A. Clairmont to be identified as the authors of this work has been asserted in accordance with law.

Registered Offices
John Wiley & Sons, Inc., 111 River Street, Hoboken, NJ 07030, USA
John Wiley & Sons Ltd, The Atrium, Southern Gate, Chichester, West Sussex, PO19 8SQ, UK

Editorial Office
The Atrium, Southern Gate, Chichester, West Sussex, PO19 8SQ, UK

For details of our global editorial offices, customer services, and more information about Wiley products visit us at www.wiley.com.

Wiley also publishes its books in a variety of electronic formats and by print-on-demand. Some content that appears in standard print versions of this book may not be available in other formats.

Library of Congress Cataloging-in-Publication Data
Names: Schweiker, William, author. Clairmont, David A.
Title: Religious ethics : meaning and method / William Schweiker, David A. Clairmont.
Description: First edition. | Hoboken : Wiley, 2019. | Includes bibliographical references and index.
Identifiers: LCCN 2019032067 (print) | LCCN 2019032068 (ebook) | ISBN 9781405198578 (paperback) | ISBN 9781118610244 (adobe pdf) | ISBN 9781118610251 (epub)
Subjects: LCSH: Religious ethics.
Classification: LCC BJ1188 .S38 2019 (print) | LCC BJ1188 (ebook) | DDC 205–dc23
LC record available at https://lccn.loc.gov/2019032067
LC ebook record available at https://lccn.loc.gov/2019032068

Cover Design: Wiley
Cover Image: © jc_design/Getty Images

Set in 10/12pt Warnock by SPi Global, Pondicherry, India

Printed and bound by CPI Group (UK) Ltd, Croydon, CR0 4YY

10 9 8 7 6 5 4 3 2 1

Contents

Preface

This book is the result of years of collaboration between the authors on work in religious ethics. The collaboration started when we published the first edition of *The Blackwell Companion to Religious Ethics* with William Schweiker as editor and David A. Clairmont as project assistant. Through the encouragement of our publisher, Rebecca Harkin of Wiley-Blackwell, it was decided that a basic text was needed on the meaning and method of religious ethics, and, further, a book that could be used in connection with the *Companion* at several levels of academic instruction: undergraduate, graduate, and in the training of religious leaders.[1] *Religious Ethics: Meaning and Method* is that book. It elaborates and expounds the account of religious ethics developed by William Schweiker as a multidimensional theory of the religious and moral life for our global times.

This history of collaboration and also the specific task of *Religious Ethics: Meaning and Method* determined its scope and purpose. In the chapters that follow *we do not survey* the moral teachings of the world's religions, *we cannot address* every issue in moral theory, and we respond to practical moral problems *only in an exemplary manner*. Each chapter engages in a comparison of Christian thought in relation to one other religious tradition. The reason for this strategy is threefold: first, Christian ethical thinking is what we know best and it is wise to play to one's strengths; second, most of the courses that will, it is hoped, use this book and the scholars who engage our arguments will have at least passing knowledge of Christian faith; and, third, with the roughly 2.3 billion Christians worldwide, it is increasingly important for Christians to understand the analogies between their moral convictions and those of other religions and for others to see the analogues to their convictions in Christian

---

1 We are happy to note that an expanded three-volume edition of *The Companion to Religious Ethics* is under production with the title *The Encyclopedia of Religious Ethics* (edited by William Schweiker, Maria Antonaccio, Elizabeth Bucar, and David A. Clairmont) and will be a valuable additional resource for this book.

ethics. However, our purpose in this book is not to compare Christian moral thought with every other religion.[2]

Some readers will say this book is so deeply Christian and Western that it cannot claim to speak so confidently about *religious ethics* as a discipline and practice. Granted, we are Christians (WS: Protestant; DC: Catholic) and we are Western as well as white, male, fathers, and university professors. What is more, we have decidedly different emphases in our work, Schweiker in moral theory and Clairmont in the history of religions. While acknowledging our sociocultural, academic, and religious locations, we plead that our readers examine the book's argument rather than its authors' lives. As noted previously, the reader will find that we engage the Christian tradition in every chapter of the book as a kind of reference point for developing the argument. Christian patterns of thought, argument, and practice are not assumed a priori to be necessarily true or good and right even though they provide a control measure in relation to which we can isolate similarities and difference among traditions. We would be delighted if someone were to test and develop our argument with reference to Buddhism, Judaism, African traditional religions, or any number of other longstanding religious and cultural traditions. Our hope, then, is that biographical facts about us and the acknowledgment of the areas and limits of our scholarly expertise do not deter the reader from wrestling with this book in order to see what contribution it brings to religious ethics.

William Schweiker,
The University of Chicago
David A. Clairmont,
University of Notre Dame

---

2 In seeking to provide an introduction to the study of religious ethics, we are mindful that readers are often introduced to the field either through a primarily philosophical lens (for example, in the widely used introductions such as William Frankena's *Ethics* or James Rachels' and Stuart Rachels' *The Elements of Moral Philosophy*) or through recent works in comparative religious ethics that focus on detailed comparisons of two thinkers from to different religious traditions (such as Lee Yearley's *Mencius and Aquinas* or Elizabeth Bucar's *Creative Conformity*, to give just two examples). Although we have benefited greatly from these approaches, in offering a more general introduction to religious ethics across a number of religious traditions, we argue that the combination of scope and depth of earlier studies (for example, David Little and Sumner Twiss' *Comparative Religious Ethics*) still have much to commend them and that a new effort in this mode is both appropriate and necessary for our global age.

Acknowledgments

Writing together is rewarding and challenging, and it takes a great deal of support from individuals and institutions for the authors to bring any project to a happy conclusion. This was certainly the case for the two of us. Rightly, then, we would like to thank three institutions for the unwavering support of this project: Wiley Publishers, the University of Chicago, and the University of Notre Dame. Rebecca Harkin at Wiley encouraged us to begin this project and waited patiently through many delays. We are profoundly grateful to have enjoyed her support and good guidance throughout the writing of this book. At the University of Chicago and the University of Notre Dame we received support and encouragement from our respective colleagues, chairs, and deans as we worked on this project in addition to our other research, teaching, and administrative duties. Without these institutions nothing much of what we do as scholars and teachers would be possible.

At Chicago, we would like to thank Deans Margaret Mitchell, Richard Rosengarten, Laurie Zoloth, and David Nirenberg. At Notre Dame, we would like to thank John Cavadini, Matthew Ashley, and Timothy Matovina for their support in their roles as chair of the Theology Department. We would also like to thank the Institute for Scholarship in the Liberal Arts, College of Arts and Letters, University of Notre Dame for a grant that made possible production of an index for this book. Our gratitude to all the editoral and production staff at Wiley who worked with us patiently throughout the project: Catriona King, Juliet Booker, Liz Wingett, Shyamala Venkateswaran, and Sandra Kerka.

The following colleagues and students at Chicago, Notre Dame, and other institutions offered us critiques, patient conversation, and their own research about the many themes and traditions explored in this book which advanced our work in many ways: Maria Antonaccio, Ebenezer Akesseh, Elizabeth Bucar, Michael Connors, Kristine Culp, Sarah Fredericks, Kevin Hector, Dwight Hopkins, Markus Hüfner, Jann Ingmire, Kevin Jung, Emmanuel Katongole, David Lantigua, Herbert Lin, Emery Longanga, Terence Martin, Jean-Luc Marion, Gerald McKenny, Richard Miller, Elena Namli, Paulinus Odozor, Douglas Ottati,

Willemien Otten, Jean Porter, Cheron Price, Bharat Ranganthan, Susan Schreiner, Heike Springhart, Jeffrey Stackert, Per Sundman, Günter Thomas, Elochukwu Uzukwu, Michael Welker, Todd Whitmore, and Charles Wilson. A special word of thanks to Maria Antonaccio and Elizabeth Bucar, our coeditors on the Wiley *Encyclopedia of Religious Ethics*, who were working with us on this much larger undertaking as we were also trying to bring this book to a successful resolution, and to Michelle Clairmont and Jann Ingmire for their patient support of this project. We owe a debt of gratitude to our research assistants, Willa Lengyel-Swenson, David Barr, Sara-Jo Swiatek, and Blaize Gervais.

Finally, we would like to thank our families whose examples prompted us to consider the ethical dimensions of religions. When two people write a book together, they discover not only interesting areas of agreement and disagreement about the research material but also a good deal about each other: where they came from, what they value, and who sustains them. We dedicate this book to the next generation of Schweikers and Clairmonts – particularly to Paul Schweiker and his wife Evelyn Buehler Schweiker and to Joseph and John Clairmont – in the hopes that they may pick up and advance in ways decidedly their own the work of respect and understanding in a wounded world.

Note on Sources, Dates, and Language Conventions

The reader will notice that this book draws from a wide variety of sources for its study of religious ethics, from primary texts of the religious traditions examined here to the work of philosophers, anthropologists, and historians of global religious cultures. We have attempted to standardize, as best we are able, the presentation of this material, which often follows a variety of conventions depending on generally accepted practices in different scholarly fields. Our goal is to follow standard scholarly conventions in the disciplines we consult wherever possible, but in some cases we have needed to make judgments for the sake of uniform presentation of the material. In these cases, we have attempted to follow the conventions employed by the contributors to *The Blackwell Companion to Religious Ethics* (Wiley-Blackwell, 2005), the revision and expansion of which this book is intended to accompany.

On the dating of historical figures, texts, and major events, we have followed standard reference works in the field such as the *Encyclopedia of Religion* (ER)[1] or the *Stanford Encyclopedia of Philosophy* (SEP).[2] Where figures are not listed in those works, we have followed the dating given in the scholarly works from which our references were drawn. In biblical translations, we follow the New Revised Standard Version (NRSV),[3] and in translations of the *Qurʾān*, we follow *The Study Quran: A New Translation and Commentary*.[4] We have followed

1 Jones, L. (ed.) (2005). *Encyclopedia of Religion*, vol. 15, 2eDetroit: Macmillan.
2 https://plato.stanford.edu (accessed 22 June 2019).
3 Coogan, M.D. and Brettler, M.Z., Newsom, C.A., and Perkins, P. (eds.) (2001). *The New Oxford Annotated Bible with the Apocrypha*, 3e, New Revised Standard Version. New York and Oxford: Oxford University Press.
4 Nasr, S.H., Dagli, C.K., Dakake, M.M. et al. (eds.) (2015). *The Study Quran: A New Translation and Commentary*. New York: HarperCollins. On technical terms in Islamic law, philosophy, and theology, we have consulted Glassé, C. (ed.) (2008). *The New Encyclopedia of Islam*, 3e. Lanham: Rowman and Littlefield. For rendering diacritic marks for Arabic terms, we have used as a guideline the IJMES Word List published by the *International Journal of Middle East Studies* which may be found at: https://www.cambridge.org/core/services/aop-file-manager/file/57d9042c58fb76353506c8e7/IJMES-WordList.pdf (accessed March 6, 2020).

pinyin method for rendering romanized versions of Chinese characters, guided by suitable reference works.[5] Although most of the material for the Igbo language is found in our sources, we have consulted the *Encyclopedia of African Religion*[6] in certain cases, aided by Michael J.C. Echeruo's *Igbo-English Dictionary*.[7] Our references to Penobscot terms follow those used in our sources, although there is one standard resource available for the two main Abenaki dialects.[8] In some cases, where complete scholarly translations are not available (for example, in the ongoing project on the Mahābhārata), we have noted in the text the translation used.

---

5 Here especially, we have benefited from Leese, D. (ed.) (2009). *Brill's Encyclopedia of China*. Leiden and Boston: Brill.

6 Asante, M.K. and Mazama, A. (ed.) (2008). *Encyclopedia of African Religion*, vols. 2. Thousand Oaks and London: SAGE Publications.

7 Echeruo, M.J.C. (1998). *Igbo-English Dictionary: A Comprehensive Dictionary of the Igbo Language, with an English-Igbo Index*. New Haven and London: Yale University Press.

8 Day, G.M. (1995–1996). *Western Abenaki Dictionary. Vol. 1: Abenaki-English; Vol. 2: English-Abenaki*. Canadian Ethnology Service Paper No. 128–129. Hull, Quebec: Canadian Museum of Civilization.

Introduction

In the religions you are to discover religion.[1]
— Friedrich Schleiermacher

The world's religions fuel the imagination and enflame human hearts. Whereas in places like Europe religion seems in retreat, there is massive growth within religions around the world. Likewise, religiously driven violence is ablaze in many nations but so too the attack on modern science. Not surprisingly, scholars, religious and political leaders, and many other people of good will, both those affiliated with or not affiliated with religious traditions, are interested in the ethical wisdom of specific religious traditions and how that wisdom interacts with and is comparable, or not, to the wisdom of other traditions. Are there ways to understand, compare, assess, and draw ethical wisdom from the religions to meet the challenges they put to this generation? This book is written for scholars, students, and, in fact, anyone interested in thinking ethically by drawing on the resources of the world's religions

More specifically, the following chapters present an account of religious ethics that defines the *meaning* of the field and also propose a *method* best suited for it. Although the book's argument is developed through comparisons between religious traditions, "religious ethics," as a discipline and field, is not limited to comparative religious and ethical reflection even if, we believe, it must include comparison within the scope of its work. In this respect, the method and meaning of religious ethics as we present it are apt for, say, Muslim, Hindu, or Jewish ethics as much as for Buddhist–Christian comparative ethics.

We are mindful of the high demands and daunting challenges of writing a book like this one. The demands and challenges facing us are well known. The religions bear untold treasures of moral wisdom, that is, practical guidance

---

1 Schleiermacher, F. (1988 [1799]). *On Religion: Speeches to Its Cultured Despisers* (trans. R. Crouter), 190. Cambridge: Cambridge University Press.

Religious Ethics: Meaning and Method, First Edition. William Schweiker and David A. Clairmont.
© 2020 William Schweiker and David A. Clairmont. Published 2020 by John Wiley & Sons Ltd.

about how to live justly and well that include beliefs and practices about the nature of human existence, social life, what is good and righteous, and reality itself. The deposit of those beliefs and practices that transmit moral wisdom is a religion's "morality." In our understanding, "ethics," religious or philosophical, is critical "metareflection" on the actual beliefs, values, practices, rituals, and social structures that inform and guide human conduct, that is, a religion's or a society's "morality." Ethics, religious or philosophical, seeks to articulate the meaning and assess the truth of moral convictions. Sometimes an ethics will criticize and invalidate moral convictions; sometimes it will revise them; sometimes an ethics will endorse inherited morality as the proper way to conduct personal and social life.

However, the distinction between morality (morals, moral convictions, moral wisdom, etc.) and ethics, as a form of metareflection, is more contentious than might first appear and will be addressed in the book. Suffice it to say that there is a good deal of suspicion in the Western academy about the idea of outlining an approach to any field of study, including "ethics." Within ethics itself, many thinkers remain within the resources of one tradition and claim its uniqueness and incomparability with other religious traditions, say, Hindu ethics or Islamic ethics. Other thinkers apply the categories of Western moral philosophy to religious resources. For instance, one might argue (and some have) that "Buddhist ethics" can be seen as a kind of virtue ethics defined in the Western world by the Greek philosopher Aristotle (384–322 BCE). We have worked against currents in scholarship in order to develop an approach to "ethics" *from within* the religions in order to explain the meaning and method of religious ethics in a way that can show the similarities and differences, the analogies, on moral matters among the religions. Our purpose is not to pit religious ethics against moral philosophy. It is to draw attention to the nuance and complexity of religious accounts of the moral life that tend to be neglected or insufficiently appreciated when discussion of morality is reduced to one specific philosophical language, method, or theory.

Global political events as well as ongoing debates about the place of religion in societies around the world have prompted people to reevaluate how best to study the moral teachings of the world's religions. Nowadays it seems obvious that societies in different ways and to different degrees are marked by a diversity of religious beliefs, institutions, practices, and adherents. In the present "postsecular" situation, as it is often called, the challenge is how best to live by the deepest moral insights of the religions and also how to understand, assess, and compare the moral teachings and practices of the religions in a world marked by a diversity of religious and moral traditions. Our approach to the meaning and method of religious ethics is, in this light, decidedly postsecular.

Sadly, too often the complexity of religious life is reduced by scholars, political figures, and the media to one or another dimension of human behavior (economic, social, political, psychological, aesthetic). Among thinkers interested in ethics, there has been a drive to interpret the religions from the perspective of Western philosophical ethics. We are told, for instance, that Christian ethics modifies elements of a Kantian ethics of duty. Other thinkers interpret the religions in terms of narratives, ideas about the Good, or virtue ethics. Admittedly, there are good reasons for interpreting Christian moral beliefs and practices in philosophical terms. The early Church Fathers during the so-called Patristic period (100–400 CE) often insisted on the harmony between Christian convictions and Plato's (429–347 BCE) conception of the Good, Stoic ideas about natural law, and philosophical accounts of human well-being (*eudaimonia*), especially widespread teachings about the virtues. In the mix, philosophical as well as biblical ideas were transformed in distinctive and decisive ways. Christians drew on and transformed Greek and Roman ideas in different ways than Muslim or Jewish thinkers did. So, the same blending of religious and "philosophical" reasoning about the moral life can be found in medieval Islam and Judaism even as Buddhism, to cite another example, drew on the philosophical resources of various Indian schools of thought, which themselves gave rise to what is now called Hinduism.

The fact that religious traditions are often marked by the incorporation of nonreligious forms of moral theory, concepts (e.g. virtue), accounts of justice, and ideas about goodness is the deep historical background to the emergence of "religious ethics" in the Western Academy. Over the last two centuries or so there emerged the study and comparison of religious moral teaching through the interpretative lens of philosophical forms of ethics. The grounds of comparison, that is, what ideas made comparison possible and fruitful, have often been the fact that the world's religions teach some version of the "Golden Rule" ("do unto others as you would have done unto you"). In Hinduism, the *Laws of Manu* (*Mānava-Dharmaśāstra*) II.161 states: "Though deeply hurt, let him never use cutting words, show hostility to others in thought or deed, or use aberrant language that would alarm people."[2] To cite another example, *The Analects* (*Lunyu*), a basic Confucian text, reads at 12:2: "'Go out into the world as if greeting a magnificent guest. Use the people as if offering a magnificent sacrifice. And never impose on others what you would not choose for yourself. Then, there will be no resentment among the people or the great families.'"[3] Further, the religions praise similar virtues and traits of character, like humility, courage, and compassion. Principles like the Golden Rule and various virtues provide the means to isolate commonalities and note the differences among the moral teachings of religions. The need to find analogies among religious traditions, that is, similarities within differences, is basic to this book. Yet we do so not only in terms of shared principles or virtues, but with respect to

---

2 Olivelle, P. (2005). *Manu's Code of Law: A Critical Edition and Translation of the Mānava-Dharmaśāstra*, 103. New York: Oxford University Press.
3 Confucius. (1998). *The Analects* (trans. D. Hinton), 127. New York: Counterpoint.

features of moral existence and dimensions of ethics that come to light once the resources of the religions help to shape a moral theory and ethics. We seek to develop the meaning and method of religious ethics *from within* religious resources mindful of the fact that those same resources bear through time the interrelation of multiple sources of moral wisdom.

In this light, religious ethics is (i) careful and critical reflection on the moral beliefs and practices of the religions in order (ii) to orient and guide the moral lives of people. However, too often work in "religious ethics," as a scholarly discipline, takes the actual religious beliefs and practices as merely the "data" for analysis and interpretation through the categories of Western moral philosophy. To be sure, we have not ignored philosophical theories, quite the contrary. Although there is some warrant for a philosophical strategy of defining the task of religious ethics, it neglects to ask the two orienting questions of this book: what do the religions *contribute* to moral theory, and, further, can one develop an approach to religious ethics *from within* the resources of the religions themselves?

Given those two questions, this book involves a hermeneutical or interpretive circle. On the one hand, we use the resources of the religions in order to develop the *method* of religious ethics, that is, how one can and should think about and evaluate the moral beliefs and practices of a religion. On the other hand, the method is applied to those same religious resources in order to clarify the *meaning* of religious ethics. The argument is admittedly circular. It draws on the religions in order to develop an account of religious ethics that uses religious resources. Our hunch is that some will find this "circularity" bothersome even though it is actually part of every kind of ethics.[4] The resources of ethics, even those that fasten on divine revelations and commands, are actual human beliefs about good and right actions and relations about which an ethics seeks to understand and to give orientation. Stated otherwise, we are involved in ethical thinking as living agents in the very task of developing an ethics to guide our lives. Yet, this "circularity," one that is banished in the hard sciences and also systems of deductive logic, is not vicious. It is, we hope to show, productive of new insight about how people can and should live. In any case, we start with the received wisdom of the religions, admit that it is credible evidence for developing a theory of ethics, and then submit it to scrutiny in order to develop that theory.

So, there are two deep convictions that undergird the writing of this book and that the book seeks to explain and to sustain. First, we are convinced that

---

4 There are of course Western forms of philosophical ethics that attribute credible claims to the religions. This was Aristotle's point in using the so-called "endoxic" (credible opinions) method, that is, to draw from prevalent moral ideas in a society and then seek to submit them to analysis in a systematic way. It was also Immanuel Kant's point when he noted, in *The Groundwork for the Metaphysic of Morals*, that he would begin the search for the supreme principle of morality by exploring commonly held moral ideas. Kant, I. (1997 [1785]). *Groundwork of the Metaphysics of Morals* (ed. M. Gregor and intro. C.M. Korsgaard). Cambridge: Cambridge University Press.

the religions provide resources for thinking about the moral life that are as complex, subtle, and persuasive as standard options in Western moral philosophy. No doubt our philosophical colleagues will find that to be an audacious claim, but one thing that it has meant is the need to develop the structure and coherence of religious ethics on its own terms. And that is why, again, this book will seem odd to some readers. In more technical terms, the book is an exercise in hermeneutical reconstruction of "religious ethics." We draw on the symbolic, textual, and ritual resources of religions in order to articulate the structure of religious ethics around basic tensions that characterize religious and human life. Culling insights and ideas from the religions we present the *meaning* and *method* of religious ethics in order to articulate the insights and problems in actual religions and also to provide some guidance for reflection on living a religious and moral life.

Our first conviction, then, is that the religions developed over millennia and in every culture on this planet have resources for deepening one's thinking about life and how one can and ought to live. This does not mean that this book is antiphilosophical. On the contrary, we explore philosophical problems, engage philosophical theories, and treat the works of philosophers. The point is that we explore, engage, and treat philosophical questions from *within* the resources of the religions in order to show the depth and subtlety of religious visions of the moral life. Our first conviction is meant to counter the trend to make the moral insight of the religions mere instances of some general theory of ethics and falsely to harmonize religious outlooks.

A second conviction cuts in the other direction, as it were. It aims to counter another trend in the academy and global social life. This trend is the belief that religious outlooks are so utterly unique that they cannot be compared. On that line of reasoning there are no similarities among religious outlooks and therefore religious ethics must always and only work within a specific tradition, say "Hindu ethics." Widespread in numerous places around the world, the idea is that one cannot pass moral judgment on other moral outlooks, religious or not, because those outlooks can be understood and rightly evaluated only on their own terms. This is potentially a form of moral relativism: the claim that there are no valid general moral ideas or beliefs that can be used to judge moral outlooks because every moral belief about what is good, bad, justice, unjust, etc. is *relative* to some people's moral outlook. The human world is then a bewildering hodgepodge of incommensurable moral and cultural value systems.[5] This also has the added effect of undermining the very religious impulse exhibited in the religions themselves that have prompted religions to engage with philosophers and with members of other religious communities. If scholars,

---

5 For an incisive critique of relativism see Midgley, M. (1993). *Can't We Make Moral Judgments?* London: Palgrave Macmillan.

religious leaders, and individuals cannot find possible ways to compare traditions and to learn from others about what makes a good, just, and right human life, then our supposed uniqueness is merely fodder for social conflict. Moral relativism may seem to be a comforting and consoling outlook but only until the point where some community has the power to dominate another under the idea that "might makes right." Relativism has the added effect of undermining the religious impulse exhibited in the religions themselves that has prompted them to engage with members of other communities about moral matters.

Religious Ethics: Meaning and Method seeks to provide readers with an account of religious ethical thinking and acting in the world. The religions, on our account, seek to articulate the structure of moral existence attuned to tensions that define human life and to orient life within those tensions. "Religious ethics" denotes a way of doing ethics in terms of the profound insights of the religions. It explains, assesses, and deploys the wisdom of the religions in order to show that, ironically, the religions explain us. The position presented in the following chapters provides then a way to interpret and to understand how the religions provide distinctive responses to the tensions that constitute the meaning and structure of human life when seen through the resources of the religions. It is appropriate, then, that we turn next to explain in more detail the "task" of religious ethics and therefore to clarify basic concepts as well as the structure of this book.

1

The Task of Religious Ethics

> *The Master said: 'The noble-minded may not always be Humane. But the small-minded–they never are.'*
> — Confucius, *The Analects* 14.6.

> *By contrast, the fruit of the Spirit is love, joy, peace, patience, kindness, generosity, faithfulness, gentleness, and self-control. There is no law against such things.*
> — St. Paul, Gal 5:22–23

Religion and Moral Convictions

The world's religions have diverse beliefs, practices, stories, and teachings as well as sages, saints, and saviors to help guide adherents in how they should live. Although one of the so-called Ten Commandments dictates "You shall not murder," other religions express the prohibition of murder through stories or prescriptions about helping others, even loving one's enemies. And although some religions ground their moral beliefs in the command of God, still other religions – and sometimes the same religions – speak about the ability of human reason or sensibilities to apprehend the demands of justice, or they look to the lives of saints and sages as the embodiment of moral perfection. The various ways to instruct and empower proper conduct constitute the "moral convictions" of a religion because in different ways each religion's morality is about right and just actions and the kinds of persons and communities one should strive to become in relation to other persons, other communities, and the divine or the sacred.

Often moral convictions among the religions are surprisingly similar. Religious people praise unselfish behavior, have codes of sexual conduct and fidelity, treasure the bonds of friendship, share beliefs about what is just and right in social life, and they even hold remarkably similar ideas about human

Religious Ethics: Meaning and Method, First Edition. William Schweiker and David A. Clairmont.
© 2020 William Schweiker and David A. Clairmont. Published 2020 by John Wiley & Sons Ltd.

flourishing and its relation to right conduct and to virtuous character. But the outlooks of the religions on the proper conduct of human life can be surprisingly different as well. Consider the examples cited at the head of this chapter. Confucius (Kong Qiu or Kong Fuzi ["Master Kong"], 551–479 BCE) related Goodness to the life of the noble-minded one. In order to be a noble-minded one, one must abide by rituals performed rightly and in the right circumstances and also follow the laws under heaven, as Confucius called them. St. Paul, the great early Christian thinker (c. 5–67 CE) from Tarsus in Cilicia, composed letters, like the one cited previously, that make up a good portion of the New Testament in the Christian Bible. (The other portion of the Christian Bible is called the "Old Testament.") According to Paul, the life of faith is lived in the power of the "Spirit" and it has no law but is manifest in love, peace, joy, and other fruits, as he calls them. Separated by time and space, these religious sages are divided not only by how they think about God or heaven but also by how they believe human life should be properly lived. The conduct of life is connected to law or to the divine spirit, abides by ritual requirements or it manifests the spirit's fruits, and it is lived under heaven or in the power of Jesus Christ's spirit.

The examples of religious similarity and difference, that is, the analogies among the religions, could be endlessly multiplied. If one casts a glance at the teachings of Buddhism in its many forms, Islam and Judaism in their many forms, and also what we call Hinduism or Christianity (again, in their many forms), ideas about how one ought to live and the practices that characterize that life would be strikingly – and shockingly – different. The devout Buddhist seeks Enlightenment and the dissolution of the "self" from its desires in order to escape *saṃsāra*, the round of suffering and rebirth. A pious Muslim, conversely, expects to stand alone before Allah on the Day of Judgment in order to account for his or her actions. And yet, again, there are similarities in moral convictions as well. The Buddhist and the Muslim agree that compassion and mercy are at the core of the moral life. A Jew and a Hindu are committed to the right ordering of social life and thus some idea about moral order and justice even while they differ of what that "order" is and what counts as a just social order. What is more, the striking similarities and profound differences in religious outlooks become more difficult to summarize when one includes so-called indigenous or native religions. Some indigenous religions involve practices of divination or the interpretation of dreams by a *shaman* for the discernment of how to live. For instance, among the Candomblé, a Brazilian African religion, the gods descend on priests and priestess during ritual dances in order to teach and protect worshippers in the conduct of their daily lives.

How are we to understand let alone assess religious outlooks on life? What resources might the religions contribute to ethical reflection? What are we to make of the amazing similarities but also befuddling differences among the religions in their teachings and practices about how one ought to live? How might the study of the religions and their moral convictions about human personal and social conduct actually enrich ethical thinking in a global age when the religions are interacting and shaping human existence around the world? How is it even possible to study, compare, and assess moral convictions? Are there constitutive features of human existence that can be analyzed and understood through the interpretations of a religion's patterns of thought and practice?[1] The study of religious ethics seeks to answer those questions for scholars, students, religious adherents, and anyone concerned about the moral life.

The similarities and differences among the moral convictions of the religions are vexing, to say the least. This is especially true in our global times when people from different religions interact, sometimes violently but mostly peacefully, and people must find common solutions to shared human problems, like, say, the environmental crisis, economic injustice, or ethnic violence (to name just a few). The root question, then, is how to develop an approach to religious ethics.

The Aims of This Book

This book presents an approach to "religious ethics," and it aims to do three things. The first aim of the chapters that follow is to define the field of "religious ethics" as a discipline of inquiry of interest to anyone who asks about the relation between "religion" and "morality." Although "religious ethics" is a relatively old idea, as we briefly explore in this chapter, it is still in need of clarity and definition. The book will present a definition of and approach to religious ethics – its *meaning* (definition) and *method* (approach) – that makes sense of the similarities and differences among the religions in their teaching and practices about the conduct of human life.

Second, the book is *not* a survey of the world's religions about their moral teachings. There are fine volumes that provide that information.[2] As noted in the Introduction, too often the world's religions are subjected to forms of

---

1 Among moral philosophers, it was Immanuel Kant who most forcibly raised the question of the *possibility* of a supreme principle of morality and then sought to find its grounds in reason itself. Our tactic is more anthropological and hermeneutical. In that respect, our argument is less foundationalist than Kant's, without, we hope, loss of scope. We contend that this approach is warranted by the religions themselves and this book seeks to make good on that claim. For a related but different approach, see Miller, R.M. (2016). *Friends and Other Strangers: Studies in Religious, Ethics, and Culture*. New York: Columbia University Press. Other works by the author of this book can be found in the bibliography.
2 In fact, cross-reference to *The Blackwell Companion to Religious Ethics* (edited by the authors of this book with an expanded edition in the works) will be possible throughout the following chapters in order to provide historical background to the work of this volume, and also the forthcoming *Encyclopedia of Religious Ethics*.

thought – say, psychological, philosophical, or sociological ones (to name a few) – developed by scholars so that the religion studied does not contribute to thinking about, say, psychology, philosophy, or sociology.[3] The religions are "data" for theories and methods of explanation, including ethics. The religions thereby do not provide the means and resources to develop these theories, including ethics.

This book significantly alters that standard approach and with surprising results. The various tensions and perplexities found in religious texts – say, the *aporia* between law and Spirit in St. Paul's writings or between the Good and the noble-minded ones in Confucius' – help us to develop an approach to religious ethics *from within* religious thought and life. A robust religious ethics, we argue, entails five interacting dimensions of thought that arise out of distinct but related tensions, *aporias* or perplexities, that religious texts and practices deploy in order to illuminate the structure of human existence. More details on those dimensions will be noted later because they structure this book as a whole. The novelty of this approach, we believe, is that it demonstrates how the religions provide resources for the development of normative ethics for how one can and ought to orient the conduct of life.

By engaging the religions and developing an account of religious ethics, the third purpose of this book is to enable people in our global times to think intelligently and clearly about religious outlooks on life and how they can and may be lived in ways that respect and enhance, rather the demean and destroy, the integrity of life.[4] We admit that the book poses a challenge to many religious adherents who believe that their religious traditions possess every moral truth and that there is, accordingly, little to learn from others. The real moral challenge for those people is how to be, say, an authentic Christian, a devoted Hindu, or an enlightened Buddhist. Learning from others is beside the point; the real task is to live by the truth of one's own religious and moral convictions. Further, the aim of this book to provide a way to address moral problems will be rejected by adherents and scholars who insist that comparison among the

---

3 The major contributors to this work are well known: Sigmund Freud, Friedrich Nietzsche, Karl Marx, Émile Durkheim, and the like. We cannot engage extensively these figures in this volume.
4 "The Integrity of Life" is our concept for the encompassing moral and religious good. Our task in this book is not to develop that idea and so we use it simply as a place-holder for the highest good, or, as we call it later, a "transcendent good." It is given different, if analogous, symbolic and narrative expression in the religions: God(s), spirits, *nirvāṇa*, *ātman*, etc. The task of religious ethical thinking is to correlate critically this concept with those symbolic and narrative forms. Likewise the two most basic norms for responsible action are the "respect for" and "enhancement of" the integrity of life. As will be shown, the religions are keen to clarify the domain of noninterference and care for others (respect) as well as actions meant to better others' lives (enhancement). For a brief but substantive account of "the integrity of life" as well as respect and enhancement see Klemm, D.E. and Schweiker, W. (2008). *Religion and the Human Future: An Essay on Theological Humanism*. Oxford: Blackwell.

religions is impossible and can add nothing to ethics. Their claim is that religious worldviews and convictions are so utterly different that there is no possibility of comparing them. It is not just that one's own tradition has all truth; it is also the case, they claim, that there is no vantage point and form of thought adequately to compare religious and moral convictions in order to develop something called "religious ethics." For both of these outlooks, then, the third aim of this book is impossible. Comparison is either morally unnecessary or it is ethically impossible.[5]

We are convinced that those two prevalent and widespread ways of rejecting the idea of "religious ethics" are neither true of the religions themselves nor a proper account of moral thinking, religious or nonreligious. One thing discovered in the following chapters is that quite often a religious community or thinker shows how their community can and must learn moral truths from the outsider, and, what is more, that human beings can and do have some basic moral knowledge, whether innate or learned. The first objection to the aims of this book is then incorrect with respect to the religions themselves, at least about moral matters.[6] The religions are not only extraordinarily different in their moral convictions, they are also and often surprisingly similar in their teachings. If that is so, then it must be possible to isolate similarities and differences and thereby to show the analogies among the religious moral convictions. The *method* we develop in this book unfolds the analogical structure of religious ethics through five dimensions of reflection that arise from within religious ways of life in response to the perplexities of human existence. In this way, we take seriously the point about religious difference without succumbing to the idea that among the religions there is only difference.

There is one other reason to pursue the third aim of this book. All ethical thinking arises in response to problems and challenges about how human beings can and should live. Certainly, in the present age one problem and one challenge is to develop ways of being religious that escape the cycles of misunderstanding and violence too often seen among religious people. At this level, the book seeks, perhaps with some audacity, to intervene into religious life in the name of responsible moral convictions. The book aims to enable the reader to see the various ways to live within and among religions and thus to make judgments about which ways are most responsible, most humane, and most

---

5 On this question see the typology of reasons for comparison (facilitative, persuasive, dialectical, reconstructive, and transformative) in Clairmont, D.A. (2011). *Moral Struggle and Religious Ethics: On the Person as Classic in Comparative Theological Contexts*. Oxford: Wiley Blackwell.

6 No doubt there are grave and maybe insurmountable differences among the religious on questions of enlightenment or salvation ("soteriology") as well as the nature and identity of the religious community. Our point is simply that granting those differences there are still similarities enough on moral matters to back the work of religious ethics.

devout. In this way, we hope the book itself serves the purpose of moral education, the sharpening of moral perception, and also character development.

Providing an account of religious ethics with these three purposes in mind is a daunting task. Yet it is a task demanded by a global age when religious people interact in many ways around our shared planet. This chapter introduces the book by expanding on its three aims. We start – rightly – with some history.

Some History

The idea of "religion" and the discipline of "ethics" are products of Western thought. What sense, then, does it make to speak of "religious ethics" and how does that field of inquiry relate to the actual religions? As a discipline of thought, religious ethics must develop a form of reflection subtle enough to explore the religions themselves. In this light, the idea of religious ethics has a specific history.

In one respect, the idea of "religious ethics" is rather ancient. During the period of what has been called the "axial age" (800–200 BCE), thinkers around the world, in China, India, Persia, and the West, developed patterns of thought, including "monotheism" or belief in one God, as well as paths to enlightenment that included moral convictions.[7] In each case there were criticisms of accepted ways of thinking and acting and proposals for new modes of thought and action. The Greek philosopher Socrates (c. 469–399 BCE), for example, advanced ethical thinking by isolating basic moral standards and concepts but was condemned for supposedly corrupting the youth and creating new gods. Analogously, the great Hebrew prophets, like Isaiah (eighth century BCE), challenged traditional religious cult and ritual with the demands for justice, especially for the poor and the outcast. Siddhārtha Gautama (the Buddha or "Enlightened One" [c. 563–483 BCE]) taught, as explored in a later chapter of this book, the Four Noble Truths for attaining Enlightenment and that the path to *nirvāṇa* (the quality of having desire "extinguished" which would lead to liberation [*mokṣa*] from suffering [*duḥkha*]) included specifically moral traits and actions. In each of these cases, and others could be noted, the validity and meaning of moral convictions were tested and even revised from *within* a religion and its way of life. The axial breakthrough in these religions was both conceptual and ethical, a fact we will also see in some of the indigenous religious we will explore.

---

7 The idea of the "axial age" was developed by the German philosopher Karl Jaspers. For a brief comparison of "axial age" thinkers see Jaspers (1962). *Socrates, Buddha, Confucius, Jesus: The Paradigmatic Individuals*, (ed. H. Arendt; trans. R. Mannheim). New York: Harvest/HBJ Book. For a recent discussion see Bellah, R. (2011). *Religion in Human Evolution: From the Paleolithic to the Axial Age*. Cambridge, MA: Belknap Harvard University Press.

Thinking about, assessing, and applying religious and moral convictions to the conduct of human life continues throughout history. The rise of Islam and Islamic law (*shariʻa*), the development of early Christianity within the context of Judaism and the Roman Empire, and the advances of Jewish Rabbinic patterns of thought into the so-called Western Middle Ages each shows the vibrancy of religious and moral thinking and thus, in early form, "religious ethics." This continued and was intensified in the early modern period in the West by thinkers as diverse as Baruch Spinoza (1632–1677 CE), David Hume (1711–1776 CE), Immanuel Kant (1724–1804 CE), Joseph Butler (1692–1752 CE), and many others. The attempt by these "Enlightenment" thinkers was to show either the independence of morality from religion (Hume), the unity of religion and morality (Spinoza), or a complex relation of religion's dependence on morality (Kant) or the inverse (Butler). Further, with these developments in modern thought the question of how, if at all, to compare the moral convictions of the religions came into focus. This interest in religion was due to the realities of the wars of religion in Europe, expanding trade, colonial domination of peoples by Western powers, and growing fascination with the history of cultures.

The current situation of religious ethics in the Western academy draws on and expands this complex and at times troubling history. Here too there are important and exemplary events. In 1993 a Parliament of the World's Religions was held in Chicago, Illinois to commemorate the original parliament convened at the Colombian Exposition in Chicago 100 years earlier. Representatives of the many and different religions met at the 1993 Parliament: Buddhists, Sikhs, Muslims, Hindus, Druids, Christians, Jews, indigenous peoples, and many more. The purpose of the Parliament, which continues to meet every four years at locations around the world, was to enhance understanding and cooperation among religious people and leaders. Yet something distinctly important happened at the 1993 meeting. The delegates gathered in Chicago issued a "Declaration on Global Ethics" that was meant to show the common moral wisdom of the world's religions and the ways in which that wisdom could help address the many moral and political challenges facing people around the world. Although the "Declaration" rightly has its critics – including the authors of this book – and has been superseded by other concords and patterns of thought around the world, it was a sign of a pressing need in our global times. In a world of cultural and religious diversity, there is the need for ways to think about the moral challenges and possibilities that affect the whole planet and are shared by human communities. To undertake that task requires not only finding points of commonality among the religions but also developing patterns of thought to interpret and to analyze the moral teachings and practices of the religions. Again, that is the task of this book and so too religious ethics as a discipline.

It was hardly surprising that delegates from the world's religions eventually had to think about a common ethics. Religious and moral challenges are found everywhere and people have to encounter the beliefs and practices of others, violently or nonviolently. There are many shared, global problems that reach beyond the power of any one nation or culture to address: global climate change, worldwide poverty, diseases, war, genocide, human trafficking, and the like. It also seems that human beings have some shared aspirations and sentiments: the desire for dignity and happiness, beliefs about justice, feelings of sympathy for others, love of one's children and family, and also outrage at senseless violence and death. Yet although global moral thinking is needed, it is exceedingly difficult to do. The customs and practices of some religions seem almost incomprehensible to others. And, in fact, in every known human society the connection between religion and morality is deeply entangled and yet at times also strongly contested.

One can easily see why that is the case. For some people, in order to be a moral individual, that is, a responsible person, one must be religious because any moral standard of what is right or wrong has its source in, say, "God's will." The divine will is revealed in texts like the Ten Commandments of the Jewish and Christian Bibles or for Muslims in the *Qur'ān*. In order to have a just and peaceful society one must follow God's will and form a morally unified society. Other people believe the opposite. They note that many nonbelieving people are good and just, often in ways that are far more obviously virtuous than religious people. They note that imposing religious and moral beliefs on people leads to tyranny, inequality, and conflict rather than peace and justice. Morality, they contend, finds its source in human reason, the social life of people, or in beliefs about what is needed in social cooperation to achieve human flourishing. Let people be religious if they like, but morality, so this argument goes, has its own source and purpose.

The debate rages across the centuries and also across cultures and religions. Each side in this well-known debate casts a skeptical eye at the book in your hands. For the religious believer, the idea of "religious ethics," rather than, say, Hindu, Christian, or African ethics, would make no sense. There is only one true religion – one's own religion – and so ethics, if it is to be valid, must be based on this true religion. The nonreligious person could hardly imagine why one would need a book on "religious" ethics. The very idea of religious ethics is confused; one ought to drop religion from thinking about how we ought to live, that is, from ethics.

Mindful of these perspectives on "religious ethics," this book seeks another way. What is this different approach to "religious ethics?" To give it a perhaps too high-sounding name, it is a hermeneutical (or interpretive) and multidimensional method of religious ethics. The method interprets and draws on the resources of religious traditions in order to articulate and explore moral understanding and the responsible orientation of human life. The book is a constructive presentation of the *meaning* and *method* of religious ethics. In order to develop the approach requires clarity about terms and also how religious ethics as a discipline has previously been conceived.

Conceptions of Religious Ethics

There are longstanding disputes about the meaning of "religion," "morality," and "ethics." For some thinkers, ethics is the philosophical analysis of the codes of conduct and beliefs about what is good, just, and right in a society, that is, a "morality." "Ethics" is a form of metareflection that seeks to interpret the meaning of some "morality" in order to assess its validity for orienting human existence. Thinkers and scholars of this type have spoken about "religious ethics" by applying some moral theory to religious sources. One might draw on the ethics of the Greek philosopher Aristotle and his ideas about "virtue" and then apply his theory to the texts and practices of a "religion," for example, Buddhism, to show that "Buddhist Ethics" is a kind of Aristotelean virtue ethics. One might use the moral theory of Immanuel Kant, the great eighteenth century European Enlightenment thinker, about practical reason and universal duty in order to show that, say, Jewish ethics is really a "deontological" ethics or a morality of duty. On this strategy "religious ethics" is an instance or kind of moral philosophy. Its distinctiveness is that religious people have peculiar beliefs about gods, the afterlife, salvation, or enlightenment. But in that case, the religions with their rich and complex heritages of texts, symbols, rituals, and practices do not provide novel and deep ways to sense, feel, and think about ethics and ethical problems.

There is a genuine problem with these *formal* approaches to religious ethics, as we can call them.[8] A formal approach begins with a definition of "ethics" and "morality" and then explores how a "religion" fits that formal definition. Typically, philosophical definitions of "morality" seek to show how it is to be understood with respect to one, singular attribute, say, that morality is about "duty" (Kant) or it is about virtuous behavior (Aristotle) or it is about consequences and utility (Jeremy Bentham [1748–1832 CE]). Ethics becomes one dimensional because its task, again, is to interpret, elaborate, assess, define, and apply "morality." Yet what if morality, or at least the moral convictions of the religions, is not one-dimensional? How might that change the very conception of ethics? Does either Confucius or St. Paul, cited in the chapter opening, neatly fit into an ethics of duty, virtue, or consequences? They seem to speak about duties, consequences, and virtues as well as other traits of a life properly lived.

Another method and approach to religious ethics is historical or *descriptive*. Here the task is to describe as precisely and carefully as possible those beliefs, values, and practices religious communities use to orient their lives and the lives of their adherents. This approach notes that different religions call reflection on beliefs, values, and practices different things. Rarely do the religions call it "ethics." For Muslims the name for thinking about the conduct of life is the interpretation of the *Qur'ān* and the Prophet's life, the

---

8 For a discussion of these issues see *The Companion to Religious Ethics*, especially the Introduction and Part I.

ḥadīth, and teaching in the form of law (*sharīʿa*). The term "ethics" derived from Greek philosophy therefore does not describe Islamic "moral" thinking. African religions, as another example, often rely on practices of divination to orient life in relation to the ancestors and changing situations. It would seem odd to call that kind of thinking "ethics." Again, Confucius is interested in the noble-minded one whereas St. Paul notes the fruits of the spirit. Are they talking about "ethics?"

From the *hermeneutical* perspective of this book, there is a genuine problem with *descriptive* as well as *formal* approaches to religious ethics. The labor of interpreting and understanding the moral resources of the religions is itself a kind of metareflection that includes but exceeds descriptive and formal approaches. "Hermeneutics," from the Greek god *Hermes* (a divine messenger from the gods to humans but also a trickster), is the art of interpretation in the service of understanding.[9] It seeks to attain understanding of texts, symbols, practices, and persons who make some claim to be meaningful but in ways that are ambiguous, tricky, and hard to decode. If the *formal* approach to religious ethics risks simplifying the moral convictions of the religions in order to find commonalities, the danger with *descriptive* approaches to religious ethics is that the search for distinctiveness can deny any commonality among moral convictions.

What if the moralities, or at least the moral convictions, of the religions reveal some analogous features? How might that change the idea of religious ethics? A hermeneutical approach to religious ethics seeks to isolate the similarities in differences, the analogies, in moral and religious understanding and the strategies of interpretation used to address life's challenges and to orient conduct. We contend that a distinctive feature of religious thinking about the moral life is the attention to tensions, the *aporias*, found in personal and social existence. Unlike philosophical forms of ethics that too often seek to elide the tensions of life, the religions seek to sustain but also to render productive and meaningful those tensions in order to provide right orientation for the conduct of human life with its oddity, joy, sorrow, conflict, confusion, and delight. The rest of this book presents that approach to religious ethics. And this requires clarity about the meanings of morality, ethics, and religion.

Morality, Ethics, and Religion

By *ethics* we mean, again, a kind of metareflection, a second order reflection on the first order morality of religious people, that provides the interpretation, elaboration, assessment, and application of a community's "morality" for the

---

9 The literature on "hermeneutics" is vast and complex. We refer to specific thinkers in the course of our argument. Yet it is no surprise that we borrowed the claim about religion from Friedrich Schleiermacher, quoted at the beginning of this book, insofar as he is recognized as the "father" of modern hermeneutics.

sake of orienting human life, individually and socially. Every religion is a form of reflection on and practice of interpreting human existence, the nature of reality, and how one should live.[10] Religious *ethics* is a specific kind of reflection on that first-order reflection. It is a metareflection analogous to other kinds of reflection on religion: e.g. historical, anthropological, sociological, philosophical, psychological, and so on. Although not every religion speaks about ethics, it is the case that every religion, and indeed every community and every human being, develops or adopts some form of metareflection on moral convictions, whatever they call that kind of thinking. *Morality*, then, is a set of convictions and practices about the proper conduct of life and the kinds of persons and communities one should strive to become. A religion's morality is found in its beliefs, practices, stories, teachings, sages, saints, doctrines, and social structures. The book is about *religious ethics* because the moral convictions that are interpreted, elaborated, assessed, and to be applied to actual life are found within the religions, a point addressed later. In other words, the subject of this book is how to think "ethically" about and also from within the moral convictions found in religions. What then do we mean by "religion?"

Ironically, none of what is usually called the world's religions call themselves a "religion." The term must be used, then, in order to indicate some commonality, some point of comparison, between vastly different beliefs and practices. The definitions of religion are legion.[11] Consider just a smattering of them. Religion is belief in a God or gods; it is a sense of the sacred; a religion is about what people believe to be ultimate, their deepest concern; religion is defined by a sense of mystery and the holy; the idea and study of "religion" is an invention of scholars to order, classify, and compare different cultural forms; and so on. Depending on the definition, religious ethics could mean the kind of reflection related to belief in gods and what the gods command, or it could mean thinking about human conduct in the light of what is sacred or some other account of religion. In that case, the beliefs, practices, and teachings of what we usually call "religion" might not be that important for religious ethics.

Again, none of the "religions" originally used the term religion to define themselves – some describe themselves as "the way," the *dharma*, submission (*Islam*), or some other conception – just as they do not usually speak of their way of life as a "morality" or thinking about that way of life as "ethics" (but, maybe, law, philosophy, or theology). The problem is that the term "religion" has to pick out similarities among the bewildering differences among "religions" and yet not blind one to those differences. And, further, it must clarify how a "religious ethics" is distinctive from a nonreligious or antireligious

---

10 Another reason we adopt a hermeneutical method in religious ethics is because the activity of interpretation can take many forms – formal treatises, ritual practices, symbolic and narrative forms, etc. – and thereby elides the simple distinction between thinking and practice.
11 For a recent discussion of the problem see Schilbrack, K. (2013). What isn't religion? In: *Journal of Religion* 93 (3): 291–318.

ethics. What the traditions, beliefs, communities, and practices examined in this book seem to share is that *they provide ways for a community of human beings to get access to, empowerment by, and orientation from something(s) believed or experienced to be ultimately real and ultimately important and related to but not isolated from other domain(s) of meaning and reality.* So, religion, we contend, is (i) about what is ultimately important and real (the sacred or divine), (ii) which some group of people or a community (iii) seek access to, empowerment by, and orientation from (iv) for the sake of the proper conduct of life, that is, their moral existence, within (v) interrelated forms or realms of reality, including alternate worlds.[12] This definition of religion is an abstraction, a rational summary (we might say), based on the world's actual religions. No one is "religious" in this general sense. One is a German Catholic Christian, a Thai Buddhist, a Hindu from Mumbai, or an American Pentecostal living in Brazil, and so on. Recall the banner quote for this book taken from Friedrich Schleiermacher (1768–1834 CE), the great nineteenth century theologian and philosopher of religion and ethics: "In the religions you are to discover religion."[13] "Religion" is, again, a construct of the scholar derived, we hold, from engaging actual religions, their histories, and sources. One needs the idea of "religion" in order to identify, relate, contrast, and evaluate the religions. And the same is true about the idea of "ethics."

Religion is about what is ultimately *important* to persons or some community of people and so what they value the most; religion has metaphysical and empirical qualities as well because it claims to be about what is ultimately *real*; existentially and socially any religion seeks access and empowerment from

---

12 We are mindful that the religions hold different ideas about what is "*real.*" For instance, speaking of *nirvāṇa* in Buddhism as "real" might seem to be a category mistake. Buddhists generally hold that the condition of *nirvāṇa* is anātman ("not-self" or "no-thing-ness") and hence not "real" as a substance, body, individual, and even material objects arise through dependent generation and therefore have no objective or permanent "essence." It is an extinguishing or "blowing out" of desire that leads to a state free from conditioned reality – a liberation. Granting that point, we use the term "real" analogically in our definition of religion and realize that the metaphysical commitments about the nature of "reality" of the religions vary in profound ways. The point of using "real" in this analogical sense is that even for Buddhists *nirvāṇa* is not a fiction or imaginary construct but is the inner truth of all things and hence "*real*" as we use the term. By a "world" we mean any determinate, bounded realm of meanings. The idea of living in and between multiple worlds is actually a common feature of human life. In addition to everyday reality marked by cause and effect, there are worlds of "play," imagination, art, deep affections, love, and the sublime that intersect with the everyday world. For the idea of religion and ethics as involving a movement between "worlds," see Schweiker, W. (2004). *Theological Ethics and Global Dynamics: In The Time of Many Worlds*. Oxford: Blackwell.
13 Schleiermacher, F. (1988 [1799]). *On Religion: Speeches to its Cultured Despisers* (trans. R. Crouter), 190. Cambridge: Cambridge University Press. For an excellent account of the major theories of religion see Pals, D.L. (2014). *Nine Theories of Religion* (Third Edition). Oxford: Oxford University Press.

what is sacred or divine as ultimately important, empowering, and real for the conduct of life. What is more, religion is deeply personal and yet also fundamentally social in character. Rituals, prayer, and sacraments have these aspects as do religious forms of thinking, reading, and writing. And the religious life entails a movement between the world here and now and some other reality, some "alternate or counterworld," even if that world is found to be the ultimate truth of the "here and now." Notice: something can be real and yet not ultimately important or even ultimately real for the conduct of life (say, the runs scored in the sixth inning of a recent White Sox baseball game); someone might have an experience that is ultimately important for them and yet not be presently real (say, a dream, vision, utopia, or a nightmare) in a conventional sense; one might acknowledge that something is ultimately important and real for others, and nevertheless not be empowered by it (how one might view some other religion). In each of these cases, that thing or experience would not be religious in terms of our definition even though they are social and personal in character.

Of course, it is popular to think that the religious are just about subjective experiences or that religious beliefs are psychological projections or ideologies. Yet for the religious person that is not the case. The proper conduct of life from a religious perspective requires *access* to, *empowerment* by, and *orientation* from and toward what is ultimately important and real and it takes place within some community of coreligionists. Religions differ in terms of how importance and reality are conceived, how to access the divine or sacred and be rightly empowered, and how life ought to be conducted by persons and communities. They also differ in terms of how they understand the "reality" within which human life takes place and how the movement between "worlds" happens. Most religions hold that there are multiple realities intersecting in human existence, some await a final coming of a divine judgment day that will end reality as we now know it, and still others teach that unseen and divine realities in fact surround and support our daily lives and which only the faithful perceive and know.

We can now say that by "religious ethics" we mean *the ethical study of the moral convictions of a religion and the comparison and assessment of different religions' moral convictions for the sake of orienting life, religiously and morally*. This is to admit that religious ethics is the labor of the scholar or an adherent within a community or those who live outside of it. How to undertake such work?

Method in Religious Ethics

This book is about the *meaning* and *method* of religious ethics. We have been writing so far about the *meaning* of religious ethics and we will return to that topic later. In thinking about the challenges posed to the study of the moral convictions of the religions, we have been naturally led to the question of how one can and should study, compare, define, and assess the moral convictions of various religions let alone undertake constructive religious ethical thinking. The question of *method* is actually related to the first two aims of the book noted previously and how this book differs from other approaches. What do we mean?

Recall that two aims of the book were, first, to define the *meaning* of "religious ethics" as a discipline of inquiry of interest to anyone who asks about the relation between "religion" and "morality," and, second, to explore exemplary convictions of religious traditions in such a way that the *method* of religious ethics is developed and clarified. In order to accomplish these aims, the book develops an account of ethical thinking that is keyed to basic tensions, or *aporias*, widely seen to characterize human existence and how the moral outlooks of different religions articulate and respond to them. This assumes, and it will have to be demonstrated, that these "tensions" are somehow constitutive features of human existence as it is known the world over and throughout history. The experiences of these tensions provide the analogical structure to religious ethics rooted in the dynamic character of moral understanding within religious traditions. The five experiences of the tensions in human existence are (i) blindness and insight, (ii) good and evil, (iii) perplexity and wisdom, (iv) freedom and bondage, and (v) truth and illusion. These tensions structure the five dimensions of religious ethics. To be sure, other scholars might isolate other tensions or perplexity. We have found that these five enable us to give a coherent and yet supple account of religious ethics (see diagram that follows).

Our contention is that the religions thrive on tensions, perplexities or *aporias*, in human existence rather than trying to resolve or do away with them as many forms of theology and philosophy often seek to do. The religions, in our judgment, try to render these tensions productive rather than destructive in human life, to make human life flourish in deeper and more profound ways. Comparison and judgment across traditions are possible because of the analogical nature of human thinking, that is, the human capacity to grasp similarities in differences and differences in similarities.[14] As noted, five "tensions" found in the religions themselves are used to structure this book; they set the framework for analogical ethical thinking, religious or not. And they give rise to five dimensions of religious ethics (descriptive, normative, practical, fundamental, metaethical).

By considering these features of experience adduced from the study of the religions, the book presents the method of religious ethics in terms of the five basic dimensions of thought each of which is treated in a chapter: descriptions

---

14 Although we will explore human moral capacities later in the book, it is not our task to establish empirically, scientifically, or metaphysically the grounds for the human ability to engage in analogical thinking. We take that as a given fact and one that is found in every human being. See Yearley, L.H. (1990). *Mencius and Aquinas: Theories of Virtue and Conceptions of Courage.* Albany, NY: SUNY Press and Tracy, D. (1981). *The Analogical Imagination: Christian Theology and the Culture of Pluralism.* New York: Crossroad.

of moral situations (Chapter 2); normative judgments about the basic, moral, and transcendent goods of human life (Chapter 3); the complexity of practical decision making (Chapter 4); the meaning of free and responsible human action (Chapter 5); and the truth status of moral judgments (Chapter 6). In this way the book provides its readers with a broad array of classic religious texts and descriptions of religious practices as well as a method to engage these critically and constructively, sensitive to the highest ideals and deepest failures of religious pursuits. Figure 1.1 can serve as a guide to the chapters to follow:

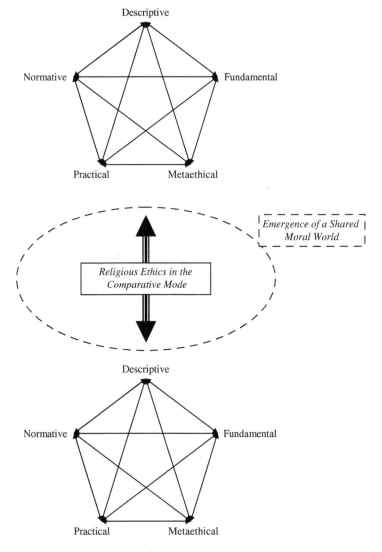

Figure 1.1 The Dimensions of Religious Ethics.

The remainder of this book makes good on the promise that these experiences and the dimensions of thinking provide a coherent, analogical, and nonreductionist account of religious ethics. It is important that the various dimensions of religious ethics be conceived in their *mutual interactions* rather than ordered into some hierarchy. Religious and moral reflection moves in and through and back and forth among these dimensions rather than ticking off answers to one and then turning in a deductive fashion to the next dimension. This is why religious ethics is a *hermeneutical* task. Like the Greek god *Hermes*, one seeks to convey meaning by crossing over and through different domains of existence. It is a movement among "worlds": realms of meaning, value, practical action, judgment, and community. The *method* of religious ethics seeks to articulate the complexity of experience while also providing a coherent way of thinking about moral problems and responsibilities. Ironically, the mere ordering of the chapters of the book can give the wrong impression about its argument. Although there is not a straight line of argument, the book does reference other chapters so the whole may be understood. We encourage readers to begin with any chapter they like and then move between them. That course of reading is more in the spirit of the method of religious ethics presented in the chapters to follow than assuming that there is a straight line of argument chapter to chapter.

In terms of moral theory, the book is making a specific and even radical point. As noted previously, ancient and modern theories of ethics tried to isolate one basic and defining feature of "morality" and then to organize ethical thinking with reference to it. From Aristotle's ideas about "happiness" and "virtue" to Kantian theories of duty and also utilitarian ideas about the greatest good, these positions, we can now say, were, in terms of method, *unidimensional*. The contention of this book, conversely, is that if one takes seriously the resources of the religions about how to explore, articulate, and orient human life, a more complex picture of morality and ethics emerges, a *multidimensional* one. By presenting a method for religious ethics, we are proposing a conception of morality and moral thinking that clarifies the profound contribution of the religions to ethics, even while this approach to religious ethics aims to provide a way to clarify and to assess the moral convictions of the religions. As noted in the Introduction, we enter a hermeneutical or interpretive circle. The aim is to show the need to enter that circle but also how it is neither vicious nor self-validating.

This point about moral theory returns us in a new light to the third and most contested aim of this book. Recall that the third purpose of this book is to enable people in our global times to think intelligently and clearly about religious outlooks on life and how they can, may, and must be lived in ways that respect and enhance, rather the demean and destroy, the integrity of life. We will have more to say about the idea of the "*integrity of life*" in Chapter 7, the book's conclusion. The lives of creatures, and, perhaps, especially moral creatures, make a demand for fulfillment; integrity denotes both the demand and a kind of completion or fulfillment. Yet if the approach to religious ethics developed in the pages of this volume is correct, and we certainly believe that it is, then two things follow. First, we will have identified an analogous structure of moral thinking across the religions and in doing so exposed the religions to wisdom found in other traditions even while overcoming the widespread idea that somehow one cannot compare moral convictions. We will have identified a structure and dynamics of thinking from within the religions and thereby avoided the frequent tactic of applying theories to the religions. In a word, we will have shown how the religions contribute to the *method* and *meaning* of moral reflection. Second, the approach to religious ethics developed in the book will also mean that religious adherents and nonreligious people as well have the grounds and the reasons to assess and even reconstruct their moral convictions in ways that respect and enhance the integrity of life. The book hopes to show how the religions can be sources of moral wisdom open to anyone in our global age even while the religions must be open to ethical criticism and revision in terms of the way their moral convictions are understood and lived. In this way, the book seeks to intervene within religious life in an age of global human interaction and endangerment.

Contents

The chapters that follow move in and through the dimensions of religious ethics attentive to the tensions found in human life. In each chapter, we place examples from Christian moral thinking and practice in conversation with examples of the moral thinking in other religious traditions. It should be clear, given our approach to the meaning and method of religious ethics, that we do not intend that the tradition illustrated in the chapter be taken as more focused on the dimension of ethics explored than any other dimension. For instance, just because Igbo religion is placed in conversation with Christian ethics in order to explore the practical dimension of religious ethics, or Buddhist religion to illustrate the metaethical dimension, does not mean that Igbo life is more focused on practical decision making than any other dimension of ethics or that somehow Buddhists are not concerned with the practical life. Our approach means that religious ethics is multidimensional and so is each religious tradition from which ethical wisdom can be drawn. Moreover, we link the traditions under discussion in a chapter to prior and subsequent dimensions and traditions we explore.

Chapter 2: Blindness and Insight takes up the central interpretive question that confronts religious people living in a changing world. How do we best describe the reality that confronts us? This question arises from the fact that human life is lived in the tension between blindness and insight about one's moral situation and true knowledge about reality. Here we seek to unfold what we mean by the *descriptive dimension* of moral thinking, and to do so we offer readers a selection of religious texts and practices that provide various answers to this question. For example, one might look to the *Qur'ān* to answer the question, "If Allah is the creator of the world and all life within it, how do we best describe the pervasive pursuit of material goods and pleasures among people worldwide?" Or we might look to the teaching of the Buddha in the *Dhammapada* to answer the question, "To what do we attribute the suffering in this world? Why do people seem constantly in a state of dissatisfaction?" In each of these questions, we present different religious readings of the human condition and our various attempts to respond to its challenges.

In Chapter 3: Good, Evil, and Beyond, we address the question of what norms and values ought to guide human life and so the *normative dimension* of religious ethics. Each religion asks basic questions about what human beings ought to pursue, what difference there is between transcendent goods and moral goods, and what principles or rules ought to govern our life together. But this dimension of reflection too is rooted in a tension within human existence between good and evil, broadly conceived, and what is beyond good and evil. For example, one might examine the revelation of God to the people of Israel in the form of "law" (*Torah*). What basic values do the commandments of God seek to protect? How do these laws function to facilitate the moral growth of individuals and a peaceful life for the community? Or one might examine the African practice of palaver, a kind of community discernment through the back and forth exchange of pertinent moral observations, through which the religious group mediates the values of past generations to address present problems. Frequently, the content of these values depends on the deployment of certain sources for moral judgment, which themselves require some account for why these sources (such as sacred texts or guidance from religious authorities in particular traditions) ought to be normative rather than other sources.

Chapter 4: Perplexity and Wisdom addresses the difficulties that each religious tradition faces with respect to its patterns of practical reasoning about actual moral problems. There is a *practical dimension* in religious ethics. Human life is marked by the tension between perplexity and the search for wisdom, that is, the capacity to discern and decide the fitting thing to do in a specific situation. Just because one has gained clarity about the problems that confront someone or the values we ought to embody in our life together does not mean that one has adequately addressed the problem of how to act here and now. How do religious traditions think about what constitutes a proper moral response to difficult moral issues? For example, when confronting unplanned pregnancy due to rape or incest, how do Buddhist and Christian responses illustrate different ways of respecting and enhancing basic goods of bodily and social life? Even within a single religious tradition we are often able to discern different patterns of practical or case-based moral reasoning. Although religious traditions often draw moral thinking into a casuistic mode, the practical dimension remains a central consideration for addressing moral problems in faithful yet creative ways.

All of the major religious traditions of the world would agree that talk of distinctly moral responses to situations, or the imputation of blame for poor decisions, makes no sense if people are not, in some sense, free to act. And yet every religious tradition probes and seeks to respond to human moral failure, in, say, weakness of the will, sin, or craving. The problem arises when one begins to acknowledge that the demands and constraints upon one's freedom go hand in hand with the recognition that one is part of a broader reality that one did not create for oneself. Likewise, religions seek to communicate the means to free people from their bondage to powers operative within human life and on human life, powers like demons, sin, or craving, to name a few. Religions differ in their account of the meaning and limits of freedom and bondage, including questions about the proper role of authority in educating people in responsible exercises of freedom.

Chapter 5: Freedom and Bondage, presents religious texts and accounts of moral agency that illuminate these differences. How do religions understand the capacities and limitations of humans as moral actors, as agents? How do practices like religious reading or education in religious law train people in the responsible use of their freedom? How do religious traditions deal with difficult problems such as individual conscience while still respecting the inherited wisdom of a tradition? Confucian approaches to ritual and filial piety, noted previously, intend to cultivate in people a disposition to act freely out of respect for one's family and friends, out of duty to ancestors, and to ensure that people of well-formed character occupy positions of leadership. Similarly, Christian attempts to balance the education in the faith with the primacy of the individual conscience before God, as St. Paul writes, echo the same difficulties of forming character and virtue. These matters are part and parcel of the *fundamental dimension* of religious ethics; they are about what it means to be a moral agent within a religious outlook on life and reality.

Chapter 6: Truth and Illusion concerns the difficult problem of the truth of religious worldviews and the possibility of deception about what is good and true, one that people wrestle with constantly as they are confronted with an array of seemingly incommensurable moral traditions. The burden of this chapter will be to demonstrate that every student of religious ethics, as well as any religious practitioner, must cultivate a sensitive awareness of the ways that various sources of moral knowledge come together to form moral judgments. This means asking on what basis particular judgments by religious communities are rendered but also about the criteria used by various communities to evaluate claims to moral truth. For example, Buddhist insights into the nature of ultimate reality are mediated through teaching traditions constituted by a scholarly class of monks and nuns. Tradition and its authoritative interpretation are taken to be authentic sources of moral knowledge. However, the Buddha frequently stated that his teachings ought to be held up to scrutiny in one's own experience and one's own practices. In Christian thought the question of the truth of moral judgment is both a matter of revealed teaching and yet there are also convictions about natural moral knowledge available to all human beings. In other words, religious judgments about truth are as complex and reflexive as any judgment made in more avowedly secular branches of society. Religious ethics in its *metaethical dimension* addresses the question of the truth of moral convictions and judgments.

Chapter 7: The Point of Religious Ethics draws together the previous analysis in order to show how our approach to religious ethics enables scholars and adherents to understand the complexity of a religion's outlook on the moral life. Specifically, this chapter shows, with reference to Buddhism and Christianity, how the various dimensions of ethics interact and shape each other: how one decides to define the moral situation, for instance, is shaped by and also shapes what a religious outlook holds to be the standard of good and evil and an understanding of freedom and so on. This mutual, reflexive interaction of the dimensions of religious ethics provides not only a salient way to understand the moral outlooks of specific religions but also the means to show the importance and relevance of religious traditions for addressing current shared human and global moral issues. In order to demonstrate the point, we address moral issues comparatively from this hermeneutical multidimensional approach. The chapters thereby show in an exemplary way this approach to current moral problems.

Conclusion

The careful reader of this introduction has already learned two important things needed to proceed through the rest of the book. Unlike geometry, engineering, or the study of, say, Sanskrit, we come to moral questions in the normal course of life and always shaped in various ways by the communities of which we are a part. Some of those communities are the world's religions and they have shaped for good and for ill the moral convictions of untold billions of people throughout history. If we are naturally interested and involved in moral problems and challenges, then it is a short step to see that "religious ethics" can and should be the interest of everyone as well, and this is especially true in a postsecular age of global dynamics.

The second lesson of this chapter is that although moral questions and challenges are regular features of our lives, how one is best to think about them, that is, how to undertake the work of "ethics," is not so obvious. The study of "ethics" is at root about how to think carefully, coherently, and truthfully about the responsible orientation of personal and social conduct. The chapters that follow provide an account of religious ethics as the way to explore and assess the moral convictions of the religions. We have tried in this chapter to give a brief description of the situation of religious ethics and to begin to introduce the normative concepts, practical distinctions, claims about human moral thinking and agency in the structure of ethics, while also posing the question of the truth of our proposal. It is our hope that readers will find this account of the meaning and method of religious ethics a goad to their own engagement with the religions, but also, and more important, a helpful approach to their own moral and religious reflection.

2

Blindness and Insight

Descriptive Dimension

Gluskabe, the man from Nothing was claimed by all … to be the first person who came upon the earth, and he was their (the people's) teacher. He taught them how they must live, and told them about the supernatural power, how it was in every living thing, and … it sent him … to subdue all obstacles which were against mankind; and to reduce the earth to such a state to become a happy land for the people.

—Nineteenth-century Penobscot leader Joseph Nicolar[1]

As he was setting out on a journey, a man ran up and knelt before him, and asked him, "Good Teacher, what must I do to inherit eternal life?" Jesus said to him, "Why do you call me good? No one is good but God alone. You know the commandments: 'You shall not murder; You shall not commit adultery; You shall not steal; You shall not bear false witness; You shall not defraud; Honor your father and mother.'" He said to him, "Teacher, I have kept all these since my youth." Jesus, looking at him, loved him and said, "You lack one thing; go, sell what you own, and give the money to the poor, and you will have treasure in heaven; then come, follow me." When he heard this, he was shocked and went away grieving, for he had many possessions.

—Mk 10:17–22

One strange fact of human life is that we can have moments of profound insight into the meaning of our lives and our relations with others. We can be moved by the claims of justice or outraged at attacks on human dignity. Yet it is equally true that we can be blind to the suffering of others and also our own complicity with injustice or the harms we have done to ourselves and to others. Blindness and insight plague human life and make it profoundly difficult to understand our

---

1 The description is by the late nineteenth-century Penobscot leader Joseph Nicolar cited in Speck, F.G. (1935). Penobscot tales and religious beliefs. *Journal of American Folklore* 48 (187): 6.

Religious Ethics: Meaning and Method, First Edition. William Schweiker and David A. Clairmont.
© 2020 William Schweiker and David A. Clairmont. Published 2020 by John Wiley & Sons Ltd.

world, others, and ourselves so that we might responsibly orient our lives. Little wonder that many cultures have stories of the blind wise person who sees the truth of things that others do not even though they have eyes to see. Or consider a movie like "The Matrix," which explores how what people think is reality is not so. Neo – the new man – must break through the illusion. Much earlier in Western history is Plato's "allegory of the cave" where people are pictured as stuck in a cave watching the shadows on the wall *as if* that is reality. It takes the philosopher to escape the cave, see reality in the light of the sun, and then come and try to help others. Conversely, our blindness might be due to sin and insight due to grace, as Christians would hold, or the entanglement of blindness and insight might be explained and explored on other grounds, as we will see.

There are many forms of human insight and blindness. Sometimes the things that we love keep us from doing what is right and good, like the rich young man in the story from Mark at the head of this chapter. Other times, people look for insight from a great figure like Gluskabe, the man from Nothing, among the Penobscot. If people are to orient their lives responsibly, they must somehow wrestle with the dogged tension, the *aporia*, in human life between insight and blindness with all of their forms and causes. This is one task the religions undertake, and it is the subject of this chapter on the "descriptive" dimension of religious ethics. In each of the subsequent chapters we add another dimension. Although each chapter adds to what has gone before, it also anticipates some of the issues that arise in the dimensions that have not yet been examined in detail. The full picture will not emerge until the end of the book, but our hope is that our discussion of the dimensions gradually fills in the details and that the comparisons developed illustrate the account we are presenting.

Describing a Moral World

Ethics is always involved in giving *descriptions* of the world and moral situations. The task, as we have put it before, is to articulate and evaluate the structure of lived reality, that is the ethical environment of a people in relation to particular situations. It is impossible to confront any moral problem without, at some point, considering the question: *What is really going on?* Are things as they appear or does the real problem reside at a deeper level, hidden from initial view, and calling for more careful consideration? How do we get true insight into a situation in order to describe it rightly and how do we avoid the many sources of moral blindness about us and within us, like sin or wrongful desires? This does not mean that ethics is only for the educated or for the spiritual elites – people with special knowledge or privileged moral perception. But it does mean that ethics requires careful thinking and more important, as many religious traditions have long acknowledged, the wisdom that comes with time, self-criticism, and a quest to respond to the realities of life.

The world's religious traditions are, however, in a difficult position with respect to giving descriptions of moral problems. On the one hand, religious traditions employ foundational stories, like the story of Gluskabe, the man from Nothing, and many stories have over time achieved the status of canonical sacred texts or "scriptures," like Mark's Gospel, that offer, among other things, portrayals of the world. In this way, religious traditions carry with them metaphysical questions and their own metaphysical accounts, using "metaphysics" in the wide descriptive sense of a picture of reality as a whole rather than in any technical philosophical sense. These metaphysical views, sometimes called "cosmologies" (i.e. ways of speaking about the cosmos or the nature of reality) purport to be true pictures of the way the reality is. They are meant to give insight and to overcome blindness about the human condition.

Religious cosmologies take many different forms. Some traditions draw these pictures from more literal readings of foundational texts or interpretations of oral traditions, whereas many other traditions assume that the way the reality is cannot be easily described through language. For this reason, religious texts must be read with an awareness of the symbolic nature of human language and interpersonal communication. Such stories may be said to be true not because they conform to an observationally verifiable picture of historical events or the demands of a positivist scientific investigation, but rather because the stories disclose something unmistakably real and accurate about the community, the world in which that community exists, and that which claims to be ultimately important and real. Recall, from Mark, Jesus' chastising the rich young man for mistaking the young man's picture of him for the true transcendent good, God. Religious traditions try to capture the complexity that people recognize to be characteristic of the human condition, but this is always work that is incomplete because it is still in the process of unfolding.

On the other hand, precisely because of their attempts to communicate truths that are not immediately apparent or easily comprehended, the religions are always in danger of losing sight of the basic symbolic nature of those religious pictures. When such pictures are taken literally and absolutized, they tend to become detached from the truthful but fundamentally ambiguous nature of the religious symbols that constitute them. The religions struggle mightily to give true and meaningful descriptions of the world, but these true descriptions are mediated by means of our common, fragile humanity. This, in turn, leads us to a profound but problematic insight about religious discourse: the very communities that seek moral insight from their investigations into ultimate realities are all too often the same communities that suffer from the very worst of moral blindness in the form violence and insensitivity to human needs. In this respect the same tension between blindness and insight found in persons' lives due to vice, ignorance, sin, and so on also permeates religious communities.

The root problem is an interpretive one, namely, how do the sacred stories, practices, texts, and beliefs of a religion, say, about divine grace or

Enlightenment, function to illuminate reality as sources of insight rather than blind people to the reality of their world and their responsibilities. More profoundly, how can forms of religious communication (rituals, speech, texts, prophecy, divination) reveal a moral situation while also, because these are human actions, conceal something of that very same situation? So, the work of the rest of this chapter is to examine some of the ways that religious traditions undertake the interpretive work of *moral description* by examining the dynamic tension between *blindness and insight*. We proceed in two parts. First, we introduce different ways that religious *discourse* offers pictures of the moral significance and complexity of our world and the difficulties involved with interpreting such discourse. Religious discourse, because of its symbolic nature, gives truthful but partial descriptions (and partial in the twofold sense of being both incomplete and also biased), and that the extraordinary varieties of such discourse, even within a single religious tradition, offer helpful guidance for how we ought to interpret this discourse. The religions mix symbolic, historical, poetic, hortatory, legal and other kinds of discourse in order to reveal and not conceal something of the complexity of the divine/sacred and of the human journey.

Second, we will also consider religious *practices*, some of which have discursive dimensions (as when practices involve stories, prayers, or the dramatic recitation of ritual formulae) but are not exhausted by their explicitly linguistic dimension even if they are forms of religious communication. Human life is, as we have said, complex and multidimensional and so we must consider how moral descriptions are generated not only from religious traditions' texts but also through the activities, gestures, images, and relationships that they contain. Here too the problems of revealing and concealing, as well as blindness and insight, have to be addressed. We will therefore need to be open to possible sources of moral description in such activities as music, visual art, funeral practices, divination, rituals marking passages to different stages of life, and so on. All of these can (and indeed have) become relevant sources for the student of religious ethics.

As we move through this chapter examining religious discourse and practices, we range widely over different forms of religious life in two focal traditions: early indigenous communities of the Americas and early Christian communities of the ancient Mediterranean world, including more contemporary examples from these communities along the way. We will keep in mind a particular moral problem that has confronted every religious tradition at some time or other and has been recognized by the global community as one of the most challenging moral problems of our age: *how to recognize the humanity of others*. The humanity of others can, oddly, be concealed in religious texts and practices thereby fostering moral blindness. The challenge, ethically, is to interpret texts and practices so that they reveal, and not conceal, the humanity of others and in doing so sharpen and deepen moral insight.

The challenge of recognizing shared humanity will allow us to examine a number of traditional accounts and later writings from various traditions that have probed this question out of the resources of their traditions. It enables us to examine thinkers for whom the difficulty of recognizing our common humanity has led in turn to deep questioning of religious descriptions of the world. And we can examine how religious discourse and religious practices are deeply interrelated, thus accounting for the linguistically mediated nature of human life and also the continuity and creativity of human action in a complex world. In order to proceed with that task, we need to clarify forms of knowing important for hermeneutical and ethical thinking.

Explanation and Understanding

In our day, it sometimes proves difficult to offer (much less to defend publicly) generally compelling descriptions of the world we share. Many current developments work against our best efforts. Modern science, both natural and social, offers descriptions of human realities that are placed in the service of solving complex medical, political, and economic problems. Yet these same habits of mind, disciplined through focused attention and patient observation, which give rise to advances in human society also occasionally run into trouble when it comes to giving explanations that are not primarily about fixing social problems or predicting human behaviors but rather about what makes for a good life.

The history of scientific endeavor shows that any effort of the mind directed at the acquisition of knowledge is bound to a significant degree to the cultural values and methods of the age and to the ways communities criticize and appropriate knowledge from previous generations. As Thomas Kuhn (1922–1996 CE) argued in his classic book, *The Structure of Scientific Revolutions*, a perspective of objectivity – that is, the disinterested acquisition of reliable information about a reality – depends in part, but not totally, on the culture in which the objectivity is sought. The method (that is, the approach) of any investigation, including religious ethics as much as the so-called "hard" sciences, is necessarily a limiting and discretionary factor in what we can know about the reality we study.

Consider, in this light, the passage from the Gospel of Mark at the head of this chapter. The rich young man's deep attachment to wealth meant that he could not understand, let alone act on, Jesus' command to him. In fact, the passage continues in this way: "Then Jesus looked around and said to his disciples, 'How hard it will be for those who have wealth to enter the kingdom of God!' And the disciples were perplexed at these words" (Mk 10:23–24a). Even the disciples could not "see" the point of Jesus' saying. In other words, how we see the world, the frameworks or "paradigms" used to organize our experience of the world are tied to interests, commitments, and values. These commitments and values can conceal as well as reveal one's moral situation, like wanting to get into heaven. Put differently, we have no completely disinterested way of knowing what are the proper questions to ask about a reality given that we cannot inhabit a perspective that would guarantee we are always asking the right questions.[2] Long before Kuhn and others, the religions were exploring the problem of human blindness and insight.

The history of the human sciences reveals much the same problem. In the late nineteenth and early twentieth century, people began to question whether we could know human beings in their behaviors and patterns of interaction in a way analogous to how we know the workings of their bodies. Studies of human behaviors sought a level of objectivity that would link observations of human life to a modest level of predictability in human affairs. As Max Weber (1864–1920 CE) questioned "in what sense are there in general 'objectively valid truths' in those disciplines concerned with social and cultural phenomena?"[3] Sociology and economics were concerned with human values but only insofar as those fields could track the origins, development, and likely future of those values and to the extent that they could be useful in predicting the likely outcomes of human behaviors. Philosophers such as Wilhelm Dilthey (1833–1911 CE) argued that the human sciences ought to develop a more comprehensive sense of their work, under the assumption that to know another person or group of people differs significantly from having knowledge of other material objects in the world. Instead of focusing primarily on *explanation*, the social scientist ought to focus on the goal of *understanding*, which Dilthey described as "the process by which we come to know something of mental life through the perceptible signs which manifest it."[4] Increasingly, the human sciences have sought to relate the tasks of *explanation* characteristic of the natural sciences and *understanding* characteristic of the humanities, yet these tasks have often been subject to the normative concerns of different cultures and historical epochs.

These different ways of knowing the world – mediating the drive to explain and control characteristic of the natural sciences and the drive to understand

---

2 As Kuhn notes to clarify the connection between communities and scientific paradigms, "Observation and experience can and must drastically restrict the range of admissible scientific belief, else there would be no science. But they cannot alone determine a particular body of such belief. An apparently arbitrary element, compounded of personal and historical accident, is always a formative ingredient of the beliefs espoused by a given scientific community at any given time." See Kuhn, T.S. (1970). *The Structure of Scientific Revolutions*, 2e, 4. Chicago and London: University of Chicago Press.
3 Weber, M. (1949). *The Methodology of the Social Sciences*, (ed. E.A. Shils and H.A. Finch), 51. New York: Free Press.
4 Dilthey, W. (1976). The development of hermeneutics. In: *Selected Writings* (ed. and trans. H.P. Rickman), 248. Cambridge: Cambridge University Press. Cited in Ricoeur, P. (1981). *Hermeneutics and the Human Sciences* (ed. and trans. J.B. Thompson), 150. Cambridge: Cambridge University Press.

and inhabit the world of others characteristic of the humanities – each enjoy a certain cultural privilege depending on the needs and anxieties of a given age. For example, many scholars think that scientific reasoning gives rise to two dangers: the danger that one begins to think of people in the same way that we think of objects, as raw material or reserve that can be used up to satisfy needs; and the danger that one remakes nature, including human nature, in the attempt to make it habitable and serviceable *to us*.[5] We might say, in a similar vein, that attempts to explain human life run the risk of changing us into creatures for whom explanation will always take priority over understanding, so that human control always trumps wonder.

Moreover, efforts at forging understanding across cultures run into significant political obstacles. For peoples whose cultures have frequently been exoticized and plundered by colonialist powers, suspicion rightly follows any attempt by people outside of a culture (perhaps especially scholars) to gather information about that culture in an effort to offer an "adequate" understanding of cultural difference. The mutual acknowledgement of regional, linguistic, and historical differences among communities often results in no more significant advance than the political marginalization of minority cultures. Often the goal of understanding – that is, mutual acknowledgement of similarities and differences that unite people rather than divide them into the users and the used – is taken to be a mask for a form of exploitation of other others' behaviors intended to silence or disarm them. On this account, understanding can be, ironically, a kind of blindness to others that also conceals them in the work of interpretation. One can imagine somebody interpreting the story of Gluskabe to back the idea that the world is just for human use. After all, the story proclaims that he came "to subdue all obstacles which were against mankind; and to reduce the earth to such a state as to become a happy land for the people."[6] That would be, on our account, not only a poor interpretation but an *immoral* one because it conceals the people who tell this story and their real beliefs.

Despite these dangers, it is possible to work toward interreligious understanding if one assumes a critical posture in reference to how understanding is achieved. Self-criticism of one's own interpretive framework is crucial in religious ethics (see Chapter 7). Furthermore, insofar as the religions use not only a vast array of interpretive strategies but also exhibit a version of moral realism (see Chapter 6), the task of interpretation and description in religious ethics must aim at understanding claims to reality and explaining their import for the moral life. So, one must seek to explain what is going on in historical developments, honor insights into profound human problems, but also adopt a critical stance toward those traditions. This is "critical" in two senses: (i) to understand

---

5 McKenny, G.P. (2005). Technology. In: *The Blackwell Companion to Religious Ethics*, (ed. W. Schweiker), 461–462. Malden: Blackwell.
6 Speck, F.G., Penobscot tales and religious beliefs, 6.

the necessary conditions under which religious discourse can be meaningful within their communities of origin, and yet also (ii) to uncover and to respond to those instances where religious discourse has been used to mystify and abuse rather than emancipate and enlighten.[7] In a word, one engages in ethical thinking (see Chapter 1).

Diagnosis and Judgment

Central to the descriptive dimension of religious ethics is the idea that judgments about what one ought to do are significantly influenced by attempts to describe what is going on. To return to the Gospel of Mark, Jesus had the insight that the rich young man's quest for heaven was actually blocked, impeded, by a love of wealth, a love that seemingly was concealed from the rich young man himself and, oddly, also Jesus' disciples. People exist in complex social relations, and so what we call social and reflective goods (see Chapter 3), and these relations, like those of wealth in Mark's Gospel, shape understanding as well as moral agency. For religious ethics, a view of the moral agent as related to herself or himself precisely through relations to others in society is important for thinking with and about religious traditions. It allows us to approach religious traditions with a healthy skepticism about the clarity that can be found in our own traditions and it appreciates the complexity of historical traditions that too often have been viewed as primitive and simplistic ways of life. The opposite is also true: the complexity of moral thinking, and the insights that come from delving into that complexity, is nowhere better illustrated than in human religiosity.

It is important to distinguish what we mean by the descriptive dimension of religious ethics from other uses of description by scholars working in the field. Religious ethics since the 1970s has moved back and forth between a more theoretical, analytical, and normative focus and a more practice-based, historical, anthropological, and descriptive focus.[8] Description was carried out largely under the methods of the human sciences with their prominent focus on adequacy and explanation. Yet as noted previously, this is only one moment in the history of the human sciences, and recent emphasis on ethnography and

---

7 We draw some of this formulation from Geuss, R. (1981). *The Idea of Critical Theory: Habermas and the Frankfurt School*, 2. Cambridge: Cambridge University Press.
8 For recent reviews of the field, see Schweiker, W. (2019). Responsibility and comparative ethics. In: *Power, Value, and Conviction: Theological Ethics in the Postmodern Age*, 111–134. Eugene, OR: Wipf and Stock (esp. 114–117); Bucar, E.M. (2008). Methodological invention as a constructive project: exploring the production of ethical knowledge through the interaction of discursive logics. *Journal of Religious Ethics* 36 (3): 355–373. (esp. 356–361); Kelsey, J. (2010). Response to paper for 'Ethnography, Anthropology, and Comparative Religious Ethics' focus. *Journal of Religious Ethics* 38 (3): 485–493. Miller, R.B. (2016). *Friends and Other Strangers: Studies in Religion, Ethics, and Culture*. New York: Columbia University Press.

descriptive ethics has not always attended sufficiently to the hermeneutical turn in thought. The more theoretical and normative studies in religious ethics over the last 40 years have been dominated by a certain philosophical style, drawn largely from British and American philosophy, which highlighted certain forms of philosophical discourse and guiding questions to the neglect of others. Epistemology, conceptual analysis, and the logic of moral systems and language-games guided the way for philosophical engagement with religious ethics. Religious ethics itself, as shown in Chapter 1, took formalist, descriptive, and, as we advocate, hermeneutical forms.

So, the place of description in ethics is determined by the meaning and method of religious ethics set forth in this book. In its constructive aim, religious ethics must be attuned to its critical and cultural task that seeks to understand and explain the structures of lived human reality for the sake of responsibly orienting human life. The descriptive dimension of religious ethics, accordingly, presents a moral description that goes beyond the explication of a moral language to communicate something about the lived quality of people's existence as creatures in a complex world of desires, commitments, and obligations.

Religious discourse and practice are forms by which moral thinking and acting are transmitted through tradition, both in the form of moral arguments through time and enacted through personal and communal action. Moral description is a reflexive activity that occurs most obviously in written discourse but also in practice. One must look both at the oral and written traditions of a community, but also examine the other activities in that community, if one wants to understand how the work of moral description happens in religion. In both the Penobscot and Christian examples noted at the outset of this chapter, there are, as we will see in more detail later, long chains of interpretation, practice, and communal organization that seek to display the insights of foundational stories and scripture, their moral cosmologies, for the ongoing life of these communities.

This leads us back to a hermeneutical standpoint from which to undertake the work of religious ethics. We conduct our investigations from a standpoint that seeks a joining of "worlds": the world of the religious practitioner, the world of the scholar, and the world of anyone willing to engage in religious ethical thinking.[9] One seeks critical moments of understanding ourselves, the religions, and the structures of lived reality because we believe that insight occurs in the reflexive relation among these. Religions offer scholars of

---

9 Note, we are using the term "world" in a hermeneutical sense, that is, it is any determinate domain and horizon of meaning, a meaningful context of life, constituted by discourse, practices, narratives, symbolic forms, social organization and institutions, and even architecture. Human cultures, and so too religions, are in the business of world-making and also provide the means to move between "worlds" within the same society or between societies. A religion, for instance, might provide ritual means to move between the present world and some hoped for and yet real "counter-world."

religious ethics a chance for deeper understanding of what they study but scholars offer religious communities and the people interested in them a chance to see what was going on in their communities that was unrecognized, concealed, or covered over by the prejudices and aggressions marking their own histories. Instead of seeing the scholar and the object of the scholar's studies as independent, closed, mutually antagonistic realities, we see them as becoming what they are in relation to one another. The world of understanding is constituted in the process of conversation, broadly understood (see diagram in Chapter 1).

We now turn to engage two religious traditions and their descriptions of moral realities mindful of the human perplexity of blindness and insight.

Native American Religious Discourse

Although the origins of religious discourse vary widely, all such discourse seems to be in some way about what human beings consider good and worthy of trust, in what is ultimately important and real at the very limits of what we can know about ourselves and the world. For example, many of the great oral traditions that would become classic religious texts began with a sense of wonder about the place of human life in the wider cosmos. Stories about the history of peoples, the powers that brought them into being, cared for and sustained them, expressed those peoples' views about their basic values and suggested the rules communities established to guard and promote those values. Ancient rituals were passed down orally through generations of religious specialists, sometimes creating and sometimes expressing the foundational religious myths of peoples. Religious rituals and myths carry within them a deep ambiguity about sacred and divine powers and the difficulties communities experienced understanding those powers, gaining access to them, and living in right relation to them.

Religious discourse (myths, stories) was closely linked with the religious practices of the people. Both discourse and practice reveal the basic dynamic that structures this chapter: blindness and insight. Giving adequate moral descriptions of the realties (human, nonhuman animal, divine) that confront people is an aspect of any religious morality and, although moral languages and norms vary and communal practices diverge across time and geographical location, the impulse to live a good life by knowing what is true about human life and responding to that truth in responses to others and to the world persists in religious communities across the globe. Each tradition pursues insight in the midst of the people, places, and events that have formed it, so it will be helpful to consider some of those figures and happenings in this chapter. Importantly, it is often the same people and events that can be the occasion of great moral

blindness that can also prompt deep insight. There is a complex and even confusing relation to the blindness and insight of individual life and of the communities. Often enough, it is individuals with special, profound insight that
reveal the blindness of others and of the community. These people are seers,
saints, and shamans in their communities.

In the remainder of this chapter and those that follow, we do not aim to give
"complete coverage" of global religious variety, but we do aim to make each
chapter comparative across traditions as we present the meaning and method
of religious ethics. Now we turn to consider one Native American religious
tradition in conversation with one expression of the Christian tradition looking
first at discourse and then religious practices.[10] Mindful of the abusive history
of empire building on the cultures and peoples of the Americas, we aim to face
squarely this history by offering respectful accounts of the moral ambiguity of
communities searching for examples of religious blindness as well as religious
insight.[11]

The Penobscot Nation inhabits about 5000 acres of land along what is now
called the Penobscot River in the northeast corner of the United States in the
state of Maine. The Penobscot Nation belongs to a confederation of native tribes
in the northeastern United States called the Wabanaki ("people of the dawn,"
which include the Maliseet, Mi'kmaq, and Passamaquoddy) who belong to the
Algonquian language group.[12] The ancient tribal lands were extensive over the
rivers of southern Maine, but were located primarily along the Penobscot River

---

10 Relatively few studies in comparative ethics have examined the moral thought of Native
American communities. One early exception is Little, D. and Twiss, S.B. (1978). *Comparative
Religious Ethics: A New Method.* New York: Harper and Row. Little and Twiss examined the
research of Ladd, J. (1957). *The Structure of a Moral Code: Navaho Ethics.* Cambridge: Harvard
University Press. See also Deloria, V. Jr. (2005). Indigenous peoples. In: *The Blackwell Companion
to Religious Ethics,* (ed. W. Schweiker), 552–559. Malden, MA: Blackwell.

11 Although we speak in several chapters of the axial religions, we do not mean to suggest by
this label that somehow indigenous or native religions are somehow "subaxial" in their moral
thinking! Quite the contrary is the case insofar as we show the complex of their moral beliefs,
outlooks, and practices. We use the terms as historical markers rather than as normative or
cognitive categories.

12 The Penobscot Nation has been particularly active in recording its history and teaching its
cultural traditions both within the community and to interested outsiders. For a summary of its
activities, see http://www.penobscotculture.com/index.php (accessed 3 July 2014). For a
discussion of the Algonquian language group, see Carmody, D.L. and Carmody, J.T. (1993).
Native American Religions: An Introduction, 15–17. New York and Mahwah, NJ: Paulist Press.
The Algonquian tribes are one of three major language groups (along with the Iroquoian and
Siouian) of the tribes collectively referred to as the "Eastern Woodlands" tribes. Other tribes in
the Algonquian language group include the "Ojibwa, Ottawa, Potawatomi, Menomini, Sauk, Fox,
Kicapoo, Miami, Illinois, Shawnees, Narragansett, Mohican, Delaware, Naticoke, and Powhatan"
(Carmody and Carmody, 16–17).

over which the Penobscot people roamed for hunting and fishing and on which banks they grew basic crops including maize, beans, and squash.[13]

One difficulty in examining the religious discourse of native peoples is the tendency to reduce that discourse both to a homogenized "Native American spirituality" and to mask the significant differences among native peoples. How temping it is to think that "[t]he 'generic Indian' holds timeless spiritual secrets, relates more intimately with nature, engages in collective production, shares commodities, and lives in an extended family."[14] Honoring this insight into the ambiguity and complexity of Native American traditions, we examine a series of Penobscot stories in this section and then consider ways that Penobscot life reflects a complex negotiation of those stories.[15] Many elements of their history enable us to grasp how the descriptive dimension moves back and forth between blindness and insight.

There are three classes of supernatural beings in Penobscot oral tradition: "(a) the quasi-human creatures frequenting the forest, bodies of water and the air, (b) the races of animals of the same realm, and (c) the phenomena which to our minds form part of the physical geographical universe without vitality, but which, to the Northeastern [Algonquian], are personalities of the air, land and water."[16] The most significant of these in oral tradition is the hero Gluskabe. This "man created out of nothing" emerged spontaneously from the dust of the ground and created many of the beings and features of the world. In some later written versions of the story, Gluskabe arose from the ground when a great spiritual force had finished making all the other creatures of the earth, from the dust shaken from the hands of the "great being" – likening him to the primeval man of many ancient creation stories like the Bible's account of "Adam."[17]

---

13 Speck, F.G. ([1940] 1997). *Penobscot Man: The Life History of a Forest Tribe in Maine*, 7–26. Orono: University of Maine Press.

14 MacDougall, P. (2004). *The Penobscot Dance of Resistance: Tradition in the History of a People*, 8. Durham: University of New Hampshire Press.

15 MacDougall notes that the Penobscots are one of the native communities to establish research protocols for scholars interested in the history and culture of their community, not to restrict access or inquiry, but "to ensure that such scholarship includes Penobscot voices and connects the past to the present." Quoting from historian Donald Fixico, while scholars should "'avoid publication of sensitive Indian knowledge (especially ceremonials) ... The most important ethical concern is for American Indian history to be included in the scope of American experience." (MacDougall, 6–7).

16 Speck, F.G. (1935). Penobscot tales and religious beliefs. *Journal of American Folklore* 48 (187): 5. For a more general discussion of conceptions of human beings see Sahlins, M. (2008). *The Western Illusion of Human Nature*. Chicago, IL: Prickly Paradigm Press.

17 See Nicolar, J. (2007). *The Life and Traditions of the Red Man*, (ed. A. Kolodny), 97–100. Durham: Duke University Press. Speck sees the variety of later eighteenth- and nineteenth-century retellings of the Gluskabe myth as cultural accommodations to Roman Catholic missionary presence but notes that it is difficult to ascertain "original" versions of stories. His views are based largely on the variety of Gluskabe stories among Algonquian tribes.

In other versions, Gluskabe arises spontaneously from the ground but is also the child, grandchild, or nephew of existing woodland or river creatures.[18] Cited at the head of this chapter, the late nineteenth century Penobscot leader Joseph Nicolar describes Gluskabe: "Gluskabe, the man from Nothing, was claimed by all ... to be the first person who came upon the earth, and he was their (the people's) teacher. He taught them how they must live, and told them about the supernatural power, how it was in every living thing, and ... it sent him ... to subdue all obstacles which were against mankind; and to reduce the earth to such a state as to become a happy land for the people."[19] The name Gluskabe derives from a word in the Abenaki language group meaning "he lies, tells falsehood, deceives" which refers to "his ability to outwit enemies through deception." The word *gluski* is used to denote both "deception" (thus the *ábe* [person] who deceives) and also "nothing" or "absence" (thus "the person who comes from nothing").[20] In this one figure, then, is found the complexity and ambiguity of blindness – he can deceive others without them knowing it – and also insight – he tells the people the truth of their origin and nature. These traits of craftiness, what we might call "prudent falsehoods," are central to the Penobscot ideal of the good man: "skilled hunter, clever and tricky, able to out-wit others, physically strong," but also one who is "capable of magical arts because of this spiritual power."[21] Gluskabe is a model of the ideal Penobscot man and hunter. These traits are among those that have made the Penobscot Nation particularly successful in drawing on cultural values to envision distinctive forms of political resistance (a point we return to later in the chapter). We see how figures like Gluskabe and their stories encode a religion's

---

18 "Penobscot mythology credits Gluskabe with some twenty major achievements for the benefit of man, to wit: distributing over the world the game animals, food, fish, hares, and tobacco; renewing the warmth of summer; protecting the eagle above who regulates daylight and darkness; moderating the destructive force of the wind; tempering the winter; bringing the summer north; reducing giant animals to a harmless size; domesticating the dog; clearing obstructions from the portages along the routes of hunting and travel; smoothing out the most dangerous waterfalls; creating the whole Penobscot river system; moderating the power of fire; making burns curable; creating sweetgrass; and serving as a source of power for those who come to his distant dwelling with their troubles. His benefits to mankind reach a climax in the mission he allots to himself to watch over his people and to return to the land at some unknown date, against which time he is preparing food and armament to save them in a crisis. By inference the Penobscot are also inclined to attribute to him the origin of their arts and inventions." See Speck, F.G. Penobscot Tales and Religious Beliefs, 10.
19 Cited in Speck, F.G., Penobscot Tales and Religious Beliefs, 6.
20 MacDougall, P. (2004). *The Penobscot Dance of Resistance: Tradition in the History of a People*, 37. Durham: University of New Hampshire Press.
21 Ibid. The reader should recall that "Hermes," after whom we take the term "hermeneutics" that is important to our argument, was both a messenger and a deceiver. The image of the trickster in this way is found in many cultures and plays on the *aporia* of blindness and insight.

account of and response to blindness and insight. Religious ethics must, accordingly, interpret and explain these figures.

Penobscot stories also offer especially helpful images of the cultural views of good and wise women that also express the religious response to the problem of blindness and insight. Two are especially prominent: Gluskabe's grandmother the "Woodchuck" and the figure known as the "Corn and Tobacco Mother." In one story, Gluskabe is living with his grandmother and, when he decides to go hunting, asks Grandmother Woodchuck to make him a bag to take with him. After rejecting a number of bags made from the hair of various animals, she makes him a bag from the hair on her own stomach (the tale doubling as an etiology of the woodchuck's smooth stomach). Satisfied with this bag, he goes hunting and tricks his prey into hiding in his bag by telling them that the sun will be extinguished and the world destroyed. Returning home, Gluskabe boasts to his grandmother that, because of his cleverness, they will no longer have to hunt for food. She chastises him for his blindness and says:

> [W]hy must you always do things this way? You cannot keep all of the game animals in a bag. They will sicken and die. There will be none left for our children and our children's children. It is also right that it should be difficult to hunt them. Then you will grow stronger trying to find them. And the animals will also grow stronger and wiser trying to avoid being caught. Then things will be in the right. *Then things will be in the right balance.*[22]

The grandmother provides for her family from her own body, but she is also critical when her gift is misused. That provision ought to be used in accordance with the gifts and skills of the hunter, but it can also be used badly if it is not used in accordance with the balance of the world. The story presents the world as bountiful yet still in need of care to achieve balance among its various parts and balance is a key to responding to blindness and insight.

The story of the "Corn and Tobacco Mother" tells the origin of the two important crops in Penobscot culture while also describing a view of the world in which the virtues of women and men are appropriate to context.[23] A young man is born from the foamy waters swirled by the winds of the river comes to live with Gluskabe. The man longs for a companion and a young woman appears the next day born from a plant. The young man and the young woman raise a family. Gluskabe leaves them some weeks later, promising to return at the appropriate time, and soon after he leaves a famine breaks out in the land. The

---

22 Bruchac, J. (1985). *The Wind Eagle and Other Abenaki Stories*, 5–7. Greenfield Center, NY: Bowman Books. Our italics.
23 Molly Spotted Elk, *Katahdin: Wigwam Tales of the Abnaki Tribe*, 17–20. Orono: Maine Folklife Center.

woman born of the plant asks the man born of the water to kill her and drag her body over the barren fields. Reluctantly, he agrees and corn emerges from where the woman's flesh falls and tobacco grows from where the woman's bones lay. After the harvest, Gluskabe returns to counsel the young man:

> Now, the words of the First Mother had come to pass. She was born of the earth and she had returned to it. She had given life and love to us, peace to our minds, and strength to our bodies. Keep a little always of what she has given you. Put it back into her bosom each growing season. She will give to it warmth from her body. Remember too, that all creatures like her must be cherished. So divide among you, my children, for you are brothers.[24]

Gluskabe counsels both the proper use of these particular crops (the nourishment from corn, the peacefulness from tobacco) and also a guiding moral principle of distribution linked to respect from a common source. Insight into what is going on discloses appropriate behavior and norms for social life.

Another story further illustrates the connection between the Penobscot description of the world and the culture's normative views of human behavior. Gluskabe sets out from his home to search for ways to make the earth better for subsequent generations. Exploring the forest and rivers, he comes to a place where the water has dried up and the people of the village are dying from lack of water. They tell Gluskabe that the great water monster Aglebemu (with the head of a bullfrog and a body of a human) has taken the water for his village and refuses to share it with other villages. Gluskabe goes to Aglebemu to request that he share the water sucked up into his huge belly. When Aglebemu refuses to share the water, Gluskabe chops down a yellow birch tree that lands on the monster causing the river water to burst forth. The water that runs from where the tree lands is taken to be the Penobscot River and the places where its branches landed smaller tributaries to the main river.[25] Gluskabe's insight about how to combat the evil Aglebemu has done to others and the common good reveals, again, the underlying moral worldview of the Penobscot, their implicit metaphysics around the idea or norm of balance and also hunting and farming skills.

However, the story is more ethically complex. When the waters burst forth, the people who had been without water, and are near death, rush to the river's edge. Depending on their reaction to the water (diving deep, swimming on the surface, drinking as much as possible), the people are transformed into various water creatures such as turtles, frogs, fish, and so on. This story is invoked to

---

24 Ibid.
25 Bruchac, J. (1985). *The Wind Eagle and Other Abenaki Stories*, 5–7. Greenfield Center, NY: Bowman Books. See also Speck, F.G. *Penobscot Man*, 216–217.

account for the diversity of families within the tribe, which is divided into two groups: those that derive from the waters and those that derive from the land. The tribal leader is elected either from the frog family of the water peoples or from the squirrel family of the land peoples. Each family has traditionally inhabited an area of the land or the rivers befitting its particular family traits that derive from its animal ancestor's habitat and distinctive behaviors or mode of survival.[26] The overall arc of this story reinforces also the story of Gluskabe's hunting bag. The world is a sufficiently bountiful place, but it will not tolerate selfishness or hoarding. Moral insight turns on this truth while blindness fails to perceive it. Further, each family (symbolized by each of the animals in the story) will have its own challenges based on its family history and its particular geographical location in the community. The world can be a harmonious place, but only if people respond to it appropriately given their understanding of their location, their history, and their particular family, its individual virtues, vices, and kinds of basic goods, as we will see in Chapter 3.

The ability of the Penobscot stories to describe the world in a way that links its description to the cultural values and practical challenges of its people shows the ethical power of myth. As the scholar of Hinduism, Wendy Doniger, writes, a myth "is a story that is sacred to and shared by a group of people who find their most important meanings in it; it is a story believed to have been composed in the past about an event in the past, or, more rarely, in the future, an event that continues to have meaning in the present because it is remembered. It is a story that is part of a larger group of stories ... myths from other peoples' cultures often provide us with useful metaphors that are more refreshing than our own."[27] Myths have a religious and a political function (or, we might say, a discourse and a practice function). In doing so, they capture the perplexity and complexity of human existence that is basic to religious ethics. This is a helpful way to express the hermeneutic standpoint in religious ethics. As it undertakes the critical, constructive, and comparative tasks of religious ethics, it does so from a standpoint of interpretation, that is, bringing moral worlds into each other. In this way, religious ethics itself is structured in part by the perplexity of blindness and insight found in the structures of human lived reality. That is, human beings do not, and cannot, grasp all of reality and

26 For a detailed discussion of the relationship between the Penobscot animal stories and the identification of families with 22 animals of the Maine forests, rivers, and coast (lobster/crab, bear, sculpin, eel, toad, insect, fisher cat, whale, beaver, sturgeon, wolf, frog, squirrel, raccoon, wolverine, water nymph, otter, wildcat, rabbit, yellow perch, and raven), see Speck, F.G. (1940). *Penobscot Man: The Life History of a Forest Tribe in Maine*, 212–29. Philadelphia: University of Pennsylvania Press. Speck was not able to trace all the family names to particular myths, but his study is still the most extensive to date.
27 Doniger, W. (1998). *The Implied Spider: Politics and Theology in Myth*, 2–3. New York: Columbia University Press.

are blinded in various ways (say, self-interest that clouds perception of reality) even as they can also have true insight into their moral situation.

Sadly, the sharing of moral worlds between cultures too often has been imposed rather than offered, temporarily accepted out of resignation rather than invitation. This has characterized the interaction of the moral worlds of First Nations (Native Americans) and nominally Christian nations. But blindness and insight are found within the Christian community as well.

Christian Religious Discourse

Early Christian communities interpreted stories that were, like their Algonquian counterparts, morally ambiguous, marked by blindness and insight. Early Christian stories, and their counterparts in others religions, can be seen as "classics."[28] Classics, as theologians and philosophers have noted, are those expressions of human puzzlement about the world and the perennial problems of our shared existence that resonate with people across times and cultures. Religious classics are those works that explore the meaning of human existence and our place in the cosmos. They are human creations believed to be inspired and that simultaneously reveal and conceal the whole of reality in a way that is given to the human community rather than being merely constructed by those communities. Persons or communities cannot simply decide to create a classic! They arise and appear in the flow of history with the power to reveal and manifest some truth of human life and community.

With this in mind, consider Christian religious discourse as an activity of moral description. Although the texts of Christian scripture include claims about historical events (the exodus of the Israelites from Egypt, the stories of kings and prophets in the Northern and Southern kingdoms, the events in the life of Jesus of Nazareth), interpreters of those stories have noticed that they are presented in many different literary forms (narrative, poems, letters, etc.). Further, "[t]hese scriptures are themselves only a relatively adequate expression of the earliest Christian communities' experience of the Risen One as Jesus. They remain open to new experiences – new questions, new and sometimes more adequate responses for later generations who experience the same event in ever different situations."[29] That early community's experience is announced in the message (*kerygma*) of the early followers of Jesus of Nazareth. Stories were told about Jesus' teaching, like the story of the rich young man at

---

28 See Gadamer, H.-G. (1975). *Truth and Method*. New York: Continuum. and Tracy, D. (1981). *The Analogical Imagination: Christian Theology and the Culture of Pluralism*. New York: Crossroad. Also see Clairmont, D.A. (2011). *Moral Struggle and Religious Ethics: On the Person as Classic in Comparative Theological Contexts*. Oxford: Wiley Blackwell.

29 Tracy, D. (1981). *The Analogical Imagination: Christian Theology and the Culture of Pluralism*. New York: Crossroad, 249.

the head of this chapter. Preaching also drew on the later formulation of Christian doctrine and other statements of the community's beliefs. Each of these, however, is only a "relatively adequate" expression of the community's experience of the God of Israel through Jesus of Nazareth. Experiences of the divine are never fully and unambiguously captured in stories that convey them. God exceeds human words and stories about God, even when those words and stories are believed to be "literally true." What is more, people living after the original experience have only a narrow selection of voices that spoke of a God who was intimately near yet painfully hidden. Those early voices spoke to (and wrote mindful of) what their communities could hear and understand.

A threefold approach helps one to understand how Christian communities engage in the work of description while attending to the other dimensions of the moral life that we explore further along.[30] First, Christians must interpret the *story of Jesus* for their own time and conduct their lives in light of that interpretation (the descriptive dimension of religious ethics). This may involve new awareness of morally significant issues (for example, the problem of greed and proper use of wealth) and changes to one's way of living in light of that awareness. Second, Christians must consider how that story forms the moral character in the community's members (for example, recall the need for the rich young man to examine the kind of person he had become, which requires attending to the *virtues* that in turn offer insight into the normative, practical, and fundamental dimensions of religious ethics). Third, Christians commit themselves to a set of *spiritual practices*, like curbing greed or fasting, which further develop character and the ability to interpret faithfully, yet critically, the community's foundational stories. This approach to the stories of the Christian community expands the scope of moral concern by cultivating a refined mode of moral perception. It is meant to open moral insight and combat moral blindness through revisiting central stories in light of new insights about the character of individuals and communities.

Stated differently, a hermeneutical approach to religious ethics is an expression of analogical thinking. As noted in Chapter 1, to think analogically about moral matters means to cultivate a certain habit of thinking that can "spot the rhyme," as William Spohn has called it, between actions appropriate to one context and parallel actions sensitive to a different context. Developing an analogical imagination means that Christians can begin to envision ways of responding to the needs and culture of their current context in a way that "rhymes" with how Jesus responded to the needs and culture of his own time. The story of the rich young man can then be used to think about the proper use of money. And that is what Christians have done. In the early Church, Clement of Alexandria (150-c. 215 CE) wrote a treatise aptly titled "The Rich Man's

---

30 Spohn, W.C. (2007). *Go and Do Likewise: Jesus and Ethics*, 12–16. New York: Continuum.

Salvation" where he made a distinction between the *use* of money and the *enjoyment* of money.[31] Christians are to use and not enjoy money, he argued. Clement's distinction has helped Christian thinking about wealth.[32] A further analogy is comparative, that is, between how Christians interpret foundational stories to provide moral insight and the parallel action of the Penobscot with their stories. This is the basic way religious communities attend to the descriptive work of religious ethics. Human beings make sense of the unknown or what is concealed through its similarity-in-difference to what is known and revealed. The mind moves from the known to the unknown, the revealed to the concealed, in the search for insight that overcomes moral blindness no matter the cause of one's blindness might be (ignorance, sin, bad karma, etc.).

In this light, consider two examples from the Christian Bible: the poetry collected in the Book of Psalms and the narratives in the Gospel of Matthew. Each offers insight into the workings of moral description in religious discourse and has an important correlate in the religious practices of Christian communities. The Book of Psalms is a collection of poems intended to be sung to accompanying music with some dating as early the time of King Solomon and the building of the first temple in Jerusalem (c. 960–920 BCE) and others dating from much later in that history after the return of the Jewish people from exile in Babylon (539 BCE). As liturgical texts in Jewish worship, these compositions are used in a similar way by contemporary Christian communities but also for private prayer. The psalms range across many topics and are usually grouped according to their style and theme. Among the most cited groupings are psalms of praise, royal/enthronement psalms, psalms of thanksgiving, psalms of complaint/lament (individual and communal), and psalms of wisdom. The Book of Psalms was organized in the Hebrew Bible into five groupings paralleling the five books of the Pentateuch and covers many of the themes examined in narrative form in those books. Accordingly, the psalms provide "an ample window on Israelite and ancient Jewish spirituality ... Succeeding generations of Jews and Christians have found in the Psalms the language to help them express both their existential anxiety and their wonder and admiration for the God of creation."[33]

In what sense are these psalms a poetic form of religious discourse offering moral descriptions in order to combat moral blindness? Consider Psalm 8 that offers a song of praise similar to the first creation story in the Pentateuch (Gen

---

31 This distinction between use (*uti*) and enjoyment (*frui*) is taken up by Augustine in various ways in a number of his works. See for example his *De Trinitate* X.11.
32 One should note, then, that the so-called "Gospel of Wealth" taught in some churches in the United States is a novel and problematic development.
33 Collins, J.J. (2004). The psalms and the song of songs. In: *Introduction to the Hebrew Bible*, 471. Minneapolis: Fortress Press.

1:1–2:3). It provides insight into the meaning of creation as the environment of the moral life.

> When I look at your heavens, the work of your fingers, the moon and stars that you have established; what are human beings that you are mindful of them, mortals that you care for them? You have made them a little lower than God, and crowned them with glory and honor. You have given them dominion over the works of your hands; you have put all things under their feet, all sheep and oxen, and also the beasts of the field, the birds of the air, and the fish of the sea, whatever passes along the paths of the seas. O Lord, our Sovereign, how majestic is your name in all the earth" (Ps 8:3–9).

The Psalm sets forth an image of the world as the community sees it: the awesomeness of God and the lowliness of his creation. And yet, the image of the world is one where the human being holds a place both exalted and precarious. In this way, the text presents a cosmology that makes sense of the reasons for human blindness and insight because of the precariousness of life, reasons like fear, greed, or ungratefulness. The Genesis creation story sets forth an image of human beings as "dust that breathes." "The glory and fragility of life – breath and yet also dust – are permanent features of existence within which persons and communities must navigate their lives."[34]

The Psalms balance the two features of the dust and breath. The dust cries out, in the words of Psalm 130, "Out of the depths I cry to you, O Lord. Lord, hear my voice! Let your ears be attentive to the voice of my supplications! If you should mark iniquities, Lord, who could stand? But there is forgiveness with you, so that you may be revered" (Ps 130:1–4). The breath affirms this fragility and glories in the intimacy with divine creative power: "For it was you who formed my inward parts; you knit me together in my mother's womb. I praise you, for I am fearfully and wonderfully made. Wonderful are your works; that I know very well" (Ps 139:13–14).

This example of poetic religious discourse offers a description of the moral space of life, a moral cosmology. As psalms that offer praise and petition, but also proffer wisdom beyond their liturgical context, these verses provide a picture of the world created and sustained by the God of Israel. Their descriptions balance the tensions of faithfulness and despair, self-care and self-doubt; they presume to speak to the God of justice and yet hold their tongues before an awesome and terrible God. These same psalms factor into Christian liturgies to express the wonder and worries of the Christian community, whereas others

---

34 Schweiker, W. (2010). *Dust that Breathes: Christian Faith and the New Humanism*, 1. Malden, MA: Wiley Blackwell.

(Ps 31) emerge from the mouth of Jesus of Nazareth as a tearful affirmation of divine providence. Religious discourse can function analogically, prompting us to see and name the rhyme between classic religious wisdom and prudent responses in our own day. Yet, the texts function not only analogically but also critically, exposing human pretension to easy knowledge and offering "explicit negations of oppressive systematic realities in church and society alike."[35]

The Gospel of Matthew was written after the destruction of the second Jerusalem temple in 70 CE and includes material from the earlier Gospel of Mark, including the story of the rich young man (Mt 19:16–26). Matthew's Gospel was addressed to a community divided on the best way forward in the aftermath of Roman oppression. It takes up issues of interpretation of the law of Moses, the identity of Jesus, the meaning of freedom and political deliverance, and distinctive values characteristic of the Jewish followers of Jesus. Traditionally, its moral vision has been distilled from the Gospel's early chapters called the "Sermon on the Mount" (5–7), an "epitome" – a synopsis – of Jesus' teaching, which has been a touchstone for centuries in debates about the distinctiveness of Christian ethics. Was the moral guidance of the Sermon intended as a moral code for spiritual elites? Does it express an unattainable ideal nonetheless useful in focusing individuals on scrutinizing their intentions, a morality appropriate only for a time of expectation of Christ's return? Maybe it means to convict sinners of their unrighteousness?[36] The context of the community that received the text is important to know if one is to grasp what might count as a potentially viable interpretation. However, if one spots the rhyme between the Gospel and the appropriate way forward, one must also venture an interpretation of the contemporary age, its problems as well as its possibilities. And that is the challenge because too easily we find ourselves blinded to the moral forces and problems in current life. Scripture can shed light and provide insight into moral reality, for example, by insisting that for Christians the poor cannot be neglected or cast aside in the quest for economic growth.

When Christian communities interpret this text, they do so with a set of questions that obviously differ from those in Matthew's community although there are some similarities as well. The figure of Jesus in Matthew is presented as the authentic interpreter of *Torah* (Jewish "teaching") and as the model of perfect obedience to the will of God. In the Beatitudes at the beginning of the Sermon, the poor in spirit are blessed as well as workers for peace and others. The community to which Matthew wrote debated the proper response to the threat of Roman power and was divided in its thinking. That response depended

---

35 Tracy, D. *The Analogical Imagination*, 416.
36 For a helpful summary of these positions, see Pinckaers, O.P., Servais (1995). *The Sources of Christian Ethics* (trans. Sr. Mary Thomas Noble, O.P.). Washington, DC: Catholic University of American Press. Also see Betz, H.D. (1995). *The Sermon on the Mount* Hermeneia Commentary. Philadelphia: Fortress Press.

on what God was doing for the people of Israel during the Roman occupation. Would there be political deliverance or another exile? Would a prophet arise in Israel to call them back to obedience to God or would there be a king who would deliver them and usher in a new age? These texts offer a picture of the world to which the character of Jesus offers a response that was to be the model for his followers. The teachings and life of Jesus reveal what is concealed and offer insight that can overcome the immoral and sinful blindness of others. God's Kingdom is promised to the meek and the poor and those who thirst for righteousness and not those with power and wealth. Here, again, is an analogue to the story of the rich young man.

Like the Psalms, Matthew's narrative offers a picture of the world (a God who acts in history to fulfill divine promises and lead people to beatitude by the example of Jesus) but also a pattern of response. Christian communities that look to this text for insight into the nature of the human condition and the world engage with it in order to form their response to that world searching for basic values and models of wise judgment. As the text offers moral descriptions, it also offers normative and practical guidance (see Chapters 3 and 4). Christian communities do not look for guidance about how to respond to the problems of the first century; they look to it for insight about how to interpret the world today. What kind of political participation is appropriate for Christians? Are they to be, as some have argued, political realists working for the best possible outcomes in a sinful world, or are they to focus inward to model a loving community and thereby to provide a counterwitness to a violent and coercive state, as others have suggested? We should not expect these questions to be easily answered or the witness of Christians brought to a naïve unity. Each age will present its questions and forms of life and Christians need to respond in a way that catches the rhyme between their day and times passed.

Comparing Moral Descriptions

A helpful way of approaching these different forms of religious and moral discourse is to focus on symbolic forms and stories. The tales of early Penobscot tribal heroes such as Gluskabe and the Corn Mother offer models for behavior for contemporary communities. However, they, and Jesus, are not only objects worthy of attention and perhaps cautious imitation. These figures illustrate and embody central community values and serve as images that guide the community. Yet, Gluskabe is not only a model for the wise and skillful leader of a hunting culture; he also invites people in the community to think creatively about what it means to come from the earth, to attend to the needs of the community, and to teach future generations to study the land and respond appropriately to its sustaining capacities and its rich variety of life. The Corn Mother reveals the importance of giving one's life to nourish the people, even to the

point of sacrifice. She also calls people to envision a world where physical sustenance is complemented by spiritual union. And Jesus not only is believed to
embody the Will of God and herald God's Kingdom but also to teach and to live
a life of love of others, even the most downcast, the sick, and the enemy.

Written and oral traditions of religious discourse provide symbols that are not
trapped by any one period in history but respond to the questions that arise in
communities as they puzzle about the meaning of their existence in each age.
They probe the feel of life – its textures, tastes, and smells – which are not
reducible to neat sets of moral values or rules. They offer moral descriptions,
but they also carry on, to each generation, the questions that prompt deep thinking in every age. In this way, religious texts, symbols, and stories provide moral
insight, analogically and dialectically, that cut through the moral blindness of
people and open new ways of conducting life, individually and as a community.

However, the descriptive dimension of religious ethics must be understood
not only in relation to the worldviews, the cosmologies, set forth in myths,
symbols, and narratives. It must also and crucially be defined in and through
religious practices. Practices, recall, ought to be understood broadly to include
not only activities that are clearly part of a community's explicit cultic activity
but also other activities "invested with explanatory and supportive meaning
through continuity of tradition ... habit ... and interpretation."[37] Because the
modern discourse about religion was developed either as a continuation of or
in reaction to Christian imagery, one ought to look as broadly as possible for
examples of religious practice, only some of which bear a structural resem-
blance to Christian ritual activity. In the next section, we continue to draw
examples from the history of the Penobscot Nation, even as, for the sake of
comparison, we return to some examples of Christian practices illuminated by
the differences we examine.

Native American Religious Practices

The ancient Penobscot tribal myths discussed earlier in this chapter form part
of the cultural heritage of the Penobscot people, although as might be reasonably argued for other religious cultures the heritage is not determined by what
is oldest. Traditions negotiate the old and the new, and often those living in
traditions need to make prudent choices about how the ancient ways will be
drawn into present practice. Part of the negotiation of tradition includes decisions about what "qualifies" as tradition and what does not, in the view of those
committed to both its maintenance and its development.

---

37 Clooney, F.X. (2005). "Practices." In: *The Blackwell Companion to Religious Ethics*, (ed.
W. Schweiker), 78. Malden, MA: Blackwell.

The Penobscot Nation, although little studied among scholars (especially in the area of religion), was the originator of one of the most significant land-settlement legal cases in the history of the United States – the Maine Indian Land Claims Act of 1980. Its origin and progress through state and federal courts illustrate what might at first appear to be a counterintuitive suggestion for how law and other forms of political engagement might best be described as loci of religious practices when religious traditions use available means to survive.[38] Moreover, these practices illustrate the descriptive dimension of religious ethics as an exercise in creating moral worlds through the workings of imagination and interpretation.

"Gluskabe's Children" returned from World War II with dreams and ambivalence about the fate of their people in the United States.[39] For most of their history, the Penobscot people lived on an island in the Penobscot River – "Indian Island" – connected to the mainland city of Old Town, Maine by canoe until a bridge was constructed in the early 1950s.[40]

The first Christian missionaries on Indian Island, who were French Jesuits, arrived in 1646 but their continued presence was not formalized until the end of the eighteenth century.[41] In the middle of the nineteenth century, the Penobscots were caught in a dispute between Congregationalist missionaries in Maine and the Roman Catholic diocese in Boston over state appropriations for public works projects on the island. Because the Penobscots were not an officially recognized tribe by the federal government, their dealings had been with the state government of Massachusetts, which included Maine until the latter became an independent state in 1820. The area north of Indian Island had been a center of the logging industry that, because of the harbors in Bangor to the south, was the central driver of the region's economy from the eighteenth century through the period of the Civil War.

The Maine Indian Land Claims Act of 1980 began as an initiative to improve living conditions on Indian Island, prompted by the cooperative work of tribal leaders and a younger generation of Penobscots who had attended college in the late 1960s and early 1970s. As the land claims cases were moving through the courts, other Penobscots were working to reestablish the cultural traditions of the early community through the revival of the Penobscot language, art, and

---

38 The recent protests against the development of the Keystone Alaska Pipeline project across the sacred lands of the Standing Rock Indian Reservation in North and South Dakota raise similar issues and have become an occasion for younger First Nation people to explore and interpret the traditions of their ancestors in light of the new ecological and economic challenges posed in our time.

39 This expression is adapted from Anastas, P. (1973). *Glooskap's Children: Encounters with the Penobscot Indians of Maine.*Boston: Beacon Press.

40 MacDougall, P. (2004). *The Penobscot Dance of Resistance: Tradition in the History of a People*, 135. Durham: University of New Hampshire Press.

41 Ibid., 116–117. The first semipermanent Catholic mission settlement on Indian Island occurred in 1791 and permanent settlement occurred in 1798. Although originally a mission territory of Quebec, it eventually became a part of the Diocese of Boston, and the original church (St. Ann's, since rebuilt) is known to be the oldest location of Catholic worship in New England.

traditional religious practices. Although there had been a school on Indian Island established by the Sisters of Mercy in 1888, it did not prioritize the study of Penobscot culture, and after the sixth grade, many students either attended school in the city of Old Town or were sent to boarding school in Pennsylvania at the Carlisle Indian School.[42]

Among the cultural traditions revived were tribal ceremonies on both a large and small scale. This included consulting knowledge of tribal elders who had an ancestor revered as a *mətə'wəlinəwak* ("person of the spiritual group"). Penobscot spiritualists (sometimes called "shamans" or "medicine men") were both individual and family spiritualists. These religious specialists [*mədeʹolinu (man of drum-sounding)* or *mədeʹolinas'kwe* (woman of drum-sounding)] often were accompanied by or directed animal helpers called *páwəhikan*.[43] There are parallels to the powers of persons figuring in ancient stories (the ability of Gluskabe to talk to animals, for example), but the practices do not appear to be focused on direct communication with people of Penobscot myths. Their goal, in many cases, appears to have been more geared toward divination, protection, and praise rather than on maintaining ancient ritual patterns. Interpretation can take many forms aimed at overcoming blindness with insight.

Penobscot religious practices have developed in a variety of ways that include protest and other forms of political activism, engaging in traditional hunting practices and in production of canoes, weapons, and baskets, along with new practices such as the annual 100-mile run north from Indian Island to Mount Katahdin. There are three core teachings of Penobscot religion: a recognition of the *spiritual power* in people and animals, a deep rootedness in the gift of the *land* and the *river*, and *reverence* for the natural world and ancient cultural ways (see Chapter 3).[44] Each of these core teachings is drawn from values contained in the community's earliest oral traditions but the meaning of these values in the lives of the people has changed over time. In which ways, then, do these practices function to offer moral descriptions of the world from traditional religious resources?

First, it is important to highlight a point made earlier about the mediation of religion through history. Religions certainly can include belief in divine beings, but it is also about the variations in belief over time in light of the stories of a community. The truth of the matter exists in the negotiation between past and present, the ideal and the real, in whatever time. Over the last 100 years, the tribe has seen knowledge of traditional stories and native language wane and wax, as a younger generation seeks knowledge of its past and wisdom from its elders.

---

42 Ibid., 21.
43 See Speck, F.G. (1919). Penobscot shamanism. *Memoirs of the American Anthropological Association* 6 (28): 240–242. Speck notes that, although the meaning of the name denotes drum-playing among the Algonquian tribes, he did not observe this among the Penobscot and is relying on the work of other scholars who did observe such practices in their studies of the closely related Passamaquoddy tribe.
44 These three core teachings, drawn from the observations of Joseph Nicolar, structure MacDougall's chapter on "core teachings that sustain resistance" but they also are a helpful way to think about the central commitments of the community through time. See MacDougall, 36–53.

However, those moments of insight are occasioned by the blindness of the time. When the Penobscots first moved to legal action in the 1980 land claim case, a negotiation ensued about how traditional teachings could illuminate the challenges of the day. There was an active debate about how best to picture the world such that individual and collective actions would be meaningful to the tribe in light of its inherited cultural values while also being economically effective. In the cultural recovery work of the traditionalists and the legal advocacy of the reformists, whose description of the present situation would prevail? Which ought to guide conduct, to orient the moral lives of the people? Was the present state of the tribe and its relation with the surrounding culture the true description of the reality the people faced, or was the reality in the memories and untapped wisdom of previous generations? Again, an interpretive and descriptive challenge faces many religious communities around the world: where is one to get insight into one's moral situation in terms of the communal resources and present life of a community?

Second, consider the response to land. The land claims case was certainly about the recovery of tribal lands that were taken unjustly in the government's failure to uphold the terms of the late eighteenth century treaties with Maine and Massachusetts. But it was also a significant religious activity, harkening back to Gluskabe reclaiming the land and water for his children from evil forces. Although it might seem odd to think about the Penobscot legal claims as religious activities, these efforts aimed at establishing the conditions for cultural recovery that far exceeded the return of acres of earth and water. What is more, the idea of "law," as seen in many chapters of this book, is important for many religions and so for religious ethics. If the land is a source of spiritual power and its human and animal inhabitants and so a model of the community's harmonious existence, then efforts to bring people to it and preserve it for future generations is a religious activity. Law becomes a practice to give people access to empowerment by what they hold to be ultimately real and important. These developments offered moral descriptions; they offered an interpretation of a reality (the land) by offering a counterwitness (reclamation for responsible use). The land was an ancient home, filled with the power, promise, and ambiguity of a people. Moral blindness conceals the context of the moral life (the land) and thus distorts moral understanding. The stories of Gluskabe and religious practices aim to overcome that blindness by means of mythic and ritual insight.[45]

---

45 One of the persistent themes in Penobscot writing is the theme of "coming back" to Indian Island. See McBride, B. (1999). *Women of the Dawn*. Lincoln: University of Nebraska Press. McBride profiles the life of four women, all given the Christian name Mary (or Molly as they were known in their community) across different time periods who experienced different passages of return to their homeland: Molly Mathilde (Marie Mathilde, 1665–1717 CE), Molly Ockett (Marie Agathe, 1740–1816), Molly Molasses (Mary Pelagie, 1775–1867), Molly Dellis (Mary Alice Nelson Archambaud/"Spotted Elk," 1903–1977). McBride's book also makes the interesting suggestion that one person's return to their homeland is strongly linked to their ancestors' experiences of return. This suggests, for our purposes, that a complex relationship exists between an individual's description of their moral space and their community's description.

Christian Religious Practices

Christian practices are also examples of moral descriptions in light of changing historical circumstances. The Book of Psalms and the Gospel of Matthew were texts that offered descriptions of the world that communicated some of the basic values of the community (their normative dimension of ethics) while also suggesting a practical response for how to live those values in light of the new situations in each age. These texts are foundational to ancient Christian practices and continue to be drawn upon to offer descriptions, norms, and practical guidance to communities today.

The Psalms are a central aspect of two longstanding forms of Catholic Christian worship: the Liturgy of the Hours and the Liturgy of the Eucharist. The latter is one of the two sacraments (the other is baptism) shared by Protestant, Orthodox, and Catholic Christians whereas the former is a style of prayer still practiced in intentional Christian – mainly Catholic – communities. The Liturgy of the Hours is an ancient practice of daily prayer of the Christian Churches structured around a daily recitation of the Psalms spread over the hours of the day. Still practiced in many Christian monastic communities, the content of the Psalms expresses the ways that the community has understood its relationship to God, drawn in part and modeled on its understanding of how the Jewish people related to God. The Psalms voice the community's response to God in various ways: praise, petition, lament, and so on. In the Liturgy of the Hours, the Christian community expresses its conviction that each of those responses is a legitimate – indeed appropriate and necessary – response by human beings to the mystery at the source of their existence. It is a way to probe the meaning and ambiguity of time through the flow of the music linked with the poetry of the Psalms. The grandeur and poverty of human beings as dust that breathes is given expression and, with it, insight beyond human blindness due to pride, greed, ignorance, and fear.

Monastic communities consecrate the hours of the day by singing the Psalms in the early morning hours, at daybreak, at midday, in the afternoon and evening, and at night. Structured around the Rule of St. Benedict, the life of the monastic community is ordered by prayer and physical labor and seeks to establish an environment of hospitality to visitors. The Psalms express both the promise and the difficulty of this form of life, offering cries of lament for human frailty and injustice while commending the pain and brokenness of the world to God's mercy. They reveal that more is going on in human time than we think. We are blind to the moral meaning and depth of human time. The Psalms, like all of scripture, are believed to disclose the reality and action of God within human time and history and thus provide an orientation for life.

The communities struggled to form their lives by the visions of the Psalms, but they were nonetheless implicated in the egos and political agendas of their age. From the early medieval period to our day, religious orders such as the

Benedictines have been criticized from without and reformed from within as they succumbed to the blindness that their own songs exposed.[46]

The movement between blindness and insight appears also in Christian sacramental practice. The Eucharist is a ritual celebration that commemorates the last days in the life of Jesus of Nazareth and functions as the central symbol of the life of the Christian community. Recorded in the Gospel of Matthew (26:17–30),[47] the story tells of the Passover meal Jesus shared with his disciples before he was handed over to the Roman authorities. The bread broken and distributed to the disciples and the cup of wine shared by those gathered with him in the hours before his death are taken to symbolize the self-giving love of Jesus and also to model the life of his Church as one people – the body of Christ united in one faith through baptism. Like the experience of the Penobscot, past and present is linked: believers are taken into "the night in which he (Christ) was betrayed" but in the present moment of the gathered congregation even as the Holy Spirit acts in the meal to make common human realities – bread and wine – into a sacrament, a sacred sign – of Christ's body and blood. In this practice, the common act of human eating and sharing food reveals the presence of the divine and access to divine power in the work of the people (*liturgy*).

The Eucharist has been a source of transformative power in the course of human history but, also, tragically, the source of great misery. Wars between Christians of different denominations have had, at their roots, debates about the meaning of this central symbol that is supposed to unite them.[48] The model of Jesus' self-sacrificial love has been used to justify silence or complicity with abuse of the powerless in families, churches, and nations. Even in academic debates in religious ethics, one too often hears the Eucharist, as a symbol for the Church, used to justify a stance of intellectual and religious superiority over those who engage in the soiled realism of politics and government. In that way, this powerful symbol does not give rise to thought but rather induces thought to sleep.[49] Sadly, what should bring insight to moral existence and its relation to the divine becomes a mechanism of blindness.

---

46 For an account of the formation of the Benedictine community and the history of its reform movements, see Melville, G. (2016). *The World of Medieval Monasticism: Its History and Forms of Life* (trans. J.D. Mixson). Collegeville, MN: Liturgical Press, 24–49 and 136–157.

47 Parallel accounts are found in the Gospel of Mark 14:12–26, the Gospel of Luke 22:7–23, and in Paul's First Letter to the Corinthians 11:23–26.

48 We cannot explore the many difference among Christian theologies of the Eucharist, or Lord's Supper, since our point is about how a practice functions in the descriptive dimension of religious ethics. Other accounts of the Eucharist or other sacred practices, say, baptism, could be used as well. And, sadly, there too there are debates among Christians about its right meaning and practice – some of which led to horrific persecutions, e.g. the violent persecutions in the sixteenth century of the "Anabaptists" by Protestants and Catholics alike.

49 The idea that symbols can give rise to thought is found in the work of Ricoeur. See Ricouer, P. (1967). *The Symbolism of Evil*. New York: Harper & Row and Schweiker, W. (1990). *Mimetic Reflections: A Study in Hermeneutics, Theology, and Ethics*. New York: Fordham University Press.

Religious Rituals and the Complexity of Life

In the cases just explored, one finds the dynamic between blindness and insight at play in religious practices. Religious discourse, just like religious practices, express the basic values of a community but over time they also pronounce on the ambiguity of pursuit of those values. Failure to recognize this ambiguity can have disastrous effects on the lives of communities and the psyches of people. This does not mean that the ambiguity of religion negates its truth or that the religious journeys of human beings are illusory. Rather, religious practices and religious discourse are implicated in life's complexity; they are part of the perplexity of human existence and thus, ironically, sources of both insight and blindness.

Our comparisons show another level of complexity, however. It points not only to the difficulty of interpreting any religious practice but also of identifying religious practices as actually religious. For those familiar with Western discourse about religion, it is no surprise that one can identify practices like the recitation of Psalms or the celebration of the Eucharist as religious practices. The important question is then: what does the comparison between the description offered by Christian practices and Penobscot religious practices yield? And although we have hinted at an answer, how are the legal cases of the Penobscot religious in the way we have defined religion? Are we left with competing and irreconcilable descriptions or is there a more constructive task before us precisely because of the approach we have taken?

Conclusion

We have undertaken one of many possible comparisons in this chapter, but we offer here a few observations on the descriptive dimension of religious ethics as a result of this work. The descriptive dimension answers the question: "What is going on?" Religious discourse and practice are complementary ways of describing a shared moral world from the perspective of debates and struggles to know and live a good life. Religious discourse answers this question through its founding myths and religious symbols; religious practices answer this question through their active response to the world of people and events. In this chapter, we have tried to illustrate the shape of those descriptions but also their depth and significance through reference to stories and ways of life of Native American and Catholic Christian communities.

The answer to what is going on gives a basic framework or paradigm for understanding values and priorities (the normative dimension of its life) and also the parameters within which its decisions will take place (the practical dimension). Its answer to what is going on entails some description of the way the world is and our ability to access that truth about our world. It also entails some account of human beings who can make free decisions within that world in a way that is meaningful to them as moral agents making choices about their forms of life in community with others (the fundamental dimension). Early Penobscot religious discourse relied on ancient tales of ancestors and heroic beings that responded to the community's desire to know themselves through knowledge of their environment. The normative status of the land that was central to Penobscot religious practice is rooted in its early stories of Gluskabe as the man who drew himself forth from the earth and taught the people to live with knowledge of its gifts and limits. Yet this same story and the others discussed in this chapter point to a quite particular account of the land: not a generalized "earth spirituality" but a desire to be connected to a particular place of origin on the Penobscot river and to the people who have inhabited that place as a homeland. That description of the land grounded creative action on behalf of the people to recover it, and disagreements arose among the traditionalists and the progressive reformers about the best way to reverence the land and maintain the tribe's values in a changing culture (the fundamental dimension intersects the practical dimension).

Unlike the Penobscots, the early Christians did not have land as a central religious value. However, there certainly were and continue to be important connections between Christians and Jews concerning the land of Israel and commitments by Christians, no less than other religious communities, to the religious significance of the planet as the shared home of all people. To this day, many Christians engage in the practice of pilgrimage to ancient holy sites, and this devotion is embraced by those Christians as a way to link a physical journey with an inner spiritual journey.[50] The early desert monks and later monastic communities valued the land as a place of retreat and purification, but its value for them lay in its terrain and location rather than in its historical connection to the community of the covenant with Abraham. Put differently, the desert was to be a place of insight and obedience to God and thereby a holy way of life freed from the blindness and distortion of life in the city.

Early Christians offered moral descriptions rooted in an understanding of land and life as gifts from a loving God that required a faithful response illustrated through the language of covenantal obligations. Christian sacraments also employ the symbol of covenant, which was the basis for descriptions of baptism and Eucharist as the signs of a new relationship between God and the people. The Psalms proclaimed a God whose faithful relationship with the

---

50 For an example of a comparative study of theologies of pilgrimage and their effects on views of religious identity and agency, see Laksana, B.A. (2010). Comparative theology: between identity and alterity. In: *The New Comparative Theology: Interreligious Insights from the Next Generation*, (ed. F.X. Clooney, S.J.), 1–20. New York: Continuum.

covenant people would occur through their free response and only in freedom would those choices have value. In the Gospel of Matthew, Jesus calls his disciples to a life of blessedness that would fulfill the people's obligations under the covenant, but it is through mercy and care for the poor that they respond to the gift of friendship with God.

The descriptions offered by each community of what is going on form their moral worlds in which basic values are proposed and defended, decisions made, and free agency realized. But what kind of moral descriptions happen *between* moral worlds? That is a crucial question for the hermeneutical or interpretive task of religious ethics. Are we not left with competing visions of the good life, of basic values and rules for making decisions? Recall that the perspective proposed in this book centers on the nature of interpretation that entails an inherent openness to the ways understanding constructs a shared space of action, a shared "world." It is from this insight that we would like to offer a description of what happens in these spaces between. "[T]he practice of comparative religious ethics contributes to the enactment of a shared moral universe in which diverse ways of being human are preserved amid the claims of responsibility."[51] In this sense, responsibility means that the one who encounters a different religious world and offers an interpretation is responding to that community and also holding oneself accountable for the interpretation offered. This means that neither the community, nor person interpreted, nor the interpreter has a privileged location from which to establish *the* moral meaning and practical truth of the religious practice or belief. Rather, meaning emerges through interpretation of what a people is saying in stories or ways of life and how what is said meets the one who sees and hears in light of their own questions. On this account, what a people is doing is never an ideal achieved or a settled cultural form; it is rather a trajectory toward a view of a good life. What is "grasped by interpreting a community's pictures of life is not the form or nature of the human as such, but precisely what that community is struggling to resemble, is using to inform its specific and historically contingent way of life."[52]

The descriptive and interpretive work of religious ethics will inevitably be partial because human beings, even at their best moments or with great breadth or depth of historical knowledge, cannot see the whole. The ethicist can at best offer relatively adequate descriptions with an appropriate level of humility about what has not been accounted for in their past and what has not yet been

51 Schweiker, W. (1992). The drama of interpretation and the philosophy of religions: an essay on understanding in comparative religious ethics. In: *Discourse and Practice*, (ed. F. Reynolds and D. Tracy), 263–294. Albany: SUNY Press.
52 Ibid., 278.

foreseen about their future.[53] Relatively adequate descriptions of a shared moral situation should not be disparaged for their incompleteness; they are also legitimate insights into shared humanity and the tentativeness of those insights and their humility are part of their virtue. To move too quickly toward a moral description drawn from only one cultural or religious tradition, without conversation across traditions and within traditions, risks perpetuating moral blindness to the humanity of others. It also risks leaving unfilled one's responsibility to be part of a broad, interreligious, and multidisciplinary conversation about the human drama.

No age is immune from moral blindness, and in no age has the fullness of insight into our human condition been reached by the majority of earth's peoples. In part this is because blindness and insight themselves are bound to being human. The Penobscot communities of ancient North America that produced that culture's great stories were offering moral descriptions of their world that revealed certain basic human values and admirable forms of life but were not without their times of blindness occasioned by their situation in history. The same can be said of early Christian communities whose Good News was conditioned by the values of their contributory cultures (Jewish and Hellenistic) and yet also chastened their positive effects in history.

In the next chapter we discuss the normative dimension of religious ethics. Yet, we should take care to remember that descriptions – the movement between blindness and insight – will condition the identification of and argument for normative positions. Indeed some normative positions will carry within them partial insight into our human situation and also the residue of moral blindness. The conversation between cultures, and periods of human history, will have the same features that are neither altogether ideal nor altogether regrettable. The moral life is the human edge of thinking that seeks to orient life within that ambiguity and promise.

---

53 We adopt and also amend the language of "relative adequacy" from Schubert Ogden and David Tracy who use it to explain the phenomenon of a symbol system (religious or some other kind) to explain our existential situation in any age. His view is that people in any historical period are looking for ways to explain "what is going on" in their world and they turn to symbols, and the larger language systems, narratives, and forms of life in which symbols are used, to help people to say what is happening in their experience, mindful that experience is also affected by culture and language. See Ogden, S. (1988). *On Theology*. New York: Harper & Row. and Tracy, D. (1996 [1975]). *Blessed Rage for Order: The New Pluralism in Theology*. Chicago: University of Chicago Press.

3

Good, Evil, and Beyond

Normative Dimension
Part 1

> Then the Lord God said, "See, the man has become like one of us, know-ing good and evil; and now, he might reach out his hand and take also from the tree of life, and eat, and live forever" – therefore the Lord God sent him forth from the garden of Eden, to till the ground from which he was taken.
> —Gen 3:22–23

> Nor should you tremble to perceive your duty [*dharma*] as a warrior; for him there is nothing better than a battle that is righteous [*dharma*].
> —*Bhagavad Gītā* 2, 31[1]

Beyond Good and Evil?

The meaning of good and evil is one of the most pressing and vexing questions in human individual and social life. In every time and place, human beings must decide how to live with respect to beliefs and values they have about what is good and evil as well as what defines right and wrong actions.[2] If people did

---

1 Flood, G. and Martin, C. (2012). *The Bhagavad Gita: A New Translation*, 17. New York: W.W. Norton and Company.
2 We speak of "having" beliefs and values in order to avoid the implication that such beliefs are a matter solely of rational selection on the part of a discrete individual in determining her or his actions. Although some beliefs are held in that way, it is also the case that we have beliefs and values that are unconscious and communal and that animate action in ways not completely known to the agent. This is a crucial point for religious ethics because the religions often give an account of powers, divine or demonic and variously conceived, acting in the agent or community. Religious ethics thereby complicates the question of agency beyond usual philosophical accounts of what defines an agent. We discuss these issues at greater length later. The important point at this juncture is that agents are moved to act by values and beliefs – variously held – that provide reasons for actions.

Religious Ethics: Meaning and Method, First Edition. William Schweiker and David A. Clairmont.
© 2020 William Schweiker and David A. Clairmont. Published 2020 by John Wiley & Sons Ltd.

not have the capacity for action, for example, if they were completely determine by someone (a god) or something (genetics; social structures and ideologies; coercion) to act in certain ways, or if one had no sense of what is good or
what ought not to be done, then they would not be *moral* agents although they
might be agents in some nonmoral sense. Moral agency is the capacity to have
beliefs and values about what to do and what kinds of people to become and
also to have the power to act (or refrain from acting) in relation to those values
and beliefs and so to give reasons for one's actions in terms of beliefs, values,
and, as seen in the previous chapter, descriptions of moral situations. The
capacity for action as well as choice will concern us in greater detail in Chapter 5
of this book. That later discussion is closely linked to this chapter. In this chapter we explore ways that religions think about good and evil, right and wrong,
and what is beyond the distinction between good and evil.

It is clear, then, that many questions are posed about good and evil. These are
the kinds of questions that take us to the *normative dimension* of religious ethics. By "normative" we mean the norms, rules, and values that ought to orient
the life of an agent or community of agents. Normative reflection, then,
demands a consideration of what those norms, rules, and values might be and
how they can and ought to orient people's conduct. A swarm of questions
thereby arise for ethical thinking. What is the origin of evil? What do we mean
by "goodness"? Is it a quality of actions, say, a just or merciful act, or is goodness right relations among people, say "justice"? Maybe, the good is some ultimate and even divine reality. Or is "good" just a term used for something
fulfilling its function well, like a "good" lawn mower or a "good" computer?
How can a person be good in a world that is scarred by violence and war? Does
the idea of a "good warrior" make sense, as we read in the *Bhagavad Gītā* about
Kṛṣṇa's speech to Arjuna? Why did Jesus chasten a man for calling him "good"
and insist that only God in Heaven is good (Lk 18:19)? Does God recognize or
perceive the Good or is "God" just another name for what we mean by the
Good? Are the types or forms of good, for example the good of our bodies,
their health and flourishing – quite distinct from moral goodness? And in any
case, what is meant by "moral" goodness? The world's religions pose the question of whether "good" and "evil" name different realities, and, additionally, if
the object of religious devotion (what is ultimately important, real, empowering) is somehow beyond the distinction between good and evil that structures
human historical and social existence or is the moral space of life defined by an
eternal opposition and even conflict between Good and Evil.

So, in this chapter we explore the *normative* dimension of religious ethics.
Several insights will be gained about the relation between religion and morality. We will see, first, that the ethics of religious traditions do not fit neatly into
the standard philosophical distinction between deontological, teleological, and
virtue forms of ethics. Rather, the religions, and in this chapter Hindu and
Christian ethics, interweave in complex ways the domain of basic goods with

moral rules (Golden and Silver) as well as obligations entailed in people's social roles. Second, we isolate a spiraling dynamic to the religious life where progress in virtue and character is recursively mediated through rules, actions, and goods leading to further virtuous character. Third, the relation between moral goodness and the transcendent good takes different forms: (i) the moral good and the transcendent good are the same for some religions; (ii) the moral good is distinct from the transcendent good in other religions; and, (iii) the moral good is a necessary but not sufficient condition for the transcendent good in still other religions.

The discussion in this chapter allows us later to outline the analogies between two traditions, Christian and Hindu, on the question of warfare. In the Vedānta school of Hinduism, *ātman* is one's true self and beyond identification with phenomena we call "good" or "evil." Salvation or liberation is found in the realization that one's actual self is *ātman* and it is identical with ultimate reality, *brahman*.[3] In the *Gītā*, Kṛṣṇa teaches Arjuna about how to live and also the truth of *ātman*. Overlooking a horrible battle, Arjuna ponders his duty to join the battle knowing that doing so will pit him against some of his family and thereby violate familial duties, like the care of one's parents and siblings. Kṛṣṇa reveals to him that ultimately salvation is liberation from the struggle and sorrow of life through the knowledge that *ātman=brahman*.[4] Arjuna is blind to the deeper reality of *ātman* and is fixated on – trapped by or in bondage to – the realities he sees in the war before him (see Chapter 2). Given that truth that *brahman* and *ātman* are one, Arjuna's task, Kṛṣṇa teaches, is to do his soldierly duty. Fighting in a righteous war is the greatest good for a warrior. It is good both to fulfill one's social function, like being a warrior, and it is good to fulfill that function in the proper way, namely to fight in a righteous war. It

---

3 In this chapter, we take as our point of reference the Vedānta school known as Advaita (or "nondual"), associated with the teachings of Śaṅkara (788–820 CE). There are, however, other prominent schools of interpretations such as Viśiṣṭādvaita ("qualified nondual"), associated with the teachings of Rāmānuja, and Dvaita ("dual"), associated with the teachings of Madhva. As Gavin Flood writes, "In complete contrast to the *advaita* of Śaṅkara, Madhva maintains that the correct interpretation of sacred scripture is dualistic: that scripture maintains an eternal distinction between the individual self and the Lord. Whereas the Advaita tradition emphasizes the non-difference (*abheda*) between the self and the absolute, Madhva insists on their complete distinction. Difference or *bheda* is a cornerstone of his theology and scriptural interpretation. Each thing in the universe is itself and unique and cannot be reduced to something else" (246). For more on the distinction among Hindu schools of interpretation, see Flood, G. (1996). *An Introduction to Hinduism*, 224–249. Cambridge: Cambridge University Press.

4 Gavin Flood explains, "In the Brāhmaṇas, the term *brahman* means the power of the ritual, apart from which there is nothing more ancient or brighter … In time, a process of abstraction occurred whereby *brahman* became a principle referring not only to the power of the ritual, but also to the essence of the universe; the very being at the heart of all appearances" (84). See Flood, G. (1996). *An Introduction to Hinduism*. Cambridge: Cambridge University Press.

is good with respect to both the reality of *ātman* and the human, historical domain of reality.

This description of the identity of all things in ultimate reality (*brahman*) found in teaching of the *Gītā* seems to be utterly missing in the Bible. God transcends the world and is not identified with reality even if God creates and acts in the world and is the ultimate reality that surrounds and permeates everything else. In the creation accounts in the book of Genesis, God knows good and evil and yet God transcends the distinction between good and evil in eternal life. God commands Adam and Eve not to eat from the Tree of the Knowledge of Good and Evil; if they do, then they will die. The text intimates that knowing good and evil is to become godlike. God's being, the story proclaims, is eternal and beyond the distinction between good and evil even if God knows good and evil and God's commands are good. What then is the meaning of good and evil for human decisions and the orientation of personal and social life? Why are Adam and Eve banished from Eden once they attain knowledge of good and evil?

Unsurprisingly, the question of the meaning of good and evil has been a dominant topic in the history of ethics. It is one topic that crosses between religious and nonreligious ethics. It is also linked, as noted in Chapter 2, to descriptions of reality providing insight meant to overcome moral blindness. Often the highest good (Latin: *summum bonum*) is defined in terms of human flourishing, well-being, or happiness (Greek: *eudaimonia*). Other thinkers, like the ancient Roman Stoics, insist that fulfilling one's moral duty is true happiness whereas the modern Western philosopher Immanuel Kant (1724–1804 CE) thought that the purpose of the moral life was to make oneself morally *worthy* of happiness. People do not agree on what defines happiness. Some think it is wealth and others power; some think happiness is about pleasure whereas others seek physical or spiritual perfection. Because of the wild diversity of ideas about happiness, Kant reasoned that morality cannot be defined in terms of happiness. Morality must be about the duties we owe to others and to ourselves as rational beings. Then again, philosophers like Plato in the ancient world or Iris Murdoch in our time, taught that the Good is a transcendent reality in the light of which reality is revealed in its true depth and complexity. The task of the moral life is to escape moral blindness through an ascent to a vision of the Good. The debate about the meaning of the "good" continues in our day.

The specific task of the present chapter is to explore how religious conceptions of what exists beyond good and evil (e.g. God, *brahman/ātman*) relate to moral convictions about good and evil, right and wrong, that are central to responsible human life. Our focus is on the fact that the religions affirm the distinction between good and evil and yet, paradoxically, deny its ultimate nature. We know that in the history of religion there are religious communities that deny any such "beyond" and insist, as ancient Manichaeism did and so too Zoroastrianism, that reality is defined by a cosmic battle between Good and

Evil. Granting this fact, we think the discussion of this chapter can also illuminate those traditions although they are not our focus of attention. And this is because human existence viewed religiously takes place in the tension between different domains of reality or "worlds," some of which are defined by our concepts of good and evil whereas others are not.

In exploring this tension and the perplexity it causes, we need to begin with a distinction important in the study of religion even though we will complicate the distinction as this chapter progresses. The distinction is between dualism and nondualism among the religions. What do these terms mean when used in ethics? And we must also clarify the way Western moral philosophy has defined types of ethics. Recall that one aim of this book is to show that the standard typology of ethics is not adequate to grasp the complexity of the moral beliefs and practices of actual religions. The usual typology focuses on the normative dimension of ethics and so this chapter is the appropriate place for us to clarify what are believed to be the basic "types" of ethics as well as some of their subtypes.[5] Before turning to the question of good and evil, we need them some clarity about "dualism" and types of ethics.

Dualism and the Types of Ethics

Dualism in ethics means the idea that good and evil can be understood and defined only in their difference, whether that difference is an opposition (good and evil are essentially opposed to each other) or complementary relation (e.g. history is a mixture of good and evil actions and relations) or necessarily related (we cannot make sense of "good" without some idea of "evil"). For example, in ancient Gnostic religion, say, Manichaeism, two ultimate realities are at war with each other, a Good god and an Evil one. Reality is defined by the conflict between these opposing realities. (In American popular culture something similar to this Gnostic outlook is found in the *Star Wars* movies: the good side and the dark side of the "Force.") Conversely, some traditional indigenous religions, which among early historians of religion was sometimes called animism, see good and evil as equal, opposed, or even complementary forces. The religious life is about appeasing the forces of evil through ritual actions and gaining access to the power of good for the purposes of health and social flourishing (see Chapter 2). The point of these dualistic outlooks is that reality is defined morally by a difference that cannot be overcome, cannot be transcended.

---

5 As thinkers from Max Weber and Ernst Troeltsch onward have noted, "types" are conceptual constructs meant to isolate the most basic meaning and relation of disparate positions. A typology does not claim to be a detailed analysis of any actual position, but, rather, serves the purpose of allowing us to grasp analogies among positions.

Conversely, nondualism, or monism, in religion is any set of convictions which denies that (ultimate) reality is defined by and understandable through the opposition or complementarity of good and evil. In nondualistic visions, ultimate reality (e.g. *brahman* or the *dharma*) is "beyond" good and evil even though good and evil remain crucial conventional ideas for the orientation of human life and the organization of human communities. The question for nondualist traditions is, accordingly, the status and meaning of the distinction between moral good and moral evil in relation to ultimate reality.

The complexity of the question about good and evil – the distinction between them and the status of each term – is aptly captured in the passages from the Bible and the *Bhagavad Gītā* cited at the head of this chapter. This is important because often the monotheistic religious traditions (Judaism, Christianity, and Islam) are supposedly dualistic in their outlooks whereas the great traditions that arose in India (Hinduism and Buddhism) and some indigenous religions are seen as nondualistic. Matters are more complicated than that easy distinction claims. How can Kṛṣṇa implore Arjuna to join a battle? For that matter, why are Adam and Eve exiled from paradise for eating from the Tree of Good and Evil only to see their younger son (Abel) murdered by his brother (Cain)? Do these stories reveal anything about ideas of good and evil in human life and thus in ethical reflection?

Before we explore good and evil from a religious perspective, a distinction needs to be explored between types of ethics. Here we want to note, and then challenge from the perspective of religious ethics, a distinction drawn by Western moral philosophers when speaking about the normative dimension of ethics. The distinction is between basic types of ethics: *teleological* ethics and *deontological* ethics and sometimes *virtue* ethics. Mountains of books have been written that assert that these kinds of ethics, and various subtypes of each, define the nature of morality as such.[6] Further, these types of ethics are believed to be at odds and thereby irreconcilable, and, as a consequence, some choice between them is needed even if the grounds for that choice are difficult to provide. If teleology, deontology, and virtue ethics along with their various subtypes exhaustively define the options within ethics, then one or the other

---

6 One of the most famous texts that make a version of this claim and that has had immense influence in the English-speaking world, on theologians no less than philosophers, is Frankena, W. (1988). *Ethics*, 2e. Upper Saddle River, NJ: Prentice Hall. One purpose of our writing *Religious Ethics: Meaning and Method* is to replace, at least among scholars of religion, Frankena's text, which we judge falsely simplifies religious ethics. For a magisterial treatment of this issue in philosophy, see Sidgwick, H. (1966). *The Methods of Ethics*, 7e, New York: Dover Books. Sidgwick does not treat the religions at all. In fact, he holds that religion is about the Ultimate Good of the universe, whereas ethics is delimited to the human good and right action. Frankena introduces a tripartite scheme of types of ethics: egoism, intuitionism, and utilitarianism. We follow and disrupt his typology simply because of its influence on religious ethics. "Any ethics, and especially Religious Ethics," must account for all of these supposed independent forms of ethics simple because human life is more complex than these types seems to allow.

outlook will be the basis for making the decision between them thereby leading, oddly, to a logical circle. That is, one would use a form of ethics (say, deontology) to define the difference between types of ethics and to show that deontology is actually the only valid type.

However, it seems clear enough to common sense that the conduct of people's actual lives always involve duties and obligations to others and to oneself, and so some "deontological" aspect, but also goals striven for, ends sought, purposes that guide human decision-making, and so "teleological" as well, and includes character traits, virtues. A discussion of these kinds of ethics will be helpful in making our main point, namely, that religious traditions have visions of what is good and right that do not fit completely into one type or another. The religions, on our account, are trying to get at, understand, articulate, and guide people's lives amid the messy complexity of actual human life. It is why we are proposing an ethics developed from within the religions in contrast to standard types of moral theory, that is, types of metareflection on the meaning and character of morality.

We now explore *teleological* and *deontological* ethics and in a later chapter *virtue* ethics in order to show why we need a better account of the normative dimension of religious ethics, an account developed from within the resources of the religions. Our task is not to give an exhaustive account of the types of ethics and their various subtypes. One can read a textbook on ethics to find a treatment of these types.[7] Our concern is to offer in broad strokes an account of the types of ethics and then turn to explore the normative dimension of religious ethics.

The Ethics of Ends

Teleological ethics says that the meaning of "Good" derives from some end or purpose or goal, sought and realized, by an individual agent or community. The term *teleology* derives from two Greek words meaning speaking or thinking (*logos*) about some end (*telos*). While the term is of Greek origin, the idea it conveys is pervasive in individual and social life. Human action, whether

---

7 For a discussion of these issues see Schweiker, W. (ed.) (2005). *The Blackwell Companion to Religious Ethics*. Oxford: Blackwell. and also the forthcoming *Encyclopedia of Religious Ethics*. Sometimes it is also argued that there are other basic type of ethics. Some thinkers champion "virtue ethics," which is focused on the formation of virtuous character and thus a kind of teleological perfectionism. The end or good sought is the good or virtuous person. A possible basic type of ethics seeks to render teleology and ideontology productive by moving beyond so-called *cathekontic* ethics, or the ethics of the fitting. The theologian Richard Niebuhr (1999) proposed this kind of responsibility ethics in his *The Responsible Self: An Essay on Christian Moral Philosophy*, new edition, Library of Theological Ethics. Louisville, KY: Westminster John Knox Press. Niebuhr's work has had immense influence on Christian ethics in the United States. Our account of the meaning and method of religious ethics has some resonance with an ethics of the fitting, but we are developing it in a multidimensional and hermeneutical way that departs significantly from Niebuhr's work.

individual or communal, aims at some goal, some end, or some purpose that the agent(s) seeks, knowingly or not, to realize, successfully or not. If one asks for the reason or justification of some action, one is asking, on this type of ethics, what end was sought, what goal realized or not. Of course, aiming at some goal also requires that one consider the proper *means* to attain or realize it. In willing some end the agent endorses the means to that end. Importantly, for some forms of teleological ethics the end, the *telos*, justifies *any means* for its attainment. If the end sought is "the greatest good for the greatest number of sentient beings," as Jeremy Bentham (1748–1832 CE) formulated the principle of utilitarianism, the means to attain that end is justified even if that would mean the suffering or distress of a minority of people or sentient beings. Other kinds of teleological ethics, say, Aristotelian or Platonic virtue ethics, would insist that a virtuous action must be done for the right reason and in the right way; there must be virtuous means to a virtuous end. Different kinds of teleological ethics make different judgments about the moral relation between means and ends, and all of them function with a means/ends logic.[8]

The brief mention of Bentham and Plato not only signals differences in how to understand justifiable means to good ends, it is also meant to indicate the defining difference between subtypes of teleological ethics. Although it is the case that a teleological type of ethics defines the "good" in terms of an end or purpose, the aim or purpose one can and ought to seek has been understood in different ways. Plato and other ancient Greek and Roman thinkers defined the "end" in terms of *eudaimonia,* sometimes translated as "happiness" but more properly understood as well-being and well-doing or "flourishing." Thinkers disagreed on how rightly to define human *eudaimonia*. Epicurus (c. 341–270 BCE), an ancient Greek philosopher, taught that the highest good was one in which pleasure is greater than pain throughout a human lifetime. The good is *hedon* or pleasure. Although Epicurus is accused of a view of life more suitable to animals than the nobility of human beings guided by reason, that criticism is not correct. The Epicurians, followers of Epicurus's teachings, realized that human pleasure is fleeting and therefore the real challenge of the good life is to avoid pain, physical or psychological. A virtuous life, they held, is the path to self-sufficiency and thus the good, that is, *eudaimonia*. Jeremy Bentham's utilitarian ethics is also hedonistic; minimizing pain and maximizing pleasure defines the end or good one should seek. Whereas Epicurus taught that individual pleasure/pain were basic, Bentham and other utilitarians proposed a universal hedonism. It is the

---

8 The relationship between teleological forms of ethics and virtue ethics is itself a complex matter that we address in more detail later in the book (see Chapters 5 and 6 on the fundamental and metaethical dimensions respectively). For our present purposes, it is enough to say that virtue denotes a good quality of character and that in order to form good qualities of character both the final ends that guide our actions and the more proximate ends (or means) for achieving those final ends must themselves be good.

greatest number of sentient beings that matters most. A current utilitarian philosopher, Peter Singer, uses the criterion of sentience, i.e. the capacity to feel pleasure or pain and to have an interest in avoiding pain, in order to develop an ethics of animal rights not limited to the human species.[9] Even the religions sometimes speak of the good in hedonic terms, say, about the bliss of heaven or other heavenly rewards for those who live devoted lives.

Part of the difficulty with these subtypes of teleological ethics (virtue, eudaimonistic, and utilitarian) is that some kinds of pleasure or pain, say, fidelity in friendship or a sense of shame, cannot be sought directly in action. One cannot choose to experience the pleasure of friendship – admittedly a quite refined and complex good. Friendship is a form of human pleasure that requires one to do other things, say, be honest, and hope a friendship will develop. Shame, whether deserved or not, is not like physical pain; it is a self-awareness of being accused of some wrongdoing, deserving or not. What is missing in some teleological ethics is a sense of what is called the "moral paradox." Some ends, some goods, cannot be directly sought but come about while attending to one's obligations and duties; they cannot be pursued with a kind of pure intention that does not also, at the same time, bring about diminutions of other goods. This is especially important in religious ethics, as we will see. If one does some good action, say helping the poor, with an eye to one's reward of heaven or out of fear of God's punishment, then one is not acting from genuinely moral motives. This is one reason that Immanuel Kant, in his *Critique of Practical Reason*, wrote that the only thing "good" in this world or any other world is a *good will*. A good will acts for *moral* reasons – that is, out of a disinterested duty to do what is right – rather than desire for happiness or the fear of pain and punishment. Further, hedonistic types of teleological ethics often seem to confuse experiences we do have, say the pleasure of sex, with what we *ought* to seek. Although sexual love is pleasurable, that does not mean that it should always be sought. Too often hedonistic ethics confuse what *is* the case with what *ought* to be done.

There are other ways to think about the good as a proper human end rather than as pleasure and pain. These forms of ethics try to avoid the difficulties of thinking about the good in hedonistic terms. Aristotle spoke about *eudaimonia* as the aim of a good life. By this term he meant that the human good was living and acting well and that requires developing and exercising virtues, like courage for a warrior. Of course there are forces and events outside of one's control that can thwart or destroy one's pursuit of *eudaimonia*, for example when a warrior is taken as a slave in battle. The truly happy life will be a combination of good circumstances, natural capacities, and virtuous action.

---

9 See Singer, P. (2001). *Unsanctifying Human Life: Essays on Ethics*, (ed. Kuhse, H.) Oxford: Blackwell.

Furthermore, Aristotle asks if there is a specific *function* of a human being, the perfection and fulfillment of which would define well-being and well-doing (*eudaimonia*). He argues that although other animals are sentient (feel pleasure and pain) and also social (they live in some kind of community, say, a herd) only human beings are rational social animals. Rationality as the capacity to direct the conduct of one's life in a reflective way is the specific function of human beings. The highest good must be the perfection of that function, what Aristotle in Book 10 of his *Nicomachean Ethics* calls the life of contemplation. There are other human goods that perfect human nature, like friendship as the good of our social being and also physical health and excellence. Yet contemplation of the Unmoved Mover (a philosophical conception of the divine) is the highest human good. Accordingly, in addition to vulnerability to forces and events that might impede or destroy the human good, only a few people – the philosophers – have the capacity, time, and luxury to pursue and to attain the highest good of contemplation.

The ancient Stoics, by contrast to Aristotle, sought to show that the highest good of the virtuous life is open, in principle, to everyone. Importantly, the slave Epictetus (c. 55–135 CE) and the emperor Marcus Aurelius (121–180 CE) were Stoic sages. The Stoics held that virtue, and virtue alone, was the highest good and to attain this good required self-sufficiency and *apatheia* about any thing, event, or misdeed that might harm one by disturbing the calmness and order of the soul. One is to live according to nature, because "nature" is ruled by *logos* (reason) and is divine. In fact, living by nature, and so reason, coheres with being human. As Marcus Aurelius put it in his *Meditations*: "A little flesh, a little breath, and Reason to rule all – that is myself."[10] The sage may attain the good of virtue despite the fact that one is bound to servitude (Epictetus) or cast into war and the death of friends and children (Marcus Aurelius). One is to do one's duty in the position that divine reason (*logos*) has assigned, practice *apatheia*, and cultivate virtue. Virtue is its own reward and therefore the highest good is open, in principle, to everyone.

Closely related to Aristotle's and the Stoics' visions there are other teleological ethics that focus on human perfection. Orthodox Christians believe that the good of life is *theosis*, becoming God-like through God's grace and the development of virtue. The Catholic theologian and saint, Thomas Aquinas (c. 1225–1274 CE), noted that human beings have two distinct but related ends and goods. There is the natural end of our lives as rational, social animals, which includes the goods of health, justice, and intellectual achievement. To attain that end, one must develop the cardinal virtues (courage, temperance, justice, and prudence or wisdom). But in order to gain the supernatural good of friendship with God and the vision of God, one needs perfection by grace

---

10 Aurelius, M. (1964). *Meditations* (trans. M. Staniforth). New York: Penguin, Bk II, 2.

(the active presence of God in the life of the believer) through the infusing on the soul of the theological virtues (faith, hope, and love). The cardinal virtues too may be brought to a higher level and further unified in the life of believer through the infusion of grace. Thomas's ethics is profoundly religious because there is a sacred domain of reality, the supernatural order that surrounds and permeates the natural and historical domain. The moral life, accordingly, must be related to both realities and also make contact with and be empowered by God. Likewise, the "natural law," that is, human practical reason that knows the first precept of the law ("seek good and avoid evil"), is related to "eternal law" (the mind of God), which includes for Christians the "new law," that is, the law of love given to the believer through the Holy Spirit. The types of *teleological* ethics differ in terms of their conceptions of the Good (pleasure, perfection, *theosis*, well-being and well-doing) and also whether the focus is the individual, community, species, and/or the divine.

The Ethics of Duty

What about *deontological* ethics? Here too we find a variety of subtypes within this kind of ethics. What they share is that the moral life is about duty and obligation and so ethics is speaking and thinking (*logos*) about duty (*deon*). What is the source of moral obligation? If some actions are intrinsically wrong are there any exceptions to those duties? How should someone apply moral rules to specific situations where duties or obligations conflict with, say, duties as a warrior and duties as a son? For deontological ethics, morality cannot be about seeking the Good simply because, as we have seen, there are so many ideas about what is Good: God, pleasure, human moral perfection, on and on. Insofar as there is little agreement about the highest good (*summum bonum*), morality must be about something else. People often praise and esteem someone who has done his or her duty despite the harm or misfortune that might bring to the actor. What is more, wrongful action can destroy the goodness of some end of action. A student might cheat in the pursuit of a high grade on an examination, and even in an ethics class! Yet once this deception is discovered, the grade loses its meaning. If teleological ethics focuses on ends, then deontological ethics focuses on laws and duties owed to oneself and to others irrespective of ends sought. The different subtypes of deontological ethics arise in terms of the source of obligation to do one's duties, which duties are most basic, and if there are universal moral duties.

Sometimes, duties and obligations, as the Stoics argued, have their source in the social role one has, say as a parent, or, in the quotation from the *Gītā*, as a warrior. There is a code of honor, rules of righteous warfare, and Kṛṣṇa seems clear that a warrior must not waver in duty to fight in a righteous war. Parents have obligations to their children and children to parents, if one thinks of the Ten Commandments in the Bible: "Honor your father and your mother" (Ex

20:12a). Of course, parental duties might be different in different cultures and the duties of soldiers are conceived differently in different religions, a topic we will explore later in this chapter. The point is that some forms of deontological ethics focus on the duties that define the obligations of social roles and ranks.

Mention of the Ten Commandments, that is, the Decalogue or Ten Words in the Bible, denotes one of the most ancient and pervasive forms of deontological ethics, namely, divine command ethics. Kṛṣṇa, a god, commands Arjuna to remember his duties as a warrior. God, in the book of Exodus in the Bible, commands the moral law in the form of the Decalogue. The *Qur'ān* is believed by Muslims to be Muḥammad's recitation of the words and commands of Allah. A divine command ethics argues that the most basic moral laws and duties come from God or gods. These commands apply to every human being, for example in the Decalogue, or they might be directed to an individual or community. In the passage from Genesis at the head of this chapter, Adam and Eve are exiled from the Garden of Eden because they violated God's commandment not to eat from the Tree of the Knowledge of Good and Evil.

The proper response to a divine command is obedience. Obedience, which has as its root meaning a form of attentive listening, means to indicate the proper motive for following the moral law or God's command: one is to obey out of reverence for God's command and respect for God's law. One must listen to the one to whom one owes one's existence in order to acknowledge proper relation. Further, God's command is categorical, that is, its meaning and application are not dependent on any condition other than the fact that God commands it. An intrinsically evil action is, then, an action that never should be performed because it is absolutely or categorically forbidden, say, the act of murder, by the command of God. One task of the ethicist or religious leader (priest, imam, rabbi, jurist) is to help make judgments about the duties that bind a community and to provide judgments about difficult cases. This task has given rise to the long tradition of Jewish and Islamic law, that is, *Halakhah* for Jews and *Sharī'a* among Muslims, and also Canon Law among Catholic Christians. We will explore these forms of reasoning in other chapters.

One challenge to divine command ethics has virtually defined that nature of moral philosophy in Western thought. It is often called the "Euthyphro problem" from Plato's dialogue with that name. In the dialogue Socrates is waiting outside of the courthouse to be put on trial and then condemned to death for corrupting the youth and inventing new gods. A young man named Euthyphro meets Socrates and says that he is taking his father to trial for negligence that led to the death of a slave. Euthyphro's plan shocks Socrates. It seems to violate familial duty. One should obey, protect, and even defend one's father. When asked why he was taking his father to trial, Euthyphro answered that the gods command him to do so. Further, Euthyphro was certain that the command from a god required denying duties to his father. The rest of the dialogue spins around the question whether something is good and pious if the gods command it, a divine command ethics, or if the gods command something because it is good and pious thereby denying the validity of a divine command ethics. The dialogue ends with Euthyphro leaving in silence. Socrates defends the idea that the gods command what is good and therefore the meaning of what is good and right does not depend on the gods. Ethics or moral philosophy is independent of religion. Religion, if it is to be moral, must accord itself with moral standards defined on nonreligious grounds. One can see why Socrates was taken to court for corrupting the young and making new gods!

If one agrees with Socrates that moral laws and duties are not commanded by God or gods, how else can one ground duties and obligation? Moral obligations arise, as we saw, with respect to social roles, like the role of a soldier or parent. Yet for some thinkers, social conventions about roles and duties are not enough to define moral duties, duties that sometimes require that one should resist social roles and duties. There might be cases, very different from Euthyphro's, where a child has a moral obligation not to obey the wish or command of a parent, if, that is, the command or wish was for the child to do something immoral. Should you honor your parents if they tell you to murder an innocent person? If not, then how would one justify and understand the moral law?

Without a doubt the most radical answer to the question of the moral law not dependent on religion is the work of the eighteenth-century philosopher Immanuel Kant. It is crucial to understand some of its features insofar as he is often seen as the purest example of deontological ethics and because the religions often speak about duties, obligations, and God's commands. Indeed, Kant claimed that his concern was to "search for and then establish the supreme principle of morality." This principle he called the "categorical imperative." As his argument develops, it is clear that the supreme principle of morality is a dictate of practical reason, that is, reason guiding and determining human action. So, there is first a claim about the scope and logical form of the categorical imperative: "So act that the maxim of your will (i.e. an internal principle of action) could always hold at the same time as a principle in a giving of a universal law [and hence binding on you as well]."[11] In order for a maxim to count as a *moral* maxim, as opposed to an immoral or nonmoral one, it must be *formal*. In other words, it is not the *content* of one's maxim, say, wanting to play the saxophone, but its logical *form*. The law must apply to everyone; it must be universal.

Next, Kant knew that human beings, as Aristotle and others said, act for ends. Kant asks if there is something whose existence is to be respected as a

---

11 Kant, I. (1977 [1788]). *Critique of Practical Reason* (trans. M. Gregor, intro. A. Reath), 28. Cambridge Texts in the History of Philosophy; German Academy of Sciences Edition: 5. Cambridge: Cambridge University Press. Additions by the authors.

good in itself and not only a means to some other end or purpose. In the *Critique of Practical Reason* he writes:

> The moral law is holy (inviolable). Man is certainly unholy enough, but humanity in his person must be holy to him. Everything in creation which he wishes and over which he has power can be used merely as a means; only man, and with him, every rational creature, is an end in itself.[12]

This allows Kant to articulate the *content* of morality: "Act so that you treat humanity, whether in your own person or in that of another, always as an end and never a means only...."

Of course, one might ask if people from diverse cultures and diverse religions really think that "humanity" is holy and whether or not such universal and formal laws are possible. Our job is not to test the validity of Kant's argument, but, rather, to show its importance for religious ethics. In order to clarify that point, we must note two other features of his ethics. One feature is that human life is social and we have to find ways for communities to be cohesive, to function as a whole, and to have some measure of peace. Kant considers the community of rational beings united through common law as a crucial idea for the moral life. The moral life, and the third form of the categorical imperative, is about the rational possibility of a "Kingdom of Ends," that is, a commonwealth of freedom, good will, and peace. The second feature is that this kingdom is obviously not an actual community. It is an ideal, a regulative ideal, to guide thinking and living. Kant argued that this is the ideal we should realize in history: a community of free people under valid laws.

With these features of Kant's ethics in hand, we can now turn to what they mean for religious ethics. In fact, we have discussed Kant's ethics at some length because it has been a dominant source for developing a religious ethics as well as criticizing and dismissing the religions as resources for ethics.[13] Obviously, Kant conceives of morality as the law of human freedom the source of which is practical reason. Freedom is a postulate of practical reason, that is, freedom is presupposed in order to make sense of the claim of the moral law on human beings. Morality is then about human *autonomy*, that is, giving a law (*nomos*) to ourselves (*auto*). If someone guides their life by the dictate of some other authority (for example, God's, one's community, or one's elders), then

---

12 Kant, *Critique of Practical Reason*, 74; 5: 87.
13 See Ronald Green's attempt to articulate the nature of "religious reason" along Kantian lines. Green, R.M. (1978). *Religious Reason: The Rational and Moral Basis of Religious Belief*. London: Oxford University Press. It is also the case that many contemporary Kantians dismiss religious ethics out of hand.

one's life is under the law (*nomos*) of another (*heteron*), what Kant calls *heter-onomy*. One is then not truly free, not truly master of one's own life.

If that is the case, and Kant argues that it is, then morality and ethics cannot be based on God's will or command. Religion and even the idea of God, if they are to be viable, must be based on morality. Indeed, Kant argues that "religion" is "acting *as if* one's duties are commands of God." We are allowed to postulate the idea of God as a perfect judge of moral action who assures that ultimately the virtuous will be happy. What is more, we are justified in postulating the idea of immortality so that we can act *as if* we have the time needed to make ourselves worthy of happiness. But these are *ideas* of reason (God; immortality). One cannot know much less prove the existence of God or immortality in any strict sense; these ideas are postulates of reason that allow us to conceive of the ultimate harmony of duty and happiness. The reason we cannot know or prove the existence or being of God – in distinction from being justified in *postulating* the idea of God – is that human knowledge, Kant argued in his *Critique of Pure Reason*, requires a synthesis between sense experiences and the forms and categories the human mind uses to make sense of experiences. Kant denied that we have experiences of God and even if we did, they would overwhelm the mind and thereby not be meaningful or even understandable.

Briefly engaging Kant's ethics, we have outlined a form of deontology in which the source of moral duties is practical reason. Kant would see divine command ethics in any form, biblical or in the *Gītā*, as a form of heteronomy, that is, "arbitrary and contingent ordinances of a foreign will."[14] Deontological ethics, no less than teleological ethics, can be given religious and nonreligious formulations. And what is more, there are even other subtypes of each of these kinds of ethics, like "rule-utilitarianism" and discourse deontological ethics and others. It is not our purpose in this chapter, or, in fact, this book, to explore every subtype of deontological and teleological forms of ethical theory.

Many philosophers and religion scholars insist both that these two major types of ethics are incompatible and that is also the case with their religious and nonreligious forms. A divine command theorist might learn a lot from Kant and yet hold that the source of morality is God's command and not pure practical reason. Aristotelians could, in principle, learn something about the roles pain and pleasure have in human life and yet reject the Epicurean and utilitarian conceptions of the Good. However, if the task of this book is to clarify the *meaning* and *method* of *religious ethics*, then one must ask: is the philosophical formulation of the basic types and subtypes of ethics, and so the nature of morality itself, adequate for the work of religious ethics? We must say "no." The remainder of this book aims to explain that answer.

---

14 Kant, *Critique of Practical Reason*, 108; 5: 129.

In order to explore good and evil in religious ethics and what the religions contribute to ethics, we need now to examine (i) the question of the *status* – the reality – of good and evil; (ii) the *knowledge* of good and evil; and (iii) we must compare different religious forms, and so, in this chapter, biblical thought and the vision presented in the *Gītā*. The comparison between the Bible and the *Gītā* will return us to the theme of dualism and monism noted previously. The chapter ends with reflection on war and religious violence, a discussion anticipated throughout the chapter. That concluding comparison is also meant to show the connection between the *normative* and *practical* dimensions of ethics. The chapter thereby picks up a thread throughout this book, namely, how can and ought religious commitments be lived in humane and responsible ways.

The Status of Good and Evil

It might seem odd to explore the normative dimension of religious ethics by beginning with the question of the *status* of good and evil. Why not begin, as Kant and Socrates did, with the *knowledge* of good and evil? After all, how can one talk about the status of anything unless one has some knowledge of it? How can someone, for example, talk about brown, medium-sized dogs or friendship unless one knows color, size, dogs, and friends?[15] The point is granted. In fact, the *knowledge* of good and evil and the *status* of good and evil are intimately interrelated. They are two sides of the same coin, as it were, and that insight is important in religious ethics. If one separates, rather than merely distinguishes, knowledge from status, a normative ethical judgment has been made, implicitly or explicitly. When someone argues that the status of good and evil are dependent on our knowledge of good and evil, then she or he could hold that good and evil are not "real" independent of the forms of human knowledge (logical, conventional, experiential). That judgment would mean that moral norms are a subset of human knowledge. Ethical positions that speak about the *status* of good and evil in terms of *knowledge* of good and evil are forms of what is called *antirealism* in ethics (see Chapter 6). Norms and values have no independent reality outside of how people know, experience, or talk about them. The idea that moral norms arise in relation to social roles would be another example of antirealism in ethics

---

15 At issue here, philosophically, is the relation between ontology (discourse about being) and epistemology (discourse about knowledge). The relation among these intellectual tasks has been hotly debated in modern thought, religious and philosophical, but on the main the religions, given their commitment to moral realism, accent ontological concerns in relation to claims about moral and religious knowledge.

and so too the belief that whatever persons and communities decide to call happiness is in fact the good.

Conversely, if one says that good and evil have status or reality *independent* of human knowledge of them, then the problem is how we come to know good and evil – say, eating from a forbidden tree of knowledge – and how that knowledge (whatever its form) motivates action. Maybe God's commands are the origin of our knowledge of good and evil, and for the believing Jew, Muslim, or Christian obviously God exists independent of our knowledge of God. Maybe Kṛṣṇa must teach us our duty by piercing illusion and ignorance (see Chapter 6). These ideas would be instances of *realism* in ethics, that is, good and evil are real and their existence does not depend exclusively on human knowing, feeling, or experience even if their "meaning" does depend on human experience, knowing, or feeling. Not surprisingly, the religions hold that the knowledge and status of good and evil must be understood together and in complicated ways. The distinction between status and knowledge is not a separation. *Status* is about the reality of good and evil; *knowledge* is about how human beings sense, experience, understand, and speak about them (see Chapters 2 and 6). So, we begin with *status* merely to indicate the predominance of *moral realism* among many religions. However, even that claim will be nuanced later in this chapter.

There is another basic distinction one must note in exploring ideas of good and evil. The distinction is between "naturalism" and "nonnaturalism" in theories of value, or, to use the technical term, *axiology*. Insofar as good and evil are value terms, that is, they denote what has worth or importance and so what human beings should seek, we can ask about the meaning and status of values.[16] By *naturalism* in ethics we mean any moral outlook or axiology that defines value and disvalue (and so what is good and what is evil) with respect to the *nature* of something and its optimal flourishing or functioning. Consider Kṛṣṇa's idea of a "good" warrior. Two conditions must be met in order to call a warrior "good," according to Kṛṣṇa's words to Arjuna, although we can imagine others as well. Beyond physical strength, courage, skill with weapons, there are other attributes of a good warrior: (i) an unwavering sense of duty and (ii) participation in a "righteous war." What defines a righteous war will concern us later in this chapter, if we can even make sense of the idea. At this point we can say that "good" in ethical naturalism names the optimal functioning and right purpose of some moral agent, in this case a "warrior," and the fulfillment of his or her nature. If the warrior wavers in his or her duty and/or she or he is part of an unrighteous war (say, genocide), then the warrior is not

---

16 Sadly, the English term "value" easily conflates two ideas that are important to distinguish in ethics, namely, price and worth. Unless indicates otherwise, when we use "value" we mean moral value or "worth" that is not reducible to monetary price.

a good warrior and maybe not a warrior at all. The term "warrior" is a moral designation distinct from "murderer," "civilian," or "ruler," for instance. Ethical naturalism understands good and evil with respect to the flourishing and functioning of an agent and therefore the need to understand the "nature" of an agent and the "nature" of some human function. One needs to know what a "warrior" is – the nature of being a warrior or what kind of thing a warrior is and does – and what her or his proper function entails. The same would be true of a good sword, dog, social order, or computer. This is why many *eudai-monistic* types of ethics are *naturalistic*. If the good is the flourishing and proper functioning of some being or even species, then one needs to know something about the nature of that being whose existence is independent of our knowledge of it.

Notice that in terms of a naturalist account of moral value, if one wants to understand the meaning of "good," one needs to know the nature of the entity in question and what its proper and optimal functioning entails. In another chapter we return to this point and ask a perplexing question: what is the nature and proper function of a human being? That is a question every religion answers but in ways that are surprisingly similar but also different among religions. We explore later the *fundamental dimension of ethics* focused on whether moral agents have a specific function (see Chapter 5).

At this junction we can see that naturalism in ethics also means, importantly, that what is meant by "good" or "evil" is an object of knowledge, that is, the knowledge of the nature of being, say, a warrior, and optimally doing one's duty in war. Because of the connection between "good" and the knowledge of something and its optimal functioning, naturalism in ethics is often linked by philosophers to *cognitivism*, that is, that good and evil are *objects of knowledge* rather than simple prescriptions of actions or the feelings, positive, or negative, one might have about an action or human relation. As a kind of knowledge, moral judgments about something being good or not is a judgment about which one can be wrong or right. Moral judgments, on this account, have truth-value; there are true and false moral judgments. In fact, Kṛṣṇa is trying to correct Arjuna's understanding of and judgment about the war. What Arjuna judges to be bad – fighting against his kinsmen – is, in truth, a duty and a good one at that. That is the case because ultimate reality is different than the reality Arjuna sees unfolding in the battle.

A cognitive ethical outlook is different than forms of *noncognitivism* in ethics that argue "good" and "evil" are emotional responses to something – judgments that express our feelings or attitudes – or that they are prescriptions for actions about what we ought to do rather than claims about the nature of something, say, a good warrior. Of course, we could interpret Kṛṣṇa's words in these ways as well, that is, he is prescribing (commanding) a course of action for Arjuna and beseeches Arjuna to think about his duty. In that case, what we mean by a "good" warrior is not some claim about the nature and function of the warrior, but, rather, the recommendation of some action, namely, doing one's duty as a warrior.[17]

It is important to realize that Kṛṣṇa's words to Arjuna can be interpreted as either an example of cognitivism, realism, and naturalism in ethics or a kind of ethical noncognitivism, antirealism, and antinaturalism. The *Gītā* shows us how the same religious tradition can be interpreted ethically in different ways. The attempt to clean up the ambiguity found in religious texts by reading them through a single philosophical type of ethics is then doomed to failure. And that fact shows us that maybe the distinction between philosophical and religious ethics is simply wrongheaded. The distinction falsifies the insight of these texts and also how they resist simplification. We can press that insight further and explain "nonnaturalism" in ethics.

One can think of any ethical position that denies a naturalist account of moral value as *nonnaturalist*. Good and evil are not terms for the optimal functioning or the flourishing of some being or creature. The meaning of good and evil is defined without reference to the nature of an agent or the action in question. For this perspective whether Arjuna is a good warrior or not does not depend on what the term warrior means and the kinds of action a fully functioning warrior does; good and evil are understood differently. Nonnaturalism in ethics can take several forms that we explored earlier in this chapter. Divine command ethics, for instance, finds the source of good in what God or the gods command. So, it is good to be a faithful warrior because Kṛṣṇa commands it so. The meaning of the term "good warrior" is simply the soldier who does what god Kṛṣṇa commands. Oddly, we can interpret the same verse from the *Gītā* in naturalist and nonnaturalist, cognitivist and noncognitivist ways.

In this light, consider the story of Adam and Eve in the Garden of Eden, the background for the quotation from the biblical book Genesis that heads this chapter. In creating the world, God pronounces that it is good after each "day" of creation. God recognizes that created value, what God brought into being, has value independent of God's own being. God does not say, "what I do is good and creation is my doing." "God saw that it was good," as the text says after each "day" of creation. This seems to suggest a "naturalist" account of value and in fact the text has been treated that way through much of the history of Christian and Jewish thought. But then, God commands Adam and Eve not to eat from the Tree of the Knowledge of Good and Evil. Here the biblical story seems to stress a nonnaturalist account of value because God's command is not

---

17 As we noted at the head of this chapter, the term *dharma* is often translated as duty (such that we can speak of someone with a given social role fulfilling her or his *dharma* for the good of the community). However, the word *dharma* is also used in the sense of the ordering of the world such to act well is to act in accordance with universal *dharma*. Both senses are at play here because the *Gītā* is concerned, among other things, with the relationship between the good of the whole world and the good for particular persons and communities.

defined in relation to the Tree, the kind of creatures Adam and Eve are, or what actions would bring flourishing to them. What is to be done, how Adam and Eve are to live, is in obedience to the command of God. Like the passage from the *Gītā*, these biblical verses are open to different ethical interpretations.

Other options are also possible. Maybe good and evil mean a subjective emotional response to some event or action. Arjuna's horror over the battlefield might lead a Hindu to think of value in emotivist terms. The evil of war is not a claim about the nature of war or what one is commanded to do, but is the emotional response (e.g. horror or grief) to some event or action that we then recommend others to adopt as well.[18] Or maybe what we mean by good and evil is a prescription for action. Evil is not a matter of feeling, the nature of something, or what a God/god commands, but it is, rather, a kind of prescription: evil is what one ought not to do. An unrighteous war, Kṛṣṇa seems to teach, is something a good warrior ought not to participate in because it is evil. A good warrior participates in a righteous war and that is what Arjuna ought to do. The good soldier is one who acts on that prescription to do one's duty.

Much more could be said about naturalism and nonnaturalism in moral theory as well as cognitivism and noncognitivism and debates about them. Our concern in this chapter is not to give an exhaustive account of theories of value or the types and subtypes of ethics from a philosophical point of view. Companions and textbooks in ethics explore these questions in moral theory at great length.[19] The point here concerns religious thinking about value, norms, and rules. The passages from the Bible and the *Gītā* raise important issues for religious ethics.

First, these passages show us how religious texts, in discussing moral questions like war or the character of human existence, indicate that humans have some knowledge of good and evil but these texts do not fall easily or obviously into one or another philosophical theory of value. They seem to blend together ideas about virtue and goodness with prescriptions of duty. The passage from the Bible at the head of this chapter is open to naturalism as a theory of value but also divine command ethics and maybe even emotivism or prescriptivism. The same ambiguity is found as well in the passage from the *Gītā*.

What are we to make of this ambiguity at the core of classic religious texts and their correlative practices? For many thinkers, inside and outside of the religions, any ambiguity about the meaning and status of basic moral terms is a *problem* to be fixed. What if the ambiguity is not a problem, but a *possibility*

---

18 Sometimes called the "yuk factor," or the "wisdom of repugnance," the idea is that some emotional responses to gross wrongs reveal a deep wisdom and moral sensibility. The idea was developed by Leon Kass, former chair of the President's Council on Bioethics (2001–2005). See Kass, L. (2004). *Life, Liberty and the Defense of Dignity*. San Francisco, CA: Encounter Books.
19 On this see Part 1 of *The Blackwell Companion to Religious Ethics*.

and an *insight*? That is the position of this book. We will see why it is the case in our discussion of war later in this chapter.

Second, no matter what the status of good and evil might be (a command of a god, rooted in the nature and functioning of human beings, a prescription for action), the domain, the space, of human existence on earth and in time is unthinkable without these distinctions. In the Bible, Adam and Eve leave a condition of "paradise" and enter a human world, that is, they enter a space of human decisions, actions, relations, struggles, feelings, and institutions with the knowledge of good and evil and yet also limited by their mortality and fallibility. They know good and evil, as God does, but unlike God they will die and they never have complete and sure knowledge of the moral challenges they face (see Chapter 4). The same is true of the world that Arjuna witnesses. It is a realm of institutions (the family), conflict and death and also a realm of the righteous and the unrighteous, good and evil. The limits on Arjuna are ones of insight and illusion. He does not really see or understand what he is witnessing, that is, the world we perceive and in which we struggle is not ultimately true and real and thus should not be of ultimate importance. *Brahman* is ultimately real and important rather than the fleeting events of human history.

Human existence is unthinkable without the ideas of good and evil and yet human perception and knowledge are limited and so too is human life. In human life and action, good and evil are related to human limitations of knowledge, action, and relations. But there is a realm, a divine or sacred realm, where the good is not limited by human perception or mortality. The question then becomes this one: what is the relation between the human world marked by limitation and also good and evil to this other, sacred, or divine realm? Is it, for instance, a relation of appearance (the battle Arjuna must join) and reality (*ātman* = *brahman*)? Maybe it is the relation between the eternal reality of God, creator and commander, and the finite, temporal realm of human life (Adam and Eve). How are human beings to live so that they are rightly related to the real and the eternal even while they struggle with the limits of their existence? What are human responsibilities within the limitations of finite existence?

We return to these questions later in discussing war and religious violence. Here one can note a third important issue for religious ethics. The biblical texts and the *Gītā* suggest that true moral knowledge is more complex than usually assumed. In the Bible, knowledge of good and evil is due to disobedience or sin. If that is the case, can we rightly know how one ought to live? Will right knowledge depend on God revealing moral truth to human beings – or at least some human beings – say, in the giving of the Law or *Torah* at Sinai (Exodus 20)? How do we know that we have properly interpreted and understood God's commandments? Maybe moral knowledge blends conventional moral rules – like what defines a righteous war – and a deeper mystical insight into true and ultimate reality, as Kṛṣṇa teaches. Much as the religions do not easily fall into neat categories like naturalism/nonnaturalism, dualism/nondualism, deontology/teleology, they also provide distinctive accounts of moral knowledge. We can pursue this point about moral knowledge further and return later in this chapter to the other matters of importance for the normative dimension of religious ethics.

Moral Knowledge

"Then the Lord God said, 'See, the man has become like one of us, knowing good and evil ....'" No matter what one believes about the *status* of good and evil (for example, that it is by a divine command or that these terms [good/evil] have to do with the nature and flourishing of something), there is still the question about how human beings can *know* the meaning of moral concepts. The religions are subtle in how they depict moral knowledge. In the biblical verse just cited, knowledge of good and evil is to become like God. Elsewhere in the Hebrew Bible, in the so-called wisdom literature like the book of Proverbs, the capacity to distinguish good and evil is the mark of wisdom and wisdom is often personified as female and divine (see Chapter 4).

> Get wisdom; get insight: do not
> forget, nor turn away
> from the words of my mouth.
> Do not forsake her, and she will
> keep you;
> love her, and she will guard
> you.
> The beginning of wisdom is this:
> Get wisdom
> and whatever else you get, get
> insight.
> Prize her highly, and she will exalt
> you;
> she will honor you if you
> embrace her.
> (Prov 4:5–8)

In an analogous way, the insight Arjuna is to have, and what the *Gītā* teaches, is that knowledge of the unity of *brahman* and *ātman* allows a person to fulfill her or his worldly duties, even soldiering in war, untroubled by the anxiety over the destiny of the soul, one's own soul or the souls of others. In each of these cases, moral knowledge, that is, knowledge of good and evil as well as the demands of one's duty and the pursuit of flourishing, are somehow related to what transcends or goes beyond the human realm. One returns, in other words, to the question of dualism and nondualism in religion, but now with respect to the character of moral knowledge. And just like the question of the meaning and status of moral values, religious accounts of moral knowledge are not easily placed within the confines of the categories of traditional Western ethics. What do we mean?

Within religious traditions, moral knowledge takes different forms. In most religions, it is held that every human being has some rudimentary knowledge of good and evil and the most basic form of justice, that is, to treat others as one would like to be treated by others and thus fairness in dealings among people. Sometimes the basic sense of justice is given in the form of a moral law or commandment. When asked to explain the whole *Torah* while standing on one leg, Rabbi Hillel (c. 110 BCE–10 CE) taught what is sometimes called the "Silver Rule": "That which is hateful to you, do not do to your fellow. That is the whole Torah; the rest is explanation; go and learn" (Talmud, *Shabbat* 31a, cf. Lev 19:18). The positive formulation of the same command was taught by Jesus, the so-called "Golden Rule": "Do to others as you would have them do to you" (Mt 7:12).

The injunction, also in the positive, is found in Islam: "No one of you is a believer until he desires for his brother that which he desires for himself." This is part of the *Sunnah*, that is, the practice of the Prophet Muḥammad that he taught and instituted as a teacher and exemplar of Islamic law *(sharī'a)*. The devout Muslim must fulfill God's injunctions, such as this one, as well as practicing religious rites (for example, daily prayers) and conforming one's life in accord with Allah's will. Not surprisingly, *"Islam"* means submission and *Sunnah* is derived from an Arabic root that means a clear and well-used path.

Whether in the form of prohibition or injunction, this basic moral maxim is not limited to the monotheistic, Abrahamic religions (Judaism, Islam, Christianity). It is found in most other religions, and, importantly for this chapter, in Hinduism as well. The *Mahābhārata*, an ancient Indian epic (the other epic being the *Rāmāyaṇa)*, is the history of the Kurukshetra war, but also philosophical reflection and devotional materials. The *Gītā*, cited at the head of this chapter, is part of the *Mahābhārata*. Elsewhere in the epic one reads: "Do not do to another what is disagreeable to yourself: this is the summary Law [*dharma*]."[20] Just like the Golden and Silver Rules and the *Sunnah*, this command is embedded in a larger textual and ritual context that is a depiction of finite and ultimate reality. The importance of those finite and ultimate settings for moral rules will concern us later.

---

20 (1978). *The Mahābhārata. 4. The Book of Virāṭa 5. The Book of the Effort.* (ed. and trans. J.A.B. van Buitenen), 281–282 (5.39.55 [5.1517]). Chicago and London: University of Chicago Press.

The basic command of morality can be stated in two different ways: one formula is a prohibition (the Silver Rule, *Mahābhārata*); the other is formulated as a positive injunction for action (the Golden Rule, *Sunnah*). In each case, despite the different formulations (prohibition; injunction), what comes into focus are actions, relations between people, basic human desires (what is wanted and what is avoided), the possibility of disinterested unselfish action, and, given the context, a religious view of life. In Hillel's case, the probation formulated as a moral law claims to be the proper interpretation of *Torah*. And *Torah*, "teaching," takes various forms (written, oral, eternal) and specifies how Jews are to live in covenant relation with God (*YHWH*), among themselves, and in relation to other individuals and communities. In Islam, as noted, the injunction is part of the *Sunnah* and thus fundamental in living a proper Muslim life. With Hinduism, we find this prohibition in the context of an epic that includes the *Gītā* and presents, aside from ritual and philosophical matters, claims about reality itself. Jesus' formulation of the "Golden Rule" is part of the "Sermon on the Mount" in Matthew's Gospel in the Christian New Testament. The "Sermon," which runs several chapters in Matthew (5–7), has been seen by Christians throughout history to be a summary of Jesus' teaching ministry.

For simplicity's sake we will designate these different formulations of the moral law as the Silver Rule and the Golden Rule. This is not a prejudice in favor of the ethics of Judaism and Christianity, because, as noted, the negative form is found in Hindu texts and the positive form in Islam. Further, we can note a shared logic to the law whether it is formulated as a prohibition, and so negatively, or as an injunction, and so positively. In both forms the rule articulates that the basic demands of morality are *equality* and *reciprocity*. The injunction or prohibition applies equally to whomever it is given. Social status, age, gender, race, religion, and the like cannot be used to exempt one from the law; moral equality is enshrined in this law. So too reciprocity: what you are morally bound to do, or refrain from doing, to me, I am likewise bound to do, or refrain from doing, to you. The principle of reciprocity in its various formulations is found in virtually every religion and culture, from ancient Babylonia and Egypt through Greek and Roman thought, and into Islam, Christianity, and Judaism as well as Buddhism and Hinduism. This fact, to recall Chapter 1, is partly what allowed the 1993 Parliament of the World's Religions to issue the "Declaration Toward a Global Ethic."

All religions seem to recognize the principles of reciprocity and moral equality from within their own beliefs and practices formulated as either the Silver or Golden Rule or both taken together. This does not mean that religious people unfailingly live by those rules! The history of religious wars and violence, sexism, oppression, colonial domination, slavery and racism betray these widespread rules. What the presence of the basic moral ideas within different religions and cultures does mean is that the world's religions should, in principle, recognize moral knowledge and truth outside of any particular religion.

In this light, questions immediately arise for ethical reflection. First, what capacity is it that allows human beings to have this basic sense and knowledge of justice? And, second, is this basic moral knowledge really sufficient for leading a responsible life? That is, how does one account for moral weakness and failure, the sad fact that we might know what we ought to do and yet not do it? Third, is there, ethically speaking, any reason for greater validity of the law when formulated positively as an injunction (the Golden Rule) or negatively as a prohibition (the Silver Rule)? Consider these questions in order.

The religions present different accounts of the human capacity for moral knowledge precisely because they have various accounts of the human mind and perception and different descriptions of human existence. Yet the religions hold in principle that every human being does indeed have some capacity for moral awareness.[21] How to describe that capacity and its limits is much more difficult, although the Silver and Golden Rules give a clue to an answer: "That which is hateful to you, do not do to your fellow" and "do to others as you would have them do to you." Both statements take the form of a command, a categorical imperative (as Kant would call it) for acting or refraining to act, and yet they are formulated (unlike Kant) in terms of human desires for happiness and to avoid harm, what is hated.[22] In other words, the Silver/Golden Rules conjoin what Kant and other philosophers sought to separate, namely, human desires and vulnerabilities – and, most generally, the desire for happiness or well-being – as incentives for action distinct from the moral law and justice. Kant's point, recall, was that for an action to be moral, it must be done for moral reasons, out of respect for the moral law. All other incentives for action, he held, are not truly moral; they cannot meet the test of the categorical imperative. The religions, in ways expressed in the Golden and/or Silver Rules, depict moral awareness not only in terms of reason and knowledge, but in the interaction of a rudimentary sense of justice and forms of desire found in oneself and in others. We need to explore these ideas in more depth.

Taken together, the Golden and Silver Rules assert that any action one undertakes in relation to *someone else* can formulate the aim or end, the *telos*, of that action in terms of what the acting agent wants or desires, some good, or, in the Silver Rule, what one does not want and hates. This is to suggest that the field of morality is defined by human *actions* and *relations* and that people exist in

---

21 This poses the important question of disability and moral knowledge and if the religions are correct to hold some more or less normative account of human capacities. The point is taken and yet it is, seemingly, an empirical and not conceptual issue. That is, the fact of disability ought to make us reconsider in specific moral situations what is rightly held as basic capacities for human action. But that a moral agent must have those capacities in some degree does not seem disputed. This is an area in which much more work in religious ethics needs to be done.

22 The philosopher Paul Ricoeur notes this point and how it alters a discussion of moral goods and moral duties. See his Wallace, M.I. (ed.) (1995). *Figuring the Sacred: Religion, Narrative, and Imagination*. Minneapolis, MN: Fortress Press.

an ethical environment or "moral space," as we can call it, defined by relations, actions, power, desire, values, and obligations. Human worlds are always moral worlds, whatever else they might be. Taken together these elements of "morality" thus constitute human "worlds" as moral spaces. The Silver Rule focuses on human vulnerability: how in relations of power we can suffer the actions of those with greater power than ourselves or they can suffer our power. The Golden Rule, for its part, also focuses on the moral space of actions, relations, obligations, values, and desires. Yet it does so by turning attention to what is desirable as a good (whatever that happens to be) from the perspective of an agent with the power to seek and realize what is desired as good. The two rules thereby direct our attention not only to desires, intentions, values, obligations, and actions but also to relations of power. If you are not to treat others as you would not want to be treated, it requires considering oneself as relatively powerless and able to suffer in relation to someone or something with the power to harm oneself. The Golden Rule also focuses on the differences in relations of power but now from the perspective of the one with the power to act. The two rules thereby present a picture of the moral world, that is, the moral meaning and structure of lived reality, defined by actions, relations to others, asymmetries of power, obligations and also human desires and aversions. The incentive for action is human desires and aversions but those incentives must be tested by their extension in the treatment of others within relations of symmetrical and asymmetrical power.

Although the moral space of life is defined by obligations, desires and aversions, values, actions, and relations of power, it is distinctively *moral* in terms of the symmetry of obligation (moral equality and reciprocity) within the asymmetry of power (actor/recipient). If I am acting for some end, I must ask what I would want done to me if someone had the power to act toward me (the Golden Rule). Or if I have the power to act, I should not do to others what I would hate to undergo, that is, suffer (the Silver Rule). The demand of reciprocity requires moral equality. I cannot make exceptions for myself not extended to others. I cannot hold them responsible for actions that I claim do not bind me as well.

We can also pose the question noted previously, that is, the question of moral motivation and moral weakness.[23] It is important to see that what is desired or what is hated is not specified in the Golden and Silver Rules. I might desire wealth; I might hate some group of people. The two rules understand the incentives and motives for action in terms of desires and aversions, yet they do not specify the *content* of those desires and aversions. This has led to important criticisms of these rules.

---

23 See Clairmont, D.A. (2011). *Moral Struggle and Religious Ethics: On the Person as Classic in Comparative Theological Contexts.* Oxford: Wiley Blackwell.

First, the Golden and Silver Rules seem to ground moral obligation, what I should or should not do to others, in *self-love*. The rules merely place a limit on how I act or refrain from acting in relations with others, but they do not seem to question the morality of a motive to act. What is hateful to me, or what I want done to me, are somehow to ground concern for others. It was for this reason that Kant thought he had to reformulate the basic obligation of the moral life in the autonomy of practical reason and respect for the humanity in oneself and others. It is why, as we saw, the categorical imperative in one of its expressions is purely formal. Put differently, the Golden and Silver Rules might not be truly moral because they root the maxim of action in an incentive for happiness or the aversion to suffering. So, Kant reasoned that there must be some way to ground the obligation to others that is not reducible to self-love or self-interest.

The first criticism centers on the motive and incentive for action (self-love, etc.) and opens a second line of criticism of these two rules. If a maxim of action is to be grounded in self-love, then one needs to clarify what is *proper* or *right* self-love. On the terms of either rule, a psychopath could act in a consistent manner. A sadist might indeed want something done to him, say, some form of physical pain, and then, on the terms of the Golden Rule, believe himself justified in inflicting pain on others. In other words, both rules seem to presuppose what moral rules are in fact meant to establish, that is, the proper intention and motive for right action. Again, this is why Kant said that the purpose of the moral life is to become *worthy* of being happy, and, further, that the only good thing in this or any world is a good will, that is, a will that is motivated to act on moral maxims alone. Yet these two rules rooted in desire seem to fail to specify a right or moral desire for action. They presuppose a good will when in fact a person with wicked will or deformed will can take them as maxims of her or his action without logical inconsistency.

At this junction we confront a third criticism of the Golden and Silver Rules. Can they account for moral failure, that is, why sometimes we do not do what we know we ought to do? If the motive for acting is self-love (most generally stated) how can I ever act against my self-love? I might be confused and others might impute to me different motives, but, in fact, at root all actions would be explainable in terms of self-love. Some version of ethical hedonism, like that of Epicurus, would be right. Refraining from some action might appear in the short term to run against my self-love, say not cheating even when it appears possible to do so without being caught. But in the long run it becomes clear that even in that case self-love ruled. Moral weakness on this account is at base confusion about one's most fundamental motive in relation to less profound incentives and preferences. How can anyone not act out of self-love? Another criticism cuts the opposite direction. The Golden and Silver Rules may imply that in acting morally I must somehow deny or qualify my own good. Even Kant, the most rigorous deontologist, did not deny the human desire for happiness. He just thought one must be *worthy* to be happy. But the rules do not seem to hold that option open but focus on what one is to do here and now. In this light, they appear unduly rigorous and maybe harmful to one's well-being, rather than lax, as the first criticism went.

Moral Weakness

Ironically, it is precisely in the face of these criticisms of the Golden and Silver Rules that something else about religious ethics comes to the fore. Religions that formulate a law of moral action in either negative or positive terms are claiming something about human existence in history and society, a claim that returns us to the text of Genesis. Can we account for moral weakness and failure in terms of a fundamental rupture in human existence that manifests itself not only in terms of moral blindness (Chapter 2) but also in the capacity to act morally (Chapter 5)? St. Paul put it well in his letter to the Romans (7:15, 18b, 24): "I do not understand my own actions. For I do not do what I want, but I do the very thing I hate ... I can will what is right, but I cannot do it ... Wretched man that I am! Who will rescue me from this body of death?" The religions locate moral weakness and failure not just in human reason or in basic motives, but, we submit, in a rupture between motives and reason's apprehension of the demands for justice. The Golden and Silver Rules thereby work on two levels: (i) a level of what one loves or hates and (ii) a level of equality and reciprocity in a basic sense of justice. The rupture between these levels in human existence – as St. Paul put it – is sometimes called "sin," as we described in the story of Adam and Eve. In other traditions, the rupture is explained as being trapped in *saṃsāra* (a recurring cycle of suffering over multiple lives) and in need of enlightenment. In the *Gītā*, cited previously, the rupture is due to illusion. We return to these matters of freedom and bondage in Chapter 6.

Religious ethics situates the problem of moral weakness not simply internal to human capacities (say, reason, or desire) but also in terms of a rupture within human existence the origin of which is a break between human life and what is sacred or divine, that is, the realm of what is ultimately real, important, and empowering. A religious ethics interprets the basic moral problem to be an issue of the relation between human beings and the divine or sacred world. The answer to the moral problem of weakness, failure, and injustice requires something more than human effort, discipline, or virtue. It requires contact with a power that is somehow beyond good and evil in order thereby to live morally, or it requires the release from illusion and bondage, true enlightenment about ultimate (non) reality.

In other words, from within the moral life we return to the question of dualism and nondualism in religious ethics and the question of Good and Evil. Let us turn in Part 2 of this chapter to that discussion but now mindful of a rupture in human existence and so the reality of human moral fault.

3

Good, Evil, and Beyond

Normative Dimension
Part 2

> Then the Lord God said, "See, the man has become like one of us, know-ing good and evil; and now, he might reach out his hand and take also from the tree of life, and eat, and live forever" – therefore the Lord God sent him forth from the garden of Eden, to till the ground from which he was taken.
>
> —Gen 3:22–23

> Nor should you tremble to perceive your duty [*dharma*] as a warrior; for him there is nothing better than a battle that is righteous [*dharma*].
>
> —*Bhagavad Gītā* 2, 31[1]

Good and Evil in the Religious Life

In Part 1 of this chapter we explored how religious teachings about the respon-sible conduct of life do not easily fall within distinctions drawn from Western moral philosophy. We saw that a single verse of the *Gītā* or Genesis can be interpreted in naturalistic or nonnaturalist ways, realist or antirealist, cognitive or noncognitive, and deontological or teleological forms. Exploring the charac-ter of moral knowledge showed that the religions have accounts that touch on human desires, senses of justice, moral equality, and reciprocity in relations of power. There were, furthermore, at least three criticisms of the Golden and Silver Rules as ways of stating the most basic duty of the moral life: first, that they rest on self-love rather than other-regard and so do not seem to be genu-inely moral; second, that they fail to specify a proper or right motive for action; and, third, their accounts of moral weakness either fail in principle to answer the problem or they root it within a relationship between human beings and some transcendent reality or state that exceeds the limits of moral reason.

---

1 Flood, G. and Martin, C. (2012). *The Bhagavad Gita: A New Translation*, 17. New York: W.W. Norton and Company.

Religious Ethics: Meaning and Method, First Edition. William Schweiker and David A. Clairmont.
© 2020 William Schweiker and David A. Clairmont. Published 2020 by John Wiley & Sons Ltd.

These criticisms have given rise to philosophical formulations of moral imperatives or the rejection of ideas about the moral law all together. Yet in our judgment those responses fail to grasp a crucial insight. The Golden and Silver Rules (as we have summarily called them) are embedded in wider and deeper convictions about what we called the moral space of life. Now we must explore what that fact means for religious ethics.

The Dynamic of the Moral and Religious Life

In order to generate and to formulate moral duty, the Golden and Silver Rules focus on *relations* to others rather than discrete actions or the self's relation to itself in the dictates of practical reason. The rules are formulated with respect to one's desires and aversions, but one ought not to act on any desire or aversion that inflicts harm or imposes some end, some good, on another. To put it differently, the Golden and Silver Rules do not purport to provide an entire account of morality or of moral weakness. There is also a whole domain of basic goods (family, social rules, education, etc.) and what we can call transcendent goods (salvation, enlightenment, supernatural goods). The rules are a test or a screen about relations of power that one's desires and aversions must pass through and withstand if one is to act morally.[2] A deontological maxim (the Golden or Silver Rule) is set between human desires and aversions and another kind of goodness that arises by acting on the rule. This dynamic is illustrated in Figure 3.1.

Yet one must understand that this structure is a *spiral*, that is, the transformed desires/aversions return to be motives for later actions, which are then

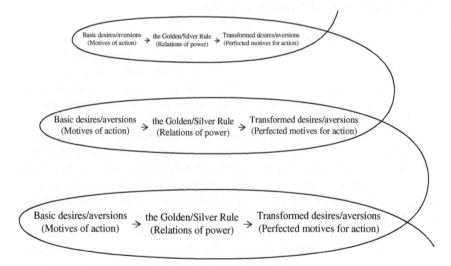

Figure 3.1 The dynamic between desires/aversions and goods.

---

2 This is formally similar to many types of "virtue ethics," that is, one cultivates and perfects one's character by doing the right thing for the right reason where "right" action is defined in terms of some paradigmatic ideal persons or some dictate of the moral law.

mediated again by yet deeper understanding of the Golden and Silver Rules giving rise to yet another transformation and empowerment of desires and aversions, and so one. (Presumably this is why Hillel could say that *Torah* is a commentary on the Silver Rule. Once one understands and acts on the Silver Rule there will begin a process of transformation that eventually encompasses the whole of life in relation to God.) And so the diagram continues:

and so on.

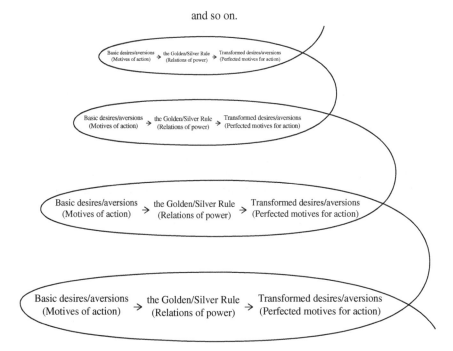

Figure 3.2 The dynamic as a continuing spiral of the moral and religious life.

In other words, the Golden and Silver Rules, and their various formulations in other religious traditions, are not meant to define the supreme principle of morality, but rather to transform and perfect one's motives and intentions for action and thereby give rise to higher, better, moral actions and motives.

These rules induce the *moral paradox* in the agent. By acting on these rules a higher, more perfect, self comes into being, but a self that cannot be the directly intended object of one's actions. This account also clarifies two dangers of the religious life. First, one can become too rule bound, insisting on strict obedience to the most minor demands of one's understanding of the moral law and thereby breed excessive pride or fear of punishment. Legalistic conceptions of the moral life miss the fact that moral rules are embedded in the service of basic goods and/or transcendent good(s). And, second, out of fear lest one understand life in too legalistic a way there is the opposite problem of laxism, that is, a vision of life without rule or standard (*antinomianism*). Repressive legalism and excessive laxism are the two dangers of religion to the moral life. Rather than exploring these threats in detail, we need to explore further ideas found in this religious dynamic as seen in Hinduism and Christianity.

So, given the dynamic of the religious and moral life and its dangers, consider some further ideas. One idea is about kinds of goods as well as their motives that are protected and advanced in the moral life. The other idea is about a basic difference within and between religious traditions, paradigmatically seen in this chapter between Hinduism and Christianity. This second idea about moral capacity and divine or sacred power returns our thought to the question of dualism and nondualism in religious ethics. Taken together these ideas help us to grasp the analogical structure of religious ethics in its normative dimension.

Figure 3.2 about the dynamic of the moral and religious life requires more detail in each of its moments and how each relates to what are called "basic goods" and also "moral" and "transcendent" goods. By "basic goods," is meant those things human beings need to flourish in some measure. Some basic goods are "premoral" in the sense that they do not depend on human choice and action; other basic goods exist only because of human choice and action. For instance, no one chooses the body they are born with and yet a body is crucial for some kind of flourishing human life. Of course, in strands of Hinduism karmic forces are built up through human choice and, accordingly, dictate the form of rebirth, say as an animal, a man, or a woman. In a sense, choice for the Hindu tradition reaches into what Christians would see as a premoral good, for example, that we have bodies. And yet even in Hinduism and its ideas of rebirth there is also a domain of premoral basic goods. If one is reborn as, say, an animal because of a previous life creating bad karmic force, that reborn animal body nevertheless requires certain kinds and amounts of food and water that are not dependent on choice but are defined by the kind of being it is. That is, there is a realm of premoral basic goods that are not dependent on choice and yet are valued and thus reasons for other choices.

"Moral" goods are ones that depend on human choice and action. Having a body or needing specific kinds of food might be premoral, but what we do with our bodies and what a tradition decides is appropriate kinds of food to eat is a moral good. Importantly, many religious traditions have particular dietary rules: kosher among devout Jews; the nonconsumption of alcohol by Muslims, and vegetarianism among Jains. Basic goods can be premoral or moral. These are values and so reasons for action. If I am a Hindu and seek to escape the cycles of rebirth, I will be motivated to practice certain dietary demands of my community as well as a discipline for the body and mind, say, practicing meditation. Importantly, thinkers and traditions have different accounts of basic goods. Yet basic goods (moral and premoral) seem to cluster around general features of human existence. What do we mean?

Goods and Reasons for Action

One can recognize various kinds of goods yet realize that traditions, as well as individual thinkers with one or another tradition, will enumerate, rank, and explain these in different ways. Our concern is not to give religiously orthodox or authoritative interpretations of these goods. That is a job for representatives of Christian communities and also Hindu communities. Of course, it is important for the religious ethicist to read and understand the interpretations of sacred texts by religious communities. But our present aim is a more limited one. We isolate analogies around kinds of goods in order to clarify the meaning and method of religious ethics. Further, part of the reason to clarify goods is that they provide a way to understand those values that the responsible life respects and enhances. And, what is more, basic goods explain the range of motives of human action and also the conflicts of motives that moral agents experience and must overcome or to which she or he succumbs. In this way, we are not applying a specific moral theory to the texts and practices of religions. As noted throughout this book, the task is to let the traditions shape moral theory and ethics.

Shown in Figure 3.2 are some of the goods and the motives they evoke as well as conflicts among motives that require moral discernment and judgment in order to decide what to do and what kind of person (or community) to become. In order to make sense of those goods and motives, let us return to the *Gītā* and the passage from Genesis in the Bible that are found at the head of this chapter. That is, different kinds of goods can be identified in the passages from the Bible and from the *Gītā* even as we will note differences in how they are conceived and lived. These goods are not given in terms of a hierarchy even though in actual moral situations when goods conflict someone – the moral agent, the religious leader or community, God or gods – have to make judgments of priority. Further, the goods can take moral or premoral form although we will not elaborate that fact in great detail. At this point it is important for religious ethics to grasp the *analogy of goods*, as we call it, in the responsible religious orientation of life.[3] One should also note, that we will isolate these goods from just two verses in the Bible and one verse in the *Gītā*! In doing so, we will see how these verses link to other passages and thus are embedded in a larger narrative and symbolic context.

The first kind of basic goods we can call *bodily goods*. Importantly, in the Genesis story God allows the man and woman, Adam and Eve, to eat from whatever "tree" they want. Yet God also commands them not to eat of the Tree of the Knowledge of Good and Evil. Basic bodily goods are then protected or prohibited by divine command (see above). Further, as the passage notes, if Adam and Eve eat of the Tree of Life – a realm of bodily and other goods – they will live forever. When they are tempted, it is by the appearance of the fruit of the Tree of the Knowledge of Good and Evil: Eve "saw" that the fruit was

---

3 For an extended discussion of these goods see Schweiker, W. (2010). *Dust that Breathes: Christian Faith and the New Humanisms*. Oxford: Wiley Blackwell. and Klemm, D.E. and Schweiker, W. (2008). *Religion and the Human Future: An Essay on Theological Humanism*. Oxford: Wiley Blackwell. We draw freely from those accounts in the present chapter.

pleasing to the eye, which motivates her action and Adam acts as she bids him to do (Gen. 3:6). Their eating of the prohibited fruit thereby opens onto another kind of good, *social goods*. Not only were Adam and Eve created as partners for each other, but their act of sin also binds them together socially. Adam took the fruit from Eve and he ate. Human beings in this text are profoundly social beings; Adam and Eve are made of each other's flesh but that is also a problem. Human sin spreads within social relations and fundamentally alters them.

After eating the forbidden fruit, Adam and Eve have a different relation to their bodies. Eve will bear children in pain; Adam has to toil in the earth that does not conform to his will. This shift that affects bodies and social relations also discloses a third kind of good, namely, the *goods of locality*. The Genesis text denotes the locality of Adam and Eve in the Garden of Eden, a realm of paradise where they live in bliss without want and without moral knowledge. After they eat the forbidden fruit, they are exiled from Eden and enter a truly human world marked by toil, scarcity, reproduction, death, love, joy, and the knowledge of good and evil. The human world, as the text goes on to narrate, is characterized by different forms of human life found in Adam's and Eve's children, Cain and Abel. Cain's life is agrarian; he toils the earth. Abel is nomadic and tends animals. As the story goes, Cain murders his brother whose blood (a bodily good and, in Hebraic thought, also a spiritual good) cries out from the ground to God. In response to God's exile of Cain, Cain asks: "am I my brother's keeper?" (Gen. 4:9) With that question we enter the realm of the moral good, a kind of good we explore later.

One interesting point about their acts of sin is that Adam and Eve, and then Cain, reveal a fourth kind of good, what we can call the *reflective goods*. When they eat the forbidden fruit, the text states "then the eyes of both were opened, and they knew that they were naked." (Gen 3:7) When Cain asks God if he is his brother's keeper, not only is a social good noted (the good of family members) and a crucial moral obligation (care for others, especially within familial bonds), but in asking the question, Cain makes himself an object of reflection. Reflective goods are those goods tied to human self-awareness and so questions about meaning, self-understanding, and recognition of others who are also self-aware. In Adam's and Eve's awareness of their nakedness, reflective goods are linked to human mortality, social relations, and the locality of life. Reflective goods are tied to the other kinds of goods. Moreover, we can see in the stories of Adam and Eve as well as Cain and Abel a negative portrayal of the dynamics of the moral and religious life diagramed in Figure 3.2. In the violation of the command of God, Adam and Eve lose their innocence and are painfully aware of their mortality: their lives are marked by pain, toil, grief, and loss. A profound disordering in the pursuit of basic goods has occurred in what ought to have been properly ordered for human life. The Bible suggests that wrongdoing alters basic motives and desires. It is the same with Cain. The murder of his brother alters the fundamental social nature of his existence. He is now banished and condemned to wander the earth and to found a city.[4] This connection between the realm of basic goods and moral obligations (paradigmatically stated as the Golden and Silver Rules) is crucial in the moralities of most religions. The violation of moral obligation alters and even distorts basic goods and inhibits the moral formation of transformed desires and aversions. One must thereby trace the diagram (Figure 3.2) in both directions, as it were, to understand not only right and good action and the perfection of character but also the dynamic of moral evil and wrong in the spiraling deformation of life.

Four kinds of basic goods are then found in the Genesis passage even as that passage is embedded in the larger narrative of the Pentateuch, that is, the first five books of the Bible. In fact, we could trace the connections out to include the great flood, exile in Egypt, the Exodus from Egypt under Moses' leadership and YHWH's power, and finally the giving of the *Torah* at Sinai and so the Decalogue.[5] Rather than following the story, we can now ask: what about the *Gītā* and basic goods? Is there any *analogy of goods* to those isolated in the biblical story?

In an interesting sense, the passage from the *Gītā* begins with where the passage in Genesis ends, ethically speaking. That is, the *Gītā* begins with the *locality* of human life marked by good and evil, violence, war, and mortality as well as *social* goods of family and social roles like being a warrior. In the text, different types of social goods seem in conflict, that is, the goods and duties of family life and the goods and duties of one's social role and caste (being a warrior). Kṛṣṇa does not answer that conflict between goods by simply ranking one higher than another, say, making family ties most important. Rather, he interrelates a deeper understanding of the locality of life and also the *reflective* good of Arjuna's self-understanding. How is that so?

Kṛṣṇa discloses that the real locality of human existence is not the illusive appearance of the war being waged before Arjuna's eyes. That world of struggle is a result of human wrongdoing. The true locality of life is *brahman*, and, what is more, Arjuna's own reflective good encompasses his role of a warrior, and the good of a righteous war, and the ultimate identity of *ātman* with *brahman* as well. Enlightenment about ultimate reality and the self provide further grounding and motive for Arjuna not to waver in his duty as a warrior.

The insight into the identity of the self and *ātman* and how ultimate reality is understood is, of course, profoundly different from the outlook presented in the biblical text. Even at the level of *social* goods the texts differ insofar as the *Gītā* presupposes the caste system, for example, Arjuna as a warrior with duties

---

4 This part of the biblical story is crucial for religious ethics in ways we cannot fully explore at this juncture, namely, that Cain has an important role in Islamic moral thought and practices. Muslims often trace their lineage back to Cain and thereby propose another reading of the story.
5 Recall that in the Hebrew scripture and Jewish tradition one is not to utter or write the name of God. The Holy Tetragrammaton (Greek for the "four letters;" in English: YHWH).

appropriate to that segment of society, along with the idea of *karma* that explains how present reality is conditioned based on past choices. Although the Bible does have some parallels to the ideas of duties specific to different segments of society (e.g. priests, kings, and prophets), there is no equivalent to *karma* in the Bible. Furthermore, the vision of *ātman* would seem, from the perspective of the biblical texts, to play down the importance of *bodily* goods, because they are not ultimately real even if they are part of *social* and *reflective* goods. But this is the point of exploring these texts within the work of religious ethics. The kinds of goods allow us to see the similarities and differences, the analogies, between the texts and traditions, what we can call the "analogy of goods."

Recall that the passage from the *Gītā* is set within the larger structure of the *Mahābhārata*, opens up another kind of goods that we have not yet discussed, namely *moral* and *transcendent goods*. We use the cumbersome designation "moral and transcendent goods" because of the deeper question, to be discussed later, about dualism and nondualism in religious ethics. The "moral" good is a form of goodness that arises when an individual's or community's life is dedicated to the moral law (Golden and Silver Rules) and thus remains within the dualism of good and evil. The "transcendent" good means to designate those traditions for which the dualism of good and evil is transcended even within the agent's or community's moral life. The reason to relate the moral and the transcendent good is that they both come into being by seeking to protect and to promote goods in one's own life and in the lives of others. That is to say, moral and transcendent goods entail the moral paradox (discussed previously). Further, it is crucial to see that most religions teach that the transcendent good cannot be attained without the moral good. (We explore this point further in this chapter and also in Chapter 5.) In a word, these are kinds of goods that cannot be directly sought, like one can with basic goods, moral or premoral. The question then arises: what is meant by these goods and what is the capacity of an agent, or community of agents, to act on and to attain one or both? In this way, the passage from the *Gītā* not only relates to its larger epic framework but also opens another crucial question for religious ethics in its normative dimension. It is the question of the highest good, the *summum bonum*, and capacities for action.

The narrative arc of the Mahābhārata makes this point as well. Kṛṣṇa "begins his answer to Arjuna's doubts by stressing the need to fulfill one's role in society and asserting that, since the self (*ātman*) is eternal and indestructible, it does not die with the body and so, because death is not final, there is no need to grieve over the immanent deaths in battle. He then goes on to affirm that all activity is a sacrifice if undertaken correctly, in a spirit of detachment, thus incorporating both sacrifice and renunciation within the context of life in the world; actions as such have no particular effect, provided one acts without interest in the result, and indeed are in reality performed by the *guṇas*, the constituents of nature, which are completely separate from the *ātman*."[6] The idea that actions have no result if – and only if – they are done without interest in their consequences is precisely the fact of the moral paradox. That is, a higher or better self comes into being from disinterested or detached acting on the moral law. How then is this idea related to the transcendent good with the normative dimension of religious ethics?

The Moral Good and the Transcendent Good

We have been tracing "good and evil in the religious life" and this has enabled us to grasp the dynamic of the moral and religious life (see Figure 3.2), an account of types of basic goods (bodily, social, reflective, local), an analogy of goods between religious traditions, and also the importance to the religions of the moral law formulated in terms of the Golden Rule or Silver Rule. Yet the passage from the *Gītā* that we have been examining opens yet two other questions and also points of similarity and difference among religious traditions within the normative dimension of ethical thinking: (i) How is the final *telos*, the highest good, conceived? (ii) What capacities must a moral agent or community possess in order to attain that good? Stated otherwise, we have so far been explaining the diagram about the dynamics of the religious and moral life by focusing on moral rules and also basic goods and motives. Now we turn to the end or perfection that in different ways relate to the moral life and so the question of the relation between the moral good, that is, respecting and enhancing the integration of the various kinds of goods of life, and the transcendent highest good.

The differences among religions are most profound at this point about the transcendent good and its relation to the moral good. Some religions conceive of the transcendent good as heaven or the vision of God, others in terms of the identity of self and *ātman/brahman*, and still others, as *nirvāṇa* and the escape from the cycle of rebirth and no-self, as in Buddhist traditions. Indeed, it would seem that we are back to the distinction between dualistic and monistic religious traditions. The great monotheistic traditions seem to retain a dualistic outlook in terms of heaven and earth or an afterlife for the human soul different than the body, and the great traditions from India appear as kinds of monism, either the unity of *ātman/brahman* or *anātman* as no-self, no-thingness. That is undoubtedly the case and many discussions of religious ethics are content to leave matters there and thereby to conclude that there is a profound

---

6 See Brockinton, J. (2003). The Sanskrit epics. In: *The Blackwell Companion to Hinduism*, (ed. G. Flood), 120. Malden, MA: Wiley.

incomparability of these types of religions. However, more is going on. There are analogies to be drawn within the discussion of the highest good once we focus on capacities for action. What do we mean?

The final *telos* of the dynamic of the moral and religious life (see Figure 3.2) is variously conceived in the religions. For Catholic Christians it is the vision of God whereas Orthodox Christians think in terms of *theosis* or divinization. All Christians await the final resurrection and the Lordship of Christ in the Kingdom or Reign of God. For a Buddhist, the focus is on *dharma* and the various practices that aim at enlightenment and thus freedom from the round of rebirth. Muslims must stand before the judgment of Allah and be judged righteous and thus fit for heaven. Hinduism, we know from the discussion of this chapter, aims at enlightenment in the apprehension that all is one. A Jew who follows the commandments along with other faithful Jews seeks to be a light to the nations about the oneness of YHWH and some believe in the final resurrection of the dead. These are, of course, vastly different conceptions of the ultimate *telos*, the *summum bonum*, of human existence. And yet, they have, as we have stressed, an analogical structure due to the paradoxical way religions understand good and evil and what is beyond good and evil. In the traditions just noted, the moral life structured by good and evil is crucial for attaining the ultimate end, but that end apparently transcends that moral space of finite life.

The conception of ultimate end in various religions has been explored before in other chapters of this book and we will return to this topic in still other chapters. At this juncture in our discussion of the normative dimension of religious ethics it is crucial to notice two differences *between* and *within* the religions. First, one difference concerns the question of whether or not God, ultimate reality, or the sacred bestows or transforms the capacity of a human agent to act and thus empowers the agent to abide by the demands of the moral life, or if, in fact, God or the sacred is the sole "agent" in attaining the highest good. And, second, one also needs to see that even *within* the same religion there are different answers to the question about human capacities and the highest good. To put the matter pointedly, is there any answer to St. Paul's lament in Chapter 7 of Romans that he does not seem able to do what is right and good? The experience of moral weakness is given a particular expression for Christians by St. Paul, but it can be found in other religions as well albeit in different form. We noted in Chapter 1 that religion is about what is ultimately real and ultimately important, and, additionally, each of the world's religions claim to give access to sacred power so that one might live a holy life within a reality surrounded and permeated by ultimate reality. How is that so?

Once we put the question in terms of what agent or agents are at work in order to achieve the highest good, then we can actually identify differences that cut through the supposedly dualist and monist traditions. Several possibilities can be identified. First, a religion can teach that a moral agent has the necessary and sufficient capacities to aim at and attain the highest good, but that accomplishment requires a time-scale longer than a single human life. This religious outlook stresses *immortality of the soul* and/or beliefs about the *cycles of death and rebirth*. Second, a religion might teach that a moral agent has neither the necessary nor sufficient means to attain the highest good. In that case, it is God or sacred power(s) or illumination that is needed to attain the final end of the religious life. The focus is on "God" as a heteronomous power who saves or redeems people. Divine power might be manifested in a savior who redeems people without any action on their part, like the way Jesus Christ is understood by some Protestant Christians, or it might come with a flash of insight in some forms of Zen Buddhism. Third, a religion might insist that moral agent has necessary but not sufficient capacity to attain the highest good. The agent must therefore *cooperate* with divine action or sacred power to attain that end. The moral life is about "making oneself worthy of happiness" but with the help of the divine or sacred. In the religions, this outlook is found in various forms ranging from ideas about the relation of justification and sanctification in Christian thought, Islamic ideas of justice and personal *jihād* as a transformation of the self, to, finally, various spiritual exercises among Hindus and Buddhists. We need not consider a fourth option that might hold a moral agent's capacities are sufficient but not necessary to attain the highest good. The reason for this omission is simple. Such a position would contend that human action is understandable without a conception of a transcendent good and in fact deny the reality of a transcendent good. Human beings act and their actions are for ends or a means to some end or responsive to some context. But such an argument is decidedly nonreligious because it constricts ends to inner-worldly ones and thus solely moral ones rather than seeing how the moral good might be the transcendent good (discussed later).

Our point, then, is that one difference among and within the religions is their conceptions of the relation between the divine or sacred power and how agents do or do not access that power in order to live the moral life and enjoy the transcendent good. This difference thereby links the normative dimension of religious ethics to its fundamental dimension, that is, the account of moral agency from a religious point of view (see Chapter 5). The second difference among the religions must be explored in the normative dimension of religious ethics. Put as a question, what is relation between the moral good and what we have called the transcendent good? Here too there are three main options: (i) the moral good just is the transcendent good; (ii) the moral good is distinct from the transcendent good; and (iii) the moral good is a precondition for attaining the transcendent good. We briefly consider these three in order. When we reach the third option, we will compare Christian and Hindu ethics of war because war, it will be seen, is a threat to moral responsibility and its relation to the transcendent good.

The Moral Good Is the Transcendent Good

First, some religions and also moral philosophies, like Confucian ethics explored in Chapter 1 or the Roman Stoic philosophers, do not make a sharp distinction between the moral and the transcendent good. Recall from our earlier discussion that Confucius related and yet also distinguished a Good man and a noble-minded one. There might be noble-minded ones who lack goodness, he taught, but a Good man is always a noble-minded one who engages in proper ritual actions. The connection between goodness as a transcendent Good of "Heaven" is thereby linked in its meaning and status to the virtue, piety, and ritual practices of the noble-minded one or moral goodness. The connection between the Good and the noble-minded one is given more precision in some basic ideas of a Confucian "ethic."[7] What do we mean?

Fundamental to Confucian ethical teaching is the ideal man, *Junzi*, who is "noble" in a profound sense. It is a person who acts from an *impersonal* ego, doing what is right because it is right, a state few might attain. Not surprisingly, some scholars compare Confucian ethics to Kantianism and its focus on the "good will." Yet in Confucian thought the "ideal man" has virtues not really explored in Kantian ethics: decorum, rectitude, kindness, wisdom, and sincerity. Further, moral wisdom (*Zhi*) depends on three other basic ideas. One is filial piety and reverence (*Xiao*). Like Socrates in the *Euthyphro* (see Chapter 3, Part 1), Confucians would be astonished at Euthyphro's claim that the gods command him to take his father to court, and for two reasons. The first reason is that although human life transpires "under heaven" and so within some sacred realm, "gods" do not command the noble-minded one what to do or refrain from doing. Every human being has a moral sense (*Yi*) and thus can cultivate the disposition to be moral and to feel in any situation what is the right thing to do. In fact, the good person acts in all cases for the sake of *Yi*, doing the right thing because it is right. *Yi* is the proper disposition to act. Second, Confucians would not understand the lack of filial piety in Euthyphro's action; filial piety and so right relations to one's elders and family are crucial for the proper conduct of life. The idea of taking one's father to court for the death of a slave that the father did not own would seem to violate *Yi* and *Xiao*. If that is so, that is, if this is not a divine command ethics, then what is the norm and guide for the moral life?

The question of the norm and guide for the moral life takes us to the two main concepts in the normative dimension of Confucian ethics. These concepts (*Ren* and *Yi*) are deeply interrelated in Confucian thought. *Ren* is what gives human beings their humanity and is found in goodness, human heartedness, and benevolence. Confucianism is, then, a deeply humanistic vision of the moral and religious life because it is human goodness and perfection, rather

---

7 For overviews of Confucian ethics, see Chan, W-T. (1963). The humanism of Confucius. In: *A Source Book in Chinese Philosophy*, 14–48. Princeton: Princeton University Press and Ivanhoe, P.J. (2005). "Origins of Chinese ethics" and Csikszentmihalyi, M. "Differentiations in Chinese ethics". In: *The Blackwell Companion to Religious Ethics*, (ed. W. Schweiker), 374–380 and 381–394. Malden, MA: Wiley. For a schematic account of main concepts in Confucian Ethics see http://philosophy.lander.edu/oriental/main.html (accessed 16 October 2012).

than divine power and glory, which is the norm of a good life. *Ren* is a sense for the dignity of human life and therefore the virtue of virtues from which flow the other virtues of the moral life. *Ren* is what makes human life worth living and therefore a person of *Ren* will sacrifice life rather than to lose *Ren*. There is a natural perfectibility to human beings, and *Ren* is the norm and guide for the moral life. One ought always to act according to *Ren*. That is the supreme principle of the Confucian life. And because the moral life is about the perfection of human life, there is, ethically speaking, no difference between the moral and the transcendent good.

If *Jen* is the supreme moral norm and if the good person acts from a disposition (*Yi*) to do what is right and good, how then should one think about the conduct of actual life, the rough and tumble of everyday existence? Here Confucian teaching uses the concept of *Li* in both personal and social life. The idea denotes gain, order, and propriety. This is why, in Chapter 1, we noted that in Confucian thought the noble-minded one must do the right act in the proper way, with propriety and order. In terms of personal life, *Li* is to guide human relationships and rules of right action that embody *Ren* even as *Li* is also the basic principle for social life and the ordering of human life.

Without entering the whole of Confucian teaching, which is not our task in this book, it is still important to explore some features of Confucian ethics at the level of practical reasoning (see also Chapter 4). As noted, *Li* in its essential connection to *Ren* is concerned with both personal and social relations. In terms of personal relations, the concern is for actions to be done with propriety and openness to others. There are five basic relations that structure human lived reality and so give shape to the moral space of life: father and son marked by love and reverence; elder and younger brothers characterized by gentleness and respect; husband and wife in relations of goodness and listening; older and younger friends whose relation is marked by consideration and deference; and, ruler and subject with benevolence and loyalty. Notice that each relation is characterized by an asymmetrical relation of power between individuals and hence the need for propriety in the terms noted. Further, it is not surprising that *Li* concerns doing positive action for others in these relations, rather than abstaining from actions. That is, *Li* can in this way be seen as a form of the Golden Rule, as explored earlier in this chapter. It should also be understood that any individual will exist within the basic relations in different degrees of power. I might be a ruler and yet a son and husband. You might be an elder brother and a father but also political subject. *Li* provides a way to conceptualize obligations within the complex matrix of relations that structures human life. Two other elements of *Li* within personal relations are truth-telling (called *Zhengming* [the rectification of names]), and the conviction that proper action is a way between extremes (called *Zhongyong* [the doctrine of the mean]).

Confucian ethics seeks to order human existence. It is then hardly surprising that *Li* also concerns social life. It is the principle of social order, ritual, and the ordering of life in ways that conform to *Ren*. Insofar as *Li* spans individual and social life as well as the complex patterns of interpersonal life, it entails a profound vision of the nature of action and human individuality. Every action affects others and therefore there are limits on individuality and the claims of self. In fact, we can say that the individual *qua* individual is not the right way to conceive of moral agents. Agents must be understood within the matrices of relations that structure human existence and the dispositions and motives appropriate to each relation. The last idea in Confucian moral teaching we can mention also pertains to the social life. *De* is the power through which people are ruled. *De* includes the power of moral example. More fundamentally good governance consists in the art of being honest; good government must maintain military and economic sufficiency in order to sustain the confidence of its people.

Of course, much more could be said and specific texts and rituals explored in order fully to characterize Confucian "ethics."[8] Our question is how this moral tradition identifies the moral good and the transcendent good. An analogous point could be made about other traditions. Recall that we noted previously the famous formulation of the "Silver Rule" by Rabbi Hillel. He also claimed, surprisingly, that scripture (*Torah*) and authoritative teaching was a "commentary" on the command not to do to others what you would not done to you. This suggests that the moral good formulated in terms of the Silver Rule is also the transcendent good, the will of God (YHWH). Rather than explore Jewish moral thought further now, it is crucial here briefly to explore religious teachings that take the virtual opposite position to Confucian ethics, that is, positions that teach the moral good and the transcendent good are completely distinct in the normative dimension of their ethics.

The Moral Good Distinct from the Transcendent Good

Classic Protestant Christianity is seemingly a clear example of an ethical outlook that draws a line between the domain of morality and the transcendent good. There are many versions of Protestantism ranging from the so-called Peace Church traditions (e.g. Mennonites) but also Anglicans, Methodists, Presbyterian or Reformed, Lutheran, and the thought of radical reformers like Thomas Müntzer (c. 1489–1525 CE). We will examine Martin Luther's thought with glances to John Calvin's teachings. The reason for this is simple. Some Protestants, like the Mennonites, drew a rigid line between their church and political society, and others, say, Müntzer, sought to have the state enforce their version of Christian faith. Still others, like John Wesley (1703–1791 CE), the

---

8 See Van Norden, B. (2012). *Virtue Ethics and Consequentialism in Early Chinese Philosophy*. Cambridge: Cambridge University Press.

founder of Methodism, taught that Christians should transform the social order. Luther and Calvin fashioned positions that distinguished but did not separate the moral good from the transcendent good of God's mercy and love. By exploring their positions, we will see another conception of the relation between the moral and transcendent good.

For Luther and Calvin, although they use different concepts to state it, human beings exist in two kingdoms (Luther) or under two governments (Calvin). Human beings exist in a moral, civil world and also the transcendent reality of Christ's Kingdom. In the "earthly" kingdom is found the institution of the State with the power to use lethal force (the "sword") in order to restrain wickedness and to protect peace. Calvin added to those two demands on government the idea that the State should support the right worship of God. So, in this secular civil realm there is found all of the relations, virtues and vices, struggles and conflicts that characterize human life since the fall and exile of Adam and Eve from the Garden of Eden. Luther and Calvin were sure that normal human capacities of thought and action suffice to govern individual and social life in the earthly kingdom. One did not need to be a Christian to be a prince or magistrate or father or mother. Further, one can speak of "civil righteousness," that is, the form of moral excellence open and possible with respect to human capacities. It makes good sense to speak of a good mother or a just judge. Yet "civil righteousness" is meaningless within the heavenly kingdom or the government ruled by Christ.[9] Indeed, Luther thought the most profound danger to Christian existence was to confuse these two realms or "worlds" and to try to rule the earthly kingdom by the Gospel of forgiveness and love in Christ, or, conversely, to imagine that the Church ought to be ruled by the Law in its various forms (natural law; civil law). Because of human sin, the earthly realm needs coercive power and should exercise it for the sake of peace and the protection of the weak and innocent.

The force of Luther's and Calvin's positions is that although human reason and a basic, if too often distorted, sense of justice is enough to shape and direct the conduct of personal and social life, on their own they do not merit God's forgiveness. Despite the righteousness of the just ruler or the moral individual, they do not merit grace. That is the human problem. People assume that good actions and moral relations somehow put a claim on God to reward them with salvation and heaven. But God is not the handmaiden of human pride and self-deception. God's grace is given freely in the life, death, and resurrection of Jesus Christ. A Christian is to place her or his faith in Christ and the

---

9 In Catholic thought there is a long history of discussion of forms of merit in relation to God's grace, including condign and congruous merit. It is precisely the focus on merit that Luther rejects. This makes moral action a living expression of one's relation to God rather than a means to perfect the self.

proclamation of his Gospel; all else is despair and damnation. The insight is that Luther insisted that the first question in moral and religious thinking is *where to look* in order to grasp how God's grace is given. Do we look to our own actions and our various forms of civil righteousness, or, does the Christian look to Christ, even his crucifixion, to know God's love and mercy? Is righteousness in oneself or oddly enough in another, in Christ, accepted on faith? (Luther called this "alien righteousness.") In order to understand these claims we need to isolate, as we did with Confucian thought, some fundamental ideas in this religious ethics.

Luther's methodological principle centers on the human relation to God. The principle is that the human is saved by grace and yet is also still a sinner (simultaneously justified and yet a sinner; *simul iustus et peccator*). Luther's method is to explore the paradoxical character of the human relation to God. The presupposition and source of Christian character and action is justification. Grace and faith are the condition and ground of love. Faith is not dead, it is not inactive, but spontaneously flows from faith in love for the neighbor. Indeed, Luther wrote that one should be as a Christ to one's neighbor. We can start to unfold the meaning of Luther's thought by looking at the Law/Gospel relation, the orders of creation, and his doctrine of the two kingdoms.

The *Gospel* is a term for God's gracious salvation of the sinner through Christ accepted in faith. Faith is the condition of this ethic, love its norm and it is structured through orders of creation and two kingdoms. The idea of *Law* is more complex.[10] First, there is natural law, that is, as stated in Romans 2:14–15 in the Christian Bible every human being has a natural sense of justice related to *conscience*.[11] Yet this natural law is affected by the fall in sin; conscience is distorted and therefore, as Calvin puts it, the natural law must be given again, republished. So, this same law, in its content, is written and preached in the Bible, it is the primal moral law that is knowledge of God's will. The content of this law is the Golden Rule–the demand for equality and reciprocity, and also the two tablets of the Decalogue, that is, the Ten Commandments. Next, the *evangelical law*, the law of love, is no different in the content of its teaching. The difference is that whereas the natural person follows the law for the sake of peace and order or fear, the Christian does so out of love for the neighbor flowing from faith.

---

10 The topic of law in Christian theology has a long history, and the discussion here is keyed to the Reformation account of law focused especially on John Calvin's discussion of law in his *Institutes* (II.7). For a different account of law, one could turn to Thomas Aquinas. Of special interest is the discussion of law in *Summa Theologiae*, I-II Q90–108, where one finds a different assessment of the extent to which natural law is obscured by sin.

11 Recall: The Christian Bible includes the Old and New Testament. In Judaism, what Christians call the "old Testament" is the *Tanakh* or, in English, the Hebrew Bible.

There are different uses of the law. There is, first, the *ceremonial* use of the law. This law is Hebrew cultic and dietary rules, no longer binding on Christians. Second, there is the *civil* use of the law. This is the use of law within the political community to secure order and preserve peace. Notice: the law that is to guide the Christian community within the Church is the law of love; the law that is to guide and govern political and social life is not love, but, rather, the civil use of the law including the possible use of lethal violence. Third, there is the *theological* use of the law, that is, convicting the sinner of his or her sinfulness and thus driving them to seek God's mercy through faith in Christ. Each of these uses of laws and types of law are crucial in Luther's and other Protestant's ethics. Yet the law however used is not the transcendent good or a means to that good. Confusion on this point, for most classical Protestants, leads to disaster. One ought not to try to rule the earthly kingdom by the law of love or to order the church's life by the civil law. To rule the civil order by love would unleash the terror of the powerful dominating the weak with impunity. Civil law concerns outward behavior only and cannot traverse and command "conscience." To rule the church by civil law is to court a return to works righteousness. The theological use is about conscience, that is, the awareness of how the human stands before God. Whereas Luther gave pride of place to the convicting power of the law or its theological use, Calvin understood the law, or *Torah*, as primarily about how to conduct and grow in the Christian life. He even thought that the Ten Commandments were a kind of portrait of the divine nature and will.

Another idea basic to Protestant teaching is station or calling. Like Confucius and also our idea of the *analogy of goods* explained previously, Luther understands human life within certain orders or estates that structure human lived social reality. There are three estates: family, secular government, and also the religious institutions like the Church. These orders created by God can and do take from in different societies, but they are how the divine rules the world, as it were. All of these callings have religious import, and Luther even understands them as all "ministries of the word." Persons are "called" into these stations; everyone has a vocation or "calling" (*Berufung*). This means that the whole secular life is rendered sacred, even as the sacred is secularized. One obeys God in and through this moral structure of human existence, but one's virtue and righteousness does not merit salvation. The moral life is not a stage on the way to the transcendent good. The moral is also not about making oneself worthy of happiness. The moral life is simply and importantly to live out one's calling(s). Thus, Christians live within the orders of creation fulfilling their vocations. And yet the motive for doing so, the dynamic power to engage in activity for the sake of the neighbor, is faith become active in love; it is not seeking the righteousness of the self. The moral good is distinct from the transcendent good.

The ideas we have briefly explored (Gospel, Law and its uses, stations, and callings) related to a basic paradox: the Christian is simultaneously sinner and saved. As noted, for Luther humans exist in two Kingdoms, two "worlds." The Kingdom of Christ is the reign of Christ through faith and the Gospel for the Christian community. The Church is present wherever the Gospel is preached and the sacraments rightly administered. The Secular or Earthly Kingdom is the governance of God working through the secular world. As noted, the Secular Kingdom has the power of coercion (what Luther call the *sword*) for the sake of peace and order. In the use of coercion, the king or Prince is the "mask of God" administering the divine judgment on the sins of the world. It is important that these kingdoms do not become confused or radically separated. These two Kingdoms meet or have their unity in God and in the human person. They are unified in that God alone is the sovereign of the universe, who rules the created order through the Secular Kingdom even in its sinfulness to minister his wrath and through the Church proclaiming the Gospel. The kingdoms are unified in human life because one is called to an earthly vocation even though a Christian is saved and yet a sinner. The idea of the two realms provides a conceptual and practical means to understand moral goods and duties and not to confuse them with faith and love, the transcendent good of Christ's grace.

Thus far we have isolated the method of Luther's ethics – how he goes about his ethical reflection – its central principle (*simul iustus et peccator*), its central ethical impulse (faith active in love), and the practical orientation of the ethic (i.e. orders of creation, vocation, the two Kingdoms). There is also a limiting principle. Luther believed that Christian beliefs about the end times (*eschatology*) mean that human beings will never bring about the Kingdom of God on earth. That transformation of reality will be God's action and God's action alone. This raises a final question. What is the place of reason in it; how is it an *ethics*? This is a crucial question because, as seen throughout this book, the moral life requires, among other things, reasoning about and giving reasons for one's actions and relations.

Luther does not deny the use of reason in the moral life if, and only if, it keeps to its proper place in the moral life. The orders of Creation, and the idea of callings and the duties and the goods that constitute them, provide resources for reflection on right conduct and good character. But there are limits to reason. When the human mind, corrupted by sin, tries to exceed its limits, tries to determine its own salvation, then reason has become a tool for evil. Outside of the revelation of God in Christ, God is an abyss, hidden, experienced as wrathful. Reason becomes, in John Calvin's terms, a factory of idols. About the transcendent good of salvation, one must hold fast to the revelation of God's mercy accepted in faith alone. In Christ alone is God known as merciful in his bearing toward people. In the light of the theological use of the law, one sees that reason and will cannot save us. Christ is savior and people are nevertheless accountable for their moral and political lives. The moral good and moral reason are not demeaned, but, rather, they are limited to the earthly realm. The Christian life is about faith and love in their proper relation. And this love and faith clarifies the proper use and domain of reason.[12] What is important for the study of religious ethics is that Luther's ethics, and similar positions in other religious traditions, draw a crucial distinction in the normative dimension of ethics between the moral good and the transcendent good. Each is understood in its proper realm and their confusion is found at the root of moral and religious evil.

The Moral Good as a Necessary Condition for the Transcendent Good

Thus far we have been exploring how religious traditions, and even different forms of the same religious tradition, relate the moral good and transcendent good, as we have called them. The aim has not been to provide an exhaustive account of any specific ethics, say, Confucian or Christian Protestant ethics. Our aim has been to clarify why and how different religious outlooks relate the domain of human existence structured by ideas of good and evil, right and wrong, and so the moral space or world of human action to what would seem to transcend that space. Because Confucius and Luther are obviously concerned with both realms of goods, we can isolate an *analogy of goods* between them, yet whereas Luther insists on the distinction, but not separation, of the moral good from the transcendent good, Confucian ethics seems to identify the two classes of goods. In that sense, Confucianism and Luther's Protestant Christianity stand at opposite ends of a spectrum, as it were.

Of course, we could explore positions that insist on the moral good but deny the *reality* of any transcendent good. Some philosophers, ancient and modern, represent that option, and we have explored briefly Kant's account of the relation between religion and morality. Yet our concern is with *religious ethics* and so forms of thought and practice that insist on a transcendent good, and, further, right access to the sacred or divine as essential to realizing that form of good. Where traditions differ is the extent to which human capacities for action are sufficient to realize that good, as in Confucianism, or if it is God and God alone who saves human beings, who, as Luther held, is the power of realizing the transcendent good. As we have noted before, we will return to the question about human agency in Chapter 5.

---

12 Luther summarizes his account of the Christian life in his seminal treatise *The Freedom of a Christian*: "We conclude, therefore, that a Christian lives not in himself, but in Christ and in his neighbor (1520). Otherwise he is not a Christian. He lives in Christ through faith, in his neighbor through love. By faith he is caught up beyond himself into God. By love he descends beneath himself into his neighbor." See Dillenberger, J. (ed with Intro.) (1961). *Martin Luther: Selections from His Writing*, 80. Garden City, NY: Anchor Books.

At this point we can note that there are, logically and historically speaking, traditions, and subtypes within the same tradition, which cast the question in yet another way. These positions contend that human action is necessary to attain the transcendent good, however conceived, but that human capacities are not sufficient to realize that good. The moral good, we can say, is a necessary condition for attaining the transcendent good, but it is not a sufficient condition. Put in Christian terms that have analogies in other traditions, human beings must *cooperate* with God in order to realize the transcendent good of salvation. The task now is to explain that kind of religious ethics. We will do so through a comparison of Hindu and Christian teaching about war. We do so for three reasons. (i) We have already explored the normative dimension of religious ethics in these traditions and now it is crucial to see what they mean for the practical dimension of ethics. (ii) This tactic allows us to return to the question discussed in Part 1 of the chapter of dualism/nondualism in religious ethics because on the surface it would seem that there is a radical difference between Christian and Hindu ethics. (iii) Our strategy allows us to address, all too briefly of course, a topic that is of crucial importance for the global age in which the religions interact with each other. Can there be, as the *Gītā* teaches, a righteous war? What does the idea of *just war* mean in Christian ethics? So, we are using a practical problem to complete our discussion of the normative dimension of religious ethics and the comparison of Hindu and Christian ethics as well.

War, *Ātman*, and the City of God

Images of religiously inspired violence fill the global media over the last decades: the smoking World Trade Center Towers on 11 September 2001, a hotel in Mumbai, India bombed, interreligious warfare in parts of Africa, the torture of prisoners by the U.S. military in Abu Ghraib prison, the global war on terrorism along with suicide bombers. Little wonder that many people believe that religion in its essence is a force for violence. Some scholars have isolated a core of violence in the ritual practices of the religions whereas others argue that the monotheistic religions are necessarily intolerant and violent toward others.[13] What, if anything, do the religions have to contribute to ethical reflection on the reality and conduct of war?

It must be said that the world's major religious traditions condemn war and violence and yet also teach when, how, and against whom war can be waged. Typically, there are teachings about what defines a righteous war or a just war.

---

13 Ward, V. and Sherlock, R. (eds.) (2017). *Religion and Terrorism: The Use of Violence in Abrahamic Monotheism*. Lanham, MD: Lexington Books.

By clarifying the ethical status of forms of human conflict, the religions actually seek to limit the use of lethal force while acknowledging the reality of war in human existence. It is this double assessment of war that forms the point of similarity among very diverse traditions, say, Hinduism and Christianity in the present chapter. In other words, there is formal similarity among these traditions: they oppose killing and the violence of war and yet acknowledge its reality and accordingly seek to clarify the ethical conduct of war. The difference between traditions is the substantial content they give to that formal structure.

We turn now to compare Hindu and Christian ethics of war drawing on the *Gītā* and claims about *just war* in the thought of St. Augustine (354–430 CE). Admittedly, there is not a precise parallel between this text and thinker. The *Gītā* is part of the main holy texts of Hinduism more akin to the Bible; Augustine is a great Christian thinker steeped in the Bible. The reason for us treating Augustine is, simply, his account of justifiable war has influenced thought around the world about the justice of war and the conduct of war. What is more, our treatment of the *Gītā* and Augustine's *City of God* cannot be comprehensive or exhaustive of these religious traditions' teachings about war. And, further, we are using the issue of war to isolate how a religion might see the moral good as a necessary but not sufficient condition for the transcendent good. In both of these traditions, one's transcendent good, namely, Enlightenment and release from suffering or the vision of the City of God, can be lost or impeded through unjust or unrighteous warfare. This also means that we will not explore strands of pacifism in either tradition, although there are many: think of Mahatma Gandhi's teachings or the long tradition of Christian pacifism.[14] The question of war, as we are addressing it, returns us to the major theme of this chapter: good and evil and what is beyond good and evil. Further, each of these traditions develops their ethics of war against the backdrop of a claim about the nature of the lived structures of reality. This is of crucial importance in the *Gītā* and St. Augustine's most influential work, *The City of God (de civitate Dei)*.

Within the Hindu tradition and thought one finds an ethic of reverence for life (*ahiṃsā*).[15] That is, to kill or harm another creature is an offense that corrupts the soul and therefore hinders and delays enlightenment. This conviction

---

14 On these issues see, for example, Fasching, D.J. and de Chant, D. (2011). *Comparative Religious Ethics: A Narrative Approach*, 2e. Oxford: Wiley.
15 Many Western thinkers have been influenced by the Hindu reverence for life, the most famous being Schopenhauer and Schweitzer; see Schopenhauer, A. (2005). *The Basis of Morality*, 2, (trans. A.B. Bullock). Mineola, NY: Dover. and Schweitzer, A. (1987). *The Philosophy of Civilization*, (trans. C.T. Campion). Buffalo, NY: Prometheus Books.The idea of the "integrity of life" as the ultimate norm and good of an ethics of responsibility presented in this book is related to but distinct from an ethics of the reverence for life. See Schweiker, W. (2010). *Dust That Breathes: Christian Faith and the New Humanisms*. Oxford: Wiley Blackwell.

naturally follows on the central conviction about the ultimate reality as *ātman* = *brahman*. If all is one, then unjust harm to any innocent also harms the wrong-doer and others as well, spinning a web of bad karmic forces. However, one must also recall that the *Gītā* is set within a larger narrative about a war and poses the question about the duties of a warrior. It is clear that the larger narrative and the encounter of Arjuna with the god Kṛṣṇa present a vision of reality. Reality – or, rather, what the unenlightened perceive as reality – is marked by struggle, conflict, and death as well as social roles (like the warrior) and intimate attachments we have to others, say, Arjuna's concern for his family, whose loss will cause him suffering. Kṛṣṇa teaches Arjuna that in fact what he perceives is actually an illusion on two levels, at least. Reality appears to be struggle and the persons we love seem to be distinct individuals. Neither claim is true. The ultimate truth about reality is *brahman* and that also means that Arjuna is one with all. His family members are one in *brahman*. Once Arjuna becomes enlightened to the truth of *ātman* = *brahman* there is no reason for him not to fulfill his duties as a warrior within the conflicts and sorrows of mundane reality. In other words, a claim about the nature of ulti-mate reality and also the actual reality of human beings is the backing, a realis-tic one, for Kṛṣṇa's teaching about a righteous war and warrior.[16]

The Christian Bible also contains many stories of war and conflict among peoples ranging from the conquest of the promised land by the Israelites (see the book of Judges) to the slaughter of innocent children and the crucifixion of Jesus (see Matthew 2 and 26–27 with parallels). Sometimes God fights on behalf of the Israelites; other times people in the midst of conflicts feel abandoned by God (see Lamentations). From within the resources of these sacred texts, it is hardly surprising that thinkers (rabbis, philosophers, and theologians) would

---

16 However, scholars have debated the extent to which Hinduism can support a just war tradition. For example, comparing the Mahābhārata and the Rāmāyaṇa, Francis Clooney notes the following. "The twelfth book of the Mahābhārata famously exemplifies the tension between the ideal commitment to not intending harm and a sober acknowledgement of the inescapability of causing pain in some circumstances. As James Fitzgerald has pointed out, it is a prolonged argument in favor of the just war. Yudhisthira, the eldest and leading prince among the five brothers who have been wrongly deprived of their kingdom and are approaching the moment of fighting to get it back, expresses horror at causing pain in war and is hesitant right up to the time of battle as to whether he should go to war ... He discusses the matter at length with his revered uncle and advisor Bhisma. The latter replies first of all that a peaceful settlement with one's enemies, even after invading their country, is preferable to causing pain. Nonetheless, when one encounters a worthy ksatriya opponent, fighting may ensue. This causing of pain is moderated by specific guidelines ... A righteous cause can be justly pursued to its conclusion, no matter how much pain is entailed. If Yudhisthira can connect the upcoming battle with the support of traditional values articulated by brahmans, then he can and must fight the battle" (117–118). See Clooney, F.X., S.J. (2003). Pain but not harm: some classical resources toward a Hindu just war theory. In: *Just War in Comparative Perspective*, (ed. P. Robinson), 109–125. Hampshire and Burlington: Ashgate. See also Subedi, S.P. (2003). The concept in Hinduism of 'just war'. *Journal of Conflict and Security Law* 8 (2): 339–361.

engage in forms of metareflection, as we have called it, on those resources to think about the conduct of war. More pointedly, Jews and Christians have sought to articulate the ethical reasons for and limits to lethal conflict. Rather than believing that every war must be total, that there are no rules or values to guide the conduct of war, and that there are no reasons to engage or not-engage in war, these traditions audaciously seek to submit the most raw form of social destruction, that is, the scourge of war, to ethical reflection and assessment. This means that for Jews and Christians the basic conviction is that peace, not lethal conflict, is the true meaning of human social life. There is a bias against war in these religions. Here too is given a complex account of the nature of reality, one in which the arena of human conflict is set within beliefs about God's power and presence and also the ultimate coming of divine rule in justice and peace.

There are other ideas about the structure of lived human reality within the *Gītā* and also Christian thought about war that must be noted. Classical Indian society presupposed in the *Gītā* is stratified by the reality of castes (*jāti*) related to *varṇa* or classes of the original Hindu creation stories. The caste into which someone is born situates him or her within society and also specifies the social role to play. Although there are many castes and subcastes, reference is usually made to five main castes in classic Vedic religion. At the top of the social structure are the *brahmans*, priests who must perform sacred rites as taught in the Vedas and also to teach and interpret the great epics, including the *Gītā*. At the bottom of society are the "untouchables" (sometimes known as "Harijans," or "children of God" as M.K. Gandhi called them, or "Dalits," the self-designation of those outside the caste system who have been "broken" or "crushed" by those within the caste system). The *Kṣatriyas* are the rulers and warriors whose social status is just beneath the *brahmans*. This is the caste to which Arjuna belongs and whose actions should fulfill the duties of that case, like being a righteous warrior. Below the warrior caste are the *Vaiśyas* who are merchants, minor office holders, and skilled laborers. Beneath that caste but above the Untouchables is the *Śūdras* caste or unskilled workers.[17]

---

17 There is a complex history to what is now known as the caste (*jāti* or "birth") system in Hindu society. The caste system is based upon the four *varṇa*s (classes) in Vedic and early Hindu religion but not coterminous with it, and the social obligations of the classes do not translate without remainder to the castes. Moreover, there have been significant social movements that have complicated the current caste system, including the political activism and self-representation of the "untouchables" signaled in their choosing the name "dalit" instead of the name "harijan" to claim political, moral, and religious agency. For an examination of the class and caste system, see Flood, G. (1996). *An Introduction to Hinduism*, 58–65. Cambridge: Cambridge University Press. For a helpful discussion of the agency in the caste system, see Rao, A. (2009). *The Caste Question: Dalits and the Politics of Modern India*. Berkeley: University of California Press. Although we cannot address the topic here, there is a complex and important history of relations between the "world religions" and the advent of postcolonial and subaltern studies, which itself requires an account of the relationship between Christian theological and missionary tradition and colonialist power and conquest. Our inclusion in this book of two religious

Ethically speaking, two ideas are important in the caste system. First, justice is the right ordering of society and social ruin would come if the caste system were overturned.[18] That is to say, justice is not simply fairness in human social dealings but concerns the way society is ordered and if it is wrongly ordered – if, say, warriors refuse to fight in righteous wars or brahmans neglect their ritual duties or outcasts try to be brahmans – then the social order is unjust, wrong. Ritual action is a way of sustaining and restoring the moral order of reality. Arjuna's actions have ramifications beyond his relations with his family. They have social and even cosmic meaning and accordingly he must do his duty. Second, one ought to act according to the duties of one's caste, and, accordingly, caste provides directions for moral action. It is not simply the caste system itself that matters, but, rather, the duties and virtues required of a member of a caste, like a warrior. So, if someone like Arjuna is born into the warrior caste, then he has a duty to fight and kill enemy soldiers in defense of the community. This also means that offensive wars are immoral, an idea shared, as we will see, in the Just War tradition in Christianity, and also noncombatants, nonsoldiers, are not to be harmed. Further, the Hindu ethics of war with these provisos about defensive wars and the protection of the noncombatant also means that total war, indiscriminate killing, is prohibited fairly consistently. The prohibition of total war along with the duty not to kill the wounded, prisoners, and other noncombatants rests on the vision of reality inscribed in a text like the *Gītā* but also the specific duties of a "righteous warrior," as Kṛṣṇa teaches.

Exploring the ethics of war presented in the *Gītā* allows us to isolate analogies between Hindu and Christian ethics. Recall that an analogy is a statement of similarity but also differences among positions. The similarities, as we will see, have to do with the justification of going to war, the so-called *ius ad bellum* criteria, and also about the just conduct of war, *ius in bello* norms. The differences between these religious visions of war are rooted in their accounts of the nature of reality and also the character of human agents. What do we mean? A quick review of St. Augustine's magisterial *The City of God*, written from 413 to 426 CE and in response to the crisis in Rome in 410 CE, will clarify the comparison between Christian just war thinking and the vision of the *Gītā*.[19]

---

traditions that have suffered under and have been largely silenced by Christian colonialism – Igbo and Penobscot – does not mean that we have even begun to address (much less resolve) the problematic issue of scholarly representations of religious and cultural difference. We hope that our readers will engage our representations and correct them where necessary, even as we challenge our readers to give an account, as we have tried to do, of religion and ethics in our global age.

18 We noted this idea of justice as order in Chapter 1. On this also see Wolterstorff, N. (2010). *Justice: Rights and Wrongs*. Princeton: Princeton University Press.

19 There is a mountain of literature on St. Augustine's thought and life as well as the idea of just war. For one account, see Bethke Elshtain, J. (1995). *Augustine and the Limits of Politics*. Notre Dame, IN: University of Notre Dame Press.

The parallel is not exact, of course. Augustine is a Christian thinker whereas the *Gītā* is a sacred text. That being said, the just war tradition flowing from Augustine's work has had profound impact on Christianity.

The City of God is an apology for the Christian faith against the charge supposedly made by the Emperor Nero that Christians caused the burning of Rome. An "apology" is a specific rhetorical form used in the ancient world and even today. The purpose of an apology is to make a case for a hearing of one's position, in this case the truth of Christian faith, against some accusation. The twist is that the apologist, St. Augustine, reverses the tables and shows how it was Rome, not Christian faith, which is the cause of its own destruction. It is within this argument that Augustine sets out the rudiments of what later becomes called the "just war tradition," although it would be better to call it a "justified war" tradition of moral reasoning. The question is what, if anything, justifies the use of lethal force in a "war."

For Augustine, the ultimate good of human social life, political or not, is peace defined as the tranquility of order. And this means, under the principle that all act for some good, that war is waged for the sake of peace. As he wrote, "War should be waged only as a necessity, and waged only that God may by it deliver men from the necessity and preserve them in peace."[20]

This idea that there may be circumstances in which war is justifiable has led to the long development in the West of just war doctrine and is still used today.[21] There is a bias against war and for any war to be justified it must be, like the *Gītā*, defensive in character and oriented to peace and the protection of noncombatants. This means that an ethics must determine the morality of end(s) of war and the morality of means or conduct of war(s). Beginning with Augustine and developing over the centuries there are two sets of criteria in just war doctrine. Although Augustine did not formulate all these criteria in this precise way, they are implied in his thought about war and peace.

The first set of criteria, again, is about the justification for entering war (*ius ad bellum*) that entails four considerations. (i) Just cause for entering war – for Augustine it has to be seeking peace – and so only defensive wars that might include retribution. (ii) War must be the last resort, or necessity as Augustine puts it. (iii) War must be declared by a legitimate authority rather than by an individual or an illegitimate power. (iv) There must be a probability of success. In the Christian tradition these criteria are important both for the justifiableness of entering war and for the peace of Christian conscience. If the conflict

---

20 See Augustine of Hippo (1892). "Letter 189" to Boniface (412 CE). In: *Nicene and Post-Nicene Fathers*. vol. I, (ed. P. Schaff), 554. New York: Christian Literature Company and Augustine of Hippo (1984). *Concerning the City of God Against the Pagans* (trans. H. Bettenson; intro. J. O'Meara). New York: Penguin Books., bk 19, chs 11–13. We will follow the custom and refer to the *de civitate Dei* by book and chapter, so CD, XIX, 11–13.
21 On this see Miller, R.B. (1991). *Interpretations of Conflict*. Chicago, IL: University of Chicago Press.

meets these *ius ad bellum* criteria then a Christian citizen can rightly join the war effort. Analogous to the Hindu idea of caste and also, as shown, the Protestant idea of "calling," some people have certain social roles to play that may include or exclude them from being a soldier: women (just war was, until recently, a patriarchal tradition), children, and the "religious," that is, priests and nuns. What is more, war cannot be total or indiscriminate. Second, another analogy between Christian and Hindu ethics of war has to do with a set of criteria about the just conduct of war, *ius in bello*: (i) noncombatant immunity and thus discrimination about who can and cannot be harmed; and (ii) proportionality, that is, the good to be achieved, must outweigh the destruction to be done. Here too there are analogues with the ethics of war found in the *Gītā* and other Hindu works rooted in similar concerns about social order – justice and peace – and the social roles of people. Both traditions ardently condemn total war and hopeless wars that cannot be justly conducted or won.

Granting all of these similarities, what about the difference in Christian and Hindu ethics of war? These differences are found within each ethics' vision of reality. In the *Gītā*, as we have seen, reality includes the illusory domain of actual life structured by caste and karmic forces as well as the truth of *brahman* as ultimate reality. That being so, war is possible because of the reality of karma and caste but it is ultimately for naught because within endless stretches of time finally the truth of *ātman* = *brahman* will be all in all. According to St. Augustine, "reality" is ultimately dependent on God's creation of all things as well as God's final rule over reality. But in terms of the moral and political life within history, reality is characterized by two interrelated but distinct "cities" or modes of social life. How does he define these two cities?

In the *City of God*, Augustine writes that "a people is an assemblage of reasonable beings bound together by a common agreement as to the object of their love, then, in order to discover the character of any people, we have only to observe what they love."[22] The two cities are define by two different loves: love of self to the exclusion of God and others (*amor sui* or *cupiditas*) and love of God and love of self and others in God (*amor Dei* or *caritas*). The Earthly City is ruled by the love of ruling and is characterized by dominion (giving and obeying commandments) that is the essence of government. Coercion (punishment, vengeance, war) is its mode of practice. The City of God is ruled by serving one another in love of God. Both cities seek peace. The earthly city seeks earthly peace and therefore must resort to domination and even to war. It is concerned with order and tranquility. The City of God seeks the peace of God and his kingdom. As Augustine writes: "Accordingly, two cities have been formed by two loves; the earthy by the love of self, even to the contempt of God; the heavenly by the love of God even to the contempt of the self. The

---

22 CD, XIX, 24.

former, in a word, glories in itself and the later in the Lord. For the one seeks the glory of man but the greatest glory of the other is God, the witness of conscience."[23]

On Augustine's account, human history is the interaction, the struggle of these two communities, founded on two loves, for two different kinds of peace that legitimatize two different ways of ordering those communities. History is an interim, a space marked by conflict and struggle, between creation and God's ultimate rule and Kingdom. Because of this character of history, Christians might be called to participate in a justifiable war out of love for their neighbor in order to protect the innocent and to restrain the wicked from their wickedness. The Christian Church as the representative of the City of God within history must work to transform, convert, the Earthly City for the sake of peace as the tranquility of order. In one of his more comprehensive statements of this proper order Augustine writes:

> Peace between man and God is the well-ordered obedience of faith to eternal law. Peace between man and man is between those of the family who rule and those who obey. Civil peace is a similar concord among the citizens. The peace of the celestial city is the perfectly ordered and harmonious enjoyment of God, and of one another in God. The peace of all things is the tranquility of order.[24]

What we have seen, then, is that for the *Gītā* and Augustine, the moral good is a *necessary but not sufficient condition* for the transcendent good. Arjuna must obey duties of caste and fight in a righteous war, but his moral good is not sufficient to reach the truth about *ātman*. Augustine insists that the individual Christian and the Christian Church must struggle to transform *amor sui* into *amor dei*, which brings true peace. And yet within the struggle of history it is finally God's grace alone that is sufficient for attaining eternal peace. Understanding the analogy between Hindu and Christian ethics of war in terms of the necessity for each tradition of the moral good but also its insufficiency to attain the transcendent good allows us to complete our discussion of Good and Evil.

Conclusion

In the two parts of this chapter we have explored the *normative* dimension of religious ethics. The discussion was set by the question of moral dualism and whether or not religious convictions are "beyond good and evil." We showed how religious traditions are committed to forms of moral "realism," but also, and surprisingly, they include both dualistic and monistic visions. The *Gītā* and a Christian text like Genesis or Augustine's *City of God* insist that the historical and mundane reality of human existence is structured by the relation of good and evil. Nevertheless, ultimate reality and ultimate goodness (*brahman*, God) is beyond that duality and a relation to that reality and goodness is the human transcendent good. The question for religious traditions thereby becomes: how ought we to live now within a reality structured by good and evil but also in relation to what is ultimately real, ultimately good, and so the transcendent good? In order to do so, the religions teach, one must receive enlightenment or salvation. And with that insight, our discussion of the *normative* dimension of religious ethics naturally opens onto its *practical* and *fundamental* dimensions about the meaning and reality of moral agency.

4

Perplexity and Wisdom

Practical Dimension

[T]he Igbo world is an integrated one in which all created beings, the living and the dead, are in communion through symbolic interactions and communication channels ... a dynamic world which demands that cosmological balance be maintained at all times to maintain social structure ... a "market place" involving a bargaining strategy but guaranteeing only "equality of opportunity" but not "equality of outcome". Individuals as a party and the spirits as another, are subjected to this bargaining process.
—Victor Chikezie Uchendu

If your right eye causes you to sin, tear it out and throw it away; it is better for you to lose one of your members than for your whole body to be thrown into hell. And if your right hand causes you to sin, cut it off and throw it away; it is better for you to lose one of your members than for your whole body to go into hell.
—Mt 5:29-30

The practical decisions of daily human life are often wrapped in perplexity. People are haunted by questions. What should I do in this situation? What kind of person ought I to become and how should I try to shape my character? What is the just thing for our community to do? Human life is in good measure about relations to others and not only about the isolated actions of individuals. That is the joy and the problem of human life because people have to decide about which relations to have, how to have them, when and how to act and what kinds of actions shape their lives. Not surprisingly people, and especially religious people, have many different ways of making practical decisions. Some religious people go to shamans, wise men and women, or priests for advice and direction on what to do. Others pray for God's power and illumination. Still others open sacred books, like the Bible or the *Qur'ān*, in search of what to do and what kind of people to be.

In some religions, like Islam, Judaism, and Christianity, there have developed complex ways of dealing with moral cases. In Islam, there is *Sharī'a* law that is

Religious Ethics: Meaning and Method, First Edition. William Schweiker and David A. Clairmont.

drawn from the words and actions of Muḥammad, the *Sunnah,* and also the Holy *Qurʾān. Sharīʿa* law cannot be altered. However, the interpretation of Shariʿa law, called *fiqh,* by imams gives some latitude to deal with specific cases. Among Catholic Christians, there developed over the centuries a tradition of *casuistry,* which deals with cases (*casus*) of conscience, and were meant, originally, to aid priests in their work of confessors in the sacrament of reconciliation. Rabbinic teaching, *Halakhah,* deals with Jewish law and ritual. As teachers, rabbis instruct about morality and the right conduct of life. Ways of decision-making differ vastly from reliance on intuitions and feelings to complex religious laws. What they share, and what allows one to see the analogies among them, is the fact that human beings must make decisions about what to be and to do. Religious ethics is the reasoned examination of human actions and relations in light of the fear, wonder, and joy of human life.

The tension or paradox of thinking about practical decision-making and practices is that wisdom is born from perplexity, but, when wisdom becomes rigidified and ossified in customs and tradition, it can blunt and impede our ability to make decisions and thereby lead us to being perplexed. Similarly, if one remains in a state of perplexity, then decision-making becomes impossible and people just muddle through life. One task of religious ethics, accordingly, is to awaken, even shock, people into awareness of the perplexity of life while seeking a wisdom that is supple enough to guide responsible decision-making.[1] The preceding chapters examined the descriptive and normative dimensions of religious ethics. In each dimension a movement back and forth within a tension, an *aporia,* was found that seems to characterize human existence and also how each dimension is implicated in other dimensions of religious ethics. In the descriptive dimension, we considered the movement between blindness and insight as communities struggled to offer pictures of their shared moral worlds, sensitive to their communities' deepest beliefs about the nature of the world and human beings within it but also sensitive to the inability of people to grasp completely the connectivity and complexity of life. The interpretation of a situation, its description, was undertaken in good measure in order to answer practical problems in human life. About the normative dimension, we examined how religious ethics considers questions of good and evil, in light of the various moral descriptions religious communities provide, but also how reflection on good and evil raises questions about how we are to act and what kind of people we should be in our pursuit of good and avoidance of evil. The relation between and among types of goods (basic, moral, transcendent) was also explored.

---

1 This is a longstanding claim, in Western ethics at least. Socrates thought that philosophical thinking begins with wonder over some of the most common things in human life, like what is happiness. The Hebrew prophets pleaded with their people to awaken to the injustice in their midst. A similar concern seems present in Japanese Buddhism and the use of a *koan* to awaken students or when Protestant Christians speak about the "theological use of the Law."

In this chapter, we add another dimension to our account of the meaning and method of religious ethics around the odd interrelation between perplexity and wisdom. We will illustrate different approaches to the ideal of practical wisdom and not just differences in content as well as the relation of oral and written forms of wisdom and perplexity in both traditions. In each case, one sees that religious ethics is best understood as an enterprise wherein the practical moral judgments move beyond the application of clear principles to cases (though this is certainly one form of moral judgment) to an appreciation of the complexity of the moral world (the descriptive dimension), the contending values expressed in different activities and social commitments (the normative dimension) and the various ways in which moral agency is viewed and the moral agent formed (the fundamental dimension). Our strategy will be to consider *practical decision-making* but also the complex notion of *practices*. Practices are the interpreting and interpreted actions of religious communities. They include religious rituals conducted in community, practices of contemplation and meditation that frequently happen individually, but also complex practical systems as one finds in the practice of law and the emergence of complex legal cultures in many religious traditions throughout the world. Following the precedent of previous chapters, we explore the Christian religious heritage in conversation with another religious tradition in an attempt to present the meaning and method of religious ethics in a multidimensional mode.

So, the focus in this chapter is the practical dimension in religious ethics. Given this focus, two issues come to the fore, one in religious studies and the other in ethics. In terms of religious studies, there is often a distinction drawn between textual and oral religions and this distinction, should it hold, seems to disallow comparison. For instance, the Synoptic Gospels of the New Testament texts of Christianity are based on the oral teachings of Jesus – his parables, stories, and *Torah* teaching – only later preserved in written form. This fact elides a strict division between the oral and the written in the foundational texts of Christianity. Analogically, we will also see in this chapter that the teachings of the Igbo find expression in oral traditions but also in law thereby once again eliding the distinction between types of religion. In this light, what we have done in order to compare these traditions is not to fall back on the textual/oral distinction, but, rather, to focus on the importance of "practices" in each religion's search for wisdom.

Second, because our focus in this chapter is the practical dimension of ethics – and because we believe that there is no sense dodging the most difficult moral issues – we explore a number of challenges that arise in the areas of economic life and in the domain of marriage and family. Indeed, because these are not (as many in our time suggest) merely matters of individual, private concern but domains of deep human and social significance, we treat them as the areas of practical concerns that will test our approach to religious ethics. The tension or *aporia* that drives religious ethical thinking in its practical dimensions is, we contend, between perplexity and wisdom in the face of the overwhelming complexity of the decisions people must make about the conduct of their lives.

Moral Problems and Religious Wisdom

Earlier in the book, we discussed the importance of thinking about the dimensions of ethics as a series of movements or developments of basic human capacities to think, desire rightly, and act well. So, for example, in our discussion of the descriptive dimension, we emphasized that answering the question "what is going on?" is best understood not as a right or wrong answer to the question but as a movement toward moral insight and away from moral blindness. Giving an adequate moral description is not a matter of giving one answer to what is going on but rather weaving together a number of different answers from different strands and even traditions of thought. Each strand or tradition represents a trajectory of development answering this question, and each offers a limited but nonetheless potentially true account of the way the world is.

Claims to truth do not mean that communities should prevent dialogue with others in order to combat moral blindness, an issue we explore later in our discussion of the metaethical dimension of religious ethics. Especially in the realm of ethics, where the object of consideration is the ever churning affairs of dependent rational animals, the truth of the matter is never entirely clear nor is it precise.[2] Nevertheless, some claims to truth can be validated (see Chapter 6) whereas others cannot, at least under present conditions. What is more, new situations arise requiring careful discernment by people in light of their distinctive times and places in history and their traditions' views about how to pursue the *genuinely* human good in the right way. What human beings desire, among other things, is that they use their powers of practical reasoning in the best possible way for the benefit of themselves and their communities, and the goal sought is practical wisdom (*phronesis*). Wisdom is the ability to discern, understand, and judge what to do and what to be within the churning and changing conditions of life that give rise to moral perplexity.

Wisdom and Moral Problems

In order to see the point about the dimensions of religious ethics, it is helpful to note the importance of wisdom in light of conditions that give rise to its pursuit. And this requires exploring instances of perplexity as well as some of

2 MacIntyre, A. (1999). *Dependent Rational Animals: Why Human Beings Need the Virtues.* Peru, IL: Open Court Publishing.

the history of ethics. The name most commonly given to that state of mind prompting the pursuit of wisdom is perplexity (*aporia*), a term, not surprisingly, used throughout this book. Often enough, people can find themselves in situations of indecision because each of the options for action seems, on their own terms, implausible, unattainable, or even wrong. In fact, one might have to affirm the goodness and truth of a possible option (I love my aged parents and should take care of them) while deciding to act on another (seemingly) equally good option (I must join the army to defend my country). Human life is wrapped in perplexity and a search for wisdom. In fact, wisdom is the ethical answer to the experience of moral perplexity. Yet oddly enough, as intimated previously, sometimes the religions *provoke* perplexity in order to force one to think again, to reconsider what one thought one ought to do and to be. Like the passages from Matthew and Victor Chikezie Uchendu at the head of this chapter, how can it be better to pluck out one's eye or what does it mean to see life as a marketplace? The religions explore the subtle and often confusing interaction of wisdom and perplexity.

Perhaps the most paradigmatic figure to examine perplexity and wisdom in the history of Western ethics was the Greek philosopher Socrates (469–399 BCE) whose self-doubt about his own purported wisdom marked him as one who had truly realized the beginning of wisdom.[3] Religious thinkers also puzzled about the nature of wisdom, linking it to the pursuit of justice but recognizing the difficulty of that goal in the midst of perplexity. This is why, as seen before, "wisdom" itself can be seen as a divine being, say in the Hebrew Scriptures. The Spanish Jewish philosopher Moses Maimonides (1135–1204 CE), writing in Arabic using Arabic philosophical commentaries on Greek philosophy, sought to reconcile Jewish teaching with philosophical wisdom. He believed that there was no contradiction between the truth revealed in the Hebrew Bible and what had been attained through the arduous pursuits of a rational mind. In his "Guide for the Perplexed" (*Dalālat al-ḥā'irīn*), he notes that Aristotle and Moses followed a similar guide to obtaining knowledge of God, suggesting that one abide patiently with perplexity in the pursuit of wisdom: "He must, however, not decide any question by the first idea that suggests itself to his mind, or at once direct his thoughts and force them to obtain a knowledge of the Creator, but he must wait modestly and patiently, and advance step by step."[4] Although practical issues demand judgments to solve complex

---

3 For a more extensive account of perplexity in the Socratic tradition (especially Plato's dialogues), see Matthews, G.B. (1999). *Socratic Perplexity and the Nature of Philosophy*. New York and Oxford: Oxford University Press. See also Matthews, G.B. (1997). Perplexity in Plato, Aristotle, and Tarski. *Philosophical Studies: An International Journal for Philosophy in the Analytic Tradition* 85 (2/3): 213–228.
4 Maimonides, M. (1963). *The Guide of the Perplexed*, vol. 1, (trans. S. Pines). Chicago and London: University of Chicago Press, I.5.

problems, we must approach the practical dimension with care to avoid false urgency. Rushed and uninformed judgments are too often bad judgments. The religions often provoke perplexity in order to give time, demand patience, in the search for wisdom in order to combat bad judgments.

There are lessons to be learned in perplexity, even if our ultimate goal is wisdom. Socrates, for example, avoided rushing to solutions to problems that had not to him emerged with sufficient clarity. In Plato's dialogue with *Meno*, Socrates considers a problem that was central to Athenian political life. Is it possible to teach virtue so that people could be educated to be good leaders in the *polis*? The Sophists, who were paid teachers claiming to be able to teach young men how to succeed, thought so, but their view of virtue was more akin to what we might now call political savviness. Socrates believed that this path was unwise and led not to virtue but to carelessness at best, viciousness at worst. That is why practical wisdom should not be viewed as the only important aspect of ethical thought but rather as one of several dimensions that together illuminate and orient the moral life.

Ethics must, in the final analysis, be practical but it should not be so at the expense of being thoughtful. Human conduct that is not guided by thoughtful reflection is dangerous. As stated elsewhere in this book, ethics is the human edge of thinking. And that means that one must see how the various dimensions of ethics are linked together. In many ways, this is what it means to cultivate wisdom. Of course, sometimes wisdom about what to do comes as a flash of insight, an enlightened vision. But the fact that this is how wisdom is sometimes experienced does not negate the reality of practical reflection already underway and preparing for that insight. That too is why the religions often provoke perplexity in order to prepare for the moment of insight as an informed intuition or discernment about what ought to be.

Cases and Judgments in Modern Philosophy

The lessons and insights of ancient thought have not always been adequately preserved or developed by recent philosophers, and this is especially true in the analysis of practical matters. Too much modern ethics, at least within the English-speaking world, focused on the analysis of the meaning of moral terms, how one justifies an ethical standpoint, or narrowly on practical problems. The domain of the practical has been a central concern of moral theorists through the ages, and even more so today when urgency and efficiency are the dominant values of the day. For example, what has come to be called "professional ethics" – that is, ethics developed by and for those in the legal, health, media, technical, and business professions – tends to prioritize the resolution of cases rather than the adequacy of moral descriptions or the nature of moral responsibility. They are instances of *casuistry* but, oddly, too often forget that in classical casuistry it was crucial to understand the "circumstance" of an action and thus to have an adequate description and interpretation of a situation. So too has the ethical thinking in some religious communities prioritized the practical at the expense of other relevant moral considerations. Frequently issues of personal decision in intimate life, particularly in sex, marriage, and child rearing, have focused on which course of action seems right rather than how moral agents develop good character or come to have adequate and sensitive moral vision.

As noted, in the western Christian context the increasingly close alignment between law and morality gave rise to a focus on *casuistry* or case-based moral reasoning.[5] The early focus on virtue and happiness gave way in the early modern period to a focus on successfully resolving cases of conscience for those who were concerned about their sins. The practice of private confession of sins, although rooted in the early Christian monastic context of spiritual direction and thereby seeking adequate descriptions of the moral life, tended toward a legalistic approach to a Christian religious ethics (see Chapter 2).[6] This early penitential practice emerged as a matter of pastoral necessity for the early medieval Church.

A different focus on the practical emerged with the discourse about natural rights among late medieval and early modern theologians and jurists. Traceable in part to the theological debates about poverty and private property among the mendicant monks in religious orders of the Middle Ages, the practical side of moral thinking became increasingly focused on what persons were owed by their neighbors and their society in their presumed natural state.[7] Whereas the early discussion of natural rights in Franciscan and Dominican debates about voluntary poverty treated rights as one element in the interpretation of a wider discussion about the apostolic, i.e. Christian, way of life, later discussions narrowed the field of concern to what one was owed in light of one's imagined original state of nature.[8] Although prefigured by Roman politicians such as Cicero (106–43 BCE) in his discussion about the obligations of government to those under its care, and further developed by Thomas Hobbes (1588–1679 CE), John Locke (1632–1704 CE), and others, law became, in fact, the primary lens through which to describe the practical expression of the moral life.

---

5 See Jonsen, A.R. and Toulmin, S. (1989). *The Abuse of Casuistry: A History of Moral Reasoning.* Berkeley: University of California Press.
6 Also see Mahoney, J. (1989). *The Making of Moral Theology: A Study of the Roman Catholic Tradition.* Oxford: Clarendon Press.
7 See for example Tierney, B. (1997). *The Idea of Natural Rights: Natural Rights, Natural Law and Church Law, 1150–1625.* Atlanta: Scholars Press.
8 For a review of the connection between voluntary poverty debates and the distinction between ownership and use of material goods, see Tierney, B. (1997). *Origins of Papal Infallibility, 1150–1350: A Study on the Concepts of Infallibility, Sovereignty, and Tradition in the Middle Ages.* Leiden: Brill.

This was further complicated by Renaissance and Enlightenment views about the place of religion in political life. Religion prior to the Enlightenment had been effectively a comprehensive worldview that influenced people's perspectives on moral meaning on all levels of existence. Later thinkers suspicious of religion and especially religious authorities after decades of religious wars were content to leave it as a private matter whose public intrusion could and should be constrained and managed by law. Even the conception of the field of Christian theology changed in response to the legal reconception of the practical. Whereas theology had once been understood to be a spiritual science aiming at wisdom (*sapientia*), in the Middle Ages it was also a unifying principle for the organization of knowledge (*scientia*) as well as the study of divine wisdom. In his *Summa Theologiae*, Thomas Aquinas, in the thirteenth century, tried to understand theology as both a "science," or domain of knowledge, and a form of wisdom.

The departmental structuring of the European university many years later marked an even more significant change. Church history and the study of the Bible informed the work of theologians but were not carried on as theological disciplines. The work of ethics fell under the label of "practical theology," which was understood as the professional application of dogmatic theology, church history, and biblical studies to the practice of ministry.[9] With the emergence of the critical academic study of religion in the nineteenth and especially the twentieth century, ethics was relegated either to the province of moral philosophy, envisioning the realm of the ethical based on the demands of practical reason apart from faith, or to the realm of positive law determined by the preference of citizens constrained by concerns for reciprocity. Theological approaches to the study of ethics coexisted but were largely maintained in Protestant and Catholic seminaries.

Practical Moral Thinking Today

Understanding how ethics is *practical* today requires that we think about these modern developments and how they still affect us and also about the history of thought. In simple form, the logic of practical judgments was first noted by Aristotle and is called a "practical syllogism." It starts with a *major premise* that states some good to be sought, e.g. health is a human good. This is followed by a *minor premise* proposed as a means to that end, e.g. exercise contributes to health. The *conclusion* is an action, e.g. I will exercise. Here is the scheme:

Major premise: (a good to be sought), e.g. Being healthy
Minor premise: (means to that end), e.g. exercise
Conclusion: (an action), e.g. actually go to the gym.

---

9 For a helpful review of these and related developments, see Maddox, R.L. (1990). The recovery of theology as a practical discipline. *Theological Studies* 51: 650–672.

But of course things are more complex. Is a proposed good actually a good? Is the means the right one for that good? What about circumstances (it's raining today so I cannot go running)? So too, one would want to explore the people involved, their character and capacities. Effective judgments require both a competent assessment of those facts, an understanding of the relevant laws or goods, and also an appropriate review of the awareness and intentions of the persons involved. More generally, the rule of law, insofar as it focuses on pursuit of justice understood as right relation between people – that is, to give each person her or his due – is directed at the practical concerns of everyday life.

However, by talking about the practical *dimension* of ethics, we are suggesting something more than the successful adjudication of cases, as important as this task may be. Rather, one is seeking the most appropriate response given the complexity of the situation. In terms of a classical account of the virtues, the practical dimension of ethical thinking should develop the virtue of *prudence*, which is the virtue concerned with the proper means to achieve a good end, for instance, the good of justice. Indeed, this classical formulation of prudence (or *phronesis*) offers a helpful way to think about the dimensions. Just as prudence is the virtue that pertains to the choice of appropriate means, so too does the practical dimension of ethical thinking inform the normative dimension of ethical thinking that identifies the good to be pursued. Although virtues are important, they cannot do all the work of religious ethics, especially when we think about the connection between its practical and descriptive dimensions. Today, the practical dimension of ethical thinking is especially complicated. Although there remain some areas where practical thinking is rightly expressed as the application of moral principles to discrete cases, too often "applied ethics" obscures the legitimate pursuit of hard-won wisdom in a perplexing world.

In this chapter, we explore two sets of human actions and relations or practices – what we term "social exchange" and "interpersonal life" – where especially careful and nuanced moral thinking is demanded. The former is the realm of commercial transactions and the human pursuit of wealth and security; the latter the realm of human relations, especially marriage, sex, and parenthood. We select these realms of practical life because within each is the intersection of basic, moral, and transcendent goods as well as moral duties that give rise to profound perplexity and thus the search for wisdom. In order to explore these realms, we follow the same approach undertaken in previous chapters, placing the Christian tradition in dialogue with another important religious culture. Here we examine social exchange and interpersonal life among in the Igbo, one of the largest tribes in Nigeria, the most populous country in Africa.

Nigerians are also the most populous African immigrant group in the United States and the second most populous African immigrant group in the United

Kingdom.[10] The presence of the Igbo people in the United States dates back to the trans-Atlantic slave trade to the American colonies, and many slaves that came to Virginia, Maryland, and the other colonies came from Igboland.[11] Here we find a religious tradition that is both local and global and also one that has been in meaningful, sustained dialogue with traditional Christian religion for many years.

Although there exists an extensive amount of scholarship on African Traditional Religions (ATR), we elect to focus on the Igbo of Nigeria in order to be as specific as possible about the forms of religious wisdom in the lives of the people. That wisdom draws on ancient religious beliefs and practices, but it also interacts with contemporary values and present-day situations in Africa and in the African diaspora including the United States. This parallels our discussion of the descriptive dimension of religious ethics by focusing on one particular Native American people – the Penobscot – rather than trying to speak generally of "Native American Religion" (see Chapter 2). Later, we will see how this point is related to the difference between missionary and nonmissionary religions (Chapter 5). Both nations (recognizing their status as sovereign peoples despite their exploitation by Christian European colonizers) – the Igbo and Penobscot – have had significant dealings with Christian missionaries and in many ways their experiences reflect the challenges of thinking about moral issues between religious cultures. Our comparison cannot step outside the historical injustice through which colonizing Christianity provided the structural conditions and power disparities through which we come to study these traditions today. Still, we aim to make accurate and illuminative comparisons with these African and North American indigenous traditions that can show something of the depth, complexity, and integrity of their religious ethical views and practices.

Igbo Religious Wisdom

We turn now to an examination of the nature of social exchange as a moral problem, drawing illustrations from the life of the Igbo. That will allow us to examine Igbo religious life as a wisdom tradition offering insight into the

---

10 http://immigrationpolicy.org/research/african-immigrants-america-demographic-overview (accessed 30 May 2019); https://www.ons.gov.uk/peoplepopulationandcommunity/ populationandmigration/internationalmigration/datasets/populationoftheunitedkingdombycoun tryofbirthandnationality (accessed 20 June 2019).

11 Korieh, C.J. (2006). African ethnicity as mirage? Historicizing the essence of the Igbo in Africa and the Atlantic diaspora. *Dialectical Anthropology* 30 (1–2): 91–118. See also Mann, K. (2007). *Slavery and the Birth of an African City: Lagos, 1760–1900*. Bloomington: Indiana University Press.

perplexity of moral life. Next, we explore Christian sources and undertake an analogous inquiry. In each case, our overall goal will be to isolate how and in what ways the religions can and must inform the very meaning and method of religious ethics in its practical dimension.

Social exchange is a broad designation about what is given and taken in a society, either voluntarily or involuntarily. These processes are grounded in material things (food, artifacts, money) and also in meaningful things (gestures, expressions, social codes, laws). Some material things are also meaningful things (as when money is used as a medium of commercial exchange or when food is shared in family celebrations). Some meaningful things (laws and social customs) are not solely material although they exert power over material things. Every culture develops a complex system of social exchange or forms of social communication.[12] These processes of communicative exchange – including gift-giving, marital relations, economics, laws, and so on – are basic to human existence and have always raised profound ethical questions ranging from just distribution of goods and burdens to matters of interpersonal trust and fidelity. They are related to the entire range of basic and moral goods (see Chapter 3).

It is important to think about social exchange descriptively and normatively: what do we mean by social exchange and how ought it to be responsibly practiced? Because the idea of social exchange is becoming increasingly prominent in applied ethics disciplines, we take it as a suitable place to begin thinking about examples of the practical dimension of ethical thinking. Social exchange is a moral problem because in the commerce of bodily or material, social, and reflective goods, we encounter perplexity when the pursuit of goods by one person or through one means or channel conflicts with others' pursuit of goods through different means or channels. Often, perplexity arises when either the goods sought are in conflict or the means employed are deemed unsuitable or inappropriate. In some cases, it is the nature of the goods in question that is at issue. For example, might certain kinds of interpersonal goods (the goods of family and friends) be sacrificed for other kinds of social goods (monetary success), and, if so, under what kinds of constraints and guidelines is it right to make such a sacrifice? Who should decide? Is it possible to reduce moral "worth" simply to "price" so that everything can have a monetary value? In other cases, the means might prove questionable. What happens if one's obligation to serve one's country implicates one in the use of deadly force?

---

12 We use the language of social exchange broadly and do not limit it to recent theoretical developments in sociology. We are, however, aware of the impact of social exchange theories on recent developments in applied ethics (especially business ethics) and therefore indirectly on our discussions of the practical dimension of ethics. For example, see Chen, S. and Choi, C.J. (2005). A social exchange perspective on business ethics: an application to knowledge exchange. *Journal of Business Ethics* 62: 1–11; Duane Hansen, S. et al. (2013). Ethical leadership: assessing the value of a multifoci social exchange perspective. *Journal of Business Ethics* 115: 435–439.

Such questions populate the moral thinking of many religious peoples. Although traditional religions (if we can call them such) were not in their origins as complex as our contemporary globalized cultures, we can isolate patterns of practical reasons that these peoples have used to engage and survive in the contemporary world.

The Nigerian anthropologist Victor Chikezie Uchendu offered the following broad characterization of Igbos' worldview. We quote him at length, having already noted this text at the head of the chapter.[13]

> First, the Igbo world is an integrated one in which all created beings, the living and the dead, are in communion through symbolic interactions and other communication channels ... Second, the Igbo world is a dynamic world which demands that cosmological balance be maintained at all times to sustain the social structure ... Third, the Igbo world is conceived in market terms. It is a "market place" involving a bargaining strategy but guaranteeing only "equality of opportunity" but not "equality of outcome." Individuals as a party and the spirits as another, are subjected to this bargaining process. ... Fourth, in a world of status instability, status seeking in Igbo society is cyclical and therefore a never-ending quest. Every elder tries to live a transparent life to guarantee himself a place of honor among the ancestors. ... Fifth ... to live a secret life from *ezi na ulo*, from the kin and social groups, is to court the charge of sorcery or other anti-social activities, personality traits that spell disorder in Igbo communities ... Sixth, although the Igbo seek explanations for social disasters through the medium of divination, they know from life experiences that their society is not "spoiled" by the spirits but by evil doers in society. ... Seventh, the Igbo live in a world of constant change and are socialized to adapt to it where possible or take a courageous exit by suicide where society or the forces do not permit individual dignity.

The religious view of the Igbo is centered on four levels of reality that are considered the most important and real in terms of their connection to human life: "*Chi/Chukwu* (source of life, giver of destiny), *personal chi* (personality emanating from *Chi/Chukwu*, the immediate carrier and embodiment of the particular individual destiny), ancestors (close to the source of life, they become the immediate givers and guardians of the life of their community), spirits (favoring or endangering the continuity of life)."[14] Each level of reality reflects a different way that the human person is impacted by what transcends immedi-

13 Uchendu, V.C. (2007). Ezi Na Ulo: the extended family in Igbo civilization. *Dialectical Anthropology* 31 (1/3): 167–219.
14 Elochukwu Uzukwu, E. (1982). Igbo world and ultimate reality and meaning. *Ultimate Reality and Meaning*, 5: 195.

ate surroundings. This view of reality, the cosmology, is profoundly moral and religious.

There are many variations in village and wider clan beliefs that we refer to collectively as Igbo religion, but, as in Christianity, there are also significant historical differences among these regions' beliefs and practices over time. A widely held account divides Igbo history into four periods, based on the prominence of the belief system of the Nri group of Igbo and the place of Eri (the cosmic ancestor of human communities) in Igbo stories: pre-Eri (prior to 650 BCE), Eri (650 BCE–850 CE), Aro (1400–1850 CE), and modern (1850–present CE).[15] Nri society recognized the central importance of *Chukwu* as the high God and originator of the natural world, but local deities figured even more prominently in religious, social, and economic life. One of the central creation myths in Igbo culture comes from the Eri period. "The Nri simply say that their founding father, Eri, and his wife Namaku were sent down from Heaven by Chukwu, the Igbo Supreme God, and that they landed at Aguleri, an Igbo village-group in the Anambara valley. There, they claim, the important features of Igbo culture were evolved or rather received as *gifts* from Chukwu."[16] How then is one to think about gift-giving as a form of social exchange, if it is one?[17]

The story goes that Chukwu observed the condition of the earth and of its inhabitants, where "men were wandering in the forest like animals."[18] So he sent Eri to the earth as a gift to humans, and Eri found that it was waterlogged and needed to be dried. Chukwu sent a blacksmith to dry the land and, after Eri offered a sacrifice (a form of social exchange), to Chukwu, offered food from heaven (they would feed on the "inner part of the sky") for Eri and his family.

Throughout the period when men lived on this substance they did not sleep. But this special food from heaven ceased after the death of *Eri* whereon *Nri* his first son complained to *Chukwu* who ordered him to kill and bury in separate graves, his first son and first daughter. After trying in vain to evade this command, *Nri* complied with it, in consequence of which after three Igbo weeks (*izu ato*) yam grew from the

---

15 Afigbo, A.E. (1981). *Ropes of Sand: Studies in Igbo History and Culture*, 27–28. Ibadan: Published for University Press in association with Oxford University Press. See also Ikenga-Metuh, E. (1985). The paradox of transcendence and immanence of god in African religions. *Religion* 15: 377.

16 Afigbo, A.E. (1981). *Ropes of Sand: Studies in Igbo History and Culture*, 37. Ibadan: Published for University Press in association with Oxford University Press.

17 There is considerable literature among thinkers in many fields about the logic and possibility of "gift-giving." For two seminal works see Mauss, M. (1922). *The Gift: Form and Function of Exchange in Archaic Societies*. London: Routledge and Sahlins, M. (1972). *Stone Age Economics*. Chicago, IL: Aldine-Atherton.

18 Ikenga-Metuh, E. (1985). The paradox of transcendence and immanence of god in African religions. *Religion* 15: 378.

grave of the son and coco yam from that of the daughter. When Nri and his people ate these, they slept for the first time. Later still Nri killed a male and a female slave, burying them separately. Again after *izu ato*, an oil palm sprang from the grave of the male slave and a bread fruit tree from that of the female slave.[19]

The story also tells how the family of Nri was asked by Chukwu to share their surplus with neighbors – another form of social exchange – who did not have enough to eat but that Nri initially resisted because the bounty of the four crops (yam, coco yam, palm fruit, and bread fruit) had come at the great personal cost of members of his household. Chukwu made an agreement with Nri that the latter would have authority over the people to grant titles, officiate at ceremonies of honor, and even make a special medicine that would ensure a hearty production of yam crops.[20] Again, forms of social exchange are made and with them practical judgments and perplexities.

There are many variations among these stories. Yet each of the stories of Nri support the revered place of this ancient city as what we call a good of locality, its status as the most significant kingdom for much of premodern Nigerian history, and the centrality of its myths to the history of Igbo religious belief.

A significant feature of the Nri stories is the relationship between Igbo cosmology and religious belief and its transition from a nomadic culture focused on hunting and gathering to a settled agricultural life. Deities that were linked to agricultural production and animal fertility (including human fertility) became more prominent in worship and the relative importance of the supreme God receded somewhat during those periods when the society became more dependent on localized agricultural and animal husbandry.[21]

The Nri kingdom was not the only one to contribute to the body of Igbo religious beliefs and moral practices. The southwestern kingdom of Aro was significant in the seventeenth through nineteenth centuries, renowned for being the only location of a shrine devoted exclusively to *Chukwu*. As a southeastern Igbo kingdom closest to the southern coast, it became an important commercial intermediary, but, more important, it functioned as an oracle that offered judgments about the guilt or innocence of those suspected of committing crimes.[22] Although each tribe of Igboland instantiated its own form of

---

19 Afigbo, A.E. (1981). *Ropes of Sand: Studies in Igbo History and Culture*, 41. Ibadan: Published for University Press in association with Oxford University Press.
20 Ibid., 42.
21 See Long, C.H. (1964). The West African high god: history and religious experience. *History of Religions* 3 (2): 332–336; cited in Ikenga-Metuh, E. (1985). The paradox of transcendence and immanence of god in African religions. *Religion* 15: 373–385.
22 Akuma-Kalu Njoku, T. (2014). Motifs from Igbo sacred texts as primary indicators of Igbo theology and religion. In *Interface Between Igbo Theology and Christianity*, (ed. T. Akuma-Kalu

social organization and procedures for ensuring social order and administering justice, and each deity was acknowledged as having its own specific laws, the Aro-Chukwu oracle was a respected source of guidance and religious inspiration. One finds, then, a connection between Igbo religion (Aro-Chukwu) and Igbo morality in the use of an oracle to make decisions and also the development of economic forms of social exchange.

The Igbo understand the person (*mmadu*, a compound of *mma* [goodness] and *ndu* [life]) to be a physical body (*ahu*) animated by a personal spirit (*agu*) assigned by Chi/Chukwu sometime after conception. The spirit may be the return of an ancestral spirit or some other spirit. "Personages associated with the physical characteristics or potentialities of an Igbo person could be ancestors respected by the community, venerable living elders, living spirits, one's dead comrades, or malignant spirits."[23] Remarkably, the "commerce" or exchange of spirit foundational to Igbo life may be found in the process of negotiation that happens before birth. "Before getting into contact with the physical body (*ahu*), [every person] walks to a crossroads (*aba uzo*) where he meets a *personal chi* specifically assigned to him by *Chi/Chukwu*. He bargains with his *personal chi* who, in a pact, defines the broad outlines of a person's (soul's) destiny. He (the soul) enters the already formed physical body at birth through a creative act of his *personal chi*, and becomes the living infant whose 'life-line' – destiny – has been 'traced on the palm of his hand' (*akala aka*)."[24] This means that at the core of human existence is some relation to sacred powers and an exchange with spirit.

Although it is perhaps imprudent to select only a few ideas from Igbo cultural practice at the risk of neglecting others and even distorting those we select, some ideas receive sustained attention in religious ethics: *mma* (goodness), *ndu* (life), *amamihe* (wisdom or right knowledge), *akankwumoto* (justice), *ogu* (innocence or guiltlessness), and *ofo* (authority).[25] As noted previously,

---

Njoku and E. Uzukwu), 66–84. Newcastle: Cambridge Scholars Publishing. The history of the Aro-Chukwu Oracle (also called the Ibin Ukpabi [after the name of the local deity to which the power of Chukwu was recognized] of Arochukwu) is complicated and much disputed among scholars. The difficulty is that the location of the Chukwu oracle made it a strategic and secretive location for the seventeenth century slave trade. Despite this misuse of the oracle, many continued to go to the oracle and found the pilgrimage "a deep spiritual phenomenon" (Ikenga-Metuh, 379) and even modern day researchers note the spiritual quality of the place where it is difficult "to not feel the awesome presence of Chukwu" (Njoku, 77).
23 Ibid., 197.
24 Ibid., 197. Many readers will be familiar with the world-renowned Igbo author Chinua Achebe's novel *Things Fall Apart*, in which the protagonist Okonkwo struggles to understand how his Chi guides him in light of his own family history (including his critique of his father, Unoka) and how his Chi also allows him to make choices, ultimately tragic ones, which turn his greatest virtues into the loneliest of vices.
25 We select these terms hesitantly because, as nonnative speakers with limited knowledge of Igbo language and culture, we must rely on the interpretations offered by Igbo scholars and

the notions of *mma* and *ndu* are central to Igbo ethical thinking, because together they communicate the reality of human beings as having vitality, destiny, and deep community responsibilities. For example, "The name *Chineke*, a concatenation of *Chi* and *Eke*, expresses the father-cum-mother divine duality of the first divine parents. The *Chi* component of the compound word *Chineke* is the vital source of life (*ume ndu*) and *Eke* the source of Goodness (*nma*). *Chi-na-eke* pass on their basic character of Goodness (*Mma*) and Life (*Ndu*) to human beings."[26] Igbo notions of goodness are strongly linked to the perpetuation and integrity of the life of the community, a value that is characteristic of many African religions.[27]

Like the foundational concepts of goodness and life, *amamihe* (wisdom or right knowledge) and *akankwumoto* (justice) are likewise closely connected. "Etymologically, 'akankwumoto' derives from three other Igbo words: 'aka' (hand), 'nkwu' (stand, remain, stay), and 'oto' (straight, erect, upright, not crooked, etc). Thus, the word 'akankwumoto' literally means keeping one's

---

scholars of Igbo language and culture. So we adopt the helpful advice of Edwin Anaegboka Udoye who, with reference to the name Chineke ("God of Creation" or "God of Providence"), notes that "Chineke is another personal name for God. It is a composition of two words – Chi and Eke. Here Chi means 'God or Providence' and Eke is a term that means 'to create'. Put together it means God who creates. Two problems might come up with regard to the word *Chineke*. Firstly, a non-Igbo reader will be entrapped on the syllogistic application of the words, when they mean other things in different usages. Secondly, the terms fall victim to what Metuh calls 'the paucity of Igbo vocabulary'. The word 'eke' has many meanings but when tone-marked the meanings become distinct ... *Ekezie* (God creates well) *Ekekwe* (God permits) *Ekejekwu* (God will decide), *Ekenweuba* (Wealth belongs to God), *Ajulueke* (Have you asked God?) and *Ekenweilo* (God has no enemy). These names present God not only as creator of life, but also as a provider of wealth, protector, and leader. He governs human events in the world. He is conceived as one who is so good that he has no enemy." See Edwin Anaegboka Udoye. (2011). *Resolving the Prevailing Conflicts Between Christianity and African (Igbo) Traditional Religion Through Inculturation*, 38. Münster: LIT Verlag. Methodologically speaking, we hope this approach to the moral ideas in other languages communicates our view that the multidimensional approach to ethics fits well with – indeed requires – a view of language as semantically flexible and inherently dialogical, as the meaning of words are revised and tested within cultures and existing language groups but also through interactions among cultures and languages groups. We take this to be true – and deeply underappreciated – of the Christian moral and theological vocabulary, which is often unhelpfully understood as a settled, insular, and inflexible "grammar."

26 Akuma-Kalu Njoku, T. (2014). Motifs from Igbo sacred texts as primary indicators of Igbo theology and religion. In: *Interface Between Igbo Theology and Christianity*, (ed. T. Akuma-Kalu Njoku and E. Uzukwu), 74–75. Newcastle: Cambridge Scholars Publishing. Echeruo notes a close connection between *eke* used to mean the creator and its use to mean fate or personal destiny. The one who creates is also the one who delivers to a person her or his own destiny, the traditional understanding of a person's Chi. See Echeruo, M.J.C. (1998). *Igbo-English Dictionary: A Comprehensive Dictionary of the Igbo Language, with an English-Igbo Index*. New Haven and London: Yale University Press.

27 Magesa, L. (1997). *African Religion: Moral Traditions of Abundant Life*, Maryknoll, NY: Orbis Books.

hand straight."[28] *Akankwumoto* is closely linked with another sense of justice that is *ikpenkwumoto* and so is important in practical decision-making.

In the same vein "ikpenkwumoto" stems from "ikpe" (judgement, case, decision, verdict), "kwu" (stand, stay, remain), and "oto" (straight, erect). Literally, "ikpenkwumoto" means judgement that is straight …. This idea of straightness in relation to justice can refer to an action or person. In the former sense, it means that one's life is straight-forward, upright, honest, predictable and impartial. In the latter understanding, a just action is one that is not crooked, is performed as it should be, is done in a disinterested manner, or has followed a due process.[29]

Both senses of justice converge on the principle that one should not be dishonest and that one should treat others fairly. This is clearly a norm for the practical life and in particular social exchange.

In early Igbo agricultural communities, the land was divided for smaller family divisions from lands held by larger extended family groups. The people would find a young man of good reputation and he would be charged by the elder member of the extended family to divide the land into equitable shares. Drawing that line in practical judgments required that one have a "straight hand" literally (so the line dividing one family's share from the other would not curve to include or exclude a certain desirable or undesirable portions of the land) and figuratively (that one would give each family that to which it was entitled). This sense of justice works on a commitment to acceptable local custom in conformity with creation (*omenala*) guided through a process of comparison with *ogu* (righteousness that is affirmed by the gods). *Omenala* ("how things are done on the land") is based on "the people's forefathers and foremothers, their ancestors who once founded the community, *Omenala*, and its underlying cosmic force and code of conduct, the *Ogu*."[30] *Omenala* denotes the prevailing culture and accepted moral standards of the community, but the morality of the community at any one time is not an acceptable standard unless it reflects the cultural memory of the people, that is, how ancestors lived in light of the challenges of their times. *Omenala* is checked and corrected by *ogu* in the sense that *ogu* is the ancestral vision of righteousness to which all people now, and even the gods themselves, are subject.[31] *Ogu* might be translated as

---

28 Oraegbunam, I.K.E. (2009). The principles and practice of justice in traditional Igbo jurisprudence. *Ogirisi: A New Journal of African Studies* 6: 56.

29 Ibid., 56–57. Notice the contrast with the idea of justice as right order (Chapter 3).

30 Jell-Bahlsen, S. (2014). The dialectics of Igbo and Christian religion in contemporary Nigeria. In: *Interface Between Igbo Theology and Christianity*, (ed. T. Akuma-Kalu Njoku and E. Elochuwu Uzukwu), 52–3. Newcastle: Cambridge Scholars Publishing.

31 Ibid., 53 n6.

"highest virtue" wherein one finds counsel to "[1] Think well of others. Do nothing but kindly deeds to all. [2] Do not cheat anybody. [3] Do not rob the blind the joy of an unusual fortune."[32] These are, we might note, in rough analogy to the Golden and Silver Rules (Chapter 3) applied to practical judgments.

In traditional Igbo society, the leader of the family or of the village takes a symbol of authority, the *ofo*, which gives that person the right to make judgments in accordance with *ogu*. As explained later, there are venues in which a person can have *ofo*, the primary one being the leader of the family, but in each case *ofo* serves the justice fully realized in *ogu* and this justice is directed to the well-being of the community. In this way, *akankwumoto* refers not only to an idea of justice as order, but to the practice of justice with proper authority that in turn requires honesty and mercy and is symbolized by the use of *ofo* in Igbo ritual and social life.

So how are these ideals to be lived? One central value of Igbo culture is the well-being of the community, both in the flourishing of the lives of individual people but also insofar as the successful individual contributes to the harmonious community. This view is captured in two complex notions in Igbo culture: (i) the primacy of interlocking kinship networks (*ezi na ulo*) and (ii) two interrelated senses of justice (*akankwumoto* understood as personal virtue or character and *ikpenkwumoto* or *ikpeziriezi* understood as wisdom or prudent judgment about complex problems of the community).[33] The cultural value of *ezi na ulo* (kinship networks) is central to the community's understanding of practical reasoning and to the people's cosmology. It reflects the goal and process of communal decision-making and the multileveled view of reality. *Ezi na ulo*, which translates as the term "family," also implies the positioning of a nuclear family within a wider reality of kinship networks (*umunna*). It is a crucial basic social good. *Ezi* is a term that can signify many different locations and so goods of locality, some more spatially defined (e.g. a courtyard of a domicile) and others more ritually defined (e.g. a location of ritual impurity) but generally implies something that is external.[34] *Ulo*, by contrast, implies something that is internal or interior. Bound linguistically to the idea of family

---

32 Akuma-Kalu Njoku, T. (2014). Motifs from Igbo sacred texts as primary indicators of Igbo theology and religion. In: *Interface Between Igbo Theology and Christianity*, (ed. T. Akuma-Kalu Njoku and E. Elochuwu Uzukwu), 72. Newcastle: Cambridge Scholars Publishing. Njoku notes that the last of these may be explained by the example "Do not deny the blind the ownership of the *udala* [fruit] found with their foot." The sense here is that one ought not to begrudge others their good fortune, especially those who have experienced misfortune, even if it challenges what the society accepts as property rightly gained through one's labors.

33 Oraegbunam, I.K.E. (2009). The principles and practice of justice in traditional Igbo jurisprudence. *Ogirisi: A New Journal of African Studies* 6: 53–85.

34 Ufearoh, A. (2010). Ezi-Na-Ulo and Umunna: In search of democratic ideals in traditional Igbo family. *Ogirisi: A New Journal of African Studies* 9: 94–105.

and kinship (*ezi na ulo*), "ulo" focuses more on the person and her or his disposition and character.

Each of these moral terms is incomplete without its counterpart, such that one cannot see the nature of what is outside without the perspective of what is inside. "The metaphysics of the Igbo and African family further informs and enhances this sense of dialogue and communal communication. In Igbo ontology, man is not an isolated being. He is a 'being-with.' He is in communication not only with his fellow human beings but also with gods, ancestors and other visible and invisible beings that are existent in Igbo world view."[35] What is "inside and outside" in the constitution of the Igbo family finds its parallel in the connectedness between the family now, the family that has gone before, and the family that will yet come to be in future generations. Social, bodily, reflective, and local basic goods extend through time and into the future such that practical decision-making must be seen in the wide field of relations. Justice acknowledges the life of the person as central and also that any individual person is incomplete without their position in the community. Justice is then about right relations, proper order, as well as right and fair exchange.[36]

Two further examples speak to the relationship between community and justice in practical decision-making. *Akankwumoto*, the term for personal virtue or character, is derived from three words: "*aka*' (hand), '*nkwu*' (stand, remain, stay), and '*oto*' (straight, erect, upright, not crooked, etc.)."[37] People are virtuous if they are straightforward, transparent in their motives, and consistent. The notion of just judgment also reflects reasoning that is straight, sensible, and not influenced by improper motives or hidden interests but keeps the good of persons and the community in mind where the word "*ikpe*' ([judgment], case, decision, verdict)"[38] signals the expression of just judgment rather than just character.

Justice therefore implies not only the good of individuals but also the proper order of the community so that members of the community have a good and fulfilling life and also that the community thrives. Here is, to recall previous ideas, a version of ethical naturalism insofar as justice is about the thriving and flourishing of the person and the community given the kinds of beings they are. Justice requires, therefore, that the individual understand her or his own good in relation to the good of the community and not as something that precedes or can be understood independent from the good of the community. Two significant

---

35 Ibid., 101.
36 Recall the discussion of two conceptions of justice (justice and right order and justice as an order or rights); see Wolterstorff, N. (2008). *Justice: Rights and Wrongs*. Princeton, NJ: Princeton University Press.
37 Oraegbunam, I.K.E. (2009). The principles and practice of justice in traditional Igbo jurisprudence. *Ogirisi: A New Journal of African Studies* 6: 56.
38 Ibid.

cultural expressions of the view of good character and good judgment are derived from the symbolic nature of two revered trees – the *ofo* and the *oji*.

Ofo has several meanings, one being the actual tree indigenous to West Africa (*Detarium elastica*) and others deriving from the reverence for the tree in traditional Igbo culture. The *ofo* "primarily represents ancestral power and authority and the key values of truth and justice. It also refers to some other significant ideas, like patriliny, the major principle of social integration among the people."[39] The *ofo* as a ritual object is a carved and adorned branch from an *ofo* tree. The *ofo* stick is usually held by the leader of the family or the respected elder of an area. There are then three kinds of uses for *ofo* important for practical judgments: religious, political, and ethical. Among the first are included the use of the *ofo* in prayers and blessing and in communication with ancestors as access to sacred power; among the second are included investment of persons with titles, conducting community deliberations, and declaring war and peace; and among the third we find included attestation to the truth of statements, as well as declarations of guilt or innocence.[40]

Another important cultural element is the kola nut that comes from the *Cola acuminata* or Oji tree. A bitter nut containing caffeine, often chewed or used in various food and beverage preparations, the kola nut is regarded as a symbol of hospitality and also as a marker of the beginning of rites and gatherings. The kola nut "signifies the beginning of every ceremony, as an object of communion between man and man and between man and spirits, it stands for love, loyalty, unity, honesty and stability of social structure. ... The kolanut is what the Igboman uses in his morning prayers to the supernatural being and veneration of his ancestors after washing his hands and face."[41] The nut has almost sacramental power and is a way for the Igbo to make contact with and receive empowerment from the supernatural and one's ancestors amid the affairs of life.[42]

In welcoming ceremonies, the sharing of the kola nut is a time when the welcoming family becomes familiar with their guests and locates them within an order of hospitality. It is an occasion for transparency in conversation, where the host discovers about the person and background of guests, including what if any relation they have to the host family and community. Hospitality occasioned by this offer become an occasion for deeper understanding that grounds any practical decisions that emerge in its wake. Practical decisions, whatever they may be, should not violate the bonds of hospitality and community.

---

39 Ejizu, C.I. (1987). The taxonomy, provenance, and functions of ọfọ: a dominant igbo ritual and political symbol. *Anthropos* 82: 457. See also Ejizu, C.I. (2002). *Ofo: Igbo Ritual Symbol.* Enugu: Fourth Dimension Publishing.
40 Ibid., 465.
41 Chidume, C.G. (2014). The symbolism of the Kolanut in Igbo cosmology: a re-examination. *European Scientific Journal* 2: 550.
42 See Achebe, C. (1992 [1958]). *Things Fall Apart*, with an introduction by Kwame Anthony Appiah, 3–6 New York and London: Alfred A. Knopf.

Not only in welcoming ceremonies but in private uses as well, the kola nut is understood to establish a connection of harmony between people (residents and their guests) as well as between oneself and one's ancestors or the gods. When broken, the nut reveals a number of sections (the cotyledon or seed leaf) that are interpreted as signs of good or bad omens.[43] This divinatory practice existed within a wider view of the kola's significance as a symbol of hospitality and a gift imparting wisdom and expressing wisdom's sound judgments.[44] Practical decision-making is linked to divination and the imparting of wisdom needed for making good decisions.

Tracking the uses of *ofo* and *oji* are significant for understanding the practical dimension of Igbo ethical life, because these disclose the close connection between the practical and the symbolic aspects of life. Consider two additional examples that illustrate this connection. First, in Igbo villages, the yam was considered one of the most important crops in the daily diet. Successful cultivation of yams provided male heads of household with community respect but also invested them with community obligations. The ability to produce more yams than was required for family subsistence allowed the farmer to fulfill obligations belonging to those wealthy enough to enjoy the surplus.[45] However, with changes in agriculture responding to changes in land fertility, yams (which had nutrient rich soil requirements) became a less significant source of sustenance and were overtaken in terms of staple diet by the cultivation of cassava because of the latter's higher yield and easy of cultivation in a period of deteriorating soil conditions.

In terms of practical decision-making, what is crucial about the transition from yam to cassava production is the impact this had on traditional male headship and community decision-making. The practice of agriculture, including the relative importance of different crops and the country's changing political and economic conditions, reveals how symbolic discourse affects practical reasoning. The changing status of a crop traditionally invested with symbolic significance (the yam as characteristic of male power to provide for the people) shows the adaptability of the social structure, demonstrating a relative emphasis between egalitarian and hierarchical decision-making in Igbo culture, especially in matters of family and local community politics. Traditional symbols like the yam are not removed or replaced in light of new ways of viewing the world. Instead symbols are expanded and transformed. The yam was a symbol of harmony, bounty, and male headship, but the community's regard for it as a primary symbol hid a deeper sensibility about the primacy of the community's

---

43 Chidume, C.G. (2014). The symbolism of the Kolanut in Igbo cosmology: a re-examination. *European Scientific Journal* 2: 548.

44 Ibid. It is within this wider symbolic view that recent scholars have argued for the traditional view of linking the two-lobed kola nut to the rejection of twins born to Igbo parents.

45 Korieh, C.J. (2007). Yam is king! But Cassava is the mother of all crops: farming, culture, and identity in Igbo Agrarian economy. *Dialectical Anthropology* 31 (1–3): 221–232.

well-being. Symbols like the yam embedded practical decision-making and social exchange within the wider domain of the community's values and cosmology. The work of families, especially rural Igbo women, to provide cassava in periods of scarcity affirmed the flexible and more egalitarian structure of local domestic economies. The practical dimension of ethics is expanded beyond typical philosophical accounts of casuistry or practical syllogisms noted earlier in this chapter.

A second example comes from ethics education in Nigerian business schools as people who were raised in agriculture and economies of small-scale exchange carry lessons from their communities into a global economy. Recall the Igbo saying noted before and at the top of this chapter: "the world is a marketplace (*uwa bu ahia*)." The saying expresses an important connection between the symbolic realm and practical dimensions of Igbo ethical thinking.[46] The human world of commercial exchange mirrors the works of just exchange on the spiritual plane of life.

> When the Igbo say that the world is a market, they usually complete the sentence by observing that when one buys to one's content, one goes home. The home referred to here is the land of the ancestors to which the Igbo believe the spirits of the dead return to bargain for a better life in their next incarnation. If one's creator dealt one a raw deal in this life, one can still bargain with his/her personal God (or Chi) and haggle for a better break in the next life. In other words, the Igbo intend the paradox that the world is a market as a description of the global world and not simply just the Igbo world.[47]

The view of the world as a market does not countenance selfish material acquisitiveness. It recognizes hard work with honorable positions and imposes social obligations on those who work and have made the most of their opportunities. The yam became an important staple of Igbo agricultural economy and its proper cultivation allowed the adept farmer to provide for his family and for his extended community. The recognition of that skill is preserved in the tile *ezeji* (yam king) given to those who were particularly good at the cultivation of yams.[48] The successful cultivation of yams was an occasion to give thanks to *Ana* (the goddess of the earth) by honoring *Ifejioku* (the yam spirit) through a community festival.[49] The festival included a series of rituals including a barn

---

46 Agozino, B. and Anyanike, I. (2007). Imu Ahia: traditional Igbo business school and global commerce culture. *Dialectical Anthropology* 31: 233–252.
47 Ibid., 233.
48 Korieh, C.J. (2007). Yam is king! But Cassava is the mother of all crops: farming, culture, and identity in Igbo Agrarian economy. *Dialectical Anthropology* 31 (1–3): 223.
49 Isichei, E. (1976). *A History of the Igbo People*, 28. New York: St. Martin's Press.

raising, a blessing of the barn that would hold the harvest, which also included the construction of a shrine to *Ifejioku*, the consecration of the first 400 yams, and a drumming ritual which was a "celebration of achievement and dignity of labour."[50] Again, a practical skill is set within a wider religious and symbolic practice and in doing so the meaning and gravity of particular judgments is deepened. Practical judgments are not deductions or inferences from higher goods, principles, duties, but ways of inscribing life in a religious, ritual, and symbolic worldview.

The logic of this symbolic significance of the yam provides a model for understanding other forms of interpersonal responsibility in Igbo religious ethics. As more people moved to commercial activities, the logic of the yam festival and the importance of honoring the provision of the earth and the dignity of labor continued. In many areas, less wealthy Igbo would apprentice their children to successful entrepreneurs, often family members, to learn the *imu ahia* ("learning" or "science" [*imu*] of "markets" [*ahia*]) in one or another specific trade – a kind of family based "guild system."[51] Parents promised that their children would serve industriously and cooperatively for the period of the apprenticeship; the employer would provide the material care and training of the young apprentice. At an extended family celebration, those gathered would advise the young person "on the virtues of honesty, hard work, obedience and respectfulness," and the expectations of both parties (parents/entrepreneurs) would be stated before those assembled.[52] The recognition of mutual rights and obligations extended not only to those who were the immediate beneficiaries of the arrangements but also to how those trained in such skills would use them for the good of the community. The change from agricultural to commercial or modern globalized economy could be an occasion for perplexity (the abandonment of traditional values, rituals, and forms of community). However, Igbo moral thought envisions ways to achieve goods through means that highlight the values communicated within traditional forms of thought but with an openness to new circumstances. It seeks to carry on ancestral wisdom (*amamihe*) in modern economic and social forms. By doing so, the Igbo provide norms and rules embedded in symbol, practice, and cosmology that inform practical decision-making. The religious context provides the wisdom needed to answer current perplexities even as those perplexities challenge the community to continue to transmit their forms of wisdom.

---

50 Korieh, C.J. (2007). Yam is king! But Cassava is—the mother of all crops: farming, culture, and identity in Igbo Agrarian economy. *Dialectical Anthropology* 31 (1/3): 223.
51 Agozino, B. and Anyanike, I. (2007). Imu Ahia: traditional Igbo business school and global commerce culture. *Dialectical Anthropology* 31: 234.
52 Ibid., 234–235.

Early Christian Religion

As seen among the Igbo, one of the challenges to understanding the practical dimension of religious ethics is the tendency of scholars to think about the practical as no more than the application of a set of principles to the facts of particular cases. That account of practical reasoning and judgment is called "casuistry," or case-method, and it is found among the religions as well. But the account of practical reasoning within the religions also takes different forms. Early Christian churches, just like the Igbo communities, faced new circumstances that called for a rethinking of traditional resources. And Christian communities also resisted the narrowing of practical reasoning. They responded to the practical demands of living well in a changing social and political landscape. In part because of the prominence of Christian religion in world affairs at different points in its history, there are many places to look for the ways it attended to the practical and sought wisdom in the face of perplexity. As with Igbo religion, social exchange is a good place to begin because it attends to the difficulties of family life and the life of the wider *oikos* (household) of humankind, including politics and economics.

The search for true wisdom is a central feature of Christian life. Wisdom is a form of knowledge, but it is not the knowledge of scientific certainty. It lifts up the best counsel of prior generations and is directed to the uncertain affairs of the present generation. In Jewish and Christian thought, the quest for wisdom links the fleeting grasp for happiness that this world promises but cannot deliver with the true and lasting good of human life. Wisdom embeds basic and moral goods in a wider conception of the good that transcends the dealings of this world, the transcendent good.

The Christian Old Testament (roughly the Hebrew Bible) has different words that are translated as wisdom. It refers to the divine governance of the universe (as in Proverbs 3:19 – "the Lord by wisdom founded the earth; by understanding he established the heavens") and also to good human judgment about difficult questions (as in the biblical pronouncement on King Solomon in 1 Kings 3:28 – "All Israel heard of the judgment that the king had rendered; and they stood in awe of the king, because they perceived that the wisdom of God was with him to execute justice.")[53] The Jewish tradition recognizes that wisdom may be found in stories about the Jewish people's struggle to keep the covenant with God, in the counsel of the prophets to trust in God rather than in human power, and in the history of Jewish law guiding the lives of the people so that they might live in right relation to God. So although certain books are recognized by modern scholars as "wisdom literature," there are many aspects of Jewish and Christian traditions that offer wise counsel in the face of perplexity.

---

53 Welton, D.M. (1897). The Old Testament Wisdom (Chokma). *The Biblical World* 10 (3): 183–189.

Not surprisingly, Christian theology attempts to preserve the same capacious view of wisdom in its own tradition. There are many places in the Christian New Testament that offer visions of and practical guidance for attaining wisdom, especially Jesus' teaching, St. Paul's letters, and the Pastoral Epistles. In each case, it is important to recall a theme introduced earlier: although the pursuit of wisdom includes within it practical solutions, it is also a necessarily truth-seeking, interpretive work that aims at human well-being for individuals in right relation with their neighbors and the divine. Consider the following examples from early Christian theology that exemplify these dimensions of the pursuit of wisdom.

Christianity emerged in a time of great social and political conflict and change. The Jewish city of Jerusalem had been occupied time and again by foreign powers since the destruction of the Temple of Solomon in 586 BCE at the hands of the Babylonian king, Nebuchadnezzar II. Jerusalem was the central city of the southern kingdom of Judah that had separated from the northern kingdom of Israel after the death of King Solomon in 928 BCE.[54] In subsequent periods, Jerusalem was controlled by Cyrus, king of Persia, who had conquered the Babylonian empire in 539 BCE, allowing many of the exiled Jews to return to Jerusalem. The second Jerusalem temple was constructed between 520 and 515 BCE, during the period of Persian occupation, and lasted until it was destroyed by the Romans in 70 CE. The period of Roman occupation of Jerusalem began in 63 BCE, when the Roman general Pompey captured Jerusalem, and it lasted through a series of kings installed by Rome through the formative years of early Christianity.

The early Christians were a small group of Jews convinced that a wandering preacher, wonder-worker, and social critic named Jesus of Nazareth was in fact the messiah or Christ and even God's son. Jesus had been executed as a criminal by the Roman authorities and was believed to have risen from the dead. His followers debated the extent of his political involvement, the kinds of social changes he envisioned, and the Synoptic Gospels (Mark, Matthew, and Luke) give a range of views about the kind of practical reforms of religious and political life Jesus envisioned. For example, the Gospel of Matthew (written sometime in the late first century) focuses on the continuities and reforming elements of Jesus' teaching, portraying a figure who sought to bring out the inner meaning of Jewish law and the forms of virtuous living counseled by that law.[55] The Gospel of Luke, written during the same period but directed to

---

54 The Northern Kingdom of Israel had fallen to the Assyrian empire in 722 BCE. See Cogan, M. (1992). Chronology – Old Testament. In: *The Anchor Bible Dictionary*, vol. 1, (ed. A.-C. David Noel Freedman), 1002–1022. New York: Doubleday.

55 For example, after the enunciation of the Beatitudes in his Sermon on the Mount, Jesus reminds his audience: "'Do not think that I have come to abolish the law or the prophets; I have come not to abolish but to fulfil. For truly I tell you, until heaven and earth pass away, not one letter, not one stroke of a letter, will pass from the law until all is accomplished. Therefore,

recent non-Jewish converts to Judaism, emphasizes the universality of Jesus' message and the revolutionary, or at least socially destabilizing, aspects of his teaching and healing.[56] The Gospel of Mark, on which Luke and Matthew are partially based, is addressed to Greek speakers with some familiarity with Jewish belief. Mark probes the meaning of Jesus as "Messiah," the nature of the "kingdom of God" ushered in by his ministry, and the effect of the "Spirit of God" on the social expectations of his times.[57] In each case, the gospel writers express an openness to what we are calling the multidimensional nature of the moral life. The teachings of Jesus challenge hearers to interpret their world in a new way and to seek truth in the midst of (sometimes in tense relationship with) the religious and political powers that set the social expectations for a good life. How does one live out loyalty to the values of the state or and the prevailing religious community?

Jesus' teaching on moral matters could be quite extreme. He told a follower that if his eye causes him to sin he should pluck it out because it is better to go to heaven blind than to have sight (Mt 5:29, 18:9; Mk 9:49). In a similar way, he called a disciple to leave his dead father; the dead can bury the dead (Lk 9:60). His parables (short stories with an almost riddle-like quality), created perplexity in his listeners. When asked who is one's neighbor, he told, in the famous "Parable of the Good Samaritan" (Lk 10:25–37), about a Samaritan (a person on the outside of Jewish society at that time) who had helped a man in distress while a priest and a Levite (important people in the Jewish establishment), did not help the man. But how could a "Samaritan" – that is, a despised an unclean person – be a neighbor when righteous religious people were not? The

---

whoever breaks one of the least of these commandments, and teaches others to do the same, will be called least in the kingdom of heaven; but whoever does them and teaches them will be called great in the kingdom of heaven'" (Mt 5:17–19).

56 The Gospel of Luke contains the infancy narrative of Jesus, emphasizing his humble beginnings (Lk 2), and an account of the opening of his public ministry that explicitly links his ministry to those who are poor and outcast. In the Temple, Luke has him read from the prophet Isaiah: "He unrolled the scroll and found the place where it was written: 'The Spirit of the Lord is upon me, because he has anointed me to bring good news to the poor. He has sent me to proclaim release to the captives and recovery of sight to the blind, to let the oppressed go free, to proclaim the year of the Lord's favor.' ... Then he began to say to them, 'Today this scripture has been fulfilled in your hearing'" (Lk 4:16–21). This emphasis on the poor has given rise to vigorous debates among historians of Christianity and contemporary theologians. We note this debate because it presents an interpretive problem we have been examining in this book: how to interpret religious traditions in ways that preserve their internal diversity, indeed sometimes ambiguity, while nonetheless allowing them to speak to the priorities and practices of our own time.

57 The Gospel of Mark, the earliest of the synoptic Gospels, begins with the penitential overtures of John the Baptist, calling his listeners to a new way of life, and announcing that "The time is fulfilled, and the kingdom of God has come near; repent, and believe in the good news" (Mk 1:15). The author of Mark's Gospel sets forth that conversion of heart will require a concomitant change in how one lives. Recall our discussion of the rich young man in Chapter 2 (Mk 10:17–22; see also Mt 19:16–30 and Lk 18:18–30).

parable evokes perplexity concerning the meaning and obligation to love one's neighbor as one's self. Recall that this formulation of the law is basic to Judaism and Christianity in the Silver and Golden Rules (Chapter 3). Yet at other times, Jesus' actions evoke perplexity, as when he dines with sinners, heals on the Sabbath, and even forgives sin. Christians believe, then, that the wisdom of Christ's teachings and actions can provoke profound perplexity and even hostility yet in the search for wisdom. Perplexity is evoked in the hearer or reader in order to force one to reconsider one's response to a situation or a person, that is, to think clearly and more deeply and thereby to gain wisdom.

The early Christian community grew and changed in status from being a religious minority under the early Roman persecutions to a pan-Mediterranean movement spread by the apostle Paul and his collaborators. It gained official standing with the reforms of the emperor Constantine (c. 280–337 CE). That change in status prompted the Christian community to face new challenges that met with a variety of responses. How could one possibly teach Jesus' radical message, say to love one's enemies, and to follow his actions in the context of a massive empire? Two examples of these responses focus on Christian views of marriage and the rise of Christian monastic communities. We can note the different ways that the practical dimension of the community's moral life is critically related to the other dimensions of ethics and how the search for wisdom in the midst of perplexity persists through the history of the Christian churches until today. Consider, in this light, marriage and family life.

Marriage was a central but not absolute value in early Christian communities. "Christ taught that marriage was created by God as a union of a man and a woman who had been emancipated from their childhood homes ... Christians were not to elevate the demands of their own temporal families beyond the demands of the kingdom of God."[58] The kingdom of God was compared to a family in the Gospel of Luke (8:21) and Jesus affirms the goodness of marriage and the demands of the Jewish law regarding marriage (Mt 19:3–12). And yet Jesus was not married (that we know of) and often scorned the family asking, "who is my mother and who my brothers" (Mt 12:48). He also ate with prostitutes and did not condemn a woman for adultery. Some, like Paul in his letters, advised abstinence and the avoidance of the responsibilities of marriage and childrearing in the service of ministry (1 Cor 7). Many others praised marriage as a model of Christian relationship more egalitarian than its counterparts in Greek and Roman culture.[59] The stability of marriage, together with the view that the family might serve as a kind of "domestic church," became

---

58 Witte, J. Jr. (1997). *From Sacrament to Contract: Marriage, Religion, and Law in the Western Tradition*, 16. Louisville: Westminster John Knox.

59 Ibid., 143–161.

central to early Christian views of marriage.[60] The Church fused the teachings and actions of Jesus as well as some Jewish convictions with the cultural patterns and wisdom from the wider political and social world, what are called "household code" (*Haustafeln*) about the relations between men and women, parent and child, and the conduct of women in worship services (e.g. Eph 5:22–6:9).

The early Church and later patristic writers saw in marriage both a series of basic goods (bodily, social, etc.) but also a spiritual significance or a transcendent good. Augustine of Hippo (354–430 CE) famously noted that marriage was "the ordained means of procreation (*proles*), the guarantee of chastity (*fides*), and the bond of permanent union (*connubi sacramentum*)."[61] Although Augustine had not worked out the full meaning of the spiritual significance of marriage, he suggested elements that would be expanded in the medieval period. *Sacramentum*, as Augustine used the term, had two meanings. One was the general meaning of a "sacred sign." The other meaning was "the specific sense of a rite or activity signifying and achieving a spiritual effect."[62] In marriage, Augustine explains, sacrament refers to "a kind of sacred bond" between the couple where the sacredness is more than the ability to produce children or even the faithfulness between the husband and wife. "It is certainly not fecundity only, the fruit of which consists of offspring," he wrote, "nor chastity only, whose bond is fidelity, but also a certain sacramental bond in marriage which is recommended to believers in wedlock. ... that the man and the woman who are joined together in matrimony should remain inseparable as long as they live."[63] Marriage became then a context within which to address practical questions about sexual conduct, family life, and even religious practice.

Later theologians, such as Thomas Aquinas (1225/7–1274 CE), would interpret "as Christ loved the Church" to mean that there is a real symbolic connection between the love of Jesus for the Church and the love between husband and wife. Aquinas explains that "the sacraments of the Church were instituted for a twofold purpose: namely, in order to perfect [human beings] in things pertaining to the worship of God according to the religion of Christian life, and to be a remedy against the defects caused by sin."[64] For Aquinas, marriage is

---

60 The terminology of "domestic Church" was common among early patristic authors such as Irenaeus of Lyons (120/130–202 CE) and Augustine of Hippo (354–430 CE). See Cahill, L.S. (1996). *Sex, Gender, and Christian Ethics*, 207–208. Cambridge: Cambridge University Press.

61 Augustine of Hippo, *On Original Sin*. Cited in Witte, J. Jr. (1997). *From Sacrament to Contract: Marriage, Religion, and Law in the Western Tradition*, 21. Louisville: Westminster John Knox.

62 Appleyard, J.A. How does a sacrament 'cause by signifying'?. *Science et Esprit* 23.2 (1971), 167–200.

63 Augustine of Hippo, *On Marriage and Concupiscence* I.11.

64 Aquinas, T. (1981 [1948]). *Summa Theologiae*, III.65.1 (trans. Fathers of the English Dominican Province). Westminster: Christian Classics.

rightly enumerated among the sacraments because it brings people to the virtue of temperance, which is the remedy against the vice of concupiscence (desire, lust) and it provides a stable structure for the procreation and education of children.[65]

A number of practical issues arose in subsequent debates about marriage and continue the transformation of parables and teachings into written books and legal codes. Martin Luther (1483–1546 CE), a leading critic of the sacramental view of marriage, followed Augustine in arguing the importance of friendship between a wife and husband in marriage but also emphasizing that marriage was an "estate of life" that was "God's good will and work," established by God as the context wherein husbands and wives would find companionship and which would bring them "delight, love, and joy."[66] Yet at Luther's time, the question of who one could marry became a source of confusion because of the differences among Roman law, Germanic law, the canon law of the Catholic Church, and also prevailing customs. Perplexity seems, once again, to abound. Luther affirmed the stability of marriage and its connection to religion but emphasized reciprocal love of spouses as the proper understanding of its reference to God's good creation.[67] He wished to avoid a valorization of clerical celibacy, which had been a regional requirement of the ordained priesthood since the fourth century (the Spanish Council of Elvira, 305 CE).[68]

From the medieval period forward, Catholic theologies of marriage were closely bound to Church law (canon law), which governed ecclesial matters, indeed the whole realm of spiritual life. Laws governing the contracting of marriage and its possible dissolution happened in ecclesial courts and were closely bound to the Church's understanding of sacramental marriage.[69] Later

---

65 Thomas Aquinas never completed his discussion of marriage as a sacrament in the *Summa Theologiae*, which was unfinished at the time of his death. A supplement to the third part was assembled from notes and previous writings after his death (see Suppl Q42, a1 on matrimony as a sacrament).

66 See Luther, M. (1962). The estate of marriage. In: *The Christian in Society II*, (ed. and trans. W. Brandt), 37–38. Philadelphia: Muhlenberg Press.

67 Buitendag, J. (2007). Marriage in the theology of Martin Luther – worldly yet sacred: an option between secularism and clericalism. *Hervormde Teologiese Studies* 63 (2): 445–461.

68 See Roman Cholij, "Priestly celibacy in patristics and in the history of the Church" http://www.vatican.va/roman_curia/congregations/cclergy/documents/rc_con_cclergy_doc_01011993_chisto_en.html (accessed 18 June 2019).

69 The famous case of the canonist Johann Apel of Nürnberg illustrates the tension between church law and civil law of marriage. Apel was an early sixteenth-century German priest and lawyer who attempted to leave the priesthood to marry a nun from a local convent. The Bishop of Würzburg attempted to annul the marriage but Apel appealed to the validity of the marriage he had contracted and resisted the bishop's attempt to invalidate the marriage and force him to return to his priestly work at the cathedral in Würzburg. Apel appealed to his conscience and the authority of the Bible in support of his marriage and resisted the bishop's attempts to annul his marriage and impose the mandate of clerical celibacy. Although eventually imprisoned and then

theologians such as John Calvin (1509–1564 CE) would critique some of the canon law interpretations of and pronouncements about marriage while still maintaining its religious significance. As Luther before him, Calvin argued that practical issues such as marriage were matters for temporal authority, the government, whereas matters pertaining to the relationship of the Christian to her or his creator were matters of the heart adjudicated in the depths of one's conscience.

> [T]here is a twofold government in man: one aspect is spiritual, whereby the conscience is instructed in piety and in reverencing God; the second is political, whereby man is educated for the duties of humanity and citizenship that must be maintained among men. These are usually called the "spiritual" and "temporal" jurisdiction (not improper terms) .... For the former resides in the inner mind, while the latter regulates only outward behavior.[70]

Medieval and early modern canon laws of marriage, and the civil law traditions at those times, address a number of perplexing practical issues. Who is allowed to marry? Under what conditions? Must marriages be public or can they be formed secretly? In which circumstances can they be dissolved and by whom? Are there real impediments to couples giving consent to marry? What if any practical guidance can be discerned from the Bible when Christians are thinking about marriage and especially about who can marry?

One of the challenges to early Christian views of marriage and family was the perplexity provoked in the call by Jesus to his first disciples to follow in his way of life. This presented practical challenges, most notably in his admonitions about the demands of discipleship and in his strong counsel against attachment to family and material possessions (Lk 14:26–33).[71] Yet the example offered by Jesus was not limited to externally observable actions. It included

---

excommunicated, Apel continued to teach canon law at the University of Wittenberg and defend the important relationship between biblical authority and secular authority mediated by canon laws of marriage. For a further discussion of the case, see Witte, J. Jr. (1997). *From Sacrament to Contract: Marriage, Religion, and Law in the Western Tradition*, 44–46. Louisville: Westminster John Knox.
70 Calvin, J. (1960). *Institutes of the Christian Religion*, I.19.15, (ed. J.T. McNeill), 847. Philadelphia: Westminster Press.
71 These passages from the Gospel of Luke have been vigorously debated in Christian communities and among scholars of early Christian texts, and they have been taken as central themes for later developments in Christian ethics. For a helpful summary of the former, see Hays, C.M. (2009). Hating wealth and wives? An examination of discipleship ethics in the Third Gospel. *Tyndale Bulletin* 60 (1): 47–68. For a summary of the latter, with special attention to the relationship between religion and modern life, see Elshtain, J.B. (2001). Bonhoeffer on modernity: Sic et Non. *Journal of Religious Ethics* 29 (3): 345–366.

also a transformation of interior life, what the Hebrew and Christian Bibles often refer to as a transformation of the heart (Heb. *lebab*, Gk. *kardia*). The search for wisdom is not only an intellectual activity, prioritizing prudence in challenging situations as many philosophers have held, but also involves an integration of mind and heart, that is, careful reasoning and discernment about what to be and to do.

In this light, consider another example of wisdom in the early Christian tradition. Early Christian monasticism focused intensely on assessing the quality of the heart, the inner motivations, and the relationship among the movements of the appetites in practical decision-making. The self-knowledge arising from monastic discipline became revered since sagacious persons whose self-knowledge produced in them a wisdom about the ways of others were often viewed as sources of counsel in perplexing situations. Athanasius of Alexandria (295–373 CE), in his *Life of Antony* (Antony of Egypt, 251–356 CE), recounts how Antony's time alone in the desert seeking self-knowledge, purity of heart, and union with God prepared him to discern the ways of others and to offer them advice in light of his discernment.[72] In his *Conferences*, recounting the advice of Abbot Moses of Scete (330–405 CE), the early monastic writer John Cassian (360–435 CE) uses examples from various practical disciplines to interpret the "goal or objective of the monk" including the work of the farmer, the merchant and the archer. These practical goals and also the life of the monk (by some accounts, a most impractical form of Christian life) aim at some good. Moses tells Cassian that "the aim of our profession is the kingdom of God or the kingdom of heaven. But our point of reference, our objective, is a clean heart, without which it is impossible for anyone to reach our target."[73] Purity of heart is not only a means to obtain a final end but also a quality of any action or decision done well, reflecting a love of goodness for its own sake, the *moral good* noted in Chapter 3. It enacts what we called the "moral paradox," that is, that a more virtuous self comes into being through disinterested conduct. The mind undistracted, devoted to the unselfish search for the good, differentiates between that which helps and that which hinders obtaining that end. In a word, practical wisdom requires a purification of mind and heart. The impure mind is wrapped in illusion and self-deception (see Chapter 6). As Cassian explains, "the mind is under pressure in this life. From all sides, temptation comes in torrents and in no way will it be free of turbulent thoughts. But the workings of zeal and diligence will decide which of those thoughts may be allowed in and cultivated."[74] Cassian's contemporary, Augustine of Hippo (354–430 CE), used similar terms to describe the virtue of "prudence." Whereas he defines virtue as "perfect love of God" and the

---

72 Athanasius. (1980). *The Life of Antony and the Letter to Marcellinus* (trans. R.C. Gregg), 94. Mahwah, NJ: Paulist Press.
73 Cassian, J. (1985). *Conferences* (trans. C. Luibheid), 39. Mahwah, NJ: Paulist Press.
74 Ibid., 52.

virtue of justice as "love serving alone that which is loved and therefore ruling rightly," prudence, or practical wisdom, is "love choosing wisely between that which helps it and that which hinders it."[75] Practical wisdom is then more complex and expansive than the intellectual virtue noted by Aristotle and other philosophers even as reaching a decision involves more than a practical syllogism. Perplexity can be the path to wisdom even as wisdom can appear to be folly or itself perplexity to the unwise person.

The early Christian monastic tradition divided along two distinct lines in later years, one more closely approximating the *anchorite* ("withdraw" from the world) model of hermits such as Antony of Egypt and one taking the *coenobite* ("community life") model given prominent form in the *Rule* of Benedict of Nursia (480–543 CE). Communities living by the Benedictine rule keep largely to the coenobitic form, while occasionally allowing some of their members to live for a time as hermits following the early anchoritic way.[76] The Benedictine way seeks wisdom in its community way of life and in the ordering of its work and prayer. Echoing its early roots in Cassian and in the monastic vision of Evagrius of Pontus (346–399 CE), the search for wisdom begins with self-knowledge, recognizing that each member of the community begins the monastic journey with a set of habits and dispositions that must be discerned, transformed, refined, and put at the service of community life. Although each monk does work to support the common life, the life of the community is a search for purity of heart through ceaseless praise to God through the recitation of the Psalms and the study of the Bible. In doing so, written texts are transformed into an oral event in order to purify one's life. This is all the more the case because for the monastics the main sin is "pride," willful self-assertion that is the opposite of love.

Like every form of human life, practical issues inevitably arise in monastic life (from decisions about daily work to the proper treatment of visitors), and the values of the Benedictine *Rule* reflect the wisdom of the community as it seeks to live with purity of heart.

> As often as anything important is to be done in the monastery, the abbot shall call the whole community together and himself explain what the business is; and after hearing the advice of the brothers, let him ponder

---

75 Augustine of Hippo. (1965). *The Catholic and Manichaen Ways of Life (De Moribus Ecclesiae Catholicae et, De Moribus Manichaeorum)* (trans. D.A. Gallagher and I.A. Gallagher), 22. Washington, DC: Catholic University of America Press.

76 See for example the allowance for hermitages among the Trappist monks at Gethsemani Abbey in Kentucky (the Order of Cistercians of the Strict Observance, a reform branch of the Benedictines), described by Kelty, M. (1994). Flute Solo. In: *My Song Is of Mercy: Writings of Matthew Kelty, Monk of Gethsemani*, (ed. M. Downey), 2–72. (Lanham, MD: Rowman & Littlefield.

it and follow what he judges the wiser course. The reason why we have said all should be called for counsel is that the Lord often reveals what is better to the younger. The brothers, for their part, are to express their opinions with all humility, and not presume to defend their own views obstinately. The decision is rather the abbot's to make, so that when he has determined what is more prudent, all may obey. Nevertheless, just as it is proper for disciples to obey their master, so it is becoming for the master on his part to settle everything with foresight and fairness.[77]

Authority is necessary for administration in the monastery and guidance of the community's decision-making, but the exercise of authority by the abbot must conform to the standards of justice and be expressed as prudence. A spirit of mutual correction and openness to the advice of all, no matter the length of time in the community, characterizes this approach to wisdom. The abbot is chosen by the whole community where possible, and leadership is entrusted to one that has an even temperament and has demonstrated "goodness of life and wisdom of teaching."[78]

One of the central features of the Christian monastic account of wisdom is its attention to *temporal* aspects of prudent action. Wisdom and judgment take time; the demand to discern what is right and fitting to do in a situation takes time to examine a situation and to deliberate about the best way to proceed. Decisions must reflect this process of discernment. For example, the early medieval Cistercian, Bernard of Clairvaux (1090–1153 CE), argued that those charged with making decisions affecting the affairs of the world could not do so effectively if they allowed the urgency of the world's concerns and its political posturing to dictate the speed of their decisions. Bernard himself counseled Pope Eugenius III (d. 1153 CE) about such matters in the twelfth-century papal court, where political alliance and monetary enrichment threatened prudent judgment in legal and ecclesiastical affairs.[79] In order to render prudent judgment about a complex situation, one must first make a "consideration" of its various aspects, asking about the background and meaning of the events and the persons involved and also imagining how God might be working through human affairs. Bernard saw a close connection between the interpretive dimension of the moral life and its practical dimension. He understood the multidimensional nature of moral thinking. And unlike some philosophical accounts of practical judgment, he knew that wisdom demands time for discernment and deliberation beyond a rush to judgment.

---

77 Fry, T. (ed.) (1982). *Rule of St. Benedict in English.*, Collegeville: MN: Liturgical Press, Ch. 3 (25–26).
78 Ibid., *Rule of St. Benedict* 64 (87).
79 See Bernard of Clairvaux. (1976). *Five Books on Consideration: Advice to a Pope* (trans. J.D. Anderson and E.T. Kennan). Kalamazoo, MI: Cistercian Publications.

In this light, it is important that Christian monastic life also gave rise to what became known as spiritual direction. A trusted spiritual guide (usually a senior monk) would talk with a junior monk about the inner life revealed in solitary prayer. Practices of "spiritual direction" have their origins among early Egyptian monks living an eremitic life but were later adapted to community contexts. Some "spiritual fathers" and "spiritual mothers" achieved great renown as spiritual guides helping others (monastic and lay persons alike) through their wise attentiveness to people's backgrounds, temperaments, and habits.[80] Analogous practices are found among other religions, for example the use of "skillful means" among Buddhists. Among the practical gifts of these spiritual parents are "insight and discernment" about the occurrences in the heart of another, "the ability to love others and make others' sufferings [one's] own" in order to accompany them on their journey, and "the power to transform the human environment" to make one's spiritual companion more deeply aware of the presence of God in everyday events and human interactions.[81] Practical reason is embedded in a vision opening the person to the empowering work of God in his life, the transcendent good.

In subsequent centuries, the practice of spiritual discernment and guidance would take various forms, and one of the most significant was in the handbooks of penance compiled as a resource for clergy hearing confessions. These "penitential books" became increasingly popular in the sixth and seventh centuries and were noteworthy because of their classification of acts based on the subject matter and gravity of the acts in question.[82] Although developed as a pastoral aid, and mediating some of the wisdom of spiritual counsel, later strands of Church practice focused more heavily on the particular features of acts, their motives and circumstances, rather than the person seeking purity of heart and union with God.[83] This was a time in the history of Christian theology where religious ethics became narrowed to one or two dimensions (for example, the normative wedded exclusively to the practical). That narrowing eclipsed other equally important dimensions of moral thinking such as the agent's interpretation of her or his situation or the nature of the freedom from which moral choice springs. Just as forms of moral philosophy can distort the full complexity of practical reasoning by focusing on just one dimension of ethics, so too can the religions.

80 Chryssavgis, J. (1986). The spiritual father as embodiment of tradition. *Phronema* 1: 19–31. See also Plattig, M. and Baeumer, R. (1998). The desert fathers and spiritual direction. *Phronema* 13: 27–40. See also Swan, L. (2001). *The Forgotten Desert Mothers: Sayings, Lives, and Stories of Early Christian Women.* Mahwah, NJ: Paulist Press.

81 Ware, K. (1974). The spiritual father in orthodox Christianity. *Cross Currents* 24 (2–3): 296–313.

82 McNeill, J.T. and Gamer, H. (1990). *Medieval Handbooks of Penance: A Translation of the Principal Libri Poenitentiales.* New York: Columbia University Press.

83 Jonsen, A.R. and Toulmin, S. (1988). *The Abuse of Casuistry: A History of Moral Reasoning.* Berkeley: University of California Press.

Perplexity and Wisdom in Interpersonal Life

In order to conclude the examination of the practical dimension of religious ethics, we turn to a brief case study from the Igbo and Christian wisdom traditions concerned with the nature of marriage and its implications in contemporary society. This case will serve to suggest new questions about the complex social reality of marriage in these cultures and the search for wise solutions to these challenges. It continues to unfold the complexity of practical reasoning within the context of religious traditions attentive to the *aporia* of perplexity and wisdom in written and oral forms.

Marriage law in the Igbo context and the difficulty of maintaining local cultural values in an increasingly globalized and multireligious world come together in the religious and legal politics of present-day Nigeria. Colonial and postcolonial Igbo history and culture have made it difficult to separate what is distinctly Igbo from what is distinctly Christian in the contemporary situation. This fact makes the discussion of marriage – particularly interreligious marriage – difficult. Since Nigerian independence from Great Britain in 1960, the country has moved toward an independent court system but is divided religiously and governmentally. The north of Nigeria is predominantly Muslim and the south of Nigeria is predominantly Christian, with the Southeastern Igboland having a higher percentage of Christians than the Southwest. With the country in its current state brought together from two British "protectorates" in 1914 and administered in that fashion until independence from British rule, the northern protectorate consisted largely of an administrative structure offering freedom to local Muslim leaders. Islam did not make significant inroads into Igboland prior to the nineteenth century, being primarily the result of religious dispersion through trade, until the middle of the twentieth century when it became more prominent.[84]

Views about marriage and family life were, prior to the twentieth century, either derived from Igbo religion or from its later contacts with Christian missionaries. The traditional understanding of Igbo marriage depends on the existence of kindship networks and various obligations that arise from them. "The Igbo child is normally brought up in his father's lineage. Later in his childhood, he is brought into contact with his mother's lineage and, as he grows up, he is made increasingly aware of the wider social world, the most important in which are his father's mother's linage and his mother's lineage. When he marries, he acquires affinal links, with his wife's lineage, which play an important role in the social life of his children. These five lineages, each of which is a distinct agnatic group, constitute for the Igbos their most important kinship network."[85] This network, the *Umunna* or "localized patrilineage," covers many

84 Rufai, S.A. (2012). A foreign faith in a Christian domain: Islam among the Igbos of Southeastern Nigeria. *Journal of Muslim Minority Affairs* 32 (3): 372–383.
85 Onwurah, E. (1989). Kinship and marriage among the Igbo of Nigeria. *Sevartham* 14 (1): 3–4.

of the realities that are recognized as local or tribal law and custom such as local office, land ownership, grazing rights for livestock as well as "title-taking ceremonies, marriage feasts, [and] second-burial rites."[86]

Although the primary social network for legal and public customary matters passes through male descendants, the matrilineage or *Umunne* is equally important. A young woman's family must be satisfied that she is being well treated by her husband's family, and one's maternal uncle enjoys an especially close relationship as mentor and friend of his sister's son. If for whatever reason a young man is exiled from his father's family, his only place of refuge is with his mother's kin.[87] Practical decision-making is embedded in kinship networks that provide guidance and support for the persons involved in deliberation and seeks to foster practical wisdom.

Kinship networks transcend biological death. "An important characteristic of Igbo lineages and clans is that their membership includes not only the living but the dead."[88] For this reason, ethical responsibility for family and family land extends not only to living kin but the deceased as well. "Even the land belongs not just to the living, but to the 'living-dead', the ancestors; and so, it will neither be sold nor given to outsiders without performing some ritual to the 'owners' of the land, the ancestors."[89] This same vigilance extends to burial of one's ancestors and the obligation to return deceased members of the kinship network to their homeland for burial. One adage concerning the responsibilities of Igbo children to their parents states that "a child who has not buried his parents 'properly' cannot boast of having conquered life's problems and so anybody who does not have the means, instead of bringing shame upon himself, his family, and his entire lineage, may defer the second-burial ceremony until such a time that he is able; may be ten, twenty or even thirty years. But it must be done, for it is believed that unless it be done, the departed will not be allowed to join his ancestors in the land beyond; and the ancestors would, of course, look contemptuously upon such a fellow."[90] A practical problem, in other words, spans space and time and connects people to religious powers. In this sense, it is a crucial element of the religion and morality of the people that the practical dimension of religious ethics must address.

In modern Nigerian politics, structured as a constitutional democracy (the Federal Constitution of Nigeria being ratified in 1999), marriage laws are governed by the National Assembly that, along with the House of Representatives,

---

86 Uchendu, V.C. (1965). *The Igbo of Southeast Nigeria*, 64–65. New York: Holt, Rinehart and Winston.
87 Onwurah, E. (1989). Kinship and marriage among the Igbo of Nigeria. *Sevartham* 14 (1): 7–8. Onwurah notes that there are some expectations to this among the Igbo, for example among the *Ohafia* in Southeastern Nigeria. The references here are to the patrilineal communities that constitute the majority of Igbo kinship networks.
88 Ibid., 4.
89 Ibid., 5.
90 Ibid., 10–11.

form the legislative branch of the Nigerian government. Marriage laws are enacted by the National Assembly with specific provisions for marriage laws originating in different religious groups. The Nigerian Constitution delegates to the National Assembly the power to make laws governing the "formation, annulment and dissolution of marriages other than marriages under Islamic law and customary law including matrimonial causes relating thereto."[91] One of the challenges to legal marriage in Nigeria has been the different views or theologies of marriage and their status under the law. In northern Nigeria, for example, 12 states have adopted Shari'a law that includes specific provisions for the regulation of marriage.[92] As Vroom argues, "The British colonial strategy of indirect rule via the existing authorities resulted in a variegated judicia system that included English-Nigerian law, Muslim law and customary law."[93] "Can multiculturalism allow room for legal pluralism?"[94] In legal decisions the written law is again translated back into real life and thereby conjoins the world of the law and the people's life-world. Religious ethics, as we have argued, has to explore this movement between "worlds."

What of Christian communities in this context and of Igbo and Christian views of marriage and marriage law in modern Nigerian politics? What lessons might it teach us about wisdom in the face of perplexity? One of the interesting features of Catholic Christian communities in Nigeria is their presence in public debate. However, Cardinal Anthony Olubunmi Okogie and Matthew Hassan Kukah, presently bishop of the predominantly Muslim diocese of Sokoto in the northwest of the country, are among the most vocal critics in public debates about democracy and corruption and the place of religious groups relative to political parties in Nigeria.[95] In the 2015 Nigerian presidential election, former military leader Muḥammadu Buhari defeated incumbent president Goodluck Jonathan on the promise of rooting out corruption and curbing the violence in the north perpetrated by the group Boko Haram. The country faces significant challenges to its political and legal systems and to its prospects of interreligious

---

91 Ezeanokwasa, J.O. (2011). *The Legal Inequality of Muslim and Christian Marriages in Nigeria: Constitutionally Established Judicial Discrimination*, 155. Lewiston, NY: Edwin Mellen Press. https://www.constituteproject.org/constitution/Nigeria_1999.pdf (accessed 20 June 2019).
92 Vroom, H. (2008). Law, Muslim majority and the implementation of Shari'a in Northern Nigeria. *International Journal of Public Theology* 2: 484–500.
93 Ibid., 487.
94 Ibid., 495. See also Nmehielle, V.O. (2004). Shari'a law in the Northern States of Nigeria: to implement or not to implement, the constitutionality is the question. *Human Rights Quarterly* 26 (3): 730–759 and Weimann, G.J. (2009). Divine law and local custom in Northern Nigerian zini trials. *Die Welt des Islams* 49: 429–465. The issue of zinā ("illicit sexual relations") has become a kind of test case for the possibility of reconciling religious law among Muslims in the north and Christians in the south of the country. As Weimann explains, "The question of how and to what extent Islamic law should be applied in the independent Nigerian state has been a recurrent issue in the Nigerian political discourse" (431).
95 Obadare, E. (2012). A sacred duty to resist Tyranny? Rethinking the role of the Catholic Church in Nigeria's struggle for democracy. *Journal of Church and State* 55 (1): 92–112.

cooperation to curb violence and political corruption. Although religious leaders face practical challenges in ministry to people disheartened by religious violence and economic difficulties, they also face generations-old problems as new religious laws meet longstanding cultural practices. Christians in the South continue to work out practical arrangements that respect Igbo cultural patterns while taking seriously new religious beliefs and practices.[96] Marriage laws, particularly those governing interreligious marriage, will be an interesting locus for the negotiation of interreligious wisdom in modern Nigeria. These negotiations can themselves be seen as the work of religious ethics.

Conclusion

This chapter examined two traditions of practical wisdom that have come together in the legal, political, and cultural life of modern Nigeria, although there are here, as in any global cultural space, multiple traditions in conversation at any one time. This approach to ethics, arising out of the religions themselves, helps to explore the odd interrelation of perplexity and wisdom in the moral life. It enables one to grasp how perplexity is a condition of practical wisdom and so how to orient life in shifting circumstances. Yet we also have seen how religious forms of wisdom provoke profound perplexity. They can appear to be simple folly or expressions of perplexity from a nonreligious perspective. Practical reasoning in a religious context moves back and forth within a tension between perplexity and wisdom. This is why it takes time, community, discernment, and deliberation.

"Being practical" is both necessary and dangerous in our global age. Appeals to practicality can easily become demands for efficiency where profound values are reduced to monetary price or convenient solution. Practicality can focus solely on the means to a desired end, without asking if those ends are genuinely good and what kind of good they might be. The rush to be practical risks reducing life and moral thinking just to rule following. The traditions examined in this chapter warn against a reduction of practicality to efficiency, worth to price as well as the danger of rigorous rule-following and unthinking acceptance of ends. This is not the only warning issued by Igbo and Christian thinkers. To be wise involves not only knowledge of the details of moral problems, legal cases, or difficult personal relationships. It also involves knowledge of practices that are meaningful to a community and an ability to extend those practices into new areas of concern acknowledged by a community as significant.

In traditional Igbo religion, the practicality of moral judgments is not to be found only in their conformity to a local rule or even family expectations but

---

96 Ebben, B. (1972). Church marriage versus traditional marriage. *African Ecclesiastical Review* 14 (3): 213–226.

also its rightness and fittingness to the situation of the community, including not just the living but the dead as well as its ethical environment. Respecting the life of individuals is central, knowing that each person's *chi* or personal spirit must, in order to live well, be in meaningful relation to others and to the *chukwu* who sets the standard for meaningful and just relationships among people. In turn, one's family kinship networks set the standard for evaluating practical decisions that require individuals to take account of the community's standards of behavior and also the various ways in which his or her action is likely to affect the community. The expansive understanding of moral responsibility guides Igbo decision-making and may indeed be characteristic of other West African communities as well.[97] This expression of the practical dimension of ethics depends on an interpretation of the situation in which the effort to understand one's moral world, one's sense of individuality and agency within that world, and relationships of mutual responsibility with others who share a common source and destiny. It depends on a construal of the world that is not just inherited uncritically from the past but tested in conversation with others in light of alternative proposals for life. Indeed, the relationship between Igbo traditional religion, Christianity, and Islam is one place where this conversation and mutual contestation occurs.

The practical dimension of religious ethics also relies on people of wisdom, people of *trustworthy character*, who demonstrate honest dealings and good judgment in difficult situations. Wisdom is found in persons but also in communities. Indeed, one of the insights offered by both the Igbo and Christian traditions is that individuals (often the elders of a community) offer counsel to people faced with challenging decisions or to groups deliberating about the best course of action in a difficult situation. These people of *sagacious judgment* offer wisdom to their own people, but the applicability of their wisdom is not limited to those communities.

Another important feature of this comparison is that wisdom requires *historical sensitivity*, wherein groups commit to a project of understanding their past and discerning the lessons it offers for their futures. Just as important a

---

97 One prominent proposal to characterize religious ethics in ATR has been the notion of *palaver* supported by Congolese Christian theologian, Benézét Bujo. For Bujo, *palaver* is the name of "the African traditional council dealing with community matters," touching on such issues as healing, family decision-making, and local administrative matters, and is characterized by a free back-and-forth exchange of views characterized by respect for the words of another. Bujo explains, "In order to understand palaver's role, one has to keep in mind the function of words in African communities. The word is powerful, and it contains highly explosive elements in Black Africa. A word can be medicine just as it can be poison; it has a life-giving power just as it is capable of bringing forth death. Words are something drinkable or edible; one chews and digests them. Badly chewed and digested, they can destroy the individual and the whole community, whereas in the opposite case they bring life." See Bujo, B. (2005). Differentiations in African ethics. In: *The Blackwell Companion to Religious Ethics*, (ed. W. Schweiker), 427, Malden and Oxford: Blackwell.

feature of the wise individual is reflexivity, that is, the ability to examine one's own thinking, especially one's presuppositions, an important feature of the wise community is its historical sensitivity to what has transpired in its family, tribal, or national histories. The medieval Christian theologian Thomas Aquinas, in discussing the virtue of prudence, explains that this virtue has as its characteristic activity the application of right reason to action.[98] However, it is not enough to apply a rule to a situation. Prudence also requires associated virtues to pursue a good course of action in a complex situation. It is important to take counsel from a range of people to understand situations from various sides, and to make sure that one is not rushed to decide by circumstances that are not central to the decision itself.[99] Moreover, one must not neglect the possibility of higher principles than justice for guiding actions that are not part of customary laws or natural law.[100] In other words, the pursuit of wisdom guided by the virtue of prudence requires a strong act of interpretation, not only to decide the appropriate rule under which to consider a particular action but also to understand "what is going on" in a broad sense, open to the historical situation of communities and the guidance offered beyond what is immediately discernable in the community's way of life.

What draws people together across cultural and religious divisions, and prompts thinking about ethical matters, is the recognition of common human problems. These challenges may be what people recognize as part of "the human condition" on which thinkers have applied their minds for millennia. These problems may also be ones pertaining to new political situations or technological developments, variations of which each generation faces, and with which religious wisdom must contend in any era. Perplexity, as we are calling it here, is inevitable in our efforts to live well, but responses to perplexity are themselves within the realm of wisdom. One response to perplexity would be simplifying the moral life just to problem solving. To be sure, there is wisdom in problem solving and there are virtues one can develop to ensure that one is prepared to solve responsibly the moral problems one encounters. Yet there is also wisdom in knowing that the moral life is not first and foremost about problem solving, as if life itself is something we could solve. This is what is at stake in arguing that religious ethics is a multidimensional project concerned as well with wisdom.

---

98 Thomas Aquinas, *Summa Theologiae*, IIa-IIae Q47 a4.
99 "For good counsel requires not only the discovery or devising of fit means for the end, but also other circumstances. Such are suitable time, so that one be neither too slow nor too quick in taking counsel, and the mode of taking counsel." Thomas Aquinas, *Summa Theologiae*, IIa-IIae Q51 a1, r3.
100 Thomas Aquinas, *Summa Theologiae*, IIa-IIae Q51 a4. This is interesting to note in part because, in light of our comparison here, Christian appeals to guidance offered by God to Christian communities in times when their form of life does not conform to the demands of civil law hold a similar place in Aquinas' thought to the place of traditional religious rites, including divination rituals, in Igbo and other African cultures.

5

Freedom and Bondage

Fundamental Dimension

I do not understand my own actions. For I do not do what I want, but do the very thing that I hate. Now if I do what I do not want, I agree that the law is good. But in fact it is no longer I that do it, but sin that dwells within me. For I know that nothing goods dwells within me, that is, in my flesh. I can will what is right, but I cannot do it.

—Rom 7:15–18

But I absolve not my own soul. Surely the soul commands evil, save whom my Lord may show mercy. Truly my Lord is Forgiving, Merciful.

—*Qurʾān* 12:53

I swear by the Day of Resurrection. And I swear by the blaming soul. Does man suppose that We shall not gather his bones? Nay! But We are able to fashion even his fingers and toes.

—*Qurʾān* 75:1–4[1]

O thou soul at peace! Return unto thy Lord, content, contenting. Enter among my servants. Enter My Garden.

—*Qurʾān* 89:27–30

---

1 The commentary on *The Study Quran* notes the following on v. 2: "The *blaming soul* is considered the middle state of the human soul in the process of spiritual growth, between the soul that *commands to evil* (12:53) and the soul at peace (89:27) ... It is called *the blaming soul* because it recognizes the shortcomings of the lower concupiscent soul and chastises it in order to transform it into the soul at peace, which returns unto the Lord content, contenting (89:28) ... Every soul is believed to be capable of recognizing its shortcomings, as expressed in the *ḥadīth*, 'There is no pious or profligate soul but that it blames itself on the Day of Resurrection; if it has done good, it says, "How did I not do more!" And if it has done evil, it says, "Would that I had desisted!"' ... Here, then, God answers by the reverent, God-fearing soul that blames itself for falling short, although it strives for obedience" (1446). Nasr, S.H., Dagli, C.K., Dakake, M.M., Lumbard, J.E.B., Rustom, M. (eds.) (2015). The Study Quran: A New Translation and Commentary. New York: HarperCollins.

Religious Ethics: Meaning and Method, First Edition. William Schweiker and David A. Clairmont.
© 2020 William Schweiker and David A. Clairmont. Published 2020 by John Wiley & Sons Ltd.

Religion and Moral Agency

Religious sages, theologians, and philosophers throughout history have rightly said that human beings are a deep mystery to themselves. Who am I? Whence have I come? Whither do I go? Who are my neighbors, my enemies, and my loved ones? To what community do I belong? Does my community really exist and what about its goodness and justice? Do "I" really exist or is the reality of the "I," my deepest sense of myself, really a fiction, an illusion, a trick of language, or a commanding self that enjoins evil? Am I free? Is my "soul" immortal? Will anyone be resurrected after death? Will I be judged and condemned to perish for my evil deeds and thoughts, or perish like other mortal beings? Why am I here? What is the purpose of my life? Human beings, as persons and communities, are questions to themselves.

The opening quotations taken from St. Paul's letter to the Romans in the Christian Bible and the verses from the Holy *Qur'ān* plunge ethical reflection into the depths of human experience and also into some of the thorniest issues in ethics. Religious ethics must clarify what it means to be a "moral agent" with others in relation to what is ultimately real and important that empowers a good and right life within some community or communities. This focus of reflection draws us into the *fundamental* dimension of religious ethics. This dimension is not fundamental in the sense that it is the ground or foundation of ethics from which every other dimension flows and to which they are derived and ordered; it is not foundationalist.[2] Certainly some formulations of religious ethics point in that direction. As we saw in Chapter 3, one way of thinking about the deepest truth of Hindu ethics is the reality of *ātman* = *brahman* around which other beliefs and values are to be understood. But a hierarchical idea of the meaning and method of religious ethics, that is, that every dimension of ethics can be reduced to some fundamental fact or insight (like *ātman*) is, as we have been showing, unhelpful for exploring, assessing, and using religious sources in ethics. The method of religious ethics developed in this book highlights the interaction among multiple dimensions of thought. Therefore, no single dimension is basic or foundational in religious ethics.

---

2 One hallmark of modern Western thought, especially in European philosophy, is precisely the attempt to find a firm, clear, distinct, and certain foundation for cognitive claims in the "thinking I," the *cogito*, as Rene Descartes argued, or in the "transcendental I," as Immanuel Kant and the German Idealists, like Johann Gottlieb Fichte, held. These so-called foundationalist arguments have been widely used by scholars of religion and ethics in ways we judge too narrow really to grasp the complexity of religious ethics. In the rush to avoid that narrowing of perspective and also the quest for certainty, many "postmodern" thinkers reject any foundation for knowledge claims and explore the creation of meaning in linguistic forms or advocate ad hoc approaches to ethics. One contention of this book is that religious ethics has a coherent but nonfoundationalist structure and thus is not simply an old-style foundationalism or an ad hoc approach to ethics. It is not our purpose to refute those options in philosophy and theology, but we are forging a different account of the structure and dynamics, the method, of religious ethics.

What is more, freedom as basic to action is also a condition for fault and wrong action. It can be in "bondage," as the title of this chapter notes. The fact of "bondage," as we are calling it, is given various names by the religions. Christian's speak of the "bondage of the will." Jews talk about the evil impulse in conflict with the good impulse. Hindu thought, as we saw with Arjuna in Chapter 3, talks about illusion and the need for enlightenment of the truth of *ātman*. A Muslim knows about the "Commanding Self."

Obviously, these are radically different conceptions of the basic problem of human freedom. Yet there are also similarities among the religions in their understanding that there is a problem of freedom. In light of it, the various religions proclaim a revelation, an insight, a teaching, or a divine spirit that liberates the agent from sin, illusion, or bondage of the will and thereby begins anew the spiral dynamic of the religious life (Chapter 3). The religions disclose the moral law in the form of the Silver or Golden Rules and they also teach a transcendent good that is related to but exceeds the moral good. This is why the world's great axial religions proclaim freedom from the bondage to sin or liberation from the cycles of death and rebirth. Yet that freedom and liberation require, as we have seen throughout this book, access to empowerment by the divine or the sacred through religious devotions and ritual as well as within a community of fellow Muslims, Buddhists, the indigenous traditions, etc. There are, again, analogies – similarities in differences – among the religions in how they construe freedom and also the problem of human freedom.

So, the question, "What does it mean to be a moral agent within a community of agents?" is a *fundamental* one in ethics in the sense that without agents of some sort, that is, beings who can and must freely direct their lives by means of moral convictions or fail to do so, there would be little point to ethical reflection.[3] The Greek philosopher Socrates (c. 469–399 BCE) thought that the pressing question of human life is this one: *how ought we to live?* The religions of the world agree with him even if, as we will see, they offer complex and even competing ideas about how responsibly to live and what it means to be a moral agent. Like the other dimensions of religious ethics, the *fundamental* dimension is an intersection where the whole of ethical reflection meets and is considered in their interrelations.[4] Insofar as we are trying to understand "moral" agents rather than say legal agents, then the *normative* dimension (Chapter 3)

---

3 There are thinkers who seem to deny this insofar as, say, *ātman* is beyond good and evil or that human beings are "modes" of God's being (Spinoza). On closer inspection one finds that these positions also have some conception of moral agency. Because of this fact, Spinoza rightly called his major work *Ethics,* and, as we have seen, Hindu thought advances a complex ethics.

4 For other thinkers who develop something like our "multidimensional" approach to ethics see Tillich, P. (1995). *Morality and Beyond,* foreword by William Schweiker. Louisville, KY: Westminster/John Knox Press and Gustafson, J.M. (1996). *Intersections: Science, Theology, and Ethics.* Cleveland, OH: Pilgrim Press.

that establishes ethical standards is involved in an account of agency but so too the *practical* dimension (Chapter 4) that focuses on situations of action and choice and the quest for wisdom. Then again, the *descriptive* dimension (Chapter 2) also intersects the question of agency insofar as agents always act with respect to some interpretation of their circumstances and also ask about the meaning of their lives or at least implicitly accept some idea of the meaning of life. Later we will see how the *metaethical* dimension of religious ethics (Chapter 6) is related to the question about the meaning of moral agency. Reflecting on what it means to be a moral being, an agent necessarily poses the question of the truth of some account of agency, religious or nonreligious.

Mindful of the interconnection between ideas about agency and the other dimensions of religious ethics, we begin this chapter with a definition of agency. With that matter in hand, we will explore yet another important distinction in religious ethics, namely the distinction between theistic and nontheistic religions, because how the sacred is conceived relates to the question of moral agency insofar as the sacred or divine are held to have some relation to, empowerment of, or action within human conduct.

The Nature and Features of Agency

How can and should one define an "agent?" As noted in Chapter 3, an agent is a being with the capacity to have beliefs and values about what to do and what kind of being to become and also the power to act (or refrain from acting) in relation to those values and beliefs and so to give reasons for one's actions in terms of beliefs, values, and descriptions of situations. We can nuance that definition a bit more. Because in order to exercise power or bring about effects guided and evaluated by moral values and norms, an "agent" must be *purposive* in the sense of being able (i) intentionally to pursue a course of action or decide how rightly to respond to some action or situation, (ii) formulate some goal(s) or end(s) deemed good or right (a so-called "life-plan") or determine what is a fitting response to the action or situation, (iii) assess and choose the necessary means to the end(s) pursed or how best to respond, and, when necessary, (iv) act with or on behalf of others. Sometimes this capacity for purposive action is further divided into claims about a moral agent being *rational* and also being *reasonable*.[5] In this more precise sense, an agent is *rational* when he, she, or it pursues some course of action or responds to actions and/or situations with respect to that agent's interests and goals or sense of a fitting response. Conversely a purposeful agent is *reasonable* when it, she or he understands and

---

5 On the idea of a life plan as well as the distinction between the rational and the reasonable, see Rawls, J. (2005). *Political Liberalism*, 2e. New York: Columbia University Press.

respects the life plans of other agents, that is, understands that others have their own interests and goals as well as patterns of responsibility that ought not to be impeded or thwarted without proper moral, legal, or other valid reasons.[6] Further, saying that an agent is purposive (rational and reasonable) explains conditions that might limit or nullify an agent's responsibility to do something or refrain from acting. If a person is lacking rational and reasonable capacities, then she or he cannot *ascribe* responsibility for actions to herself or himself, and, further, others cannot *impute* responsibility to him or her. Responsibility is lessened if these capacities have been diminished due to coercion, ignorance, lack of information, age (e.g. a child who is still developing capacities to reflect on her or his actions), or personal fault.[7] Recall that this was true even of the *Gītā's* teaching about Arjuna's duties as a warrior that we explored in Chapter 3.

Beside the power of rational and reasonable action, there is, second, another capacity often identified as basic to the idea of "agency," that is, *freedom.* Stated differently, if a person is coerced into acting or limited in their capacities of rationality and reasonableness, then, given the degree of that coercion and the extent of those limits, their agency and power to act morally is diminished. Not only must agents be able to hold life plans and respond to changing situations and actions, they must also have the ability to act on and carry out those plans and to respond to circumstance. If one is coerced, determined, or predestined to act a certain way against one's will, then he or she is not a responsible moral agent, albeit he or she might be seen as an agent (representative) of the power coercing, determining, or foreordaining his or her action. For example, the war criminal who claims that he was "just doing his duty" may not bear full responsibility for his crimes, but he does bear responsibility as an agent of the state in its criminal treatment of people. Put simply, an agent is not only the puppet of someone else's power and plans or if she or he is such, then one counts that person as the agent of whomever or whatever determines her or his actions

---

6 In this book we have to leave open the question of whether or not animals are moral agents, for two reasons. First, the topic is massive in scope and important for current environmental and animal ethics. The scope of the issue escapes brief treatment. But, second, the topic is in many respects answered by the religions themselves, many of which do see animals and other beings as "agents." Our point, then, is that whatever is called an "agent" must have, in some form, the attributes we are discussing with respect to human agents. In fact, they might have those attributes to a greater extent than humans (e.g. angels and heavenly beings) or to lesser degree than humans (nonhuman animals and some spirits). What matters to us are the attributes of an agent much more than who is an agent. For a helpful discussion of the moral standing of animals, see Korsgaard, C.M. (2018). *Fellow Creatures: Our Obligations to Other Animals.* Oxford: Oxford University Press.

7 The distinction, but relation, between *ascribing* responsibility to oneself and *imputing* to someone else is crucial in practical judgments about responsibility and culpability. The forms of logic of imputing and inscribing accountability for actions are also exceedingly complex. On the question of assignments of responsibility see Schweiker, W. (1995). *Responsibility and Christian Ethics.* Cambridge: Cambridge University Press.

and relations. If I tell you the whereabouts of my relatives because you have put a gun to my head and threatened me with death, then I might be judged not to be fully responsible for giving the information because I was coerced into doing so. Again, if I am a soldier under orders, then my actions are not only imputed to me; I am also the representative of my commander who also bears responsibility for the execution of orders.[8]

The reality of "coercion" and limits on responsibility has led to a crucial distinction about moral freedom in modern Western philosophical ethics. A moral agent must be *autonomous*, that is, to be ruled by the law (*nomos*) of his or her own (*auto*) making. True moral freedom is autonomous; one's actions and the maxims of those actions are not coerced or only given by someone else. One must accept and endorse the forces that have shaped one's character and intentions. Conversely, if the moral rule or law (*nomos*) of one's maxims for action is given by another (*hetero*) then one is not genuinely free and thus not fully moral. For instance, if some "god" predetermined that you were to read this book at this time, then your freedom and agency would be diminished in some way. Or, to use another example, if social norms about wealth and poverty set the goal of your life plan as the continual search for more and more wealth while the scope of your responsibility is limited by the market forces, then, again, your freedom would be diminished but not destroyed by the heteronomous power (social norms; a god; the market). Granting that many forces are working on and in an agent's life (social norms, religious convictions, genetic predispositions, gender roles, social systems [e.g. the market], etc.), the minimal degree of freedom an agent must possess to be considered a moral agent is to endorse as her or his own actions that are part of an integral self. For instance, if I lack the power, desire, or capacity to act otherwise than how my parents tell me to act or what social ideas about wealth or status require of me, then I am not a *moral* agent in any profound sense of the word. If I am a puppet of God's will or a dupe of social *mores* then God or society decides. Am I then truly a moral agent?[9] We return to this question about autonomy later, especially in light of the passages from Romans and the *Qur'ān* found at the opening of this chapter. Some philosophical accounts of *autonomy* are too thin to catch the insights of the religions about human freedom.

There is a third area of dispute about what defines moral agency. As the eighteenth-century English thinkers put it, the topic here is the "springs of action." We need to consider what in fact does move an agent to pursue its, her,

---

8 One of the oldest and best accounts of the struggle between soldier and commander is found in Homer's *Iliad* and the conflict between Achilles and Agamemnon. On this see Alexander, C. (2009). *The War that Killed Achilles: The True Story of Homer's Iliad and the Trojan War*. New York: Penguin. Similar issues can be found in the great Indian epics.

9 See, Baggini, J. (2015). *Freedom Regained: The Possibility of Free Will*. Chicago, IL: University of Chicago Press.

or his goals; to be responsive and responsible; and so to exercise freedom. Several options are found in religious and Western philosophical thought with analogues, as we will see, to other religious traditions, including Islam.

First, *rationalists* argue that reason can and ought to move an agent to act and only in that way is one genuinely autonomous, self-ruling. Socrates thought that "knowledge is virtue" by which he meant that, if you truly knew what was the virtuous thing to do, you would act in that way. If you did not so act, then you obviously did not know the virtuous thing to do.[10] Knowledge is a motivating power and therefore the basic task of ethics is to enable some knowledge of what is good, just, and right. Stoicism arose in the Greek world, originating with Zeno of Citium (344-262 BCE) in Athens. The ancient Roman Stoic philosophers also thought that reason, *logos*, should and could guide one's conduct with respect to one's duties and to seek tranquility in life. In the *Gītā*, as we saw in Chapter 3, Arjuna's enlightenment is the necessary and sufficient empowerment to fulfill his duty of caste. The Stoics, Socrates, and the *Gītā* could scarcely understand what St. Paul was talking about in the letter to the Romans cited previously. Obviously, for them, St. Paul did not really know what he ought to do. They would also be confused by the *Qur'ān's* ideas about different "selves." A moral agent, the ancient philosophers and texts like the *Gītā* would argue, is someone who acts as a coherent self and with a coherent life-plan.

Next, *voluntarists* believe that the *will* moves one to act and that the will, accordingly, must be free in some basic way. Reason might know what one is to do, what is responsible conduct, but in order to act in the moral sense of the term the will must be involved. Moreover, we must will to do some actions even if we do not desire to do so. The moral life includes duties and obligations, after all. This is, to recall, the "moral paradox." Christian thinkers from St. Augustine onward have argued about the extent of human freedom of will in light of human sin and "the bondage of the will" but also the reality of God's grace operating in the Christian's life. So too, as seen later, some Muslim thinkers insisted that the human will, ultimately speaking, is not free. Allah knows and determines every human action. In brief, the will is related to but different from reason and desire as capacities for action.

Some thinkers speak of the will as a "rational appetite" to get at this point.[11] Can one have a duty to feel some way, say, to desire to tell the truth? And, what is more, theoretical reason can tell us what *is* the case, but it is powerless to command what we *ought* to do – namely, our duty. Just because I know that

---

10 For a powerful example of this argument that also distinguishes philosophy from rhetoric, see Plato (1952). *Gorgias* (trans. and intro. W.C. Helmbold). New York: The Library of Liberal Arts.
11 In the Christian tradition St. Thomas Aquinas, along with others, called the will a "rational appetite" meaning that the will mediates between reason and desires. Some thinkers, following St. Paul, held, as Martin Luther, John Calvin, and, on some readings St. Augustine, that due to sin the will was in bondage. There are analogues to these positions on the will as a distinct "faculty" of the soul and also its bondage in other religious traditions.

2 + 2−1 = 3 in a base 10 system does not mean I will be moved actually to do the proper computation in a business transaction. In fact, someone who knows that mathematical truth may nevertheless ignore it for some other purpose, say, fudging with a business's accounting books. The human capacity to act under valid moral obligations is the "will" or, as Immanuel Kant calls it, practical reason.[12] To put it another way, *voluntarists* want to show that "will" is reason in its practical use, that is, practical reason (will) can intend and motivate action in accord with properly moral maxims that it has legislated for itself. Kant understood Paul's dilemma, but he thought that we can nevertheless will to do right. Augustine, conversely, thought that St. Paul was right about human experience, full stop.

Third, *hedonists*, in the strict sense of the term, argue that desires are the most basic springs of human action. Neither the dictates of reason nor the exercise of the will actually motivate human action. We are creatures of desire and our actions and responses are moved by desires and loves. The moral challenge of human existence is not the maxim to act rationally or the duty to will the right norms for our action, but to desire and love what is good and just. As the eighteenth-century philosopher David Hume famously put it in *Enquiry Concerning the Principles of Morals*, "reason is and ought to be slave to the passions." Reason is not self-motivating. Without denying the importance of reason in the moral life, Hume along with other British philosophers tried to show that we have a "moral sense" and that benevolence and sympathy, or "fellow feeling," is basic to morals. As Hume wrote, "Truth is disputable; not taste: what exists in the nature of things is the standard of our judgment; what each man feels within himself is the standard of sentiment."[13] The moral life is more about sentiments and fellow-feeling (sympathy) than standards for theoretical judgments. Hume would tell St. Paul and the *Qur'ān* that they are confused. Knowledge of what is good and right never motivates action and it is curious that Paul thinks knowledge would have that role in human conduct. Hume would hold that our sentiments or feelings are what move us to act. The moral life must work to cultivate moral sentiments like sympathy, benevolence, and a sense of justice.

So, the task of clarifying what or who is an agent includes (i) claims about moral purposiveness (rationality; reasonableness); (ii) freedom and what lessens responsibility through coercion or other limiting factors on freedom (ignorance, fault); and (iii) the domain of motivations, the "springs of action," that have been understood in terms of reason, will, desire, or some combination of those human capacities. We have also begun to see certain points where the religions complicate matters. This should not be surprising. Chapter 1 noted

12 See Kant, I. (1997 [1785]). *Groundwork of the Metaphysics of Morals*, (ed. M. Gregor; intro. C.M. Korsgaard). Cambridge: Cambridge University Press.
13 Hume, D. (2004 [1777]). *An Enquiry Concerning the Principles of Morals*, 3. Amherst, NY: Prometheus Books.

that *religion* is about what is ultimately important and real and that some group of people or a community seek access to, empowerment by, and orientation from for the sake of the proper conduct of life, that is, their moral existence, within interrelated forms or realms of reality, interrelated "worlds." On that understanding of "religion," it is clear that a religious tradition will have impact on agency, inside and out. Religious beliefs and practices will touch the most inward parts of a person or other creature that is an agent and what they think, desire, will, and do.

Most religions have intense concern with the *inwardness* of persons' lives, that is, the constant flow of consciousness, emotions, and evaluations that are the energies of character. Religions typically seek to transform, sanctify, and/or enlighten persons in ways that are shown in action and in which responsible action furthers the process of transformation, sanctification, or enlightenment. Recall that in Chapter 3 we outlined the spiral dynamic of the religious life in order to make sense of this process of transformation, sanctification, or enlightenment. That discussion also showed how ideas about virtue and law were important in connecting the religious dynamic with the moral life. We have also seen in the descriptive dimension of religious ethics that beliefs and practices will inform an agent's understanding of the contexts, the situations, outside the person and her or his power of action, within which the agent or community of agents must responsibly act. Insofar as an agent always acts at some time and in some place, then beliefs and practices about the lived structures of time and place will affect what the agent can, must, and will be able to do (see Chapter 4). Those structures bear on the depth and scope of moral agency. And with that insight we see how reflection on agency implies metaphysical questions, that is, questions about the most general features of reality and some account of that reality in which agents live and act, or, as we have called it, the moral space of life, an ethical world or environment.

The religions usually hold that there are other agents in reality than just human agents. These other agents (God, gods, demons, angels, spirits, ancestors, Jinn, ghosts, karma, cycles of rebirth, the religious community itself as well as other social forces, etc.) are acting inside and outside human actors. That is, religions hold that there are forces (agents or not) working within a person's life and also in and through the world that have impact on what we mean by a moral agent and what an agent can and cannot do.[14] Priests and shamans in different religions are often media through which a spirit or god acts within mundane reality. People can be subject to demon or spirit possession and religious rituals are the means to release them from bondage to the demon or to learn some message of healing from the spirit. Refuge in the

---

14 We have noted this before in terms of the gods' actions in Indian epics, the Jewish and Christian Bibles, and also the Iliad, but they are readily found in all of the religions.

dharma is, for a Buddhist, a means to quell the fires of desire and to escape the fateful cycle of rebirth within the domain of *saṃsāra*, the domain of suffering as the moral space of human life. Further, if one takes the passages from the *Qur'ān* and Romans cited at the head of this chapter, it is clear that an agent might have multiple "selves," be overtaken by an alien power (sin), and also exist and act in relation to God/Allah. In these ways, reality is peopled with various agents, some good and some evil, even while the human self is not an internally singular entity in the quest for complete *autonomy* and self-sufficiency.

When the topic of moral agency is raised in the context of religious ethics, the question is this: how is a conception of agency to be developed from within these kinds of religious sources? The purpose of this chapter is to answer that question. Just as with Chapter 3 and the distinction explored there between dualism and monism, we turn to another distinction between types of religion and relate that distinction to the power of God or gods or some other force(s) to act within creatures lives. The distinction is between *theistic* and *nontheistic* religions. Yet we will see that things are more complicated than an easy distinction between types of religion might imply. At issue for religious ethics is how best to think about human agency in the context of other powers or agents, divine or not.

Theistic and Nontheistic Religions

The understanding of religion used throughout this book focuses on what a person, creatures, or a community holds is "ultimately real, important, and empowering" for the "conduct of life." The idea of what is "ultimately important, empowering, and real" is an intellectual construct. It is scholarly "shorthand" for a formal similarity among the religions even as it acknowledges that the religions will use myriad symbols, stories, and rituals to speak about their convictions. The religions have much more specific and practical ways of construing their ultimate focus. The main division is between religions that focus on a God or gods as what are ultimately important, empowering, and real and so *"theistic"* religions from the Greek term for "God" (*theos*), and those religions that do not focus their practices and beliefs on God or gods, so *"nontheistic"* religions. Further, within theistic religion there is a difference between *monotheistic* traditions, that is, belief in one God as paradigmatically found in Islam, Christianity, and Judaism, and traditions that have many gods, like Hinduism and some indigenous religions, which are *polytheistic*. Usually, these two forms of theism (monotheism and polytheism) are taken to be exhaustive of the forms of "theistic religion," that is, religions that understand what is ultimately important, real, and empowering as a God or gods. Further, the distinction between theistic and nontheistic religion is taken to designate the possible forms of religion found among the peoples of the world. However, things are, once again, a bit more complex.

The distinction between monotheism and polytheism might be misleading if the contrast blinds one to the actual complexity of religious ideas about the divine or sacred. For instance, Hindus believe that the many gods of their tradition, on some accounts millions of them, are manifestations of the supreme God. The Supreme God exists in and through living things and gives life to all things. *Śiva*, the supreme God, is omnipresent (present everywhere) and omnipotent (all powerful), but to understand *Śiva* one must know the other basic gods and the forces they represent. Different aspects of God are then worshipped depending on the form of the Hindu tradition to which someone belongs. These deities who help the supreme God *Śiva* are also worshipped. What is more, the deities in Hinduism are highly advanced spiritual beings represented in human (male and female) or partly human form.[15] In Hindu mythology, three gods are especially important for human life: *Brahmā* the Creator, *Śiva* the Destroyer, and *Viṣṇu* the Preserver.

Conversely, there are within the monotheistic traditions many ways of "naming" God that provide a highly differentiated way of speaking about God and God's actions. Although Christians believe in One God, their conception of God is internally complex, Triune. Somewhat analogous to the central gods in Hinduism (*Brahmā, Śiva, Viṣṇu*), the Christian conception of the Godhead is Father (creator and sovereign), Son (redeemer and judge), and Holy Spirit (sustainer and empowering force). Christians have debated for centuries how to understand the persons of the Godhead and their relations in one God. And that is a crucial difference from Hindu thought. Christians do not usually conceive of God as "destroyer" and, further, the Trinity is not a relation of three gods. The Godhead is One even though Triune. The doctrine of the Trinity, we should note, arose from the conviction that Jesus Christ was in some way divine and therefore must be related to the One God of Judaism, the mother religion for Christianity. Even within Islam, easily the world's most consistent monotheistic tradition, there are 99 names of God that point to Allah, the one God. So too, Judaism has a long tradition of rabbinic reflection on the names and manifestations of God's being not to mention the equally powerful elements found in mystical forms of Judaism.[16]

So, on closer inspection a hard and fast distinction between theistic and polytheistic religions also breaks down or one must at least grant that there

---

15 For an account of the development of what is called "Hinduism" see Doniger, W. (2009), *The Hindus: An Alternate History*. New York: Penguin Press.

16 For a discussion of this point see Fishbane, M. (2005). *Biblical Myth and Rabbinic Mythmaking*. Oxford: Oxford University Press, Rahman, F. (1979). Islam, 2e. Chicago, IL: The University of Chicago Press and McGrath, A.E. (1990). *Understanding the Trinity*. Grand Rapids, MI: Zondervan.

are varying emphases among the world's religions. Recall that religions typi-cally explore an agent's relation to the sacred or divine internal to the agent and yet also with respect to the structures of lived reality within which that agent (or community of agents) must responsibly orient his or her (or their) life (see Chapters 2 and 4). Insofar as religions with all their ritual actions, beliefs, texts and scriptures, leaders, communities, and symbols are about relations and access to what is ultimately real, empowering, and important, then it is hardly surprising that the divine or the sacred would be found in and on the internal and external domains of agency. The divine is active *in* and *on* the human self and the human "world."

For example, traditional Theravāda Buddhism is a nontheistic religion. It teaches that reality arose out of the fires of desire and by means of the code-pendent origination of things. Immoral action and wrongful desire give rise to karmic structures of the realm of suffering (*saṃsāra*) and also the cycles of rebirth. The path out of suffering is to take refuge in the Buddha's *dharma*, quell the fires of desire, show compassion for all that suffer, and to be enlight-ened by the truth of not-self (*anātman*), that there is, in fact, no self to which to cling. Monks, dressed in robes to symbolize the dead among us, acquire merit through ritual practices and then communicate that merit to others, say, the village people around the monastery who, for their part, support the monks. That conception of the "self" trapped in the realm of suffering and clinging to wrongful desires is radically different than St Paul's account of the self in Romans or the teaching of the *Qur'ān* cited at the head of this chapter. Nevertheless, there is a connection between the internal domain of an agent's life – her or his desires, wants, and reasons – and the structures of lived reality, the realm of *saṃsāra*. What is ultimately empowering, important, and "real," *nirvāṇa*, is in relation to the depths of the human person but also the structures of reality.[17] Furthermore, in some forms of Buddhism (Tibetan; Mahāyāna; Pure Land) there are gods, spirits, and demons. Yet these realities do not deny the character of a Buddhist idea of moral agency and the structures within which human agents conduct their lives.

Consider also Islam, a religion that prides itself on being the purest form of monotheistic belief and practices. The *shahādah* is a profession of faith and sometimes called an Islamic Creed that focuses on the oneness of God and

---

17 Of course, speaking of *nirvāṇa* as "real" might seems to be a category mistake. Buddhists, as we have noted before, generally hold that the condition of *nirvāṇa* is outside of the realm of conditioned things, that all conditioned things have the quality of *anātman* ("no-self" or "no-thing-ness") and hence are not "real" as a substance, body, or individual and even material objects arise through dependent generation and therefore have no objective or permanent "essence" (*ātman*). Recall from Chapter 1 that we use the term "real" analogically in our definition of religion and thus underscore that the metaphysical commitments about the nature of "reality" of the religions vary in profound ways. The point of using "real" in this analogical sense is that even for Buddhists *nirvāṇa* is not a fiction or imaginary construct but is the inner-truth of things.

also that Muḥammad is God's prophet, the seal of the prophets. It is one of the five so-called "Pillars of Islam." In its shortest form it reads in English: *There is no god but God (Allah), Muḥammad is the messenger of God.* The other "Pillars of Islam" include ritual prayer five times a day (*ṣalāt*), fasting and self-control during *Ramaḍān* (*ṣawm*), alms giving to the poor of 2.5% of one's savings (*Zakāt*), and if one is able the pilgrimage to Mecca at least once in a lifetime (*Hajj*).[18] Along with *shahādah*, these other "Pillars" show how Islam, which means "submission," is a life dedicated to the worship of and obedience to Allah, care for others, a life of self-control, and a deep commitment to justice.

For Muslims, the will of Allah orders and structures all things, and, further, Allah's mercy and compassion are fundamental to a holy life. The animal self can command one's innermost being and is prone to evil. "But I absolve not my own soul. Surely the soul commands evil, save whom my Lord may show mercy. Truly my Lord is Forgiving, Merciful" (*Qur'ān* 12:53). Further, every human being will stand before God's judgment over their acts of justice and their virtues and vices. In this sense, the self witnesses against itself. "I swear by the Day of Resurrection. And I swear by the blaming soul. Does man suppose that We shall not gather his bones? Nay! But We are able to fashion even his fingers and toes" (*Qur'ān* 75:1–4). Here too Allah's mercy is needed. "O thou soul at peace! Return unto thy Lord, content, contenting. Enter among my servants. Enter My Garden" (*Qur'ān* 89:27–30).

What is more, there have been debates throughout Islamic history about the reality of human free will. Many verses in the *Qur'ān* state the power and might of God: "Unto God belongs sovereignty over the heavens and the earth and whatsoever is therein, and He is Powerful over all things" (5:120). "Have they not journeyed upon the earth and observed how those before them fared in the end, though they were greater than them in strength? Naught in the heavens or upon the earth can thwart God. Truly He is Knowing, Powerful" (35:44). And yet the *Qur'ān* is also clear that human beings are accountable to Allah and to others for their actions. So, again, what is ultimately real, important, and empowering, that is, Allah, works in the depths of the human self and also gives structure and order to lived reality. Although that is the case, it is still right and proper to impute accountability to human agents and/or to have them ascribe it to themselves.

The point at this juncture is not to deny any distinction between theistic and nontheistic religions. Obviously, there are differences and some of them will prove significant when thinking comparatively about the fundamental dimension of ethics. Still, with respect to the moral life and thus religious ethics as

---

18 See Rahman, F. (1986). Islam: an overview. In: *The Encyclopedia of Religion*, vol. 7, (ed. M. Eliade), 303–322. New York: Macmillan.

well, these different religious forms (theistic and nontheistic) function analogously to each other in order to indicate how the object of religious devotion and piety is operative or acts within the moral agent and externally to the agent in the structures of lived reality. We might say that any "ethics" that recognizes within its account of agency the reality of other powers than the human agent that are at work in the agent and acting in the world must be seen as at least quasi-religious in character.

Ancient Roman and Greek moral philosophers argued that real "atheism" was not the denial of the existence of the gods as such, but, more significantly, the denial that God or the gods cared about moral distinctions between right and wrong, just and unjust actions and that those distinctions, along with reward for virtue and punishment for vice, structure the human world.[19] In terms of the meaning of religion, one can deny or affirm that the "gods" are ultimately "real" but what is crucial, for these thinkers, was the claim that they were practically "important and empowering," that is "gods" cared about the moral and political life. The ancient sages knew that one could believe in the existence of a deity or deities and yet deny their concern for the moral and political life. In doing so, one is a "practical atheist." The question of moral agency has a human and a divine or sacred side for the religions. On the human side, the concern is to show how human powers or capabilities for action, that is, human agency, are related internally and externally to what is divine or sacred. And on the side of the divine or sacred, the issue is whether or not and how God/gods or the sacred is related to moral distinctions that structure human lived reality and are active in that reality, that moral space.

Thus far in this chapter we have noted certain powers, capacities, or capabilities needed for a being to be considered an agent: purposiveness (rationality and reasonableness), freedom, and motivation (reason, will, and/or desire). Moral agency, as the focus of the fundamental dimension of ethics, is an account of those capabilities in relation to the normative dimension of ethics (values and norms) as well as the focus of other dimensions of ethics (descriptive, practical, metaethical). The religions complicate accounts of moral agency by relating the inward life of agents and the structures of lived reality to the ultimate object of religious devotion in theistic or nontheistic form. This account of agency showed the analogy between theistic and nontheistic ideas of the divine or the sacred and thus their similarities and

---

19 One should recall the argument of Chapter 3 in which we explored the exile of Adam and Eve from "Eden" with the knowledge of good and evil that then gives moral shape to human existence outside of "Eden." In this respect, the origin of the distinctly human world is co-constituted with the "Fall" into sin. We can now see how the normative and descriptive dimensions of religious ethics are necessarily related to but distinct from its fundamental dimension, the topic of this chapter.

differences. Moreover, we have begun to unfold the understanding of agency found in two religious traditions that also articulate the fallibility and fragility of the human self, namely, a Christian account in St. Paul's letter to the Romans and also an Islamic vision given in the *Qur'ān*. Of course, those outlooks, *Qur'ānic* and *Pauline*, are embedded in the larger structure of each text as well as the millennium-long traditions of interpretation and doctrinal dispute about how rightly to understand them and their place in the Muslim or Christian life. Because of that interpretive history, it is not possible to summarize in one chapter or even one book every Christian and Islamic account of moral agency!

In order to compare and contrast Islamic and Christian accounts of moral agency we can build on similarities between them, namely, that each tradition is a form of *monotheism*. Further, each tradition underscores the importance of human moral responsibility while also explaining the presence of God at work in the depths of a person's life as well as in the structures of moral reality within which human beings must orient their lives. Yet this discussion will also shed light on *nontheistic* traditions, like many forms of Buddhism, insofar as those traditions, we argued previously, are also concerned to show how what is ultimately important, empowering, and real (for example, *nirvāṇa* in Buddhism) touches the human agent as well as the structures of reality within which the Buddhist life of compassion and detachment is to be lived. Little wonder, then, that religions have sought to create social realities in which their lives can rightly be lived, for example, monasteries, the Church (in its various forms), the global Islamic *ulamā*. It is this dual perspective in the fundamental dimension of religious ethics, what we have called the internal and external perspectives, that is crucial to a religious account of moral agency.

Of course, there are profound differences among theistic and nontheistic religions, and also among monotheistic and polytheistic religions as well as among the monotheistic religions themselves. In terms of our discussion here, profound differences must be acknowledged between Islamic and Christian thought. Christians believe in the Trinity; Muslims do not. Christians believe in Christ as redeemer and also the work of the Holy Spirit in persons' lives to sanctify them; Muslims obviously do not; Muslims believe in the truth of the *Qur'ān* and Muḥammad as the "seal" of the prophets; Christians do not. Muslims look to the Last Judgment where every person will be judged by Allah as righteous or not; Christians believe that Christ has taken away the sins of the world and await the return of Christ "to judge the living and the dead." Still, we will isolate sufficient points of similarity between Christian and Islamic thought to enable us to outline an account of moral agency within religious ethics.

Muslims and Christians believe that God and God alone is the ultimate sovereign and that human agency must thereby be understood as lived *before*

God, coram deo.[20] In fact, at its depths an account of moral agency within religious ethics is a way to talk ethically about God's action or the presence of the sacred in the moral space of life. We will also isolate through the comparison between Romans and the *Qur'ān* positions that parallel the discussion in Chapter 3 about the relations between the moral and the transcendent good, but now with respect to the relations among human and divine agency. In doing so we explore the central "tension" that structures the *fundamental* dimension of religious ethics, namely, *freedom and bondage*. We turn first to freedom and the sovereignty of God, then move into purposiveness and the divine mind, and finally to moral motivation and the will of God.

Freedom and the Sovereignty of God

Monotheism is the belief in one God and only one God. This religious form means at least three things for ethics. First, insofar as there is in truth only one God, then other supposed gods, demons, and spirits (natural or nonnatural) either are not real but rather projections of the human imagination, or they are manifestations of the One God (as in Hinduism), or they are subservient to the will and purpose of the One, a supreme God in a pantheon of gods, say, in Greek and Nordic religions, or semidivine beings (e.g. spirits, demons, Jinn). The task of the religious life, accordingly, is to make contact with the one real God in ways that empower a life commanded by and pleasing to God. For monotheistic traditions, the most fundamental religious "sin" is idolatry, that is, treating something that is not divine (one's nation or one's own life) as if it were divine and therefore denying the reality and supremacy of the true God. Idolatry, furthermore, is believed to lead to moral failings. Misplaced reverence misdirects human conduct. If someone believes that their nation is somehow divine (e.g. "America, right or wrong"), then other peoples and nations are sinful and immoral. One meaning of *jihād* in Islam is a spiritual exercise of Muslims rightly to order their devotion to Allah rather than idols. Christians too, especially relying on the Hebrew prophets, believe there is a strong link between idolatry and injustice.

---

20 The claim that human life is lived before God can be problematic, ethically speaking, but also rich in meaning. If "before God" means that human finite life is denigrated in the face of divine power and goodness, then the idea would seem difficult to sustain, ethically speaking. However, if the term means (i) that human flourishing and well-being must be considered prior to any claims about the divine and yet (ii) human life also transpires within an ethical environment defined in relation to the divine or sacred, then, the idea is ethically and religiously important. It thereby shows both the dignity of human beings and also how the divine or sacred limits and yet sustains existence. This double meaning decenters human beings when thinking about moral worth but also sets people within an ethical environment that endorses their dignity and responsibility.

Second, monotheism is important for ethics insofar as the one God is real and is in some relevant sense an "agent" creating, ordering, and sustaining reality. The moral life must be interpreted and understood in relation to this divine "agent." In order rightly to answer the descriptive interpretive question of religious ethics (see Chapter 2 on the question "What is going on?"), one must give an account of God's actions in every aspect of a moral situation. Not surprisingly, Christians and Muslims have developed nuanced ways to speak of God's action through a host of names and attributes of God in relation to mundane reality. The 99 names of Allah in Islam include ones like The Exceedingly Compassionate, The Magnificent, The Giver of Life, The Bringer of Death, The Preserver, The Bringer of Judgment, and so on. Each name points, it is believed, to the unity of God, the oneness of Allah. Furthermore, the greatest name of Allah under- scores not only the unity of Allah's being but also Allah's relation to the religious and moral life. That Greatest Name means the one which, if someone prays to Allah, then, Allah will answer the prayer. Human life and conduct transpire within the scope of Allah's sovereignty and action. This is the case for Christians as well. The various names of God (father, lord, creator, judge, sovereign, etc.), Christ (son of God, lamb of God, savior, messiah, redeemer, etc.) and the Holy Spirit (comforter, sustainer, sanctifier, perfecter, etc.) articulate the divine unity but also God's manifold relation to reality. What is more, the Christian doc- trine of the Trinity (variously understood) is a metatheological doctrine that specifies the rules and grammar for speaking of God's relation to material and spiritual realities as well as to God's own being.[21] Put simply, for Muslims and for Christians the moral "space" of human life is one defined by the being and activity of Allah/God. To affirm God's existence and yet to deny the working of God and the care of God for what is good, right, and just in human existence is, as noted previously, a form of practical atheism that misconstrues the ethical space of life and the agency of persons and communities.

The third important thing for ethics about monotheism is that, insofar as there is only one, real God who is sovereign and good, then moral goods and moral duties must in some way relate to and be derived from God, say, in God's commandments or union with God as the human highest good. Christians pray, in the so-called "Lord's Prayer" believed to be taught by Jesus to his disciples, that God's kingdom will come and God's will is done on earth as in Heaven. The moral standard is God's justice and love made known in the life and teaching of Christ. The vision of God (*visio dei*) was conceived to be the highest human good by many medieval Christian theologians. The content of the moral law

---

21 Some Christian thinkers, like St. Augustine, hold that the divine Trinity has an analogue in the human soul, say, memory, will, and reason. Other theologians, one thinks of Karl Barth, deny that analogy and look solely to God's self-revelation testified in scripture. These differences, although theologically important, become ethically germane within Christian ethics, but we cannot explore them or debates within Islamic theology in this book.

revealed by God and knowable by human beings, the so-called natural law (see Chapter 3 on the Golden and Silver Rules), is found in the Ten Commandments, including duties to God and duties to human beings. Christian ethics, then, for some is rooted in God's commands whereas other thinkers argue that because of human sin the Ten Commandments republish natural moral knowledge. That is, Christian theologians have disagreed about the place of the natural law within ethics. Some thinkers, like the medieval theologian Thomas Aquinas, insist that human beings have a natural moral knowledge. Others, like the twentieth-century Swiss theologian Karl Barth, focus on the command of God.

Muslims also believe that human beings have some basic sense of justice. The citations from the *Qur'ān* that head this chapter indicate some basic knowledge of good and evil. Muslims believe that Allah is the first teacher of right knowledge that includes knowledge of just obligations. This further means that *'ilm* (roughly translated as "knowledge" but wider in meaning) is an obligation for Muslims and covers the wisdom imparted to the community (*Ummah*) by the Prophet but also the knowledge found in the disciplines of ethics, law, politics, philosophy, and theology. Further, *'ilm* takes three forms: information, natural laws, and conjectures. The first two forms are considered "useful" and the third as a means to knowledge. The medieval Muslim thinker Abū Ḥāmid Muḥammad ibn Muḥammad al-Ghazālī (c. 1058–1111 CE and known as al-Ghazālī) confronted skepticism and drew a distinction, sometimes disputed, between useful and harmful knowledge. Importantly, al-Ghazālī asserted that Allah is immediately active in each and every moment of existence. He bitterly attacked the use of Greek philosophy in Islamic thought and thereby turned Islam away from philosophical speculation. In the next century the Islamic thinker ʾAbū l-Walīd Muḥammad bin ʾAḥmad bin Rušd known as Ibn Rushd and in Latin Averroës (1126–1198 CE) sought to combat al-Ghazālī's attack on philosophy, but in many respects the argument for revelation had already shaped Islamic thought and law. Analogous debates are found in Christian thought.[22] At issue, just as it was in the normative dimension of ethics, is the use of nonreligious sources of knowledge (philosophy, law, etc.) in a religious ethics.

---

22 In fact, Thomas Aquinas, in Christianity, Averroës in Islam, and Moses Maimonides among medieval Jews also sought to utilize the resources of Aristotelian thought in their religious and ethical works. Indeed, it is clear that these thinkers drew insights from each other and thus created a community of discourse not unlike what is badly needed in our global age. For a helpful discussion see Rubenstein, R.E. (2004). *Aristotle's Children: How Christians, Muslims, and Jews Rediscovered Ancient Wisdom and Illuminated the Middle Ages*. New York: Houghton, Mifflin, and Harcourt). It should not be surprising that against those who seek to fortify ethical thinking solely within the confines of their authoritative tradition, others like Aquinas, Maimonides, and Averroës engaged forms of thought outside their traditions in order to present their ethics. In this book we seek that kind of engagement with other traditions similar to these great medieval thinkers in the monotheistic traditions even as we also seek, in ways they did not, to avoid within the domain of ethics the need to refute the claims to salvation or enlightenment found in other outlooks, religious or otherwise. We are trying to show that some basic moral knowledge is simply part of the human condition and that moral wisdom and virtue, wherever found, should be acknowledged.

Monotheistic religions must show how God is related to every dimension of ethics even as each dimension is important for understanding moral agency and the moral space of life within which agents must responsibly orient their lives. This is what is meant by calling this dimension of religious ethics the *fundamental* dimension. Yet more must be said. In both Islam and Christianity, God's sovereignty is known in relation to the natural world but also the world of human actions and relations and distinctly moral goods and values. Because of this conception of God's sovereignty, in the sacred texts of Islam and Christianity natural events are imputed to God's power, like the movement of stars in the heavens, but also that moral wrongdoing, say, injustice, has consequences through God's action on the natural world.

It was believed in the ancient world that the sins of a person bring physical suffering and trauma. For instance, we read in the Gospel of Mark (2:1–5):

> When he returned to Capernaum after some days, it was reported that he was at home. So many gathered around that there was no longer room for them, not even in front of the door; and he was speaking the word to them. Then some people came, bringing to him a paralyzed man, carried by four of them. And when they could not bring him to Jesus because of the crowd, they removed the roof above him; and after having dug through it, they let down the mat on which the paralytic lay. When Jesus saw their faith, he said to the paralytic, "Son, your sins are forgiven."

Not only does this story reveal something about the faith of the paralyzed man's friends, it also shows the close connection in the ancient world between sin, moral wrong, and physical consequences in the natural world. In the Bible this idea is most forcefully explored and criticized in the book of Job where a righteous man (Job) is made to suffer physically and emotionally in order to test his faith in God.

The passage from St. Paul presented previously in this chapter is somewhat more complex. Paul is talking about a disruption within the self and its capacity to do what is good and right rather than physical consequences brought about by sin. Nevertheless, it is important to grasp this connection between "moral causation" and "physical causation." It is found in other monotheistic traditions (Judaism and Islam), but it is also expressed in Hindu and Buddhist ideas about *karma*, suffering in this world, and also the cycles of rebirth that are to lead to liberation from the realm of *saṃsāra*. In order to understand these traditions and their conceptions of the sovereignty of God or the working of *karma* one must see this connection between physical and moral causation. Moral wrongs or sins in these religions can and do have effects in the natural world understood as God's reward or punishment or the logic of *karma*. Of course, within the modern world this close connection between moral wrongdoing causing consequences in the physical world as well as claims that God caused some natural disaster (e.g. hurricanes, diseases, earthquakes, etc.) due to the sin of people is no longer widely held. There are also within the primary texts of traditions challenges to this idea. And for many modern people, albeit not for everyone, the link between moral and physical causation is scientifically implausible and has been mostly abandoned.

God's sovereignty over the natural world in classical Christian and Islamic traditions is understood as the creator, preserver, and final orderer of everything that is as it is. Some Christians and also Islamic thinkers understand God's sovereignty in terms of God's willing at every moment to sustain reality as we know it. God's will is supremely sovereign both morally and physically, and, accordingly, the good moral life depends on obedience to God's will and commands. Other thinkers in both traditions emphasize God's mind in talking about divine sovereignty. Thomas Aquinas, for example, in his *Summa Theologiae* argued that the divine mind rules and orders reality in and through interlocking laws: eternal law (the divine mind itself), divine law (God's special commands revealed in scripture), natural law (human participation in the eternal law through reason), and human law (the laws of human communities).[23] By doing moral acts and forming just communities, human beings participate in God's sovereign, providential ruling of the world. As noted, analogous ideas can be found in theistic and nontheistic religious traditions. Human moral fault, and ultimately human sin against God/Allah, as well as good and right conduct have consequences in the human social world and also in the natural world.

The Islamic and Christian traditions insist that human beings possess the freedom necessary to live a pious and just life, granting, in the case of Christianity, the reality of human sin, or, as in Islam, the influence of one's social environment on one's intentions and conduct. In a word, human beings are responsible for their conduct even though God is ultimate sovereign power. Mindful of these ideas about divine sovereignty in the physical and moral worlds, we can begin to see how Muslim and Christian thinkers might consider those conditions that limit or lessen human moral responsibility. What lessens or nullifies responsibility, as noted previously, are situations of coercion, social factors that can rob an individual of full responsibility (for example, abject poverty), the limitations of natural human capacities, such as ignorance of a situation or the physical inability to act. We explored some of these "limits" earlier in this book. Here one can ask: what about human agency, our topic in this chapter?

Noted previously, the minimal level of freedom needed for a being to be a moral agent is not to be completely determined by some other being (e.g. God)

---

23 On this see the "treatise on Law" in I-II, Q90–97 of the *Summa Theologiae*. One can find analogous discussions of law among medieval Jewish and Islamic thinkers, a topic we cannot pursue.

or the structures of reality (genetics, *karma*, etc.). Yet we intimated before that there are different accounts or theories of freedom, two of which we can now explore.[24] First, a *voluntarist* conception of moral freedom means that a moral agent can act on a principle of choice and her or his choice is not determined by the situation to which the agent responds, her or his own inclinations or desires, or a power foreign to his or her act of choice (e.g. an all-determining God). What the voluntarist conception of freedom insists on is that if an agent's actions, intentions, and motives can be understood and explained without reference to the agent as the origin of the choice, then the agent is not actually free. The voluntarist holds that for an action to be free an account of that action must have reference to the agent in such a way that the description does not picture the agent as a causally determined event in the world. If the agent is so determined, then her or his action is not really an *action* but it is, rather, an *event*. An agent is free if and only if the grounds of the agent's choice are constituted in the act of choosing or in the act of self-legislating his or her maxim of action.

Recall that Immanuel Kant's claimed that freedom is a "transcendental" idea rather than an empirical reality. "Freedom" is the condition for the possibility of human action rather than a "reality" in the world. Kant thought, following Isaac Newton, that the natural world was a system run by unchanging laws that made freedom impossible, but in the domain of morals one can "postulate" freedom as a transcendental condition for action. Given what has been said about the "action" of the divine or the sacred internal to the agent and externally in the structures of lived reality (say, God's providence or the cycle of rebirths), it is not surprising that the religions often reject a voluntarist conception of moral freedom or see it as a condition of the possibility of action. To be sure some accounts of enlightenment, perhaps in Zen Buddhism, *might* tend in this direction, but by and large the religions work with a different conception of freedom.

The insight of a voluntarist idea of moral freedom is that for moral action, discourse, and judgments to make sense, an agent must in some way "own" her or his acts and their effects in the world. It must be possible for the agent to *ascribe* to himself or herself responsibility for an act or have it rightly *imputed* to him or her by others. When I say, "I did that action" I mean to signal that I am the point of origin of the action and I confess that to be the case. If you say, "Charlie told a lie," then you mean to impute responsibility for the act of speaking a lie to Charlie as the origin point of the action and also its consequences. All of this makes sense and it protects a robust idea of moral agency. The difficulty with the voluntarist conception of moral freedom is that it focuses on the relation between an agent and his or her act and choice and thereby too easily does not give sufficient attention to the fact that an agent

---

24 See Schweiker, *Responsibility and Christian Ethics*, esp. ch. 6.

always acts *somewhere* and at *some time*. Agents are situated within some world or, as we have put it, the structures of lived moral reality. Insofar as that is necessarily the case, that is, an agent is always acting in some "world" or "worlds" as a "moral space," then a conception of freedom must consider not only the relation between the agent's choice and the act but also the situation or context of action and the various relations (religious or not) that structure it.[25] As noted, for the religions the divine or sacred is, ultimately speaking, the inner truth and reality of the situation of action by any and every human agent. Another account of freedom is thereby needed insofar as religious ethics is developed from within religious resources.

Along with a *voluntarist* conception we can also speak about an *evaluative* idea of moral freedom. This conception is one that focuses on human wants, desires, values, and loves the norm of which, we saw in Chapter 3, is the Golden or Silver Rule as well as desires, reasons, and relations of power. It is consistent with the insight of the religions insofar as they focus on what an agent holds to be ultimately empowering, important, and real where the act of "holding" includes emotional (i.e. wants, desires, loves) aspects as well as being an act of reason and/or will. The *evaluative* conception of freedom is found in St. Paul's words from Romans and is always set in the context of human wants, desires, beliefs, and ideals. An evaluative idea of freedom claims that an agent is truly free if and only if she or he acts on what is most basically valued or loved, what matters most to the person or community, and not what happens in the moment to appeal to desire or want. Granted that everyone has immediate and occasional desires and appetites, but freedom is linked to settled dispositions and wants. In a term used previously, freedom is always in relation to some life plan important to an agent. This freedom is rational and/or reasonable when what is most basically valued is the agent's own flourishing and/or concern and love for others and their flourishing. The difficulty, of course, is that what one loves and what one desires can conflict. An alcoholic father, for example, might value his family above all else as a central feature of his life plan and yet because of his alcoholism act in ways that harm himself and his family. In that case, the father manifests *weakness of will* and is under the power of addiction in ways that limit his freedom; he is in bondage.

The "problem of free action arises because what one desires may not be what one values, and what one values may not be what one is finally moved to get."[26] One can also talk about "second-order" desires and volitions to make the same point, that is, desires and volitions we want to order our first-order desires and

25 See Gabriel, M (2015). *Why the World Does Not Exist* (trans. G.S. Moss). Cambridge: Polity Press.
26 Watson, G. (1986). Free agency. In: *Moral Responsibility*, (ed. J.M. Fischer), 85. Ithaca, NY: Cornell University Press.

which help to constitute one's identity.[27] A life plan from that perspective is just a settled set of second-order desires. Further, it is clear that these basic wants and desires, what one cares about as most important in a life plan, is not a delimitation of freedom precisely because free action expresses our most basic wants. It is not, for instance, a denial of my freedom to say that I ought to be truthful with my friends. I am not coerced in speaking truthfully to them because my friendship is a second-order desire that orients and directs my first-order desires, say, a desire in a particular situation not to tell the whole truth. Basic desires orient the will that then chooses in specific situations. So, although I might find it difficult to tell the whole truth in a situation due to the pull of my other desires (temptations!), it is not a denial of my freedom to live with that obligation.

Recall that one of the advantages of the Golden and Silver Rules (see Chapter 3) is that these rules focus on relations among people who have desires and wants. They assume that a fundamental second-order desire is that we want reciprocity of respect and care in relations of power. If that is the case, then we can see that reorientation in life requires a redirection of what we want, what we care about, and progresses through the dynamics of the religious life charted in Chapter 3.

This kind of multileveled account of human desires and moral freedom is found among the religions and so too this account of moral conflict. St. Paul's plea in Romans is about not understanding himself because of a conflict between what he wants to do and how he in fact does act. Fault or sin is not only doing a wrongful act, as it is for the voluntarist model of freedom; it is having a disoriented desire or want that ought not to hold as a second-order desire that then disorients one's conduct and relations to others. Consider again the plight of the alcoholic father. Or consider the "Commanding Self" in the *Qur'ān* that enjoins evil. In the condition of fault or sin one is still free. One is not under a foreign and heteronomous power. In fact, one's choices are directed and enlivened by what one values and cares about. The problem is that one's loves and values are distorted and wrongly placed and therefore one is bound, enslaved, to those values and loves.

An *evaluative* account of freedom commends itself for religious ethics insofar as it makes the religious relation, that is, the agent's relation to what is *most important, real, and empowering,* central in an account of freedom and moral agency. Yet this account of freedom is not without a problem, and it is a problem that the religions address through their distinctive texts, teachings, and ritual practices. The difficulty with an evaluative conception of freedom is this one. If one's freedom is bound to what one most basically values, and human

27 See Frankfurt, H. (1988). *The Importance of What We Care About.* Cambridge: Cambridge University Press and Taylor, C. (1982). Responsibility for self. In: *Free Will,* (ed. G. Watson), 11–26. Oxford: Oxford University Press.

valuing is too often misplaced and misdirected, how, in fact, does one come to know that he or she is in a condition of misdirected and misplaced valuing? Part of the mystery of being human is that we might not understand that our most basic loves, desires, and wants are radically distorted, wrapped in illusion, bound to what is immoral. We might be perplexed about ourselves and need to seek wisdom (see Chapter 4). How are we then rightly to understand ourselves and others? How are we responsibly to live? Further, if our actions flow from and give expression to our basic value orientation, then we cannot by our own will or reason overcome our plight. Every act, every thought, and every decision merely expresses and reinforces the problem of wrongful valuing and reinforces its grip on our lives. An agent neither knows the depth of the problem nor can act alone to overcome it. This is the problem of human freedom and bondage.

In order to clarify the meaning of human freedom within the framework of Islamic and Christian monotheism, we can usefully explore other aspects of thinking about agency. Specifically, we must examine, as noted previously, moral *purposes* and also moral *motivation*. This will clarify, we hope, how it is that Muslims and Christians believe in the ultimate sovereignty of God and yet also insist on human free action and how people are responsible for the conduct of their individual and social lives. God's sovereignty is another power beyond human capacities that nevertheless works on and through those capacities. Yet that claim about God does not mean that a *heteronomous* power rules a Christian's or a Muslim's life. The idea that somehow God is an alien and heteronomous power before which human beings are supposedly powerless needs to be explored within ethics insofar as human beings really are responsible for the orientation and conduct of their lives.[28] With those discussions in hand the chapter concludes by returning to freedom and bondage that is the tension lodged in the heart of the *fundamental* dimension of religious ethics.

Moral Purposes and the Divine Being

A conception of freedom (voluntarist or evaluative) holds that if freedom is to be distinguished from acting willy-nilly or construed as nothing but moral license ("do your own thing"), then it must be oriented by some purpose, goal, or encompassing situation that provides direction to actions and relations, and also rules, norms, or laws about responsible and obligatory action in relation to

---

28 Some modern Christian theologians have spoken about "*theonomy*," that is, the law of God at work through grace in the lives of people. Their point is that the theonomous power of God does not destroy but actually realizes true autonomy insofar as genuine human freedom is only found in relation to God. For a brief statement see Tillich, P. (1995). *Morality and Beyond*, foreword by W. Schweiker. Louisville, KY: Westminster/John Knox Press.

oneself and others. We saw that the *normative* dimension sought to specify basic, moral, and transcendent goods that should orient life and denote the true flourishing of human existence even as some form of the Golden or Silver Rules are the norms for responsible conduct and relations with others. This chapter explores many of the same questions but now from the perspective of the acting person, the moral agent, in relation to others. The reasonable person, recall, was someone who recognized and took it as important in their own conduct to respect and enhance other people's own distinctive life plans, say, to abide by the Silver Rule. The just society or community is thereby a reasonable one insofar as peoples and groups are respected and enhanced with regard to the full scope of their life plans together. Immoral action, on this account, entails seeking an immoral aim, say, a life of crime, or the denial of the claims of others, perhaps a violation of trust or kinship relations, or some combination of irrational and unreasonable behavior in the structure and purposes of a community. Religiously motivated violence, for instance, is patently unjust and morally evil when it destroys people's otherwise peaceful lives.

However, an *evaluative* conception of freedom, in contrast to voluntarist accounts, found among the religions complicates claims about rationality and reasonableness. This conception of freedom is not only an evaluation of specific actions (say, a suicide bomber or the giving of alms) or relations (like, the oppression or liberation of a religious community). It is also concerned with the desires, wants, needs, and beliefs that motivate action and places much of the weight of moral judgment on them. Further, it cannot be assumed that for the religions one's own flourishing should be the basic overriding value that orients life. In most of the religions, theistic or nontheistic, human acts of self-giving through love, compassion, and care are judged especially important and even saintly. They enact the "moral paradox." Jesus, for example, taught not only the Golden Rule but also that people should love even their enemies. In Buddhism acts of compassion for all that suffer are especially important for those who seek to follow the Buddha's path to enlightenment. Likewise, reasonableness might mean more than simply respecting the rational life plans of other people. Reasonable conduct entails respecting and enhancing the integrity of others' lives in relation to Allah, Christ, *ātman*, ancestors, or *nirvāṇa*. The religions recast what are deemed rational and reasonable moral purposes by understanding those purposes with respect to relations to what is ultimately real, important, and empowering, that is, the divine or the sacred. How is that the case? Consider Islamic and Christian accounts of moral purposes.

Islam and Christianity have both a universal conception of God (God is the God of all reality, all people) and also an exclusive one (only the one God is truly God). A central conviction of Muslims is the oneness of Allah and that Allah alone is God. The highest human good is thereby a right relation to Allah and the hope of heavenly bliss. The transcendent good of a relation to Allah and heaven is the context within which moral goods and duties are to be understood and given meaning. This fact means two things in Islam.

First, because Allah alone is the God who creates, sustains, and judges every human being, whether he or she acknowledges it or not, everyone and everything has some relation to Allah. Insofar as humanity has a relation to God/Allah, then every human being possesses dignity and worth that can and must be acknowledged with respect, justice, and compassion. Importantly, a human being has dignity and worth that follows from a relation to God/Allah as his or her creator. To violate a human life is thereby also to act against Allah/God and therefore to sin. Further, all things, living and nonliving, have worth through a relation to God/Allah even if human beings bear special dignity and responsibility. Indeed, because of the prohibition of images in Islam but also the specific dignity of human beings, Muslims speak about human beings as the vice-regents of Allah. Christians hold that human beings are made in the image of God, a teaching found in the book of Genesis (1:26–30). Not surprisingly, within Islam justice and compassion become central moral goods and duties, a fact shown by the importance of giving alms as one of the "Pillars of Islam."[29]

If we consider compassion and justice one can see the link in Muslim ethics between the normative dimension and the fundamental dimensions of religious ethics in terms of moral agency. Compassion is one of the most frequently occurring terms in the *Qur'ān*. Each of 114 chapters or Sūrahs of the *Qur'ān*, other than the 9th Sūrah, begins with "In the name of God, the Compassionate, the Merciful...." Even the hope of paradise rests on Allah's compassion and mercy: "O thou soul at peace! Return unto thy Lord, content, contenting. Enter among my servants. Enter My Garden" (*Qur'ān* 89:27–30). The compassion of God is also seen in the giving of the *Qur'ān* and the teachings of Muḥammad because these contain the teachings and wisdom about how to live in submission to Allah and thus to be able to stand justly before God at the Judgment Day. Likewise, al-Ghazālī, and many other sages, taught in his *The Duties of Brotherhood,* that one should love others and that through such love every human being is embraced by Allah. This is why Islam can teach a positive form of the moral law, the "Golden Rule: "No one of you is a believer until he desires for his brother that which he desires for himself." It is also part of the *Sunnah,* that is, the practice of the Prophet Muḥammad that he taught and instituted as a teacher and exemplar of Islamic law *(sharī'a).* In terms of moral agency, a life plan would be patently irrational if it was devoid of compassion for others and obedience to Allah and the teachings of the *Qur'ān*. One's abiding disposition and so second-order desire can and should be to live a life characterized by

---

29 See Schweiker, W., Jung, K. and Johnson, M. (eds.) (2006). *Humanity before God: Contemporary Faces of Jewish, Christian, and Islamic Ethics.* Minneapolis, MN: Fortress Augsburg Press.

mercy and compassion for others that finds expression in care for the poor (almsgiving) as well as the pursuit of peace and friendship.

What is true of compassion in Islam is also the case for justice. In one sense, justice means putting things in their right place and thus right order among people and in relation to God.[30] Justice requires equal treatment among people. Justice is a moral virtue, an excellence of human character, and it also creates a condition of the proper distribution of rights and duties. Every person should seek to encourage the virtue of justice as part of a consciousness of God. "Be just; that is nearer to reverence. And reverence God...." (*Qur'ān* 5:8). Just as compassion is an attribute of Allah so too is justice. What is more, the standard of justice transcends questions of religion, race, creed, or color. One is to treat friends and foes with justice. "O you who believe! Be steadfast maintainers of justice, witnesses for God, though it be against yourselves, or your parents and kinsfolk, and whether it be someone right or poor, for God is nearer unto both. So follow not your caprice, that you may act justly. If you distort or turn away, truly God is Aware of whatsoever you do" (*Qur'ān* 4:135). Moreover, the *Qur'ān* itself sets principles of justice and faith. The claims of justice pertain to everyone and justice is an inherent right of every human being under Islamic law. "The Word of thy Lord is fulfilled in truth and justice. None alters His Words, and He is the Hearing, the Knowing" (*Qur'ān* 6:115). Justice also pertains to economic dealings, relations among women and men, and the interaction of peoples. As with compassion, so too with justice and the Golden Rule. The virtue of justice and the standards of justice mean, we can infer, that asymmetries of power between people are not the norm for human interactions. The norm is justice and it moves toward equality of concern and treatment for people.

For Islam, then, justice means equality and fairness but also the right ordering of society. Not surprisingly, throughout most of the history of Islam there has been a close connection between Islam and the state. In order to live a truly Muslim life, the social and political order must also adhere to Islamic teaching and law (*sharī'a*). *Sharī'a* is the moral and religious code of Islam. There are two sources of *sharī'a*: the *Qur'ān* and also the *sunnah*, that is, the example set by Muḥammad. *Sharī'a* addresses basic social issues, like crime, politics, and economics, but also aspects of personal life including sexual relations, fasting, and the like. In those places where *sharī'a* has official state status, it is interpreted by jurists (*qadis*) with responsibilities for the *imām* (religious leaders).

---

30 Recall that, at least in Western thought, two dominant ideas of justice are found. One is "justice as right order," which one sees in Islamic thought and also in ancient thinkers like Plato, the Stoics, and in Christianity in St. Augustine. There are also contemporary examples of this argument with respect to notions of tradition. The other dominant conception of justice is the idea of justice as rights and thus claims of an individual to protection from political powers but also the claim of the state on human responsibility.

What is more, Islamic jurisprudence (*fiqh*) teaches that every human act falls into one type or another: what is obligatory (*farḍ*), recommended (*mustahabb*), neutral (*mubah*), discouraged (*makrūh*), and forbidden action (*haram*). Given this, legal rulings are important for every aspects of a Muslim's life because it specifies what is permissible, obligatory, or not. The idea of justice that is expressed in *sharīʿa* differs from secular law. This is because Allah's laws that govern human conduct are a part of the law governing reality. Violations of *sharīʿa* are then against Allah and human nature.

The status of *sharīʿa* and the idea of justice that it enshrines raise questions about the compatibility of Islam to modern, secular, democratic nations. The relation between Islam and modern political conditions has been intensified by the struggle among some Islamists to introduce *sharīʿa* in the nominally secular political order. Behind these issues is a deeper ethical and political matter often noted by Islamic scholars. As the Iranian political philosopher and theologian Abdolkarim Soroush has noted,

> The language of religion (especially that of Islam as exemplified by the Qurʾan and the Tradition) is the language of duties, not rights. In these texts, human beings are given commandments by a supremely sovereign authority. The language of *sharīʿa* is that of commanding, as the picture of humanity in the mirror of religion is that of a duty-bound creature.[31]

Neither Soroush's conservative critics nor his supporters would disagree with the idea that in Islam and many other religions too, human beings are duty-bound creatures and this idea is in stark contrast and even tension with modern Western ethical and political ideas about the centrality of *rights* in the moral and social life. We return to the theme of "rights" later in this chapter. For now, note, once again, that the backing for Islamic ideas about justice is the being of Allah, the absolute sovereign authority of God.

As Allah's vice-regent on earth, every human being should submit their lives to Allah around the "Five Pillars," the *Qurʾān*, and the teaching of Muḥammad. The Muslim's life is also to be characterized by virtues like compassion and justice. Importantly, one can see that these virtues focus on asymmetries of power, as we put it before: compassion for the suffering and the poor, and hence the duty of almsgiving, and justice which seeks equity. These obligations are not "heteronomous" because they cohere with and enhance the nature of human existence as a duty-bound creature. Further, the virtues and teachings implicitly acknowledge the fallible nature of human beings, asymmetries of power, and so the need for teaching and learning in moral matters. In these ways, the Muslim holds that the mind and will of Allah mercifully guides human life.

---

31 Sadri, M. and Sadri, A. (eds. and trans.) (2000). *Reason, Freedom, and Democracy in Islam: The Essential Writings of Abdolkarim Soroush*, 62. Oxford: Oxford University Press.

Are there analogues to these Islamic claims about moral agency within the Christian tradition? Christians also understand human beings to be creatures of God; humans are made in the "image of God" (*imago dei*). Throughout its long tradition, Christian theologians have disagreed about how best to understand the "image" of God: is it found in human reason, in the human capacity to love and be loved, in our moral and spiritual capacities, or something else? Furthermore, theologians in this tradition long debated the effects of sin, attributed to Adam's and Eve's sin in the Garden of Eden, on the *imago dei*. Did sin utterly efface the image so that Christian faith requires a virtual re-creation of people through Christ's sacrifice and the work of the Holy Spirit in the believer's life? Did sin distort reason or, as St. Augustine taught, did sin flow from a disordered love that then warped the human will bending it toward an inordinate love of self? These various theological accounts of sin sought to make sense of St. Paul's cry about not understanding his own actions and also to clarify what redemption through faith in Jesus Christ meant for the moral life.

Throughout these discussions and debates about sin and redemption a central facet of Christian moral thought was the importance of love as exemplified in Christ and the early community. Given the effects of sin on human knowing, willing, and feeling, the moral law needs to be revealed. Not only had Christ taught the great command to love God and neighbor. He also instructed his followers to love as he loved them (Jn 13:34) and even to love their enemies. In the so-called "Sermon on the Mount" one reads in Matthew chapter 5, 43–45:

> You have heard that it was said, "You shall love your neighbor and hate your enemy." But I say to you, Love your enemies and pray for those who persecute you, so that you may be children of your Father in heaven; for he makes the sun to rise on the evil and on the good, and sends rain on the righteous and on the unrighteous.

The "Sermon on the Mount," as noted before, is an epitome, or summary, of Jesus' teaching and thus of central importance to Christian ethics. St. Paul also makes love basic to the Christian life. In 1 Corinthians, a letter to the Church at Corinth, Paul writes in 13:1–13 a virtual hymn to love that culminates in 13:13 with a statement of what became the central virtues of the Christian life. "Now faith, hope, and love abide, these three; and the greatest of these is love."

Given Jesus' teaching, Paul's letter, and also the claim in 1 John 4:16 that "God is Love," it is not surprising that Christianity has been called a religion of love even if Christians are not always loving. Yet Christian theologians have long insisted that the nature of Christian love (Greek: *agape*; Latin: *caritas*) is actually a gift from God. The ability to love as God loves, revealed in Christ and manifest in God's sustaining power, is possible only through divine grace working *in* the individual. Once again we see how the working of God interior to the moral agent, empowering and fostering *agape* love, is related to God's working in the external world and in the mission of Christ. Faith, hope and love, Catholics teach, are thereby called "theological virtues" and are understood to be gifts of grace. Protestants teach, based on Paul's thought, that faith becomes active in love on behalf of the "neighbor."[32] In this respect, Jesus' Golden Rule (see Chapter 3) redresses asymmetries of power not simply with reference to an individual's control over wants and desires, but the rule is grounded in a powerful deity who nevertheless loves the creature, who is not, relatively speaking, powerful. For Christian faith, to love as God loves is to care for all people, but especially the weak and the downtrodden.

If love is the Christian analogue to Islamic ideas about compassion, what about justice? There is also a longstanding idea of the distinction and separate functions of church and state that culminates in modern democratic societies. St. Paul argued, in Romans 13:1–3 that God is the source of all authority, but there are distinctions between the religious and the political community.

> Let every person be subject to the governing authorities; for there is no authority except from God, and those authorities that exist have been instituted by God. Therefore whoever resists authority resists what God has appointed, and those who resist will incur judgment.

Likewise, Jesus supposedly said about the justice of taxes, "Give therefore to the emperor the things that are the emperor's, and to God the things that are God's" (Mt 22:21). There is then a relation but distinction between God's sovereign rule and the governing political authorities. Indeed, throughout much of human history and in many different cultures and societies there has been some connection between religion and the political order. The modern idea of the "separation of church and state" is indeed modern and Western even if within Christianity it is foreshadowed in Jesus' and St. Paul's teaching.

In Christian ethics there is a relation and yet distinction between justice and love (*agape*). Justice is to approximate love in the political order, but love cannot replace justice in political life. While love is a central motive and virtue in the Christian life, and should be shown even to the enemy, the turmoil and

---

32 Although it is beyond the scope of this book to explore these differences between Catholic and Protestant ethics in detail, we can note one doctrinal difference among Christians important for the moral life. Catholics typically see "love" (*agape; caritas*) as the mother of all the virtues that together perfect believers in holiness and unite them to God as the human highest good. Protestants typically do not speak of faith, hope, and love as "virtues" nor is "faith" formed by love. "Faith" is trust in Christ and the promises of God from which love flows to the neighbor. Granting these differences, it is still the case that love is basic in Christian moral thought and often paired with justice.

conflict of political life demands justice in order to protect the weak and the innocent. In this respect, most modern Christians distinguish the domain of religious authority where love should rule in Christians' lives and political authority with the demands of justice. This seems to suggest that love is an intra-Christian good whereas justice pertains to the domain of politics.

However, love and justice are in fact related. As the twentieth-century Protestant theologian Reinhold Niebuhr put it, "Equality is always the regulative principle of justice; and in the ideal of equality there is an echo of the law of love, 'Thou shalt love thy neighbor AS THYSELF.'"[33] As we saw before in Chapter 3, "natural law" is the human natural capacity to know the basic moral law expressed in the Golden or Silver Rules and also a rudimentary sense of justice. Human beings, for this line of thinking, are born with the capacities for moral agency. As created by God, human beings are moral creatures with the task and capacities to orient their lives responsibly. Although those capacities might be distorted by sin or overridden by the lust of self-love and the sin of pride, human fault cannot and does not destroy some remnants of the moral capacity to recognize justice and to act in just ways. Stated differently, although love is, for the Christian, a gift of God and God's working through the Holy Spirit in the lives of believers, the rudiments of justice can be apprehended by human reason and used to guide social life. Justice is also a virtue that means the right ordering of the human soul and the settled disposition to give others what is their due. In this way, the political and religious realms or "worlds" meet in the human person whose innermost being is open to God and yet who lives amid complex social and personal relations. One of the misunderstandings of Christian ethics (the same is true for Islamic ethics) is that the virtue of justice in the individual can somehow be separated from the moral law and the demand for social justice. Although it is the case that in some forms of ethics (one thinks in the ancient world of the philosopher Aristotle), the whole of ethics is conceived with respect to virtues as excellences of character, that is not the case for the monotheistic religions where law and virtue must be considered with respect to the responsible purposes of human life. Again the purposes that should guide the moral life are a reflection for Christians of God as sovereign judge and also loving redeemer. God is then active in the depths of human action.

Moral Motivation and the Will of God

How is this question of motivation posed by the monotheistic religions? "Islam" means "submission." The term also derives from an Arabic word for "peace." "*Dar al-Islam*" means the "House of Peace" and only a society ruled by Islam

---

33 Niebuhr, R. (1979). *An Interpretation of Christian Ethics*, 65. New York: Seabury Press. Emphasis in the original.

can be truly at peace. Human life outside of Islam and its social establishment is called *Dar al-Harb* ("House of War"). The mission is to spread *Dar al-Islam* and thus to spread peace under the sovereignty of Islamic rule and thus God/ Allah. The "House of Safety" (*Dar al-Amn*) denotes another category of Islamic social relations. These are nations, in the West and elsewhere, in which Muslims live as a minority and are allowed the freedom to practice their religion, submission to Allah and the rule of *sharī'a*. These various social conditions are important for Islamic ethics insofar as they denote conditions under which the Muslim life is lived freely (*Dar al-Islam*), utterly against the social rule (*Dar al-Harb*), or in a tenuous but stable and religiously tolerant condition (*Dar al-Amn*). One sees again how important are the structures of lived reality (social and natural) as a moral space for human life.

If we turn to the question of moral motivation within Islamic teaching, we must note that Allah alone is master and sustainer of creation and everything functions under his command. Allah is perfect and holy in every respect. Human beings are to worship, serve, and obey Allah who has provided human beings with guidance for how responsibly to live through Jesus, the great Hebrew prophets, the *Qur'ān* and Muḥammad's life and teaching, the seal of the prophets. Further, a person's life is lived in anticipation of Allah's judgment on her or him for life (actions as well as thoughts and feelings) in heaven, the hereafter. The proper motive of the Muslim life is seeking the pleasure of Allah. The true sanction for every moral law and the aim of every moral virtue is the love and fear of Allah along with a sense of accountability on the Day of Judgment and also the promise and hope of eternal reward and bliss in the hereafter. Through *sharī'a* a Muslim is given guidance for every aspect of life, from the smallest detail of family life to the demands for social justice and even life in the Hereafter. If hope of bliss and fear of punishment are ingrained in an individual, then one will follow and not disobey Allah's will.[34]

Of course, the Islamic and other monotheistic conceptions of moral motivation might seem to be heteronomous; they appear to some people to be a form of bondage and servitude. After all "submission" hardly seems to mean freedom. Further the Islamic account of right moral motivation might appear to be driven by a desire for reward from an all-powerful and sovereign God who knows the tiniest details of a person's thoughts, loves, and intentions. Moral duties would not flow from a human being's own will, freedom, and intention but remain bound to Allah's will. That is not the case. For Muslims people have a natural desire to worship and obey Allah, and the moral law and teachings of

---

34 Here is another instance where the religions enrich the work of moral theory. On many philosophical accounts, divine command ethics would not be seen as concerned with *eudaimonia*, human flourishing and happiness. In fact, hope for reward and fear of punishment would be taken, if they motivate action, to be contrary to the absolute obedience owed God's command where the sole morally valid motive is obedience itself irrespective of goods or consequences. Clearly, in the case of Islam, and the same can be said for Judaism and Christianity, matters are more complex.

Islam are not foreign to or against human nature. In this respect, the teachings of Islam are neither heteronomous, that is, given by some foreign power to human nature, nor autonomous, legislated by the human self to itself. There is a harmony between Allah's will and the perfection and bliss of human nature created by and for Allah. Human bliss is in relation to Allah but it is nevertheless *human* bliss.[35]

In terms of moral motivation, a religious conception as found in Islam does not easily fall within Western philosophical categories. Allah is working within human life in terms of the instructions of the *Qur'ān* and the example of Muḥammad, but also in the structures of lived experience and, indeed, all of reality. Although that is true, a Muslim is responsible for her or his choices and will have to answer for them on the Day of Judgment (*Yawm ad-Dīn*). This will be the final Day of Reckoning and with it the end of all life, resurrection, and judgment. Like the Christian New Testament, the precise time of this final day is not foretold even if there are signs of it. Sūrah 75 of the *Qur'ān* (*al-Qiyāmah*) is about the resurrection and tribulation. Islamic thinkers have made extensive comments on these passages. Without doubt, for Muslims a human being is indeed responsible for the conduct of his or her life.

For Islam, the will of Allah is not against or contrary to human flourishing and thus the human highest good. Right relation with Allah *is* the highest or transcendent good. Furthermore, Allah wills that good, provides instruction and orientation for how to live such a life, and is the final judge of every human being's life. To recall Soroush's words, the language of Islam is a language of duty and not rights. This means that a truly moral act is one that is done *from duty* and not simply an action that despite the agent's intention *accords with duty*.[36] The religions, and certainly Islam, are interested not only in "outward" obedience to God's law but also the inner intention, the dispositions, loves, and fears of the agent. A wrongful intention, an act that is not motivated by reverence for Allah for example, can mar the moral goodness of that action. Further, an action that might be partially unsuccessful in terms of its actual moral consequences, say, helping the poor in one's city, might nevertheless have great moral rectitude due to the agent's intention and motivation. The question of moral motivation is then complicated insofar as Islam has a double perspective

---

35 For a recent study showing how some Muslim and Christian women conceive of freedom neither as autonomous or heteronomous but as "dianomy" see Bucar, E.M. (2011). *Creative Conformity: The Feminist Politics of U.S. Catholic and Iranian Shi'a Women* Washington, DC: Georgetown University Press. Christian theologians often speak of "theonomous freedom" to make the same point, that is, true freedom is from God but this is neither self-legislated by the agent (autonomy) or a foreign rule of to the acting agent (heteronomy).

36 Immanuel Kant who held that religious morality is by definition heteronomous makes the same point in his *Critique of Practical Reason*: "No other subjective principle must be assumed as incentive, for though it might happen that the action occurs as the law prescribes, and thus in accord with duty but not from duty, the intention to do the action would not be moral, and it is the intention which is precisely in question in this legislation." Kant, I (1956 [1788]). *Critique of Practical Reason* (trans. L.W. Beck), 85. Indianapolis, IN: Bobbs-Merrill.

on action. God/Allah sees the inner disposition and intention of the agent but also judges the outer, public actions of people.

Insofar as Islam does not have a doctrine of original sin, then the problem of moral weakness or bondage of the will is not formulated in St. Paul's terms. As noted in the passages from the *Qur'ān* that head this chapter, moral weakness is due to the power of the "animal self," the Commanding Self. The failure to do what is right and just flows from the fact that human beings have tensions or struggles within themselves: human beings are themselves, it would seem, an aporia. If one were to ask, and many have, why Allah created human beings in this way, one can only answer that it was Allah's will and that it underscores that human beings are religious and moral beings through and through. Ideas about the good, justice, and compassion are written into the structure of reality by the will of Allah. Following the way of Islam – submission to Allah – is then to bring harmony or justice to the self and also to accord with Allah's will just as, socially, it is to bring about the "Land of Peace." Here one grasps, again, how the divine will can act within the agent's own life to conform it to its proper end and duty. The various "Pillars of Islam" are the means to live in submission to Allah and thereby to attain the highest human good of Heaven with Allah.

The question of moral motivation is equally complex in Christian thought, which also seeks to understand the working of God in a person's life. Christians believe that Jesus Christ, son of God and as Logos is part of the Triune Godhead, is the messiah and redeemer who saves people from sin. What does that mean and how does it relate to moral motivation? Recall the passage from St. Paul. For Paul and subsequent Christianity, sin is a power that infects human life making the human will enslaved and in bondage to it and thus unable to love God and others, to act justly, and to have faith and hope. Put differently, "sin" is a condition in which the emotional, cognitive, and volitional capacities of a person are at odds with each other. Paul does –he wills – what he does not want – desires – to do. He knows – cognitively – what is right and good and yet does not willfully do it. *Sin* is thereby a "condition" of human existence, rather than just wrong actions or evil intentions, which nevertheless gives rise to *sins*, wrongful acts like hatred, murder, deceit, and theft (violations of the Ten Commandments as well as reciprocal justice) that reflect back on the self and reinforce the sinful condition. Merely avoiding sinful acts is then not enough to overcome the condition of Sin. Insofar as human action has cognitive, emotional, and volitional elements, as well as other facets, then human beings cannot by themselves and under their own powers of agency free themselves from the deadly bondage to "Sin." This is why Christianity is resolutely a religion of redemption. Humans cannot save themselves. God has graciously saved them in and through the works and teachings of Jesus Christ accepted in faith and lived through a life of love.

Perhaps the most direct way to understand Christian conceptions of moral motivation is to note, first, that these ideas entail the usual ways of speaking about the "springs of action." Christians speak about the will moving one to act or desire or, again, reason. The various human powers act together to motivate action. One of the most elaborate Christian accounts of the motives in human action is found in St. Thomas Aquinas's *Summa Theologiae*. In the second part of this massive work is his treatise on human acts, Thomas explains how reason, will, and desire work together to motivate and direct action. Insofar as we are speaking about action, there must be some goal or end sought as well as the means to that end chosen. Reason, according to Aquinas, apprehends the end and presents this to the will as a good to be obtained, which in turn moves the agent to act in order realize the specific end. Because we are speaking about action, and so "ends," those "ends" are apprehended as "good" and so also an object of desire. The rightly functioning human being manifests a complex interaction among human powers and these, over time, can be trained thereby developing habits and virtues. Moreover, the virtues, for their part, are good habits, at least the so-called natural or cardinal virtues (justice, courage, temperance, prudence).

And yet, human beings have fallen into sin, the consequence of which is, in terms of action, that the intricate working of the moral agent is wrecked. Will does not follow reason or empower action. Reason has a mistaken or distorted apprehension of goods. Desire is warped, as St. Augustine taught, into self-love rather than love of God and others in God. Grace is then needed to restore and reform the self and to liberate the self from bondage to sin and thereby to enable virtuous action. Granting the incredible complexity and diversity of Christian theological accounts of action, two "models" or general accounts of grace in relation to human action have dominated at least Western Christianity and both of them are drawn in good measure from St. Paul's writings.[37]

One model of the relation of grace to human action is widely found in Catholic ethics, and Aquinas nicely presents it. The Pauline background to this "model" is found in St. Paul's first letter to the Corinthians. In Chapter 13 of that letter, Paul concludes: "And now faith, hope, and love abide, these three; and the greatest of these is love" (1 Cor 13:13). Aquinas, outlining what might be called the "Catholic model" of the relation of grace and action, aims to show how faith, hope, and love as theological virtues are related to the cardinal virtues which a human being attains through their own learning and habitual behavior.[38] By theological virtues, Thomas means those excellences of human powers that have God as their

---

37 The idea of a conceptual "model" is widely used in the natural and social sciences and also in the comparison of moral systems. By a conceptual model we mean a construct composed of various concepts that are meant to enable us to understand, interpret, know, or simulate some subject matter, in this case the relation of divine grace to human action.
38 There is considerable debate among scholars of Aquinas's thought on the question of the extent to which the cardinal virtues themselves depend on grace insofar as Thomas calls love (*caritas*) the mother of all the virtues and yet cardinal and theological virtues would seem to have different ends, the natural and the supernatural ends of human life. St. Augustine understood all the virtues as merely forms of Christian love (*caritas*) and in this respect what appeared to be virtues among non-Christians are really nothing by "beautiful vices." It is not our purpose to settle this scholarly debate but merely to note how Christian thinkers must, especially in the Catholic model, puzzle through the relation between kinds of virtue.

end and therefore must be infused by God on the human soul in order elevate human beings to their supernatural perfection, the *beatific vision* or vision of God. More specifically, Thomas shows how faith is the supernatural perfection of knowledge, hope of the human will, and love as the deepest longing of human existence for God. In this way, the human powers of reason, will, and desire that are needed to explain human action are healed and properly related by divine grace and human cooperation with that grace even as divine grace transforms a person into a friend of God. The end or purpose of human transformation is the justification of the believer and eternal bliss and friendship with God.

The point of the "Catholic model" on the relation of grace and human action is that grace perfects human nature and thereby allows and requires good moral action to cooperative with grace ending in the supernatural destiny with God. To recall the dynamics of religious life from Chapter 3 (see diagram), the "Catholic model" of the relation between human action and grace is one in which God's grace is operative at each moment in the dynamic even while believers must *cooperate* with that grace through the practices of religion (sacraments, good deeds, prayer, confession, etc.) by which the believer is perfected in love.

A somewhat different model of human action, the "Protestant model" (as one can call it), also draws on St. Paul but much more in terms of the bondage of the will to sin, as in the quotation from Romans but also from two chapters earlier in Paul's letter. "But God proves his love for us in that while we still were sinners Christ died for us" (Rom 5:8). In a succinct form of the Protestant outlook, Martin Luther argued that human beings are saved by God in Christ not when they are perfected in love, but, as St. Paul argued, while they were yet sinners. This means that Luther did not conceive of faith as a "virtue," and so a perfection of some human power, but rather as trust in God's promises of mercy. Luther and other Protestants worried that if one stresses the need for persons to cooperate with God's grace there are two dangerous consequences. Either (i) the believer comes to think that they somehow helped to save themselves and that because of their good deeds God owes them salvation (Luther called this "works righteousness"), or (ii) the believer will realize that she or he will never be perfect, fall into despair, and come to resent God as a moral tyrant demanding a kind of perfection beyond human capacities. In each way, the person is bound by, enslaved to, either (i) their pride or (ii) despair. Reading in Paul's Letter to the Romans, Luther came to believe that God's righteousness is actually the divine mercy in Christ, and, further, a Christian is saved not when they are perfect but while they are still sinners.

What does this "Protestant model" of grace and action mean for moral motivation? Luther, in famous treatises like *The Freedom of the Christian* and his biblical commentaries, began a revolution in thinking about human action. Luther and other Protestants believe that what God's mercy and grace do is to accept the believer as a sinner and free that individual from the burden of trying to be perfectly holy. When freed from such relentless self-concern about one's holiness ("works righteousness"), the believer is then freed for loving the neighbor. Importantly, this freedom to love means that the Christian does not love others *for the sake of acquiring his or her own virtue* but simply out of a radical care for the needs of others. Faith, hope, and love are not "virtues," they are not, on the terms of the Protestant model, excellences of human capacities. Faith is trust in God's promises, love is faith active in the world caring for others and fulfilling the demands of ordinary life, and a hope in God's kingdom. In this way, Protestant Reformers (e.g. Luther, John Calvin (1509–1564), Huldrych Zwingli (1484–1531), Philipp Melanchthon (1497–1560), and others) helped advance the modern concern for the human person and political freedom. For them, God's grace releases the believer from endless demands of perfection and thereby frees them to do acts of love for others. Action is moral, then, when done in free expression of love, bounded by the moral law known through the Decalogue (the Ten Commandments) and testified in conscience. In this way, faith is not formed by love, as Aquinas taught, but, rather, faith becomes active in works of love.

Much more could be written about various Islamic conceptions of moral motivation as well as the similarities and differences among Catholics and Protestants and even among Protestant Christians themselves. Further inquiry into these various "models" of human action from Christian perspectives is not needed for our purposes in this chapter. Clearly, religious traditions share with philosophical accounts of moral agency attention to human powers or capacities (such as desire, will, reason, and the like). They complicate the idea of moral agency by showing how the divine or the sacred "acts" *within* the agent's life as well as *within* the structures of lived reality. In religious ethics the question of moral agency is also a question of how the divine or the sacred relates to acting human beings and social life as well. Insofar as accounts of virtue or practical reason that exclude any conception of the sacred or the divine working within the agent and through the structures of lived reality or even the hope that God can do so, would miss much in a religious conception of moral agency. The task of the religious ethicist, accordingly, is to explore the accounts of agency found within the religions and also to develop a conception of agency informed by religious sources. That twofold task has of course been the purpose of this chapter in and through outlining the similarities and differences among Christian and Islamic thought.

Rather than delving deeper into specific religious accounts of agency, we conclude this chapter, as with other chapters, by turning to a topic of practical concern for peoples around the world. There is little doubt that one of the major ethical achievements of the twentieth century has been the development and spread of ideas about "human rights." Although often criticized as an incoherent doctrine and rejected by some Muslims and others due to a focus on rights rather than duties, the fact remains that human rights discourse has become a powerful global force for the interactions among peoples. At stake is how to protect and promote the humanity of people, including the person and social agency. Insofar as that is the case, it is appropriate in a chapter on the *fundamental dimension* of religious ethics to engage this discourse about human rights.

Religion and Human Rights

A lecture series held at the University of Chicago in 2002–2003 under the auspices of the Pew Forum on Religion and Public Life was provocatively titled: "Does Human Rights Need God?" The editors of the volume succinctly formulate the question as well as the idea of human rights. "Human rights," they observe, "are a bundle of claims each person has simply because of his or her humanness. These claims have been enumerated in international declarations and agreements. How does God enter into it?"[39] Human rights constitute claims on behalf of persons essential to their respect and well-being as persons. These "rights" have been variously enumerated in declarations and agreements beginning, most famously, with the United Nations Universal Declaration of Human Rights in 1947.[40] Further, there have been theological, historical, and cultural approaches to the relation between religion ("God") and human rights. There have also been criticisms of human rights as distinctly Western, Christian, and individualistic and so not applicable to other cultures, theologically and philosophically untenable, and also practically unworkable since it is difficult to see what kind of political, legal, or social institution can back human rights claims and punish violations of those rights.[41] Still other thinkers find human rights discourse hopelessly anthropocentric and thereby hindering ethical concern for animals and the natural environment. The criticisms of human rights are well known and yet as noted it remains the case that human rights discourse provides one way to address shared moral and political problems.

In light of the discussion of "agency" in this chapter, human rights discourse illuminates the way ideas about agency are an intersection for the dimensions of religious ethics. Rather than engaging specific religious or philosophical debates about human rights, we can show how our approach to religious ethics opens human rights discourse to religious and ethical reflection, criticism, and reconstruction. This will complete the work of the present chapter even as it will move the reader back to previous chapters as well as forward to the next chapter on the *metaethical dimension* of religious ethics.

The idea of human rights is that human beings, by virtue of their humanity, have certain fundamental and inalienable rights and that these rights make a claim against other persons, communities, and institutions to respect for humanity and also to aid in human flourishing. The rights are "fundamental" in the sense that they are basic to the humanity of a person rather than nonessential or preferential. For example, I do not have a human right to own a BMW automobile even though I like them; a person does not have a right to a 40-room mansion

---

39 See Bucar, E.M. and Barnett, B. (eds.) (2005). *Does Human Rights Need God?*, 3. Grand Rapids, MI: Eerdmans.
40 The declaration can be found on the United Nations website: http://www.un.org/en/documents/udhr (accessed 18 June 2019).
41 For a recent discussion see Joas, H. (2013). *The Sacredness of the Person: A New Genealogy of Human Rights*. Washington, DC: Georgetown University Press.

even if the right to a "home" could be seen as a human right. These rights are inalienable in the sense that they cannot be given to or taken away by others because they are part of what it means to be a human being. To deny unjustly or illegally a person's freedom of movement or bodily integrity is to deny something about their very humanity in virtue of which she or he has a claim to respect and care. Notice then that the idea of a human right links the *normative* and *fundamental dimensions* of religious ethics. The link between these dimensions of thought connects agency with what is morally normative and thereby specifies an account of moral agency as opposed to some other kind of agency. And that is why human rights have been hotly debated among the religions. How is that so?

Recall the words of Abdolkarim Soroush cited previously: "The language of religion (especially that of Islam as exemplified by the *Qur'ān* and the Tradition) is the language of duties, not rights." That is to say, religious traditions, and especially theistic traditions, insist that human beings do not make right-claims against God(s). The divine is the supreme good and also sovereign over reality. Human worth is understood not simply as an attribute of humanity as such, but constituted through a relationship to God(s). This is why, as noted, some Protestant thinkers worried about seeing the moral life in terms of "virtue." Does the virtuous person have a claim against God for the right of salvation? Furthermore, if God is at work within the human person as well as within the structures of lived reality can one really say that a human right is grounded just in our humanity and our various powers of thought and action? And if a religious ethics does claim to ground these rights – and their related duties – it will be from a perspective on humanity different than a nonreligious perspective. The religions, as noted, contend that the deepest truth about human beings is not their relation to themselves or others but their relations to the divine or sacred. The idea of human rights thereby poses normative and fundamental questions within religious ethics that must be addressed from within religious resources. In fact, religious ethics may allow us to see the complexity of the idea of human rights too often missed from other perspectives.

Human rights also pose crucial questions for the *descriptive dimension* of religious ethics. As many commentators note, the idea of individuals bearing rights and the conception of the social and political order as organized to protect and promote those rights are distinctly modern and Western, even liberal, ideas. Some religious and cultural traditions put emphasis on the common good rather than on individual rights, as Catholic thinkers argue, or the ordering of social life through hereditary bonds and obligations, or in Islamic conceptions of the House of Peace amid the House of War as a form of common life that transcends the modern nation state. From a religious perspective, human rights discourse may entail an interpretation of the structures of lived reality in a way that conceals or endangers other facets of reality. An interpretation of moral or political situations for a devout person is going to be thicker than contemporary disputes about rights, say when Muslims speak about various "Houses" or Christians contrast the Church and the World. Additionally, the *practical dimension* of religious ethics draws on resources for addressing the actual questions of human conduct that will exceed the resources of human rights discourse. Islamic jurisprudence, Buddhist teachings, Christian uses of biblical texts as well as Church teaching and critical reflection are used in these various traditions to address the practical questions of human life. Human rights discourse can thereby illuminate the complexity of resources that the religions use in practical reflection.

We have tried briefly to show how the question of "religion and human rights" can be used to demonstrate the insights of a multidimensional conception of religious ethics and also some of the points of criticism of human rights from religious perspectives. That being said, the force of the present chapter was to show the depth and power of the religions to think about the meaning, value, and conduct of human life, personal and social. Insofar as that is the case, then the religions might also have resources to join cause with human rights discourse for the sake of respecting and enhancing the integrity of life, human and nonhuman. In fact, religious discourse not only criticizes some conceptions of human rights but also provides deep resources for conceiving of human worth and those actions and policies needed to protect and promote human well-being in relation to other domains of life, finite but also transcendent forms. In this light, one task of religious ethics is the ethical reconstruction of religious convictions and practices so that as global forces the religions can be lived in their most humane forms. That task is at the outer limits of this book.

Conclusion

This chapter has sought to unfold the *fundamental dimension* of religious ethics in and through exploring the analogies between Islamic and Christian accounts of moral agency and the *aporia* of freedom and bondage. Although the religions address topics about moral agency included in philosophical ethics, and especially about various human capabilities, they nevertheless bring their own distinctive sources and perspectives that enrich and deepen an understanding of human beings as moral agents whose conduct takes place within the complex structures of lived realities. And here again one might ask if religious ethics is really a form of ethics. If ethics is delimited to human agents and human agents alone and if the structures of lived reality are limited to the social and political institutions that human beings create to protect and promote their lives, then the idea of religious *ethics* seems like an incoherent one. However, if one turns to the full complexity of the religions along the lines of a multidimensional method of thinking, one finds, surprisingly, that *religious ethics* is not only a coherent idea but one that enriches ethical reflection in novel and profound ways. And that is, of course, what we have been outlining as the meaning and method of religious ethics. We turn next to ask, how, if at all, one can show the validity and truth of this conception of the discipline of religious ethics.

6

Truth and Illusion

Metaethical Dimension

Then, when the Bodhisattva had entered his dwelling alone, in a secluded spot, he thought, "This world, alas, is in a sorry state: There is birth and decay, there is death and falling into other states and being reborn. And no one knows any way of escape from this suffering, this aging and this death. When will deliverance be found from this suffering, this aging and death?"

—*Mahāpadāna Sutta*[1]

When through wisdom one perceives, "All dhammas are without self," then one is detached as to misery. This is the path of purity.

—*Dhammapada*[2]

In the beginning was the Word, and the Word was with God and the Word was God. He was in the beginning with God. All things came into being through him, and without him not one thing came into being. What has come into being in him was life, and the life was the light of all people. The light shines in the darkness, and the darkness did not overcome it.

He was in the world, and the world came into being through him; yet the world did not know him. He came to what was his own, and his own people did not accept him. But to all who received him, who believed in his name, he gave power to become children of God, who were born, not of blood or of the will of the flesh or of the will of man, but of God. And the Word became flesh and lived among us, and we have seen his glory, the glory as of a father's only son, full of grace and truth.

—Jn 1: 1–5; 10–14

---

1 *Mahāpadāna Sutta* 2.18. Dīgha Nikāya 14; *The Long Discourses of the Buddha: A Translation of the Dīgha Nikāya* (1995). (trans. M. Walshe), 210–211. Boston: Wisdom Publications.
2 *Dhammapada* 20.277–9. *The Dhammapada*, (1987). (ed. J.R. Carter and M. Palihawadana). New York and Oxford: Oxford University Press.

Religious Ethics: Meaning and Method, First Edition. William Schweiker and David A. Clairmont.
© 2020 William Schweiker and David A. Clairmont. Published 2020 by John Wiley & Sons Ltd.

Human beings are animals that interpret their worlds, asking "What is going on?" We seek the good, in material comfort and in meaningful relationships, asking "What are we to do and to be?" People want to navigate well the complexities of life, asking "What is the best way for us to act, given these difficult situations?" Humans contemplate their existence and the meaning of their freedom asking, "What kind of power and agency do we have?" Each of these questions point to a different dimension of ethical thinking about the moral life, what we have labeled the descriptive, the normative, the practical, and the fundamental dimensions of religious ethics.

In each of these dimensions, the human person or community and their ethical thinking moves back and forth between two equally important truths that are in tension with each other. Human beings are creatures that seek insight about themselves, their relationships, and the complex environments they inhabit. Yet human beings are blind to much of what happens in the world, and, often enough, willingly so. People seek what is good, but they are aware of the many ways that in fact humans pursue evil, often under the guise of the good. We long for wisdom but live much of life in a state of perplexity as each age seems to heap further complications and confusion upon the previous one. We crave freedom and the formation of individual character and community integrity through our choices together, and yet we are limited, imperfect creatures whose finitude poses a limit to our freedom.

Now we consider a different sort of question that in many ways flows from all the others and is intertwined with them. Here too the religions complicate ethics because they explore the odd intermixture of truth and illusion. The great Jewish philosopher Emmanuel Levinas once said, "Everyone will readily agree that it is of the highest importance to know whether we were duped by morality."[3] Has everything our communities taught about what is just, good, and responsible just been a falsehood or a ruse of the powerful? Is our own thinking so limited and faulty that we cannot know what is morally true? Maybe there is no such thing as moral truth but only preferences, recommendations, and emotions that, no matter how noble, are not true or false in any sense. What counts as being morally true, that is, how does one define moral truth, and then set out to demonstrate it? The question is how to validate, show to be true and right, moral convictions.

Following standard terminology in ethics, we call this the metaethical dimension. But unlike some philosophies, in our usage, following religious insights, it names the human capacity to seek *truth*, even as we are often, and to our detriment, satisfied with *illusion* about the good and our search for it. Furthermore, the central claim of this chapter, and indeed of this book, is that an ethical position or judgment is validated not with respect to a single perspective or

---

3 Levinas, E. (1969). *Totality and Infinity: An Essay on Exteriority* (trans. A. Lingis), 21. Pittsburgh, PA: Duquesne University Press.

dimension of thought, say, from a single rational principle like Kant's categorical imperative or even just one divine revelation. Rather, a position or judgment is validated through the ongoing movement among the dimensions of religious ethics with the result that one finds it (i) more coherent than other positions, (ii) able to answer questions that rival positions or judgments cannot and so is error-reducing, (iii) resonates with the rest of a person's or a community's moral outlook, (iv) is undertaken with the openness to allow the better argument to prevail, and (v) meets procedural demands of honest human communication.[4] We return to the *method* of validation throughout the chapter and also note its relation to the "spiral" of the religious life outlined in Chapter 3. As in our previous chapters, we place into dialogue different traditions, Buddhist and Christian, and their views on the search for truth amidst the pervasive presence of illusion.

What does the term "metaethics" mean in modern moral philosophy? Simply put, metaethics is part of moral theory not about normative ethical judgments, say, what is right, responsible, or good, but, rather, what is the nature of moral properties (like, good or responsible), what is their meaning, and what are the moral attitudes and judgments moral properties entail. In short, metaethics focuses (i) on questions of the nature of morality, its connection to the world as it exists and as human beings experience it, and the conditions affecting the person who acts; (ii) on the nature of moral choice itself, as a person considers options to choose and evaluates the actions she or he undertakes; and (iii) on the standards of moral truth and the extent to which we can know them. How can we know that our accounts of our moral worlds and of our choices are true or valid? If ethics is second-order reflection on morality, as we have argued, then, put abstractly, metaethics is second-order metareflection on each of the dimensions of ethics.

Our aim is to show why it is more helpful to think of metaethics as a dimension of religious ethics arising from thinking with the religions about the good life rather than as a necessary starting or ending point for ethics. To do so we show how the metaethical dimension is found in and shaped by religious thinking about the good life by considering Buddhist and Christian accounts of truth and their connection to the good, the responsible, and the right. The different moral vocabularies of each tradition are used to illustrate an approach to moral truth that is multidimensional. Finally, we illustrate how the metaethical dimension is connected to the other dimensions by considering the natural environment and threats to its ecology. In each section the argument shows how religions offer a way of answering the central question of metaethics – "What is

---

4 These criteria of validation are widely used among contemporary thinkers and do not purport to be a novel account of how to validate a position. For a discussion of this method of validation see Schweiker, W. (1995). *Responsibility and Christian Ethics*. Cambridge: Cambridge University Press.

moral truth and what are the standards of moral truth?" In this way, our discussion intersects with previous discussions of realism and antirealism as well as cognitivism and noncognitivism in ethics even while charting new ground (see Chapter 3). The chapter addresses many of the concerns raised in moral philosophy while also offering a picture of human life as truth-seeking. Yet that seeking is carried out by creatures who are always to some degree blind in their quest even as they seek insight into their lives and the shared space they inhabit.[5] One can then see this chapter as the counterpart to Chapter 4 on Perplexity and Wisdom insofar as here we explore the objects of wisdom (truth) and perplexity (illusion) just as Chapters 3 (Good and Evil) and 6 (Freedom and Bondage) were conceptually linked. Remember, our claim is not to pit religious ethics against moral philosophy but rather to draw attention to the nuance and complexity of religious accounts of moral truth that tend to be overlooked or insufficiently appreciated when discussion of moral truth is reduced to a particular philosophical language and method.

Metaethics in Recent Moral Philosophy

Questions about moral truth are basic to any religious or philosophical ethics. From the brahman's hymn in the Ṛg Veda for ritual knowledge in the midst of the vast unknowable realms of the universe, to Plato's account of Socrates' question to Euthyphro about the source of his piety, religious truth and moral truth have been deeply intertwined. Religious persons across the globe, in their worship and wisdom traditions, seek the truth about the world and their place in it. The difficulty is that the quest for insight into what is true is not without frequent, indeed sometimes tragically destructive, instances of moral illusion. Rooting out the frequent and most harmful expressions of that illusion is a common calling of religious ethics.

The difficulty in approaching metaethics as a set of theoretical questions within moral theory, rather than as a *dimension* of ethical thinking, is that metaethical questions, if not considered with sufficient human sensitivity to the experiences of moral failure, struggle, and transformation, can easily obscure the quality of the moral life worth thinking about in the first place. What is a good life? What makes a life good? To what extent is the goodness of human life related to the goodness of other animal life? What are the complex meanings that people draw forth from or construct for their lives by their actions and relationships? How do we form a just community? What is the right thing to do in this situation? How do we maintain a sense of integrity in

---

5 For an earlier formulation of the metaethical dimension, see Schweiker, W. (ed.) (2005).
The Blackwell Companion to Religious Ethics, 1–16. Malden, MA: Blackwell. See also van Roojen, M. (2015). *Metaethics: A Contemporary Introduction*. New York and London: Routledge.

Metaethical Dimension
(What, if any, are the standards of moral truth?)

$\downarrow$

Epistemological Question
(Can moral claims be rationally validated?)

$\swarrow$ $\searrow$

Cognitivism   Non-cognitivism

$\downarrow$

Ontological Question
(Do moral properties/facts exist?)

$\swarrow$ $\searrow$

Realism   Anti-Realism
(moral properties are real)   *(moral properties are not real)*

Subjectivism
Expressivism
Emotivism
Prescriptivism
Nihilism

$\downarrow$

Semantic Question
(Do moral statements have truth value?)

$\swarrow$ $\searrow$

Naturalism   Non-Naturalism
(Moral properties are natural properties)   *(Moral properties are*
            not natural)

Reductive   Internal Realism
    (Moral properties are natural ones
    and of an observable kind, e.g., pleasure)   Intuitionism

Non-Reductive   Divine Command Ethics
    (Moral properties are natural ones
    of a distinct kind, e.g., religiously ordered
    basic goods)

$\downarrow$

HERMENEUTICAL REALISM

$\swarrow$ $\searrow$

NATURALIST   NON-NATURALIST

Figure 6.1 Philosophical approaches to metaethics and religion.

the midst of moral diversity and interpersonal commitments? There are important questions about moral knowledge and the basis of moral knowledge that
persist in any ethical discussion, and we cannot ignore them.

There are different angles that thinkers have taken on moral truth.[6]
Sometimes, the ontological angle is primary: "Do moral facts exist?" At other
times, the semantic or meaning angle is primary: "Do moral statements have
truth value?" Often, the epistemological angle is primary and the starting point
for metaethics: "Can moral claims be rationally validated, shown to be true?"
Organizing metaethics in this way can be represented in the diagram on the
previous page (Figure 6.1).

For example, one can begin with the question of whether or not moral claims
can be rationally validated (the epistemological question). If one answers that
they cannot, then one would be in a group of thinkers often described as metaethical *noncognitivists* (see Chapter 3). Noncognitivist positions together share
the view that moral claims cannot be rationally validated because it is impossible to come up with universally accessible and agreeable truth conditions
through which people could come to an agreement about what would make
such conditions true. Such thinkers might argue that moral claims are just
expressions of basic emotional states (emotivism) or statements of personal
preference (prescriptivism). Others argue more radically that there is finally no
such thing as morality at all (nihilism).

Cognitivist positions hold that moral claims can be rationally validated –
although the meaning of validation (the semantic question) and the means by
which that validation occurs (the ontological question) differ among cognitiv-
ists (see Chapter 3). For example, if one focuses on the ontological question – do moral facts exist? – we can either answer yes (moral facts do exist;
they are real things in the world) or no (moral facts do not exist; they are not
real things in the world, and so our everyday use of the world "moral" must
imply something else besides there being some independent realm of moral
reality). For this reason, answers to this ontological question are classified
either as realist (moral facts are real) or antirealist (moral facts are not real).
Antirealist positions are, for the most part, classified also as noncognitivist (see
Chapter 3).[7]

---

6 Antonaccio, M. (2005). Moral truth. In: *The Blackwell Companion to Religious Ethics*, 29.
Malden, MA: Blackwell.
7 There are various trajectories of thinking about antirealist positions in metaethics: the first is
noncognitivist; the second is error theory, and the third is nonobjectivism. Richard Joyce explains
the relative differences in the following way. "Moral noncognitivism holds that our moral
judgments are not in the business of aiming at truth … The moral error theorist thinks that
although our moral judgments aim at the truth, they systematically fail to secure it. The moral
error theorist stands to morality as the atheist stands to religion … it would seem that when a
theist says 'God exists' (for example) she is expressing something that purports to be true.
According to the atheist, however, the claim is untrue; indeed, according to her, theistic discourse

If, on the other hand, we ask the semantic question – do moral statements have truth value? – we are asking a question that stems from a basically cognitivist position. If we believe that moral claims can be rationally validated (the cognitivist position), we must also ask how they are rationally validated. In other words, by what means does the rational validation happen? So if one follows the line in Figure 6.1 from the cognitivist answer to the epistemological question, to the realist answer to the ontological question, one arrives at two options for the semantic question. Either moral claims are real because they have some connection to the way things naturally occur or they are real because morality is some kind of independent reality perhaps connected to, but not the same as, "nature." For example, some so-called communitarians hold that in order for a moral claim to be rationally validated, we must have a shared understanding of the structures of meaning – how meaning is established and communicated in a community – such that a moral claim can mean one thing and not another. This is the semantic question, and to this question one could answer yes, for example because moral statements cohere with a community's convictions about reality that exists independent of the judgments human beings make about it.

Moral naturalists are those whose answer to the semantic question requires some connection to the way the world is and how human beings operate – their basic desires, capacities, and their connection to other creatures and their environment. Nonnaturalists are those who believe that morality is real but it is a reality that is not explainable with reference to nature (see Chapter 3). There are several varieties of nonnaturalist moral realists, all of whom believe that moral reality in some way exists but is moral not because of its connection to the natural world or the basic conditions in which human beings find themselves. Rather morality is real because the moral exists as some non-natural but nonetheless real property of actions or relations. One might claim that human beings have a moral intuition – a kind of trustworthy connection to the morally real – that can pick out the moral from the immoral or the amoral even if that moral property cannot be defined with reference to something else. Or one might claim that there exists a single source of all things that have or will come to be (and without which nothing would exist – what some call God) that has so established existing things to follow a certain order that will guarantee their harmonious relation. We have seen this before in so-called divine command ethics. That order

---

in general is infected with error. The moral error theorist claims that when we say 'Stealing is wrong' we are asserting that the act of stealing instantiates the property of wrongness, but in fact nothing instantiates this property (or there is no such property at all), and thus the utterance is untrue ... Non-objectivism (as it will be called here) allows that moral facts exist but holds that they are, in some manner to be specified, constituted by mental activity." See Joyce, R. Moral anti-realism, *The Stanford Encyclopedia of Philosophy (Fall 2015 Edition)*, (ed. E.N. Zalta, http://plato.stanford.edu/archives/fall2015/entries/moral-anti-realism (accessed 30 June 2019).

may have nothing to do with the natural state in which human beings or other living things find themselves, but it can be obtained if we understand the order that can be achieved if certain things are pursued in a specific way (for example, obedience to divine commands). Or one might argue, as Immanuel Kant did, that morality is a dictate of pure practical reason and thus not a part of the "natural" world. In each case, the moral as an aspect of reality may exist with the natural but its meaning *as moral* does not depend on natural properties.

We also note, at the bottom of the chart, another option called hermeneutical realism that can take naturalist or nonnaturalist forms. The idea here – and the position advanced in this book – is that human beings can use only human means – reason, understanding, interpretation of cultural forms (symbols, narratives, practices, etc.), insight, and experience – to understand themselves, the world, and moral claims, but this does not deny the fact that what is sought is what is real, including the reality of moral properties, ideas, and values. In its naturalist form, which, again, is the position of this book with respect to axiology or the *realm of goods*, moral goodness is bound to the natural characteristics of human beings and their world. Nonnaturalism, which, to be honest, is also the position of this book with respect to the character of *moral norms* and the *transcendent good*, is not bound to, if still related to, natural characteristics. To use older terminology, we advance a naturalist conception of the "good" related to a nonnaturalist account of the "right." This means that what is right (e.g. just, fair) is validated with regard to those natural basic goods one ought to respect and enhance for the integrity of life. The transcendent good is manifest in and through acting on the moral imperative to respect and enhance the integrity of life. In this respect, this book as a whole is the outline and defense of a specific moral theory, including a metaethics, drawn from religious resources. Some will disagree with us. We hope that many more will agree with us for the sake of a reorientation of religious ethics.

Although there is much more that could be said about discussions in metaethics, it is important to note the ways that religion does and does not factor into this classification of metaethical inquiry. One can ask how the three questions guiding metaethical reflection noted previously (ontological, epistemological, and semantic) are ordered and the meaning commonly given to each. The ordering is anything but self-evident. These questions – or questions like them – arise in the life of religious persons and institutions. So, for example, if one takes the epistemological question first (Can moral claims be rationally validated?), one could pose the following challenge. In seeking to answer the basic question of the metaethical dimension – What is moral truth and what are the standards of moral truth? – why should we begin by asking about rational validation? In the way discussed in Chapter 3, if one begins with how we know good and evil, then the answer to their existence might already be determined. Further, is the mode of rational validation a historically contingent project or is it something that operates in basically the same way from one historical period to the next? Does reason take the same form in every culture or is reason bound up with the traditions and cultures in which it operates? Is religious faith necessarily irrational, or are faith and reason in some way complementary in the search for moral truth? Are reason and faith complementary in the same way across religious traditions or are there important differences? How is rational validation connected to other deeply human ways of thinking through symbolic or other poetic forms? How is rational validation related to an honest acknowledgement of the limits of human thought, perhaps even a tragic aspect of human existence?

In a similar way we could ask about the ontological question (Do moral properties exist?), considering how the facts and meaning of existence have been considered in various religious traditions. Although the religions do offer answers to this ontological question in metaethics, they often situate this question in different terms. One could ask how our account of the real affects what we know and even what we think it is possible to know. Changing the order of questions further illustrates our basic thesis that religious ethics ought to be treated as a multidimensional project. In order to answer the question of whether or not moral properties exist, it seems reasonable to ask what is going on (the descriptive dimension) and what norms and values one ought to pursue (the normative dimension). In other words, our answer to the three metaethical questions posed in this chapter requires us to consider the questions posed by the other dimensions of religious ethics. Traditionally, both the religions and classical philosophical traditions have sought answers to these questions in discourse about ontology (inquiry into the meaning of being) and metaphysics (inquiry into the basic foundations or structures of reality). The answers to those questions come from (and are critically evaluated by) the complex mythical, legal, and ritual discourses that one finds in religious communities.

The semantic question (Do moral statements have truth value?) offers another way to think about the metaethical dimension. In the history of modern philosophy, one of the more puzzling questions has been to ascertain what it means for a statement to be true. Is a statement true because it communicates something about an existing state of affairs in the world (a correspondence approach)? Or is a statement true because of its relation to other statements that make it part of an intelligible whole (a coherence approach)? An intuitionist would claim that if one intuits a moral property, then it is true because that is how moral properties appear to us. If one opts for a correspondence approach, how is the state of affairs about the world to be determined? By appearances? By scientific testing? Is truth best understood in terms of statements or declarative sentences or is truth a quality or even, as some religious traditions hold, a being? How do our capacities to see and understand the world relate to our judgments about truth?[8] In each case, the answers to these

---

8 See Glanzberg, M. Truth. *The Stanford Encyclopedia of Philosophy (Fall 2014 Edition)*, (ed. E.N. Zalta), http://plato.stanford.edu/archives/fall2014/entries/truth (accessed 30 June 2019). Glanzberg offers brief historical accounts of what he terms "neo-classical correspondence

additional questions would likely push us to another way of thinking about the original topic. Inquiring about the extent to which moral statements have truth value (the semantic question) is certainly related to whether or not moral properties exist (the ontological question), although it would be strange to inquire about the truth value of moral claims if moral properties did not exist at all. Moreover, the extent to which moral claims can be rationally validated (the epistemological question) would be an odd sort of inquiry if moral properties did not exist, which is precisely the sort of objection raised by those who take moral claims to be nothing but assertions of certain desires or preferences or power relations. Religious-ethical discourse tends to begin metaethical investigation with the ontological question and then takes up together the epistemological and semantic questions.

Here too the religions complicate things. Maybe what we take to be real – say, that you are an enduring self or that the Grand Teton mountains exist – is in fact an illusion and that the truth is not-self/no-thing-ness, as in Buddhism, or *ātman* in Hinduism (see Chapter 3). Or, maybe what is ultimately real is beyond and yet related to this world, say, the Kingdom of God, and we live with a mixture of truth and illusion. If the real is defined by empirical sensation, then what kind of experience is it to live in a kinship network with the dead (see Chapter 2)? Conversely, is the real known by divination or mystical insight, and how is that communicated to others (see Chapter 4)? Human beings in their incredible complexity subtly move back and forth between truth and illusion in thinking about moral matters.

The other dimensions of religious ethics have their own ways of intersecting with the epistemological and sematic questions, but each in some way argues a positive answer to the ontological question. Religious traditions tend to be expressions of moral realism, although, as noted, it is not clear that they are all naturalists. To be sure, there are certain scholars of religion

---

theories of truth" along with "neo-classical coherence theories" and pragmatist theories among others. Glanzberg notes the important connection between theories of truth and metaphysical views that support those theories, suggesting that modern discussions of correspondence theories of truth were at least partially predicated on an inadequate account of modern critiques of classical approaches to truth. One of the central issues has to do with how two different forms of idealism were developed in the modern period: the "metaphysical" or "ontological" idealism associated with George Berkeley (1685–1753 CE) and the "epistemological" or "formal" idealism associated with Immanuel Kant (1724–1804 CE). See Guyer, P. and Horstmann, R.-P. Idealism. *The Stanford Encyclopedia of Philosophy (Fall 2015 Edition)*, (ed. E.N. Zalta), http://plato. stanford.edu/archives/fall2015/entries/idealism (accessed 30 June 2019). The debate about correspondence theories, with its background of debates about idealism, was carried on by Bertrand Russell (1872–1970 CE) and F.H. Bradley (1846–1924 CE) in the twentieth century. See also Candlish, S. (2007). *The Russell/Bradley Dispute and Its Significance for Twentieth-century Philosophy*. New York: Palgrave Macmillan, and Hylton, P. (1990). *Russell, Idealism, and the Emergence of Analytic Philosophy*. Oxford: Clarendon Press.

who would disallow this classification of religious ethics, maintaining that religious discourse, like other kinds of normative discourse, cannot be realist because moral realism, they maintain, is not a viable philosophical option. They are left to consider how moral language (religious or otherwise) works in human life and that is a challenge considered in more detail below. Much of this debate hinges on other disputes about the viability of metaphysics (religious or otherwise) and the relationship of the human mind to the external world, all of which are questions that religions have examined for quite some time.

It is tempting to suppose that the question of truth in religions depends on how one resolves a series of either/or distinctions. Does one side with reason *or* religion? Does one side with a religion of "enlightenment" *or* a religion of "salvation"? Does one assume that the real religion is the religion of history *or* the religion of myth? Does one find "true religion" in doctrine *or* ritual? Does one begin thinking about ethics by starting with metaphysics *or* conceptual genealogy?

To examine the metaethical dimension in religious ethics, as one of five interrelated dimensions, frustrates any attempt to take an either/or approach to these questions. Those religions, like Christianity, directed at salvation, for example, also have accounts of enlightenment or insight into the nature of the world, and those directed at enlightenment, say, Buddhism, also posit basic human problems from which people must be delivered (either through their own effort or some other kind of assistance). Although there are certainly elements of religion which move beyond reason – especially reason understood in a limited technical sense – religions are not irrational insofar as they probe the usefulness, indeed the necessity, of rational discourse to reflect on belief and the perplexity of human life. Metaethics is certainly one dimension of religious ethics, but it must be related to the other dimensions in order to draw an accurate picture of human life, discern the reality of good and the tendency to evil, and form proper bases for moral judgments.

We turn now to an examination of two religious traditions that have taken seriously the metaethical questions examined here. In one sense, these are paradigmatic examples of religions of redemption (Christianity) and enlightenment (Buddhism). Yet as noted these traditions in fact complicate that neat and simple distinction. This is why it is important and interesting to compare them around the metaethical dimension of ethics. Thinkers in these traditions approach the question of truth and illusion, the human perplexity that founds metaethical reflection, in conversation with their religion's resources of thought and practice. Not surprisingly, these religious traditions yield different answers while raising similar concerns and illustrating similar dynamics. In a word, one can chart the analogies between Buddhism and Christianity on the metaethical dimension of religious ethics.

The Metaethical Dimension in Buddhism

Buddhism arose in southern Asia in the sixth century BCE, although the precise dates of the historical Buddha, Siddhārtha Gautama (Sanskrit)/Siddhattha Gotama, (Pāli) have been disputed for a number of years.[9] Beginning in India and spreading from there to Sri Lanka and on to other Asian countries and later to Europe and the Americas, Buddhism remains one of the statistically dominant traditions in much of Asia although it is also a recognizably global religion. There are many varieties of Buddhism, representing its historical and geographical diversity in Asia and in western countries. The development of distinct Buddhist traditions over the first several hundred years of its history produced three trajectories interpreting the Buddha's message (*sāsana*): *Theravāda* (the "way of the elders" which is the prominent form of Buddhism in Burma/Myanmar, Cambodia, Thailand, and Sri Lanka), *Mahāyāna* (the "great vehicle" which is the prominent form of Buddhism in China, Japan, Korea, and Vietnam), and *Vajrayāna* (the "diamond thunderbolt vehicle," which is the prominent form of Buddhism in Tibet).

The focus in this chapter will be on the early Theravāda and monastic interpretation of the tradition. Yet many of the elements introduced in the discussion of Theravāda Buddhist metaethics hold for the other Buddhist traditions as well.[10]

A basic feature of Buddhist teaching is the belief that Buddhist wisdom comes from three sources (or "three jewels" [*tiratana*]): the person of the Buddha, his law of life (Dhamma [Skt. Dharma]), and his community of followers (the Buddhist monastery or Saṅgha).[11] The Buddha is the source and living

---

9 Narain, A.K. (1993). Review of *The Dating of the Historical Buddha. Die Datierung des Historischen Buddha*, Part I (Symposien Zur Buddhismus Forschung, IV. I), Edited by Heinz Bechert. Gottingen: Vandenhoek & Ruprecht, 1991. *The Journal of the International Association of Buddhist Studies* 16 (1): 187–201. As Narain notes, "Although many dates have been proposed in the past for the death of the historical Buddha, the two most commonly accepted now are 543/44 and 483/86 BCE; the first by most Buddhists and the second by most modern scholars," (187) whereas Heinz Bechert who convened the symposium himself argued at a somewhat later date that "he is convinced that 'the *parinirvāṇa* of the Buddha must have taken place sometime before Alexander's campaign, i.e. between ca. 400 and ca. 350 BCE' and, while 'a somewhat later date is not inconceivable,' he considers Alexander's Indian campaign as the '*definitive terminus ante quem*'" (190).

10 Because we are drawing primarily from the Theravāda tradition, our references to Buddhist terms in this chapter will employ Pāli terminology from the Pāli canonical literature. The Pāli terms are close to the Buddhist Sanskrit terms that will be familiar to many readers (for example the Pāli term Dhamma denotes the same word as the Sanskrit term Dharma).

11 There are many ways of introducing the central "doctrinal" elements of Buddhist teaching, and many good introductions to Buddhist teaching and Buddhist life. Our introduction offers many of the same elements found in Clairmont, D.A. (2011). Why does the Buddha close his eyes in my Eden: a Buddhist ecological challenge and invitation to Christians. In: *Green Discipleship:*

exemplification of the wisdom of the Dhamma, and that wisdom is preserved, interpreted, taught, and further (if imperfectly) exemplified in the members of the Saṅgha. Stories of the person of the Buddha and his teaching come to us through early Buddhist writings. These are, again, divided roughly into three kinds: discourses between the Buddha and his followers, rules and stories from the establishment of the early monastic community, and a more systematic presentation of the early Buddhist community's analysis of human existence and its relationship to the natural world. Each of these is preserved in a different collection of Pāli writings of the Theravāda: the first is Sutta-piṭaka (the "basket of discourses"), the second is the Vinaya-piṭaka (the "basket of discipline"), and the third is the Abhidhamma-piṭaka (the "basket of highest wisdom"). Many of the stories and conversations between the Buddha and his disciples are repeated in various forms in Suttas and in the Vinaya.[12]

The canonical stories of the Buddha portray him teaching his followers what he had discovered about the world through his ascetic disciplines and the insights attained through meditation. Because Buddhist cosmology maintains that Buddhas ("enlightened ones") have arisen over several eons of history, with the historical Buddha of our era – Siddhattha Gotama – being the most recent teacher of Buddhist truth, the canonical stories often focus on the Buddha's memories of his previous lives. For example, in the *Mahāpadāna Sutta* (the Great Discourse on the Lineage, which is found in the canonical collection of longer discourses, the Dīgha Nikāya), the Buddha Gotama discusses the past life of the Buddha Vipassī.[13] As a prince whose father tries to insulate him from the sufferings of this world, Vipassī discovers on his chariot rides outside the palace four sights that prompt him to renounce his royal life: an old man, a sick man, a dead man, and "one who has gone forth from home to homelessness," the ascetic life. Upon questioning his chariot driver about these sights, he learns that even royal persons will grow old, will experience sickness, and will die so as never to see their family and friends again. The one who has renounced the world – who has "gone forth from home to homelessness" – is one who, as Vipassī's chariot driver explains, "truly follows the Dhamma, who truly lives in serenity, does good actions, performs meritorious deeds, is harmless and truly

Catholic Theological Ethics and the Environment, (ed. T. Winright), 340–358. Winona, MN: Anselm Academic. Among the most useful introductions to the relationship between Buddhist teachings and ethical matters that have informed our thinking about Buddhist metaethics, we recommend Gethin, R. (1998). *The Foundations of Buddhism*. Oxford: Oxford University Press, Keown, D. (1992). *The Nature of Buddhist Ethics*. New York: Palgrave, and Harvey, P. (2000). *An Introduction to Buddhist Ethics*. Cambridge: Cambridge University Press. Also see the chapters on Buddhism in *The Blackwell Companion to Religious Ethics*.

12 One could note analogy here between Jesus and his followers and the eventual codification of the "synoptic" Gospels (Matthew, Mark, Luke) and the Gospel of John.

13 Dīgha Nikāya 14. *The Long Discourses of the Buddha: A Translation of the Dīgha Nikāya* (1995). (trans. Maurice Walshe), 199–221. Boston: Wisdom Publications.

has compassion for living beings."[14] Here the problem of illusion and truth is inscribed in the life-story of Buddha himself. Is the seeming reality of this world and of death "real," or are these illusions?

A similar story is recounted of the Buddha Gotama in the work of the second-century Indian poet, Aśvaghoṣa, who in his *Life of the Buddha (Buddhacarita)* recounts the Buddha's journey from palace life to wandering asceticism to find a solution to the problem of suffering. Searching for those who might be able to provide him with the truth about the nature of the world and the human plight, he comes upon a forest ascetic who describes the goals of life for which the future Buddha's insight will provide a path. "'Desiring liberation in a world subject to destruction, I seek that happy indestructible abode, isolated from [humankind], with my thoughts unlike those of others, and with my sinful passions turned away from all objects of sense. Dwelling anywhere, at the root of a tree, or in an uninhabited house, a mountain or a forest, I wander without a family and without hope, a beggar ready for any fare, seeking only the highest good.'"[15]

The stories of the Buddha's struggle for enlightenment present him as going forth in search of an answer to a universally recognized human problem of suffering. He comes to a significant realization about the way the world is and how human beings ought to respond to it if they wish to address that problem. "Then, when the Bodhisattva had entered his dwelling alone, in a secluded spot, he thought, 'This world, alas, is in a sorry state: There is birth and decay, there is death and falling into other states and being reborn. And no one knows any way of escape from this suffering, this aging and this death. When will deliverance be found from this suffering, this aging and death?'"[16] What he discovered through sustained meditation was an insight into the true nature of reality and of the human plight situated within this world. The problem is how people should respond, given the nature of the world. The *Dhammapada*, an early Pāli text in pithy verses summarizing the Buddha's teaching, asserts that "When through wisdom one perceives, 'All saṅkhāras [conditioned realities] are transient,' then one is detached as to misery. This is the path of purity. When through wisdom one perceives, 'All saṅkhāras are suffering, then one is detached as to misery. This is the path of purity. When through wisdom one perceives, 'All dhammas are without self,' then one is detached as to misery.

14 Ibid., 210.
15 Buddhacarita III.18–19. Max Müller, F. (1894). *Sacred Books of the East*, vol. 49, 52. Oxford: Clarendon Press. See also Aśvaghoṣa. (2008). *Life of the Buddha* (trans. P. Olivelle). New York: New York University/JJC Foundation; Aśvaghoṣa. (2009). *Buddhacarita: In Praise of Buddha's Acts*, (trans. C. Willemen). Berkeley: Numata Center for Buddhist Translation and Research.
16 *Mahāpadāna Sutta* 2.18. Dīgha Nikāya 14; *The Long Discourses of the Buddha: A Translation of the Dīgha Nikāya* (1995). (trans. M. Walshe), 210–211. Boston: Wisdom Publications. In Christianity, see St. Paul's plea in Romans 7:24. "Wretched man that I am! Who will rescue me from this body of death?"

This is the path of purity."[17] These are the so-called three characteristics (*tilak-khana*) of all reality: impermanent [transient] (*anicca*), unsatisfactory [suffering] (*dukkha*), and not-self (*anattā*). Each of these characteristics is true of every thing that exists and of the most basic components of all things that exist. In this way, the nature of human beings, so the Buddha argues, is continuous with the nature of other things and so entails a complex form of realism, as we will see.

The most commonly referenced expression of these characteristics is an expansion of the second characteristic (unsatisfactoriness), and is commonly called the Four Noble Truths basic to Buddhist metaethics, especially about the nature of reality:

1) Suffering/unsatisfactoriness (*dukkha*) is the truth of all things.
2) There is a cause (*samudaya*) of suffering/unsatisfactoriness and it is found in craving (*taṇhā*).
3) There is a cessation (*nirodha*) to unsatisfactoriness and it is the cessation of craving.
4) There is a path (*magga*) of eight steps that leads to the cessation of this unsatisfactoriness.

The craving that is the cause of suffering has three roots, the Buddha argues: greed (*rāga/lobha*), delusion (*moha*), and hatred (*dosa*). Suffering (and liberation from it) depends on one's response to the world as it really exists. This means that one must understand rightly what is being experienced and why one is experiencing it in the way that one is. As Thanissaro Bhikkhu explains, "These four truths are best understood, not as beliefs, but as categories of experience. They offer an alternative to the ordinary way we categorize what we can know and describe, in terms of me/not me, and being/not being. These ordinary categories create trouble, for the attempt to maintain full being for one's sense of 'me' is a stressful effort doomed to failure, in that all of the components of that 'me' are inconstant, stressful, and thus not worthy of identifying as 'me' or 'mine'."[18] The usual ontological categories for understanding reality (e.g. being/non-being; I/not-I; thing/no-thing) in fact breed illusion and therefore suffering. The Buddha offers a view of how the world is and what is going on in our typical response to it (the descriptive dimension of ethics) and offers a vision of what we ought to do in response to this situation (the normative dimension). Within this response is an argument for how we determine the truth of the world (metaphysics) and how we determine the truth of our proper response (metaethics). The Buddha also offers a program for living this response. This program is a version of the "spiral of the religious life" explored in Chapter 3.

---

17 *Dhammapada* 20.277–9. *The Dhammapada*, (1987). (ed. J.R. Carter and M. Palihawadana). New York and Oxford: Oxford University Press.
18 Thanissarao Bhikkhu. (1999). "Introduction" to "The Four Noble Truths." http://www.accesstoinsight.org/lib/study/truths.html (accessed 20 June 2019).

Traditional Buddhist teaching unfolds this spiral path or program of life through a series of lists, the first of which is the Noble Eightfold Path. This path is divided into three groups: morality, concentration, and wisdom. *Sīla*, which we translate as morality to mark the accepted standards of proper Buddhist behavior, is universal in the sense that it is understood to be an applicable solution to everyone who recognizes with the Buddha the perennial problem of suffering.[19] It has three parts: right speech (*sammāvācā*), right action (*sammākammanta*), right livelihood (*sammājīva*). The admonition to right speech counsels that we refrain from any speech that is knowingly false, meant to defame the reputation of another, harsh in tone or content, or speech that has no purpose but to fill time or perpetuate rumors about others (what we commonly call gossip). The admonition to right action focuses on avoiding any kind of harm to other living beings. This element of the path is further unfolded in the list of five precepts (*pañcasīla*) incumbent upon all Buddhist lay persons (the same list, with some additional elements, is also required of nuns and monks): that one not take the life of another, that one not take what is not given, that one avoid wrong conduct in sexual matters, that one not use false speech (a link to the previous elements in the eightfold path), and that one avoid intoxicants which lead to reckless and hurtful behaviors of many kinds.[20]

---

19 Bhikkhu Bodhi gives the following summary of canonical uses of the term *sīla*. "The Pali word we have been translating as 'moral discipline', *sila*, appears in the texts with several overlapping meanings all connected with right conduct. In some contexts it means action conforming to moral principles, in others the principles themselves, in still others the virtuous qualities of character that result from the observance of moral principles. *Sila* in the sense of precepts or principles represents the formalistic side of the ethical training, *sila* as virtue the animating spirit, and *sila* as right conduct the expression of virtue in real-life situations. Often *sila* is formally defined as abstinence from unwholesome bodily and verbal action. This definition, with its stress on outer action, appears superficial. Other explanations, however, make up for the deficiency and reveal that there is more to *sila* than is evident at first glance. The Abhidhamma, for example, equates *sila* with the mental factors of abstinence *(viratiyo)* — right speech, right action, and right livelihood – an equation which makes it clear that what is really being cultivated through the observance of moral precepts is the mind. Thus while the training in *sila* brings the 'public' benefit of inhibiting socially detrimental actions, it entails the personal benefit of mental purification, preventing the defilements from dictating to us what lines of conduct we should follow. The English word "morality" and its derivatives suggest a sense of obligation and constraint quite foreign to the Buddhist conception of sila; this connotation probably enters from the theistic background to Western ethics. Buddhism, with its nontheistic framework, grounds its ethics, not on the notion of obedience, but on that of harmony. In fact, the commentaries explain the word sila by another word, samadhana, meaning 'harmony' or 'coordination.'" See Bhikkhu Bodhi, "The noble eightfold path: The way to end suffering," Access to Insight (Legacy Edition), http://www.accesstoinsight.org/lib/authors/bodhi/waytoend.html (30 November 2013). However, as we know from previous chapters, this is far too simple an account either of "Western" or of "theistic" ethics.

20 The list of five precepts is extended for monks and nuns to include a total of 10 precepts. The list includes the practices of not eating after midday, avoiding frivolity and ornamentation, sleeping only in modest beds, avoiding monetary exchange of gold and silver, and wearing

The admonition to right livelihood links the previous two elements to the ways that one earns a living, and counsels Buddhists to avoid any means of material support or accumulation of wealth that is intrinsically harmful to oneself or others. "One should acquire it only by legal means, not illegally; one should acquire it peacefully, without coercion or violence; one should acquire it honestly, not by trickery or deceit; and one should acquire it in ways which do not entail harm and suffering for others. The Buddha mentions five specific kinds of livelihood which bring harm to others and are therefore to be avoided: dealing in weapons, in living beings (including raising animals for slaughter as well as slave trade and prostitution), in meat production and butchery, in poisons, and in intoxicants (AN 5:177). He further names several dishonest means of gaining wealth which fall under wrong livelihood: practicing deceit, treachery, soothsaying, trickery, and usury (MN 117)."[21]

The second major section of the eightfold path is concentration (*samādhi*) and focuses on those actions that develop a quality of mind that is tranquil, focused, and wholesome. Here epistemological metaethical questions are addressed. Focusing the mind is aided by morality and has as its goal sustaining insight and wisdom (the third division of the path). There are three steps in the concentration section: right effort (*sammāvāyāma*), right mindfulness (*sammāsati*), and right concentration (*sammāsamādhi*). The first of these steps points to what we might recognize as the will (*cetanā*) or effort (*viriya*) to do something, which can be either wholesome or unwholesome in that to which it is directed.[22] The second step is mindfulness that is a practice of awareness of the body and its surroundings without being attached to any of the objects or events of which one is aware. Its purpose is both to settle the mind and free it from distractions (which requires the effort of the previous step) in order to be able to attain a single pointed focus on the present reality from which insight springs. The step begins with meditation on the body before progressing to the feelings and states of mind that arise in relation to the body. The third step is a kind of attentiveness or singular focus on the directed mind that arises in meditation. It has two goals – serenity (*samatha*) and insight (*vipassanā*) – and their own objects of mental focus that have been developed through Buddhist medi-

---

clothing only in a dignified way. Canonical reference to this list may be found in the Brahmajāla Sutta. (1995). *The Long Discourses of the Buddha: A Translation of the Dīgha Nikāya* (trans. Maurice Walshe), 67–90. Boston: Wisdom Publications.

21 See Bhikkhu Bodhi, "The noble eightfold path: The way to end suffering," Access to Insight (Legacy Edition), http://www.accesstoinsight.org/lib/authors/bodhi/waytoend.html (accessed 30 November 2013).

22 The section of the Pāli canon called the Abhidhamma offers a highly technical explanation of the nature of reality and the place of the human being's mental life within that reality. The basic schema proposed there classifies reality according to kinds of *dhamma* (basic units of reality). Among these one finds a list of 52 mental factors (*cetāsikas*) of which one is effort or energy (*viriya*).

tative practice ranging from the foulness of bodily processes to events in the life of the Buddha. Each is understood to produce a particular effect in meditation depending on the temperament of the one beginning the practice (some are understood to be more appropriate beginning points than others).

The third section of the eightfold path – insight wisdom (*paññā*) – is both the beginning and the end of the path (so we could have placed these sections at the beginning rather than at the end of our explanation). As the beginning of the path, it marks the content of Buddhist teaching about the Four Noble Truths, and so semantic questions, but also the roots of unwholesome acts. As the end of the path, it marks the goal of Buddhist practice that is insight into the nature of the human problem (suffering caused by attachment) and the proper context for understanding the other divisions of the path (*sīla* and *samādhi*). It has two components: right view/understanding (*sammādiṭṭhi*) and right thought/intention (*sammāsaṅkappa*). The former is linked to the Buddhist teaching on wholesome and unwholesome actions and the fruits of those actions which will necessarily follow as an effect from a cause (a process called *kamma* [Skt., *karma*]). In this way it provides a summary of the Buddhist view of morality as a universal causal system or what we might call a certain expression of natural law that links moral and physical causation.[23] The latter – right thinking – links the content of Buddhist wisdom with the active process of moral transformation in the other parts of the path.

Because this Buddhist account of wisdom is rather far-reaching, and because it is closely linked to an account of causality with significant moral implications, it is tempting to describe this as a metaphysically grounded approach to religious ethics. The Buddhist account of causality is formulated in the teaching on the Law of Dependent Co-Origination (*paticcasamuppāda*). Often depicted as a circle of linked causal elements, this teaching purports to show how mental events are linked to human suffering and also how lives continue one to the next depending on the kind of karmic fruit that ripens as a result of prior conditions – a process called the cycle of rebirth (*saṃsāra*). The 12 points on the circle are:

1) Ignorance (*avijjā*)
2) Mental Formations (*saṅkhāra*)
3) Consciousness (*viññāṇa*)
4) Mind–Body (*nāma-rūpa*)
5) Six-Sense Bases (*saḷāyatana*)
6) Contact (*phassa*)
7) Sensation (*vedanā*)

---

23 For an examination of Buddhist ethics as a kind of natural law which explores important differences between Buddhist and Christian appropriations of the term, see Payutto, P.P. (1995). *Buddhadhamma: Natural Laws and Values for Life* (trans. G.A. Olson). Albany, NY: SUNY Press.

8) Craving (*taṇhā*)
9) Clinging (*upādāna*)
10) Becoming (*bhava*)
11) Birth (*jāti*)
12) Death and Decay (*jarā-marana*)

These 12 causal conditions are linked to the process of successive rebirths.

> This account, the twelve-linked chain of dependent origination, is tradi-
> tionally understood as describing a sequence that takes place over three
> successive lives. In one life there occurs (1) ignorance (namely ignorance
> of the fact that all sentient existence is characterized by impermanence,
> suffering and non-self), and because of its occurrence there occur (2)
> volitions (*saṃskāra*) [Pali, *saṇkhāra*], understood as the active forces in
> karma. It is in dependence on these volitions in the one life that there
> occurs (3) consciousness in the next life. That is, rebirth (in the form of
> the first moment of consciousness in a new life) occurs because of the
> desires that led to the performance of actions in the past life. On this
> consciousness in turn depends the occurrence of (4) a sentient body.
> That is, it is due to that first moment of rebirth consciousness that the
> organized matter of the fetal body comes to be a sentient being. On the
> existence of the sentient body in turn depend (5) the six organs of sense
> (the organs of the five external senses plus an 'inner sense' that is aware
> of inner states such as pain). On these depend (6) contact or sensory
> stimulation. And given sensory stimulation there arises (7) feeling, that
> is, the hedonic states of pleasure, pain, and indifference. Feeling in turn
> causes (8) desire, and desire leads to (9) appropriation (*upādāna*), the
> attitude whereby one takes certain things as being 'me' or 'mine.' In
> dependence on appropriation there originates (10) becoming. This con-
> sists of the volitions that bring about the next rebirth, as well as the psy-
> chological elements making up the sentient body in that rebirth. In
> dependence on this there is (11) birth, that is, rebirth into the third life.
> And in dependence on birth there is (12) old age and death, here stand-
> ing for all existential suffering.[24]

These conditions account for the basic kinds of causes that affect the life process, both physical and mental. However, one might also ask what it is that
finally exists in the world that is subject to this life process. This explanation of
existence is crucial to a Buddhist metaethics because it is attempting to give a
comprehensive account of life that is coherent, resonates with the experience

---

24 Siderits, M. (2007). *Buddhism as Philosophy: An Introduction*, 22. Indianapolis and
Cambridge: Hackett Publishing.

of suffering, and avoids and answers the errors of other positions (addressed previously).

To this question, Buddhist teaching argues that sensible realities (both human beings and other creatures) are composed of five aggregates (*khandhas*). These units, although they can be further analyzed into the more specific kinds with specific functions, remain the most basic categories of reflective human experience, and, when combined in various ways, give rise to the whole range of conditioned experience (both pleasant, unpleasant, and neutral) that constitutes human life.

1) Name-Form (*nāma-rūpa*)
2) Feeling (*vedanā*)
3) Perception (*saññā*)
4) Mental Formations/Active Thinking (*saṅkhāra*)
5) Consciousness (*viññāṇa*)

Buddhist thinkers engaged in further exposition of these basic units of analysis by considering how the mental factors on this list give rise to certain kinds of consciousness, as indicated in Figure 6.2. For the five *khandhas* that offer the main categories into which reality is grouped, there is a further division into more precise kinds of physical and mental realities. This more precise classification is an analysis of how the *dhammas* (elements/phenomenon), when combined in various ways, give rise to the *khandhas* (aggregates). There is also a question about what if any realities exist that are not conditioned. Figure 6.2 presents the relationship between the aggregates and the elements.[25]

In offering this analysis of reality for the sake of the spiritual life, the question for thinkers was threefold: (i) Are there different kinds of conditioned reality, and, among these kinds, is there anything that is real yet not subject to the casual conditioning that the teaching on dependent co-origination addresses? (ii) When one analyzes conditioned realities into their most basic components, do those most basic units (*dhammas*) have some kind of stable essence that, one could argue, violates two of the three characteristics of reality noted earlier: that is, impermanent (*anicca*) and not-self (*anattā*)? (iii) Given that this system of analysis is closely related to what Buddhist thinkers claim to have discovered through meditative practice, to what extent is the mode of analysis

25 This table, with additional tables offering a more detailed analysis of this particular line of Theravāda Buddhist teaching, is presented in Clairmont, D.A. (2010). Theravada Buddhist Abhidhamma and moral development: Lists and narratives in the practice of religious ethics. *Journal of the Society of Christian Ethics* 30 (2): 171–193 and Clairmont, D.A. (2011). *Moral Struggle and Religious Ethics: On the Person as Classic in Comparative – Theological Contexts.* Malden, MA: Wiley-Blackwell. These were developed from the treatments of Theravāda Buddhist Abhidhamma philosophy in the edition of the *Abhidhammattha Sangaha* edited by Bhikkhu Bodhi (Onalaska: BPS Pariyatti, 1999) and from Gethin, R.M.L. (2001). *The Buddhist Path to Awakening.* Oxford: Oneworld.

Khandhas (aggregates)	Dhammas (things: phenomena)	
	Conditioned	Unconditioned
Rūpa (material/form phenomena)	Rūpa	Nibbāna [Skt., Nirvāṇa]
Vedanā (feeling)	Cetāsika (mental factors)	
Saññā (sensation)		
Saṅkhāra (mental formations)		
Viññāṇa (consciousness)	Citta (kinds of consciousness)	

Figure 6.2 The relationship of Khandhas to Dhammas.

within the system derived from that practice or is it, rather, a logical elaboration of what Buddhists discover in meditative practice? This last point is worth pondering in terms of the metaethics of a Buddhist moral outlook. At least in theory, *Theravāda* Buddhist thinkers are suggesting that an account of metaphysics is both deeply experiential, that is, drawn from the experience of meditation by anyone who will commit themselves to this form of training, and universal in scope because anyone can enter into this practice of meditation and, at least in theory, understand the exposition of basic elements and their aggregates offered in this account.

"[T]he path evolves through its three stages, with moral discipline as the foundation for concentration, concentration the foundation for wisdom, and wisdom the direct instrument for reaching liberation."[26] Yet we should not think about each element as something to complete before moving on to the next one. As with the "spiral" of the religious life (see Chapter 3) and the method of validation by moving in and through the dimensions of religious

---

26 Bhikkhu Bodhi, "The noble eightfold path: The way to end suffering," Access to Insight (Legacy Edition), http://www.accesstoinsight.org/lib/authors/bodhi/waytoend.html (30 November 2013).

ethics, there is not a rigid direction of thought or life. "The eight factors of the Noble Eightfold Path are not steps to be followed in sequence, one after another. They can be more aptly described as components rather than as steps, comparable to the intertwining strands of a single cable that requires the contributions of all the strands for maximum strength. With a certain degree of progress all eight factors can be present simultaneously, each supporting the others. However, until that point is reached, some sequence in the unfolding of the path is inevitable."[27] And so it is, analogously, with the method of validation in the movement among the complex dimensions of religious ethics. This suggests that the eightfold path, and the method of validation proposed here, include not only standards for right behavior, but a way of thinking about moral development or virtue. In order to see the world rightly, one must commit to a certain way of life through which one comes to see oneself and one's environment as it truly is, and thus one returns to these foundational disciplines with a deeper awareness of the connection between what one does and what one knows and values.

To what extent does Buddhist teaching, including the analysis just offered, track familiar questions and categories in Western ethics? In an essay on approaches to Buddhist ethics, one scholar posed the question "Is there a moral theory in Theravāda Buddhism?" Focusing on the diversity one finds among different kinds of Buddhist narrative and philosophical analysis, Buddhist ethics is characterized by what is called *particularism* with respect to the problem of criteria. This is the epistemological view according to which "in order to know the criteria for knowledge (i.e. to distinguish between correct and incorrect criteria), we must already be able to recognize its instances."[28] On this account, particularism may be differentiated from *methodism* in establishing epistemological criteria. Here the view is that "in order to recognize instances, and thus to determine the extent of knowledge, we must know the criteria for it."[29] A *particularist* would hold that we must first recognize acts of greed

---

27 Ibid.
28 Hallisey, C. (1996). Ethical particularism in Theravāda Buddhism. *Journal of Buddhist Ethics* 3:37–38.
29 Ibid., 38. Hallisey draws these distinction from the work of the twentieth-century philosophers Roderick Chisholm and W.D. Ross. Observing a tendency in recent Buddhist ethics, Hallisey notes that "Most studies of Buddhist ethics seem to have approached their task as if it were clear the first proposition is true ['[I]n order to recognize instances, and thus to determine the extent, of knowledge, we must know the criteria for it'"] and the second false ['[I]n order to know the criteria for knowledge (i.e. to distinguish between correct and incorrect criteria), we must already be able to recognize its instances.'] – apparently assuming that only by theoretically knowing the criteria for ethical knowledge can we recognize any particular instance of morality as such. In approaching their task in this manner, they have embraced what Roderick Chisholm calls *methodism*, since their concern has been with identifying the method by which Buddhists have decided whether a particular action or character trait is a good one; one of the

before defining the "criteria" for a greedy act, like a wealthy man hoarding gold. The *methodist* would insist, contrariwise, that we have to have a criterion of a "greedy act" in order to recognize instances of greed as in fact instances of greed. So, one needs the concept "greed" and some idea of why it is a moral vice in order to see the wealthy man's hoarding of gold as an example of "greed." Ethical knowledge is thereby tied to the knowledge of and questions about moral meaning.

Resisting attempts by scholars to portray Buddhist ethics as either a species of consequentialism[30] or a variety of virtue ethics,[31] Charles Hallisey argues that Buddhist ethics can be rightly understood only if one examines the various genres through which one can glimpse the many ways in which Buddhists attend to moral questions. This includes Buddhist narratives and the commentaries on Buddhist narratives and philosophical treatises that themselves often appeal to stories to clarify the use of particular moral terminology. "As a historical phenomenon, the Theravāda Buddhist tradition (not to speak of Buddhism more generally) has been internally diverse, just as Islam, Christianity, Judaism, or Hinduism have been; and just as it is certainly inappropriate to speak of all of Christianity as teleological or deontological, so it is with the Buddhist traditions."[32] That has been a point, of course, of this entire book about the religions in general.

What do we make of this discussion of Buddhist ethics in light of the overview of metaethics noted here? First, a focus on religious texts (and especially narratives) will put on display the variety of values recognized by a community and the many ways they look to pursue those values consonant with their moral understanding of the world. This does not mean that theoretical approaches to these religious accounts of the good, the responsible, and the right are somehow out of place. Quite the opposite: the search for the good, the responsible, and the right happen within a given cosmology that makes claims about the "search for the good in light of the limits and possibilities of the real."[33] This has been our point about the penchant for *realism* among the religions. Second, religious ethics is characterized, as noted previously, by an interplay among the

---

characteristics of methodism is a high regard for consistency, a characteristic that has been a guiding principle in much of our work" (37–38).

30 Kalupahana, D. (1976) *Buddhist Philosophy: A Historical Analysis*, 61. Honolulu: University Press of Hawaii and de Silva, P. (1991). Buddhist ethics. In: *A Companion to Ethics*, (ed. P. Singer), 62. Oxford: Blackwell cited in Keown, D. (1996). Karma, character, and consequentialism. *Journal of Religious Ethics* 24:330. Also see the various articles on Buddhism in *The Blackwell Companion to Religious Ethics*.

31 Keown, D. (1996). Karma, character, and consequentialism. *Journal of Religious Ethics* 24: 329–350.

32 Hallisey, C. (1996). Ethical particularism in Theravāda Buddhism. *Journal of Buddhist Ethics* 3: 35.

33 Reeder, J.P. Jr. (1998). What is a religious ethic? *Journal of Religious Ethics* 25 (3): 160.

interrelated dimensions of thinking about moral questions. The metaethical dimension is simply that dimension of thinking that articulates criteria and movement among dimensions in response to other and even rival positions.

So, to hold that the metaethical is one dimension in a consideration of religious ethics means that debates about moral theory are connected to the other dimensions on which they depend for their meaning and application. And this account of the metaethical dimension should be seen as informed by the substantive engagement with Buddhist and other religious traditions. But this also means that although we judge that Buddhism resembles a kind of naturalist moral realism, classifying it this way does not override those moments when its particular forms of moral discourse do not fit neatly within that classification. Moreover, the relationship between the metaethical, normative, and practical in the case study of ecological ethics examined next will show moments when the practical concern will press on aspects of the metaethical by way of challenge and further clarification. This is what it means to think multidimensionally and hermeneutically in religious ethics.

The Metaethical Dimension in Christianity

Before we move into a consideration of how the metaethical, normative, and practical dimensions relate in ecological ethics, let us address briefly the metaethical dimension in Christian ethics. There are at least four dominant and often interrelated trajectories of moral reflection that have developed in Christian ethics and each of these finds precedents in certain philosophical emphases that have been joined to Christian views: the divine command trajectory, the natural law trajectory, the highest good trajectory, and the trajectory of virtues.[34] Given the complex interaction among the early Christian movement and the surrounding Greco-Roman world, each trajectory bears a certain connection to metaethics in classical philosophy. Yet each also has a distinctive quality when compared with other expressions of the metaethical in religious ethics, especially the Buddhist expression explored previously. As a discussion in metaethics, the question tends to be focused on what if any grounding exists for the moral norms articulated in the Christian community, and how, if at all, those norms can be justified across cultures and traditions. Each of these trajectories also offers a different way of thinking about the relations of the other four dimensions to the metaethical dimension. Further, each gives its own specific account of the "spiral" of the religious life (see Chapter 3)

---

34 See Porter, J. (2005). Trajectories in Christian ethics. In: *The Blackwell Companion to Religious Ethics*, (ed. W. Schweiker), 227–236. Malden, MA: Blackwell. We have added the "highest good" trajectory to Porter's discussion.

and, at their best, a multidimensional method of validating their claims. Our task is not to adjudicate among these strands of thought but to see how they approach questions in metaethics.

Let us begin with divine command ethics, a mode of ethics that returns us to the famous Euthyphro Problem explored in Chapter 1. In its most simple and direct forms, a divine command ethics claims that something is good or bad, or right or wrong, or just or unjust (and so involving a whole range of moral concepts) because it is commanded or forbidden by God. Murder is wrong, because that is God's command. Justice is good for the same reason. God's commands can come in many forms: a direct command to an individual, through sacred revealed texts, and, for Christians, in the life and teaching of Jesus Christ. Other theistic traditions that speak of God's command also have specific ways or forms in which the command of God is given and heard. Furthermore, in the monotheistic traditions (Christianity, Judaism, Islam) the command of God is an expression of God's will and being and therefore per-fectly good and perfectly right. Because God is that which is ultimately real, important, and empowering, following the commands of God (say, through *Torah* for Jews, the *Qur'ān* in Islam, or discipleship to Christ) is a way to make contact with divine power. "Divine command theories are characterized by the fact that they distinguish God's will or authority from other aspects of divine reality and identify this aspect as the ground of morality, or as the sole source of morality, which is set over and against other putative sources of moral obligation."[35] What distinguishes divine command approaches to ethics from other approaches in the Christian tradition is their insistence on the priority of God's commands as the grounding of what people are obliged to do and to be.

Not surprisingly, there are many versions of the divine command approach, some of which focus more on the properties of the God who issues commands (God is loving; God is just), others on the epistemological necessity of a divine lawgiver (or some kind of equivalent foundational source of moral norms), that is, how we know what is just is that God has commanded it and we receive this command in specific form. Some medieval Christian approaches to analyzing the nature and quality of God's commands, say, the Franciscans John Duns Scotus (1266–1308 CE) and William of Ockham (1285–1349 CE), focused on the attributes of God in which human beings shared as creatures created in the image of God such as the faculties of reason and will. They argued that God's free will could in theory command actions that contradicted what human beings could know about God and God's standards of goodness and right con-duct through reason and prior revelation. The danger, not unlike the Euthyphro problem, is that God might – at least in theory – command what we would

---

35 Ibid., 228.

commonly understand as wrong or even evil, say the murder of the innocent.[36] If God commands the action, it is good and right by definition. This problem has led to other developments.

Recent approaches to divine command ethics have emphasized theoretical questions, such as the one just noted: the possibility that God's command could "suspend" a rationally accepted standard of human morality or that human attempts to establish a moral order apart from God's commands, based on human reason alone or even an account of human beings' basic natural capacities, ultimately are betrayals of God and of God's place as the author of the moral order.[37] In such approaches, we can discern how divine command theories exhibit a metaethical dimension. By prioritizing the command of God at the expense of an account of human nature or the workings of human reason, divine command theories can be accused of focusing exclusively on one dimension (the normative) at the expense of attending sufficiently to the other dimensions (for example, the descriptive or the practical). Nevertheless, one could imagine a divine command metaethics that would focus on God's command expressed through the dimensions of religious ethics and, further, that the whole "spiral" of the religious life is commanded by God.

A second line of approaches to metaethical questions in Christian ethics comes from the tradition of natural law theology. Natural law should not be confused with what modern sciences has called the "laws of nature," although, we will note, there is some connection. Specifically, "natural law" refers to (i) the capacity of the human mind to grasp the most basic of moral principles, say, justice and seeking the good, and (ii) that the good of a living being must be understood with respect to the flourishing of its specific nature, that is, *moral naturalism*. So, natural law approaches argue that "[w]hile moral norms were thought to reflect God's will, they were also seen as reflections of God's wisdom and benevolence, insofar as they reflected exigencies of reason or human nature."[38] At issue, then, is the moral significance, if any, of the connection between human reason and the natural world. This includes reflection on the moral significance of naturally occurring biological patterns (e.g. the

---

36 The command to Abraham to sacrifice his son Isaac is an example. The story has generated thought among Jews, calling it the Binding of Isaac or the Akedah (*Aqedah*). It is also found in Islamic thought. Among Christians it has been hotly debated since the publication in 1843 of Søren Kierkegaard's seminal work, *Fear and Trembling*. He argued that God's command entailed a "teleological suspension of the ethical" where the individual's God-relation (Abraham's) can suspend normal ethical relations, say, father to son. We cannot explore these issues here. However, it is important to note that each of the so-called Abrahamic religions (Islam, Judaism and Christianity) must wrestle with this question. The various interpretations are instances of the religions seeking to render productive, rather than destructive, a perplexity or *aporia* of religious life, that a loving God could command the sacrifice of an innocent son, Isaac.

37 Porter, 228–229.

38 Ibid.

human reproductive cycle), and social groupings in human communities (e.g. families) but, more significantly, on the transcultural conversation about wisdom and the shared quest to live a good life and help neighbors also to seek and achieve some degree of human flourishing. Discussed in Chapter 3, the idea is that in order for any living creature to flourish, one needs to know its range of needs and the goods that fulfill them. That is the point of "naturalism" in ethics.

There were many precursors to the natural law tradition in Christian thought, including the Greek and Roman Stoics and the tradition of Hebrew wisdom literature. "What these have in common, however, is a view of morality which grounds it in intrinsic, ordered structures of being, in contrast to approaches that emphasize authoritative will."[39] Although natural law writing characterized medieval legal thinking as well as theology, perhaps the most well-known account was offered by Thomas Aquinas. "Aquinas also endorses the almost unanimous view that the Decalogue (the 10 Commandments) offers a summary of the precepts of the natural law."[40] For natural law thinkers like Aquinas, it is not contrary to human reason or experience or our knowledge of living things that God commands a summary of the natural law. Natural law thinking of various kinds assumes a rationally intelligible world from which various human projects can be developed which are either conducive to, or ultimately in contradiction with, a basic desire for human happiness. Aquinas even insists that God's grace does not destroy or recreate human nature but rather perfects nature.

In the account developed by Thomas Aquinas, natural law is a *law* in the sense that it is an "ordinance of reason directed to the common good promulgated by the one who has care of the community."[41] Thomas identifies four interlocking kinds of law: eternal, natural, human, and divine law. Natural law, again, is simply the human mind's participation in the eternal law of God. Reason which grasps the precepts of natural law, is a basic capacity of human nature by which people can discern what is good for them, both individually and for the familial and social groups that support and sustain them. It is connected to a divine ordering of the world, the *Logos*, that is then incarnate in the Christ, and the particular commands issued by a divine promulgator to sustain the world in that order, but, again, it is not in contradiction with them. Indeed, some commandments provide a summary of what that rational ordering would entail in a form that would be broadly acceptable to those who do not share the same religious framework. In this way, natural law ethics seeks a universal outlook while being attentive to the needs and goods for the flourishing of creatures, including persons and communities.

---

39 Ibid., 229.
40 Ibid., 230.
41 Thomas Aquinas, *Summa Theologiae*, I-II Q90 a4.

More recent appropriations of the earlier natural law tradition have linked it with different metaphysical systems, and its status today is disputed based on the relative weight it gives to reason and to the moral significance of naturally occurring biological processes. In terms of religious ethics as a whole, a natural law approach can, but need not, give priority to the descriptive and the practical dimensions of ethics in that it offers an account of human life that is recognizably structured through the pursuit of basic goods, offering modest practical constraints on those goods based on principles that tend to establish broad public agreement.

With respect to the typology of metaethics noted previously, natural law accounts are viewed as naturalist versions of moral realism, whereas divine command accounts tend to be viewed as examples of moral realism of a non-naturalist variety. In both cases, the moral order is real because God, who is being and goodness itself, is the source of morality and reality. Yet the means by which one has access to morality differs based on the extent to which one views human reason as a reliable guide for knowledge of God and human well-being. Here then are interesting similarities and differences, and so analogies, with Buddhist metaethics. Divine command ethics, like the Buddhist version noted, insists that what us ultimately good is beyond or transcends the processes of the "world" even as it provide structure to and refuge from that "world." Yet, a divine command ethics relies on the idea of an all-knowing and all-powerful God that is unintelligible in the Buddhist outlook and in fact could lead to suffering if one clings to one's beliefs about God. Contrariwise, natural law thought, like Buddhist metaethics, claims that we must grasp the nature of creatures and even reality as a whole if we are to see happiness or avoid suffering. Yet natural law thinking, unlike Buddhist thought, holds that these realities are substances that have ultimate existence and perfection in God rather than being phenomena arising from codependent origination and ultimately fleeting. The question then becomes, which of these positions best meets the four criteria of validation noted earlier in this chapter?

A third trajectory of metaethical reflection explores human aspirations to pure goodness or perfection rather than divine commands, natural law, or virtues. This third strand is interrelated with other Christian metaethical approaches simply because Christians hold that God is the highest good and a proper relation to the God revealed in Christ defines human flourishing. Still, many ancient Christian thinkers, like St. Augustine, as well as some modern thinkers explore the perfect of human being through divine grace and proper love of God and neighbor. Indeed, Orthodox Christian believe in the divinization of human beings, *theosis*, as the highest good that is knowable in Christ, is ultimately real, and is the perfection not the destruction of human nature.

A pointed example of this trajectory of thought is found in Augustine's treatise *On the Morals of the Catholic Church* (*de Moribus Ecclesiae Catholicae*) and other works. Augustine asked, in trying to refute other positions and thus establish the truth of Christian faith, that if one seeks ultimate happiness or well-being, it must be some state or reality that (i) is permanent and so unchangeable, (ii) supremely good or nothing is better than it, and (iii) cannot be lost against one's will and thus can truly be one's own. The highest good, so defined, is an object of human love and thus the question becomes, what is the proper object of that love, what is the highest good?

Augustine examines first the nature of human beings as a composite of body and soul and points out that the best part of humans is the soul, which is created eternal, rather than the changeable human body. If that is the case, then the issue is what is the highest good of the soul. This must be God, Augustine reasons, because nothing is better or more real than God, God is unchangeable in his will, and the soul can be related to God through the love of God as well as others and oneself in God. Yet in order to be united to God, and thus not to lose the highest good against one's will, the soul must be perfected, which it is through the virtues of temperance, fortitude, justice, and prudence. But these virtues, he argues, are nothing but forms of Christian love, *caritas*. And through the love of God, the neighbor (body and soul) and oneself in God (body and soul) one is united to God and thus to the highest good. And this highest good, that is, God, is what is ultimately real, important, and empowered through grace.

Notice the metaethical argument made by Augustine. Examining the concept of the highest good, a semantic analysis, and attitude or aspiration entailed in the concept, he links this understanding to an ontological claim about human beings (we are body *and* soul). Given those insights he then asks, how it is that humans can attain the highest good, become united with God? The perfection of the human is through a life of love that is also and at the same time a life of virtue and one of happiness, a union with the highest good. But how do we know this God, and that God is gracious to us? Augustine answers this epistemological question by turning to Holy Scripture that reveals in Christ the love and grace of God for human beings. And in this way, he contends, Christian faith is the most valid morality against all rivals.

"Blessed are the pure in heart, for they will see God." The idea of a union with God, seeing or beholding God, as the highest human good goes back to Jesus' teaching in the Sermon on the Mount, especially, Matthew 5:8 as just cited. In the early theologians after the Apostles we find Irenaeus making the claim that then reaches until the twentieth century in Anglican theologians like Kenneth Kirk: "The glory of God is a living man; and the life of man is the vision of God."[42] To ask, what is the true end or purpose of human life, thinkers in this trajectory do not focus on obedience to God's commands, natural law, or the virtues, although these can and have been included. They focus on purifying human life and enjoying God. But this means, as Kirk notes, that for Christian ethics "the question is, therefore, How is disinterestedness, or unselfishness, to

---

42 Kirk, K.E. (1934). *The Vision of God: The Christian Doctrine of the* Summum Bonum, abridged edition, 2. London: Longmans, Green and Co.

be attained?"[43] That is, seeking perfection and union with God is not an act of brute self-love, but a transformation of the self into God's likeness from which one can love others, even the enemy. The answer to the question, Kirk states, is the way of worship. "Worship lifts the soul out of its preoccupation with itself and its activities and centres its aspirations entirely on God."[44] One can note some analogies to Buddhist thought and practice. The disinterestedness of worship is also found in Buddhist detachment and care for all sentient beings. And worship is like a meditative practice since its aim is union with the highest good just as the aim of Buddhist practice is a transcendence of self.

Dominant in the ancient and medieval Church, the metaethical trajectory that focuses on the highest good by love, worship, and the vision of God continues to inform ethics.[45] And, as we have seen, it is closely related to the discourse of virtue and so the perfection of human capacities. So, the fourth trajectory of Christian approaches to the metaethical dimension of ethics, one also found in Augustine, Thomas Aquinas, and others, is through a discussion of virtue. The focus here is on the formation of character traits, virtues, rather than the commands of God, the highest good, or natural law. "A virtue is a disposition to act, desire and feel that involves the exercise of judgment and leads to a recognizable human excellence, an instance of human flourishing."[46] Insofar as these excellences are expressions of a stable, well-developed character and not just instances of momentary good action, they are virtues in another sense. Virtues are acquired gradually through the solidification of certain latent dispositions to act in recognizably good ways. Often this process of solidification is closely connected to central orienting narratives (including religious narratives) by which people organize their lives, and to the imitation of exemplary figures both within and outside a person's community. This means that although virtue language has the merit of recognizing moral commonality as we observe commendable behaviors by people from different social and cultural backgrounds, not to mention historically remote periods, it also is uniquely bound in its semantics (the meaning of moral terms) to particular communities. A certain set of character traits might seem praiseworthy in certain religious groups, think of the warrior Arjuna discussed in other chapters, but those same character traits might be viewed in the context of modern democratic political life as a hindrance to participation in civic deliberation.

43 Ibid., xi.
44 Kirk, K.E. (1934). *The Vision of God: The Christian Doctrine of the* Summum Bonum, abridged edition, xi. London: Longmans, Green and Co.
45 The most brilliant philosophical example is the work of Murdoch, I. (1992). *Metaphysics as a Guide to Morals*. New York: Allen Lane/Penguin Press. For the most compelling example in religious ethics see Antonaccio, M. (2012). *A Philosophy to Live By: Engaging Iris Murdoch*. Oxford: Oxford University Press.
46 Lee Yearley, cited in Spohn, W. (2007). *Go and Do Likewise: Jesus and Ethics*, 28. New York: Continuum.

Moreover, in traditional Christian virtue ethics, say, in Aquinas or Augustine, all virtues are related to the ultimate Christian virtue of love (*agape* in Greek; *caritas* in Latin). This means that virtue is related to the transcendent good of Christian faith, that is, the God who is love (1 Jn 4:8). Augustine saw the virtues as different forms of love while Aquinas drew a distinction between the natural cardinal virtues formed by learning and habit and concerned with basic and moral goods, and the "theological virtues" (faith, hope, and love) that are infused by God in the believer and lead to friendship with God and the human transcendent good. The question then becomes whether or not the idea of the unity of the virtues, that is the unity of all forms of human excellence, is a plausible idea outside of a theistic framework focused on the grace of God. Yet the claim of Augustine and Aquinas is less focused on the fact of the unity of the virtues and more on how the Christian grows closer to the divine power, union with which is the goal of living the Christian life.

The return of virtue ethics as a distinctive theoretical option in metaethics relates to (as do our other options) what one perceives to be the most significant dimension of ethical thinking. If one focuses on the prevalence of seemingly intractable moral disagreements in modern society, one might opt for virtue ethics because it prioritizes questions of community coherence and consistent moral witness over the ability to give arguments that reach outside of specific community narratives and standards. One who values clear standards by which one can make difficult decisions in changing social and political contexts might view virtue ethics as not practical enough, or one who values a textured interpretation of the priorities and preoccupations of our own age might view virtue ethics as not sufficiently attentive to the intellectual and political trends in a global community.

In a word, there is some difficulty in assigning virtue approaches to one or another element in the established typology of metaethics. Many virtue ethics positions have elements of moral realism because they emphasize observable human excellence. However, these positions do not typically foreground the kind of epistemological concerns in which these typologies are grounded. Moreover, they tend to focus on the fundamental dimension of religious ethics and so on the relationship between freedom, moral identity, and the formation of character. But there is an analogy to Buddhist ethics we can note. Just as the Buddhist outlook seeks enlightenment through various practices, so too a virtue ethics is concerned with those practices that rightly shape human character to act in virtuous ways. The focus is then on practice rather than simple obedience to a command or rational deliberation about the choices one faces. The difference between a Christian virtue ethics and the Buddhist position is, again, the impermanence of the self in the Buddhist conception whereas virtue ethics seeks to establish enduring traits of a person's character.

Although we have described Christian and Buddhist approaches to metaethical questions as varieties of naturalist realism, we have also signaled that thinkers in these traditions (and thinkers looking at these traditions from the outside) have offered other classifications of their metaethical responses. On our reading, this shows the flexibility and dynamism of religious traditions as they join conversations with other religions and with modern academic positions.[47] For example, the review of trajectories of Christian ethics noted that there is no uniform agreement about how Christian theology grounds moral norms. Is it some version of a divine command theory? Is natural law the approach most conducive to Christian claims about the relationship between divine creation and divine precepts? Does the tradition rather resist such questions, opting instead to see the moral life as a life of virtue, configured through stories, moral exemplars, and practices that form the members of the Christian community into a set of recognizable human excellences but also into a distinctive set of qualities not so widely regarded as virtuous? Perhaps the real issue is how the highest good is conceived and how to achieve union with it.

As one thinks about the relationship among the dimensions of religious ethics, it is worthwhile to keep in mind those dimensions that, at first glance, seem to fit rather uncomfortably together. The focus in this chapter has been the metaethical dimension, and readers may wonder whether anything could be more removed from a discussion about the rational grounding of moral claims than the kinds of questions signaled in the discussion of the practical dimension (Chapter 4).[48] Yet through this discussion we have noted four criteria of validation and also clarified why metaethics is one among five dimensions of ethics and how this shift in thinking, drawn from religious sources, provides a more supple and complex way to assess ethical positions than is often found in most discussions of metaethics. Consequently, it would be the task, one beyond the scope of this book, for a developed religious ethics to demonstrate its validity over against rival options by undertaking the work of metaethical reflection in the way we have outlined.

---

47 For example, some modern interpreters of Buddhism have suggested that Buddhism is not a form of moral realism but rather a form of idealism. This theoretical positioning comes from the observation that the foundation of Buddhist metaphysics is an analysis of mental events and that those mental events are ultimately reducible to a single kind of element (*dhammas*). To the extent that this kind of classification represents a kind of monism combined with philosophical idealism, this would bring Buddhism close to a philosopher like F.H. Bradley (1846–1924 CE). See Jayatilleke, K.N. (2011). *Facets of Buddhist Thought: Collected Essays*, 230. Kandy: Buddhist Publication Society.

48 By examining the relationship of the metaethical and the practical dimensions, we mean to focus on the ways that grounding moral claims relate to living by particular moral values and principles in the many different situations that arise in our complex, globalized, temporally and spatially compressed world. We acknowledge, however, that there has been another line of thinking in religious ethics concerning the relationship between the metaethical and the practical, namely the importance of practical strategies for adjudicating disagreement about moral issues in public discussions in modern democratic political life. See Stout, J. (2004). *Democracy and Tradition*. Princeton and Oxford: Princeton University Press and Weithman, P. (2016). *Rawls, Political Liberalism, and Reasonable Faith*. Cambridge: Cambridge University Press.

Buddhist and Christian Ecologies

In this final section of the chapter, the focus is on the metaethical and the practical in Buddhist and Christian religious ethics by examining a case study that touches on basic goods, the moral good, and ideas about the transcendent good. The relationship between human beings and their environment has become a focal point of reflection for people around the globe. Religious communities have turned with renewed energy to study their own histories of ecological responsibility and those instances where they have not attended sufficiently to the effects of their actions on the environment and through these cumulative effects on the needs and rights of their neighbors.

The language with which ecological concerns are addressed has also changed. Modern discourse centered on human beings living in an environment to be manipulated and controlled for human benefit. Nowadays, there is concern to understand the distinctive and interlocking human ecologies existing within and related to an equally complex global ecology of life forms. Such a change in moral language, and so semantics, has allowed religious communities to draw insights from their own traditions into conversation with secular philosophies and ecologically engaged scholars from the natural and social sciences. This has shown the layers of interconnected meaning that have been latent but underutilized in these traditions. Although it is certainly true that ecological concerns are manifest in different religious languages and that the geographical regions each with its own dominant religious groups have experienced varying kinds and degrees of ecological change, there are sufficiently similar dynamics to warrant a comparison between Buddhist and Christian ecological ethics.

Buddhist Ecological Ethics

Buddhist engagement with ecological ethics can be roughly divided into three kinds, each of which seeks to show the validity of its ethical outlook and thereby express metaethical stances: (i) retrieval of tradition-specific resources and their corresponding modes of response in the historical situations of their origin; (ii) development of tradition-specific resources for new responses in light of new questions not anticipated by Buddhist communities in the past; and, (iii) collaborative extensions of traditional themes (questions and responses) to meet present-day ecological challenges.[49] Each of these three has drawn upon the

---

49 This section extends an approach first developed in Clairmont, D.A. (2011). Why does the Buddha close in eyes in my Eden: a Buddhist ecological challenge and invitation to Christians. In: *Green Discipleship: Catholic Theological Ethics and the Environment*, (ed. T. Winright), 340–358. Winona, MN: Anselm Academic.

narratives about the Buddha and the theo-philosophical thinking developed by the early Buddhist community (in terms of the three sources of Buddhist ethics noted earlier, these would track to the Buddha and the Dhamma). They also draw on the practices that communities have maintained to cultivate individual spiritual attainment and pass on Buddhist wisdom to subsequent generations (an admittedly wide understanding of the Saṅgha as a source of Buddhist practices).

The first kind has been unfolded both by Buddhist practitioners and scholars of Buddhism, who note certain characteristically Buddhist ecological themes found in their traditional teachings and identify the ways that Buddhists have drawn comparisons between Buddhist views of human life and Buddhist views of the natural world. Here are five areas in which Buddhists have drawn on traditional teachings to think about present day challenges to the environment: humanity's place in nature; nonharming of animals; positive regard and help for animals; a positive if guarded view about the moral significance of plants, trees, and forests; and a history of thinking about and developing innovative practices of conservation and environmentalism.[50] A central element in the first of these themes is the belief that all life is connected through the round of rebirths. Human beings bear a special responsibility among sentient creatures "because they have greater freedom and understanding than animals,"[51] we nonetheless have "a vision of sentient beings and their environment co-evolving (or co-devolving)."[52] A central element of the second theme is the value of noninjury (*ahiṃsā*), which is prominent in Buddhism and other religious traditions of Indian origin. This value draws special attention to instances where animals are caused undue suffering or killed unnecessarily, including animal consumption, experimentation, certain kinds of animal husbandry, and even the cumulative effects of pest control.[53] A central element in the third and fourth of these themes is the conduciveness of the forest and other variations in the natural landscape to progress in the Buddhist path to enlightenment.

The second kind of response seeks to develop traditional Buddhist teaching in light of the distinctive kinds of problems facing Buddhist communities today. This form of response has been labeled "Eco-Buddhism," a strain of "Engaged Buddhism," developed by Buddhists and Western scholars of Buddhism. The latter term, often traced to the activist Vietnamese monk Thich Nhat Hanh (1926–present),[54] refers to Buddhist movements that arose in

---

50 Peter, H. (2000). Attitude to and treatment of the natural world. In: *An Introduction to Buddhist Ethics: Foundations, Values and Issues*, 150–186. Cambridge: Cambridge University Press.

51 Ibid., 150.

52 Ibid., 153.

53 Ibid., 156–170.

54 Queen, C.S. and King, S.B. (eds.) (1996). *Engaged Buddhism: Buddhist Liberation Movements in Asia*. Albany: SUNY Press, 2, 34 (n6).

response to particular instances of social injustice perpetrated on or within Buddhist communities. Engaged Buddhism is "a fundamental commitment to making Buddhism responsive to the suffering of ordinary Buddhists."[55]

In the Theravāda countries that draw most explicitly on the canonical resources reviewed above, one finds a number of engaged Buddhist responses to the ecological changes in Southeast Asia. Buddhists have responded to the commercial use of Thai forests by calling on resources from the tradition in which kings who were viewed as ruling in accordance with the Dhamma issued decrees to protect forests except as was necessary for the care of the people.[56] In Thailand, "'ecology monks' are those actively engaged in environmental and conservation activities and who respond to the suffering which environmental degradation causes,"[57] as Sue Darlington explains, "Environmentalism in Thailand is not equivalent to the Western distinction between development and pristine natural areas that must be preserved. In Thailand nature is inextricably linked with economics. The critical issue is access to land and resources and the need to maintain sustainable livelihoods. The debates revolve around whose concepts of sustainable livelihood are to be upheld."[58] In an effort to protect wooded areas from exploitative timber harvesting, some monks have undertaken the practice of "ordaining" trees – in effect, wrapping a monastic garment around their trunks – to discourage logging.

In other Theravāda countries, monks and lay people have engaged in broad-based educational movements and partnerships with global development organizations. The Mlup Baitong ("Green Shade") movement in Cambodia is a good example of these collaborations. "Their projects focus on water resource management, tree nurseries, vegetable gardens using natural agriculture (comparable to integrated agriculture), and environmental education for monks. Although they have sponsored an occasional tree ordination, the Cambodian monks emphasize the use of Dhammayatras, or dhamma walks, to promote social issues, including environmental problems."[59]

The Sarvōdaya Śramadāna in Sri Lanka, founded in 1958, also uses a variety of ecologically sensitive development techniques to help rural populations establish environmental standards for their own communities. "They aim at appropriate development, based on an economics of sufficiency, free from 'pollution' by materialist values. Accordingly, they concentrate on ten 'basic

---

55 Ibid., x.
56 Harvey, 177–178.
57 For a more developed description of this practice and the history leading up to it, Darlington, S.M. (1998). The ordination of a tree: the Buddhist ecology movement in Thailand. *Ethnology* 37 (1): 1. See also Darlington, S.M. (2012). *The Ordination of a Tree: The Thai Buddhist Environmental Movement*. Albany: SUNY Press.
58 Ibid., 2.
59 Darlington, *The Ordination of a Tree*, 240.

needs,' including a clean, safe and beautiful environment, and activities include cleaning canals and building roads, wind-pumps and biogas generators."[60] These approaches and the others noted are drawing on analogies to what we have called basic, moral, and transcendent goods in their practical responses to the environmental challenges they face.

The third kind of approach involves explicitly religious cooperation around ecological issues and other social problems that contribute to destabilizing environmental factors. Both Thich Nhat Hanh as well as the fourteenth Dalai Lama have encouraged broad-based, collaborative ecological work. Nhat Hanh, who established the Order of Interbeing (Tiep Hien) in 1966, focuses on the connection between the practice of mindfulness and the ability to recognize the effect of one's actions on the actions of others, including the environment shared by all sentient beings.[61] The Dalai Lama has spoken frequently about the need to foster interreligious collaboration on ecological challenges. He notes that "[w]hen global warming threatens the health of this planet that is our only home, it is only by considering the larger global interest that local and national interests will be met."[62]

In addition to the leaders of Buddhist communities, scholars of Buddhism have themselves drawn some of these connections, arguing with each other about what counts as legitimate developments of Buddhist teachings in light of new threats to the integrity of global ecology. Scholars have argued that certain Buddhist doctrines, when properly ordered and taken together, offer a coherent view through which we can view the environment and our own place in it. "The crisis that threatens our planet whether seen from its military, ecological, or social aspect, derives from a dysfunctional and pathological notion of the self. It derives from a mistake about our place in the order of things."[63] It is the

---

60 Harvey, 179.
61 Harvey, 185. For more information on Thich Nhat Hanh and the Order of Interbeing, see www.orderofinterbeing.org. Training in this community is grounded in 14 mindfulness practices: (i) openness, (ii) nonattachment to view, (iii) freedom of thought, (iv) awareness of suffering, (v) compassionate, healthy living (vi) taking care of anger, (vii) dwelling happily in the present moment, (viii) true community and communication, (ix) truthful and loving speech, (x) protecting and nourishing the Sangha, (xi) right livelihood, (xii) reverence for life, (xiii) generosity, and (xiv) true love (with different practices commended for monks and lay persons). This list incorporates material from a number of different Buddhist lists. The traditional Theravāda list, drawn from the *Satipaṭṭāna Sutta*, identifies four foundations of mindfulness: body, feeling, consciousness, and mental states (tracking to elements of the five aggregates).
62 The Dalai Lama, "Why I'm hopeful about the world's future," *The Washington Post*, Opinions, 13 June 2016. He goes on to explain that his own home country of Tibet suffers from climate change in an acute way. "I have a personal connection to this issue because Tibet is the world's highest plateau and is an epicenter of global climate change, warming nearly three times as fast as the rest of the world. It is the largest repository of water outside the two poles and the source of the Earth's most extensive river system, critical to the world's 10 most densely populated nations."
63 Macy, J. (1990) The greening of the self. In: *Dharma Gaia: A Harvest of Essays in Buddhism and Ecology*, (ed. A.H. Badiner), 57. Berkeley: Parallax Press.

Buddha's teaching on dependent co-origination, supported by the insight into the three factors of phenomenal existence (unsatisfactoriness, impermanence, and not-self) that ground an argument for a Buddhist approach to ecological concern uniquely fitted to the challenges that the global community must address if we are to escape our illusions. As Joanna Macy argues, the "'conventional notion of the self' is being replaced by wider constructs of identity and self-interest – by what you might call the ecological self or the eco-self, co-extensive with other beings and the life of our planet. It is what I will call 'the greening of the self.'"[64] This ecological interpretation of Buddhism has parallels in other world religions, as the recent movement of "spiritual ecology" demonstrates.[65] Because no religious community has been without blindness or illusion to the effects of cumulative moral problems, all of the world's religions are being pressed by these significant earth and climate changes to dig into their histories for resources to contribute to the global conversation.[66]

This third approach has not been without criticism, however, from those who read the tradition's early sources as ambivalent on ecological matters or at least not as easily linked to current problems as others believe. Premodern societies were more fearful of the natural world than reverent of it and so, some scholars argue, one cannot draw Buddhist ecological wisdom from Buddhist ideas without examining the doctrinal logics inherent in those earlier sources. Some approaches to ecological issues exhibit a characteristic form of American Buddhist modernism. "Firstly, the movement represents a dissolution of traditional boundaries between the mundane and supramundane realms, the universalization of the *saṅgha* concept being a good example of this process at work. Secondly, environmental activity, proceeding, as it clearly does, from a scientific observation of changes in the natural world reflects a 'tacit elimination of traditional cosmology.'"[67] The chief difficulty with eco-Buddhism, from this perspective, is its tendency to adapt Buddhist doctrines to the needs of modern social movements without sufficient critical engagement with what those doctrines can and cannot support, or without sensitivity to changing those traditional teachings into something they are not.

What is more, the problem with such ecological interpretations of Buddhism is the implied values these movements have that bestow on nature higher worth than the early Buddhist interpretations could reasonably permit. "The ultimate

---

64 Macy, J. (1990). The greening of the self. In: *Dharma Gaia: A Harvest of Essays in Buddhism and Ecology*, (ed. A.H. Badiner 53. Berkeley: Parallax Press.
65 See Vaughan-Lee, L. (ed.) (2013). *Spiritual Ecology: The Cry of the Earth*. Point Reyes: Golden Sufi Center, which includes essays by Joanna Macy and Thich Nhat Hanh among others.
66 For a discussion of cumulative moral problems, see Clairmont, D.A. (2013). Medieval consideration and moral pace: Thomas Aquinas and Bernard of clairvaux on the temporal aspects of virtue. *Journal of Religious Ethics* 41 (1): 79–111.
67 Harris, I. (1995). Buddhist environmental ethics and detraditionalization: the case of EcoBuddhism. *Religion* 25: 203.

analysis and evaluation of existence in Early Buddhism does not seem to confer any value on nature, neither on life as such nor on species nor on eco-systems. The ultimate value and goal of Early Buddhism, absolute and definitive freedom from suffering, decay, death and impermanence, cannot be found in nature." Early Buddhism "only motivates the wish and effort to liberate oneself (*vimutti*) from all constituents of both personal existence and the world."[68] The Transcendent good seems, in this light, to be pursued at the expense of basic and moral goods.

Christian Ecological Ethics

Consider now some Christian ecological ethics in order to examine similarities and differences, analogies, in how the metaethical dimension relates to the practical life. Whereas Buddhist ecological ethics depends on its metaphysical and ontological views about the nature of the world (impermanent and not-self) and the basic problem of the human person within that environment (suffering caused by attachments to false views), Christian ecological ethics also depends on certain metaphysical assessments of the world, namely, beliefs about creation, the activity of God in human history, and the redemptive work of Jesus the Christ. Forgiveness and mercy are central to a Christian view of divine action, and human beings are called to responsibility in relation to their fellow women and men and to their shared environment that they view as a gift from a loving God. William French observes that "Christianity shares with Judaism and Islam a common set of core beliefs stressing the transcendence and sovereignty of God, the goodness of God's creation, and the primacy of the human over the rest of creation." However, "through their histories, the stress on human primacy was balanced by an understanding that humanity remains part of the broader order of God's creation."[69] The challenge for a Christian ecological ethics is to keep the well-being of humans in view, resist the deification of nature, and also articulate how creation bears the trace of the divine and therefore must be respected as having its own integrity, not reducible to its usefulness or as material for consumption by human beings. How does one avoid the reduction of worth to price, as we put it before?

New though this challenge may seem, it was not unknown to earlier generations of Christians. The most iconic of Christian figures to be associated with ecology is Francis of Assisi (1181/2–1226 CE). Francis wrote very little and much of the material we have about his early life comes from hagiographies. Still, his vision of a cosmic harmony was grounded in a deep conviction that care

---

68 Schmithausen, L. (1997). The early Buddhist tradition and ecological ethics. *Journal of Buddhist Ethics* 4:11.
69 French, W. (2005). Ecology. In: *The Blackwell Companion to Religious Ethics*, (ed. W. Schweiker), 470. Malden and Oxford: Blackwell Publishing.

for creation was fundamentally an act of obedience to the command of God expressed in the Decalogue and the fabric of the universe. His biographer and companion, Thomas of Celano (1200–1255 CE), offered the following hagiographic portrayal that illustrates the connection between care of creation and obedience to God: "After the birds had listened so reverently to the word of God, [Francis] began to accuse himself of negligence because he had not preached to them before. From that day on, he carefully exhorted all birds, all animals, all reptiles, and also insensible creatures, to love the Creator, because daily, invoking the name of the Savior, he observed their obedience in his own experience."[70] Respect for creation is not independent of the distinctly human good and the high value placed on all human life, because in Christian belief human beings are capable through reason of knowing and loving God, to experience mercy and forgiveness, and to understand the meaning of salvation. For Francis, all of God's creation is being drawn toward its eventual perfection, a theme found in aspirational ethics.[71] Yet the means by which human beings will participate in the "new creation" is through obedience to God.

Thinkers such as Aquinas understood natural law as drawing people toward a recognition of a divinely created order through their capacity to reason about the natural world and to ask questions about its patterns, purpose, and origin. As Daniel Scheid notes, there are several aspects of Thomas's thought that seem remarkably fitting to developing a Christian ecological ethic: "(1) the intrinsic goodness of creation, (2) the importance of ecological diversity, (3) the order of creation as the greatest good, which aligns with the modern understanding of sustainability, (4) a common good that applies to the entire cosmos, and (5) humanity's vocation to become 'cocreators' with God and bring creation to a greater flourishing."[72] For Aquinas, knowledge of the natural law implicates one in thinking about the kind of creature that could live in accordance with the insights discovered through reason or specifically revealed by God. Obedience to this law, and to the higher divine law that perfects the natural law, requires the maturation of one's basic desires – a perfection of one's naturally occurring powers – so that one can approach oneself, other people,

---

70 Thomas of Celano, "The Life of Saint Francis" cited in Keith Douglas Warner, O.F.M. (2011). Retrieving Saint Francis: tradition and innovation for our ecological vocation. In: *Green Discipleship: Catholic Theological Ethics and the Environment*, (ed. T. Winright), 122–123. Winona, MN: Anselm Academic. The translation is from Armstrong, R.J., Hellman, J.W., and Short, W. (eds.) (1999). *Francis of Assisi: Early Documents, vol. I: The Saint.* New York: New City Press.
71 For a discussion of Pope Francis encyclical on the environment, Laudato Sí, see *The Journal of Religious Ethics* 46: 3.
72 Scheid, D.P. (2011). Saint Thomas Aquinas, the Thomistic tradition, and the cosmic common good. In: *Green Discipleship: Catholic Theological Ethics and the Environment*, (ed. T. Winright), 129. Winona, MN: Anselm Academic. See also Scheid, D.P. (2016). *The Cosmic Common Good: Religious Grounds for Ecological Ethics.* Oxford and New York: Oxford University Press.

and one's surroundings (in short, all of creation) in a way that is respectful rather than exploitative. A Christian ecology rooted in obedience to divine command and a Christian ecology rooted in knowledge of the natural law both assume a framework of growth in virtue that will order individual capacities and social relationships for the common good and in this way various trajectories of metaethical thinking are interwoven.

One can also note that there are forms of Protestant and Orthodox ecological thinking that also draw on their traditions to meet the practical challenge of climate change and other ecological problems. We cannot survey these here. Suffice it to note that they will also engage in metaethical reflection in order to warrant and validate their ethical judgments. And, as just intimated, they will in different ways draw on the discourse of divine command, natural law, aspiration and the highest good, and the search for perfection through virtue in doing so. In each case, there is the demand to meet the criteria of validity noted earlier in this chapter even as thinking and living that process aims to advance the religious life.

Thinking About an Ecology of Practice

The metaethical dimension is best understood as an expression of the deeply human desire to search for truth, tempted though we often are to be satisfied living in a world of illusion. Do not we all want to know if we have been duped by morality, to recall Levinas' words? Yet metaethics in modern philosophy focuses on certain aspects of the search for truth: to have true knowledge about morality, to know the meaning and reach of moral claims, and to provide justification for moral beliefs. Religious ethics shares with philosophical ethics the search for true knowledge about the reasons why people ought to be moral and what such standards mean in a morally and religiously pluralistic world. However, religious ethics seeks to know something more about the moral life than the rationality of its standards and the certainty of its beliefs. Religious ethics aims at an accurate picture of the moral life as something we think and feel, at which we struggle and strive. Religious ethics is a work of shared interpretation concerning what is true about the human person and human communities, recognizing that often what is most true about human life comes only through the struggle to live truly in the midst of illusions. Those truths do not always come through the formation of declarative sentences or well-formulated propositions. Often they come just as much though story and image, community and collaboration.

Illusion no less than truth can take different forms. It can be about moral claims or the nature of moral truth but it can also be about a view of ourselves or our time in history (the descriptive dimension). It can be about illusory rather than real human goods (the normative dimension). It can be about the difficulties of prudential judgments in situations we find perplexing (the practical dimension). It can be about the challenges of developing character and moral responsibility under conditions that seem to emphasize our finitude and moral weakness rather than our freedom (the fundamental dimension). The multidimensional approach to religious ethics developed in this book confronts these puzzles without giving any one of them a leading role to the exclusion or minimization of the others. The reason is that religious ethics seeks to articulate the structure of lived reality in and through its dimensions.

The consideration of Buddhism and Christianity in this chapter has explored how each of these traditions speaks about the quest for moral and religious truth in a world where illusions come from within and from outside the traditions themselves. Buddhist teaching cautions against attachment to any view, seeing the danger even in an excessive attachment to the Buddha himself, his teaching, or his monastic community. Buddhist teaching, in stark contrast to Christianity, marks off as especially dangerous attachment to views about a single, all-powerful creator god. Buddhist ethics focuses on the karmic results of actions, classifying those actions and the conditions that give rise to them as either wholesome or unwholesome. The standard of what counts as wholesome depends on how those actions do in fact – in the past, present, and future – give rise to a desire for attachment in the form of craving. Any belief, person, or part of the material world could, in theory, become an object of excessive attachment, including "God," and therefore an occasion for suffering. Analogically, a Christian worries that any belief, person, or part of the material world can, in theory, become a false object of faith, including doctrines about "God," and thus an instance of idolatry leading to injustice.

Traditional Buddhist teaching is arguing for a strong *metaphysical* view – the world does, Buddhists believe, show this teaching about unwholesome action and attachment to be true – that interrelates with a strong *metaethical* view. If you want to know the truth about morality, examine the effects of wholesome and unwholesome effects of action on individuals and their communities. In this way, the Buddhist is arguing for a strong connection between the metaethical and the practical dimensions – the truth of one points to the truth of the other as Buddhist ecological teaching builds on these basic views about attachment and suffering. Although there is significant debate among Buddhist communities (scholars and practitioners alike) on the kind of ecological activity that is commended by Buddhist teaching, it is clear that the metaphysical views influence the parameters for these communities' practical solutions. Any solution to the problem of suffering, including the suffering human beings inflict on each other and their environment, will in one way or another be traceable to greed, hatred, and delusion and will operate according to the causal logic of dependent co-origination. Herein we have another example of how the metaethical and the practical are linked. Disagreement among Buddhist communities on this point exemplifies the difficulty but also the necessity of linking the metaethical and the practical dimensions to the descriptive dimension.

In Christian ethics, the tradition developed lines of thinking about the truth of moral questions, exemplified by the approaches of natural law, virtue ethics, the highest good, and divine command. Much of this thinking was picked up in the later debates in philosophical ethics. Thinkers questioned whether natural law could be a basis for moral norms and knowledge of those norms and similarly inquired whether something like a grounding of moral norms in a divine legislation was necessary to give them certain foundations and resistance to abuse by human caprice. Both Christianity and Buddhism seem to embrace a certain kind of moral realism, and each tradition also supports a kind of naturalist realism. Yet we also judge there to be sufficient warrant in these traditions and in the depth and diversity of human experience to develop other lines of moral realism.

Important for the hermeneutical approach of this book is the consideration of the features of moral existence that highlight the coherence of character and moral selfhood and also of the reflexivity that characterizes attempts to make sense of moral worlds in conversation with others. This "hermeneutical realism" seems all the more important when employing a multidimensional approach from the comparative standpoint that we have been developing. The moral world that is real is not only something we discover, that is, a moral order that characterizes the world and provides the boundaries within which we navigate our life projects. It is also something people construct through our interactions with other people and the interpretation of the complex and diverse realities we call the religions with their myths, symbols, institutions, and practices. The reality of the moral space of life is discovered through the interpretive means people use to understand and orient their life. We discover through interpretation; this is the claim of hermeneutical realism.

The kind of realism to which the metaethical dimension points requires conversational interpretation, and not just accurate description, since each of us is in some way part of the moral world of every other. Our own attempts to describe the world, to identify and pursue what is good, to seek a right and fitting course of action, to use our freedom responsibly and thereby develop good qualities of character, to seek the truth about ourselves and our world, are together a kind of offering that adds to and thereby changes the moral worlds of our neighbors. Their actions, pursuits, interpretations, and judgments shape our world as well. We are not duped by morality because, understood in and through the interactions of the various dimensions of ethics, one finds a true account of the structure of lived moral reality and guidance for the orientation of life. This is another way of saying that the religions and religious ethics disclose the many ways persons and communities inhabit a multidimensional moral space, and each of the dimensions of our moral lives return to us, echoing with the promise and puzzlement of every other life.

7

The Point of Religious Ethics

> I call heaven and earth to witness against you today that I have set before you life and death, blessings and curses. Choose life so that you and your descendants may live, loving the Lord your God, and holding fast to him ....
> —Deut 30:19–20a

> I am the gate. Whoever enters by me will be saved, and will come in and go out and find pasture. The thief comes only to steal and kill and destroy. I have come that they may have life, and have it abundantly.
> —Jn 10:9–10

> But what sort of thing would make us enemies, angry at each other, if we disagree about it and are unable to arrive at a decision? Perhaps you cannot say offhand, but I suggest you consider whether it would not be the just and unjust, beautiful and ugly, good and evil. Are not these the things, when we disagree about them and cannot reach a satisfactory decision, concerning which we on occasion become enemies – you, and I, and all other men?
> —Plato, Euthyphro, 7c-d[1]

The Point of It All?

The chapters of this book set forth an account of the meaning and the method of religious ethics. Our purpose is nothing less than to define a field of study in which religious sources contributed to thinking about normative moral convictions and practices and also the responsible orientation of life. This account means taking a different approach than much work in religious studies wherein the religions are seen as "data" to which various theories, ethical or otherwise,

---

1 Plato (1984). *Euthyphro*, 7c-d In: *The Dialogues of Plato*, Vol. 1, 47 (trans. R.E. Allen). New Haven: Yale University Press.

Religious Ethics: Meaning and Method, First Edition. William Schweiker and David A. Clairmont.
© 2020 William Schweiker and David A. Clairmont. Published 2020 by John Wiley & Sons Ltd.

are applied. In order to challenge that approach to religious ethics, the chapters isolated five dimensions of reflection that arise out of basic questions human beings ask about the conduct of their lives. Along the way we have noted fundamental differences among the religions, say, the difference between religions of redemption and religions of enlightenment, and also how the moralities of the religions do not fall into easy types of ethics often used to categorize the world's religions, like monism and dualism. Similarities were also explored, for example, the place of the Golden and Silver Rules in the religious life and also basic, moral, and transcendent goods.

The driving moral impulse of the religious life, we have argued, is how persons and communities are to obtain contact with what is ultimately real, important, and empowering whether the "object" of that contact is conceived in terms of gods, one God, or the sacred, and how this motivates responsible conduct in diverse and yet interacting domains or "worlds."[2] Religious ethics can draw from and contribute to the religious and moral life whether the specific religion is a form of monotheism, polytheism, pantheism, or relativizes the importance of divine beings in the moral life. Understood in this way, religious ethics is a form of hermeneutical and normative inquiry aimed at understanding the meaning and orienting of the moral life as well as a form of "metareflection" on the moral and religious resources of the religions. Religious ethics assesses and prescribes how religious beliefs and practices can be lived responsibly by adherents of a specific religion, say, liberal Judaism or Zen Buddhism, but also, conceivably, how anyone might draw from various religious resources for the sake of taking responsibility for the integrity of life.[3]

The question for this last chapter is this one: "What is the point of it all?" After all, the purpose of ethical reflection is not simply to know what is good, right, or responsible but to become good, act rightly, and to live in a responsible way. The question about the "point" of religious ethics actually entails three distinct but interrelated questions. First, why should anyone undertake the study of religious ethics? Second, how are we to understand the formation of people's religious and moral identities within a specific religious community? Third, how might such reflection on religious resources and moral identity

---

2 Recall that this account of "religion," a broadly cultural hermeneutical one, is a scholarly construction drawn from actual religions and has similarities to other theories of religion. We note, in particular, Riesebrodt, M. (2010). *The Promise of Salvation: A Theory of Religion* (trans. S. Randall). Chicago: The University of Chicago Press and Geertz, C. (1966). Religion as a cultural system. In: *Anthropological Approaches to the Study of Religion*, (ed. M. Banton ASA Monographs), vol. 3, 1–46. London: Tavistock Publications.

3 One should note that many of the moral "saints" of the twentieth century freely drew from various religious traditions while remaining deeply committed to their own tradition: Gandhi, Martin Luther King, Jr., Mother Teresa of Calcutta, Desmond Tutu, Nelson Mandela, and others. These "shared saints," as they are called, show that a devout person can draw moral wisdom from many traditions and yet remain faithful to their own.

provide orientation for the responsible religious life whatever religion – if any – one actually inhabits? In this chapter we address this cluster of interrelated questions by focusing on the question of religious identity and membership, even as we draw into the discussion the related questions. Our task is to show that from within religious sources there are warrants for the criticism and reconstruction of traditions and so the work of ethical thinking. By the end of the chapter we will have formulated a principle of religious self-criticism, what we call "The Principle of Integral Convictions." It is a way to test religious moralities and identities for distortions and unethical teachings and practices.

We have organized the chapter in this way because nowadays what defines religious identity is complex and disputed and often gives rise to conflicts within a single religion, say Sunnī against Shīʿa Muslims or Catholics against Evangelical Protestant Christians. How best to understand and define religious identities? And furthermore, can we identify an idea or principle that warrants, makes valid, the work of self-criticism from an ethical standpoint? If we can isolate a norm of religious self-criticism from within the moral convictions of the religions, then we will have an answer to why one should undertake the work of religious ethics and also the contribution of religious ethics to anyone's moral life and community, religious or not.

It is important to note, then, that our approach to the religious identity of persons and/or communities is not strictly sociological or institutional, because, once again, we want the religions to help inform and shape an account of their moral and religious identities. That is to say, we are not exploring how many people in the world call themselves "Hindus," "Jews," or "Buddhists," nor do we intend to survey how religious institutions, for example, temples or churches, define themselves over against other social institutions, whether religious, political, or economic. It is also not our intention to examine the emergence of new religions (say, nature religion or Gaia worship) or the phenomenon of Internet chatrooms, new age spirituality, and online religion.[4] Finally, we will also not explore the waning of religious membership in some parts of the world or religious revivals in other places or even the emergence of the so-called "nones," that is, those people without any religious identity, in places like the United States.[5] Those are important matters to address within the scope of religious studies. They are not the focus of our discussion in this chapter.

Our approach to the question of religious identity in this chapter, and, indeed, this entire book, is from a religious and ethical perspective, that is, from the perspective of the account of religion adopted in Chapter 1 and our understanding of ethics as normative reflection on the meaning and truth of religious "moralities." In what follows, we address two major problems about "religious identity" in

---

4 See Kripal, J.J. (2007). *Esalen: America and the Religion of No Religion*. Chicago: University of Chicago Press.
5 See http://www.pewforum.org/2012/10/09/nones-on-the-rise (accessed 18 June 2019).

relation to the moral life and so from the perspective of religious ethics. The first problem arises when ideas about religious identity lead to violent extremism and the destruction of others, the problem here is violent fanaticism or what we prefer to call "moral madness."[6] The other problem arises when religious people try to compensate for the threat of moral madness within their tradition either (i) through assimilation to the wider culture or (ii) the accommodation, even identification, of their beliefs with other cultural and religious institutions. In both cases, the threat of moral madness or fanaticism leads to responses that, ironically, negate the distinctiveness of a specific religion's way of life. A religious life becomes simply an expression of wider social and cultural values and beliefs, say, the identification of Christianity with American "values" or the accommodation of Hindu life to extreme Indian nationalism. Stated otherwise, *is there a way to undertake the criticism of religion and the surrounding culture from within a religion without destroying religions distinctiveness distinctiveness and thereby its contribution to the religious and moral life?* The challenge of this chapter is, then, not only to isolate these problems for the religions but also to show that religions provide resources that enable forms of self-criticism in which religious distinctiveness is not elided but that also provides a trenchant criticism of moral madness.

Let us begin by explaining the terms just noted and also the idea of "self-criticism" within the religions before turning to explore those ideas in an exemplary nonmissionary religion (Judaism) and a missionary religion (Christianity). It may come as a surprise to critics and proponents of the religions to learn that the religions sustain a rigorous and yet refined norm of self-criticism. This norm of self-criticism, we further hold, is what validates ethical reflection on religious sources as developed throughout this book. It specifies the stance of religious ethics in the orientation of the responsible religious life.

Moral Madness and Religious Self-Criticism

By the term "moral madness," we mean those instances when persons or communities act on their convictions in ways that, ironically, reject their own deeper moral beliefs. Moral madness is a way of having or holding convictions that demand rigid and indiscriminate application to human relations.[7] For example,

---

6 For a brief discussion of these ideas see Schweiker, W. (2004). *Theological Ethics and Global Dynamics: In the Time of Many Worlds*. Oxford: Blackwell, especially Chapter 9 "On Moral Madness." On the "integrity of life" see Klemm, D.E. and Schweiker, W. (2008). *Religion and the Human Future: An Essay in Theological Humanism*. Wiley Blackwell. Also see, Neiman, S. (2002). *Evil in Modern Thought: An Alternate History of Philosophy*. Princeton, NJ: Princeton University Press.

7 Recall our footnote in Chapter 1 about "having" and "holding" beliefs. The importance of this idea here is that someone might hold beliefs in ways that guide their conduct and yet are profoundly at odds with what they claim are the norms and values of their actions. That is to say, "moral madness" is a (violent) form of hypocrisy. One's actions contradict one's stated values.

the *Lex Talionis* from the biblical text, "An eye for an eye and a tooth for a tooth," is a law of retaliation. (See Deuteronomy 19:21 and Matthew 5:38 for contrasting expressions of this law.) The punishment inflicted on the wrongdoer should correspond to the degree of the wrong done thereby abiding by norms of equality and reciprocity. In the Jewish and Christian biblical texts, the law is basic to retributive justice. Admitting the reality of conflict and wrongdoing, the law of retaliation was meant to limit and curtail the possibility of endless cycles of reciprocal revenge and the continued increase of levels of violence. Retaliation cannot exceed what is suffered but must be on parity to that suffering thereby reconstituting some measure of equality between persons or groups.

However, the *Lex Talionis* is not unambiguous. As Mahatma Gandhi is reputed to have said, "An eye for an eye only ends up making the whole world blind." That is, this "law" demands strict equality in treatment, but it does not provide limits to the possible ongoing, and equal, revenge. This gives us a deeper understanding of moral madness. It is the assertion of the sanctity of one's identity and conviction over claims of responsibility that might limit cycles of revenge.[8] Moral madness is moral because it is the denial of commitments, like respect for and care of human and nonhuman life. Sadly, if anything defines negative religious forms in the global age, it is the violent clash between religions when adherence to some "orthodoxy" or "orthopraxy" override moral convictions and give credence to the idea of a "clash of civilizations."[9] Our contention, conversely, is not in terms of religious "orthodoxy" or "orthopraxis," that is, having the right beliefs and right form of action, but that religious identity ought to be measured against the transcendent good, what the religions call the sacred or the divine and we have called, ethically speaking, "the integrity of life," an idea that we will elaborate later.[10] We will see how this idea of the

---

8   Some scholars have argued that the "sacred" is best defined by the use of violence, the sacrifice of some "holy" victim, in order to bring to an end on-going cycles of violence. Most famously, see Girard, R. (1977). *Violence and the Sacred* (trans. P. Gregory). Baltimore, MD: The Johns Hopkins University Press and Janowski, B. and Welker, M. (eds.) (2000). *Opfer: Theologische und kulturellen Kontexte.* Frankfurt: Suhrkamp. For a recent attempt to explore contemporary societies and their forms of violence from this perspective of the "sacred," see Dupus, J.-P. (2013). *The Mark of the Sacred* (trans. M.B. Debevoise). Stanford, CA: Stanford University Press. Although they make important contributions to the anthropology and sociology of religion, we judge positions that equate the "sacred" with sacrificial violence too narrow in their conception of religion and its relation to ethics and politics. It is for this reason we want to explore the idea of "moral madness" as more adequate for the work of religious ethics.

9   This idea was made famous by Samuel Huntington; see Huntington, S. (1997). *The Clash of Civilizations and the Remaking of World Order* New York: Touchstone. From Jewish and Christian perspectives, see, respectively, Sacks, J. (2002). *The Dignity of Difference: How to Avoid the Clash of Civilizations* New York: Continuum and Marty, M.E. (2005). *When Faiths Collide.* Oxford: Blackwell.

10   Here we just note that "God" or the "Sacred" are religious symbols and ideas or characters in a story whereas "the integrity of life" is an ethical concept. Religious ethics requires both interrelating and critically comparing religious symbols and ethical concepts. The "Highest Good" is then given conceptual and symbolic expression.

good formulates insights from both Jewish and Christian ethics with analogues in other religions as well. Importantly, this transcendent good also entails a principle of self-criticism and the criticism of culture. It allows, first, the religions to counter moral madness within themselves, but, second, to do so without loss of their distinctive identity through assimilation or accommodation to the wider social order.

Before exploring that possibility of self-criticism within Jewish and Christian moral thought, we need to clarify what we mean by the "self-criticism" of religion and show that it serves the ethical aim of respecting and enhancing the integrity of life. In making an argument about religious self-criticism, we agree with the philosopher and economist Amartya Sen and also the passage from Michel de Montaigne (1533–1592 CE) on the title page of his famous *Essays*. We cite Sen first and then Montaigne:

> The point at issue is not whether *any* identity whatever can be chosen (that would be an absurd claim), but whether we do indeed have choices over alternative identities or combinations of identity, and perhaps more importantly, substantial freedom regarding what *priority* to give to the various identities we may simultaneously have.[11]

> There is nothing so beautiful and legitimate as to play the man well and properly, no knowledge so hard to acquire as the knowledge of how to live this life well and naturally; and most barbarous of our maladies is to despise our being.[12]

The contention of this book, and, we think, any viable religious ethics, is that responsibility is the rule of individual and communal freedom that can and must have *moral* priority in the choices about the formation of religious peoples' identities, no matter how complex those identities might be.[13] The claim of responsibility is what makes humans moral creatures that must shape and,

---

11 Sen, A. (2006). *Identity and Violence: The Illusion of Destiny*, vol. 38. New York: Norton. Also see Schweiker, W. (2010). *Dust that Breathes: Christian Faith and the New Humanisms*. Oxford: Wiley Blackwell, esp. Chapter 1: "The Specter of Religious Identity."

12 Michel de Montaigne, *Essays* III:13 cited in Bakewell, S. (2010). *How to Live or A Life of Montaigne: In One Question and Twenty Attempts to Answer It*, 201. New York: Other Press.

13 It is important that we are speaking only about their *moral identities*. Of course, every religion will have complex accounts of the relation between its adherents' religious, moral, political, and economic identities. These cannot be explored in this book. We are interested in the relation of religious convictions to moral identity. It might be that *in some cases* moral convictions and actions are not entailed in a religious conviction, say, in Christianity, beliefs about the order of prayers in meditation. In those cases, the religious beliefs or practices are morally indifferent, they are nonmoral.

therefore, responsibility must orient their identities rather than their identities grounding and defining the nature of moral responsibility.

This rule of freedom, we hope to show, is nothing other than a principle of self-criticism found *within* a religious tradition. That principle is not imported from some other cultural or social sources nor is it grounded in a supposed purely rational or metaphysical scheme. The religions will, to be sure, find the source of their critical principle in God's command, the teachings of the Buddha or Jesus, the insight that *ātman* and *brahman* are one, or some other argument about the sacred source and aim of self-criticism. Differences are to be expected. Yet the connection between responsibility and self-criticism is just another way of saying that to live well requires that an individual or a community in their actions and relations respect and enhance, not despise or destroy, people's own being and other living things.[14] The inverse claim, that is, that identity has priority over responsibility, is the specter of moral madness: one is responsible only for those like oneself. True moral and religious self-criticism is a bulwark against such madness. Stated otherwise, the work of self-criticism within the religious life is part of the dynamic of the religious life explored in Chapter 3. Self-criticism, whether by the individual or the community, is part of the dynamic spiral of mediating basic, moral, and transcendent goods through a normative principle of responsibility. Religious self-criticism aims to show when the character and conduct of a person or community is not advancing and elevating human life to its proper end due to violations of moral norms.

What then is meant, more precisely, by self-criticism? Criticism can mean several things. First, at the level of common sense, criticism means the disapproval of something or someone because of what are seen to be faults or mistakes. Often religions fall subject to this meaning of criticism. Someone might argue that the religions breed ignorance because they are supposedly against science. Someone else might contend that the religions have bad psychological effects or devalue the body. A believer can criticize the leader of the community because of his or her moral failings. Second, criticism can also mean the analysis and judgment of literary, artistic, or performative/ritual works for the sake of explaining their meanings and making judgments about their faults and merits. One important development in the Modern West has been the use of

---

14 We realize the practical complexity of this claim. For some religious traditions the demand of responsibility for the integrity of life means, as it does in Jainism in India, the demand for harmlessness and thus the prohibition of any killing of any living being. Some Buddhists as well seek to enact compassion for all beings that can suffer. Other religious traditions, say Judaism and Islam, have rules about which forms of life can be consumed and conditions under which a human life can be taken, say by capital punishment or justified warfare. Still other religions, one thinks of Christianity, have a range of positions on this question from strict vegetarianism to no dietary restriction and from pacifism to just war thinking. We return to this later in this chapter.

forms of literary and historical criticism to analyze, explain, and assess biblical texts. This has led to new insight into the origin of various texts and their sociohistorical contexts. In the last few decades there have been many studies of religious ritual and practices in the formation of a community's life. Of course, some religions will not allow these types of criticism of their sacred texts and practices; others have engaged in the ongoing analysis and criticism of those writings and ritual practices.

Although these two forms of criticism, the common sense and explanatory meanings, are widely practiced with respect to the practices, texts, and convictions of the religions, we are concerned with yet another and different form of criticism. This form of criticism has two interrelated elements that can be distinguished but not separated.[15] The first element of this kind of criticism is the attempt to isolate and to correct illusions or misunderstandings that distort a moral agent's or community's moral perception, judgment, and decision-making. For instance, inordinate pride can distort how someone perceives a moral situation and thus lead to bad decisions and wrong judgments. A mother who believes her child can do no wrong easily misses situations in which the child must be corrected or disciplined. The hypocrite is someone who judges the actions of others and yet does not live by those same standards himself or herself.

The second element of this idea of criticism is more complex. Here the concern is to isolate and to articulate the conditions (social, psychological, economic, etc.) that make illusions, misunderstandings, and fault possible. A Buddhist might say that because of our desires, that is, because we cling to things and especially our sense of self, we become trapped in *saṃsāra* and thereby do not perceive what is really the case and therefore falsely judge by mistaken ideas about good and bad behavior. A Jew might argue that the condition that makes moral illusions and misunderstanding possible is the constant struggle within each human being between the good and bad impulses. Christians might speak of moral weakness, that is, the inability to carry through on some action or commitment, or the bondage of the will due to sin (as Martin Luther called it). In this case, we might know what we ought to do, what is right and just, but lack the willpower to act in those ways. Some thinkers argue that the condition of possibility for moral weakness, illusions, and misunderstanding are the social forms that shape human character and association. Karl Marx made this kind of argument in terms of the means of production in a society and the ideologies economic relations generate. Friedrich Nietzsche found the roots of Western moral decay in what he called the "slave revolt" that lives on

---

15 This type of criticism is longstanding in Western thought and other traditions as well. In the West it begins philosophically with Socrates' question of people about basic ideas and then in Plato's complex dialogues. It continues into the modern world in Kant's so-called method of "critique," in Karl Marx's thought, in Nietzsche and many others. The point is that forms of self-criticism are longstanding in religious and nonreligious ethics.

in Judaism and Christianity. Obviously, this second aspect of criticism, that is, seeking the conditions that make possible illusion, misunderstanding, and moral fault, can take and has taken various forms.

For present purposes it is important, at least with respect to ethical reflection, that these two elements of criticism are interrelated and are undertaken by an individual or a community in order better to orient the responsible life. In order to clarify this claim, we turn now to different forms of religion and their ideas about how one ought rightly to access what is ultimately real, important, and empowering for the responsible orientation of life. This will enable us to isolate the threat of moral madness within Judaism and Christianity as well as the impetus of self-criticism in a robust, moral meaning of that term.

Forms of Religion and Identity

Seen within the context of the development of Judaism and Christianity, there are longstanding disputes about what makes someone a "Jew" or a "Christian."[16] Among Christians it would seem that one becomes a Christian by confessing that Jesus is the Savior, the Christ, and, further, joining a church through baptism – a symbolic, ritual death and rebirth – and also participating in the life and worship of the church and taking its sacraments. Christians seek to follow Christ as his disciples and to walk in the ways that lead to life, as the Bible puts it. But Christians disagree on virtually every one of these marks of membership. Some Christians believe in "infant baptism" whereas others insist on adult believer baptism. There are Christians who do not recognize the legitimacy of other Christian communities, or the ordinations of their ministers and priests, or even the number of sacraments, if there are even things called "sacraments."[17] Some Christians claim that the only right way to follow Christ requires pacifism; others, as we know from this book, can imagine a Christian fighting in a "justified war." When one begins to peer into the world of Christianity, one sees that there are vast differences among Christians and

---

16 We cannot explore the moral claims of those who profess to be "spiritual but not religious," and for two reasons. (i) Religion is, on any viable understanding, deeply social in nature. The idea that one can be religious – or spiritual – without communal ties and bonds is simply impossible. (ii) It is not clear that various "spiritualties" have distinctive moral outlooks. Most of the time they reflect or reject the morality of the dominant culture or some version of current moral convictions.

17 For Christians a "sacrament" is a holy sign and some believe, as St. Augustine put it, that this sign is one that gives what it signifies. That is, on this account a sacrament communicates divine grace. Finite things (e.g. water in baptism; bread and wine in the Lord's Supper [or Eucharist]) can bear and communicate infinite things, God's grace. Other Christians do not speak of sacraments in this way but understand them as signs of faith and remembrances.

Christian communities that have been occasions for Christians to violate Christ's commandment to "love one another." If within "the religions you are to discover religion," as Friedrich Schleiermacher noted in his *Speeches*, then it seems that within the Christianities one discovers Christianity.[18]

The same must be said about Jews. There are different Judaisms arising in the course of history (Orthodox, Reformed, Conservative, and others) and there are disputes about Kosher (dietary taboos) as well as the teachings of *Torah*. Jews tend to define being Jewish in terms of birth, say that one's mother is Jewish, and there are also religious definitions, like being part of Israel, God's elect people. Throughout history there have been disagreements about what Judaism is. Still, analogous to the two central features of being a Christian, that is, faith in Christ and participation in some church, being a Jew is at least marked ethnically through birth and religiously by being part of God's holy people. Some scholars draw a distinction, but not a separation, between ethnic and religious Judaism. Whatever the case, being a Jew and being a Christian entail a way of life.[19] Our concern, accordingly, is the connection between that way of life and religious identity.

Although we find similarities between ways of life that are lived in different ways and give rise to distinctive forms of Christianity and Judaism, there is a more basic difference between these religions. Drawing on a distinction in religious studies, we can designate missionary religions, like Christianity (Buddhism and Islam, too) and nonmissionary religions, say Judaism (or Hinduism, indigenous religions, and Confucianism, if it is a religion).[20] These ideas are different ways of conceiving how to be religious that have implications for religious identity and the problem of religious violence sparked by moral madness. The distinction between these forms of religion is easily stated and with it in hand we will explore in more detail Jewish and Christian moralities as examples of each type. This tactic will allow us to isolate an analogy between these different types of religion and how that analogy relates to the problem of religious violence and the point of religious ethics. Like other chapters of this book, we also note the ways that the distinction between religions often breaks down under careful examination.

Briefly, nonmissionary religions are ways of life in which one's membership in some ethnic group, say, Jews, or caste – like the warrior caste in traditional

18 Schleiermacher, F. (1988). *On Religion: Speeches to Its Cultured Despisers* (trans. R. Crouter), 190. Cambridge, UK: Cambridge University Press. Recall that this passage is cited on the title page of this book, *Religious Ethics: Meaning and Method*.

19 For a brief discussion of the question of Judaism, see Neusner, J. (1993). Judaism. In: *Our Religions*, (ed. A. Sharma), 291–356. New York, NY: HarperCollins.

20 See Sharma, A (2012). *Problematizing Religious Freedom*. London: Springer esp. chapter 10. One should note that at some points in history Judaism was also a missionary religion. However with the development of Rabbinic Judaism in whatever form the mission of the Jews has not been to make converts, but, rather, to display to others the Holy People of God.

Hinduism (see Chapter 3), or sacred space and tribe in some indigenous religions (Chapter 2) – is what defines one's religious identity.[21] One might not be a "practicing Jew" and yet one's ethnic identity suffices for being a Jew. Similarly, one's caste demarcates the duties and obligations that ought to guide conduct and also define one's identity. In Hinduism, and also some indigenous religions, a temple must be built on a specific place just as Native Americans often have sacred places, say, the Black Hills in North Dakota or fishing sites in Northern Wisconsin. Nonmissionary religions thereby define religious identity in ways that demarcate group and sacred place (i.e. forms of what we called in Chapter 3 "social" and "local" basic goods). Religious rituals, moral guidance, religious leadership are set within the context of identity so defined and the rituals, guidance, and leadership are meant to strengthen identity and protect the purity of the community. This is why, recall, ritual is so important for the Confucian "noble-minded one" and his life under heaven.

A Jew, for instance, follows *Torah* and keeps Kosher because the Jews are to be the holy people of God. The land of Israel was promised to the Jews by YHWH (God), and so settling in the land has moral and religious importance. In fact, the passage from Deuteronomy in Hebrew scripture that heads this chapter contains the words of Moses to the people just before they are to cross over into the land promised to them by God. Yet as daily newspapers show, conflicts over the ownership of the land, conflicts also found in the book of Judges in the Hebrew Bible, can stem from the tight connection between religious identity and "place," sacred land. Similarly, for many Hindus, temples must be built on a sacred place. Sadly, in the last decades among fundamentalist and nationalist Hindus, if some other structure is built on that spot, specifically, a mosque (the Islamic house of prayer), then violence might break out over the rightful place of the temple. In other words, nonmissionary religions define religious identity in such a way that without some religious and moral counterbalance they are open to violence toward or exclusion of others and repression from within the bounds of the community. This is the threat of moral madness found within nonmissionary religions; it is the flip side of the problem of assimilation as a threat to this kind of religion. Furthermore, it is the possibility of moral madness that exposes the need for religious ethics within the religions themselves. We return to this point in our discussion of Jewish morality.

Missionary religions (like Christianity, Islam, and Buddhism) are likewise ways of life that are, sadly, open to distortion and violence, yet in different ways than nonmissionary religions. As the name implies, "missionary religions" are

---

21 The classic study about the importance of community in defining religion is Emile Durkheim, *Elementary Forms of Religious Life*. For a recent discussion along these lines see Taylor, C. (2004). *Modern Social Imaginaries*. Durham, NC: Duke University Press. For a helpful discussion of the issues, see Lear, J. (2008). *Radical Hope: Ethics in the Face of Cultural Devastation*. Cambridge, MA: Harvard University Press.

those communities for which religious identity is not bound to ethnicity, place, caste, or even language. To be sure, they may have sacred places, say, for Muslims the Ka'ba in Mecca, Saudi Arabia. According to tradition, the Ka'ba mosque was built by Abraham around a black stone and the Prophet Muḥammad named Mecca the Holy City of Islam.[22] Muslims also believe that the Qur'ān dictated to Muḥammad is the literal word of God (Allah) and therefore must be learned in the original Arabic and not translated into another language. Similarly, Buddhists give reverence to the Bodhi (or Bo) Tree under which the Buddha achieved Enlightenment. Sacred texts and commentaries are written in Sanskrit, the language of the elites, or Pāli. Christians of every sort give homage to the Church of the Holy Sepulchre in Jerusalem supposedly built on the site of Jesus' crucifixion and burial. Catholics also look to Rome as a sacred space and some still adhere to the Latin Mass and so Latin as the proper language of worship.

Whereas missionary religions have sacred places, languages, and spread initially among certain peoples (say Indians and the Chinese with Buddhism), religious identity, what makes one a Christian, for instance, is not defined most basically by those places, languages, or ethnicities. Given this fact, Muslims, Buddhists, and Christians can be found around the world, often engage in missions, and sometimes, especially in Islam and Christianity, establish governing regimes that are both religious and political. How then is religious identity constituted in these missionary religions? Here we can note some analogies among the missionary religions and then turn to explore religious identity in Judaism and Christianity as examples of nonmissionary and missionary religions, respectively.[23]

For the missionary religions, identity is constituted by beliefs and practices that establish access to higher power(s). A Buddhist, for instance, seeks refuge in the *Dharma*, that is, the teaching of the Buddha, and also follows the "Middle Way" explored in Chapter 6. There are also certain practices (prayer, meditation) that shape one's identity as a Buddhist. A Muslim must abide by the Pillars of Islam and, most importantly, confess that Allah (God) is One and Muḥammad is his Prophet.[24] One becomes a Christian through the ritual of

---

22 Although it cannot be explored in detail it is important to note that all three of the monotheistic religions (Judaism, Christianity, and Islam) claim Abraham as important to their faith traditions. This leads some scholars to speak about the "Abrahamic religions." Although true, it is also the case that the figure of Abraham provides a point of analogy between these religions since each of them understand his importance in different ways and also in relation to a central figure distinctive to that tradition: Muḥammad in Islam, Moses in Judaism, and Jesus Christ in Christianity. See Peters, F.E. (2005). *The Children of Abraham: Judaism, Christianity, Islam*, (new edition). Princeton, NJ: Princeton University Press.

23 We realize that the Jewish community has at certain times and places engaged in missionary activity. That said, our concern is with the legacy of modern Judaism mainly in the West.

24 Remember that although Islam has some 99 names for God, in the crucial confession the oneness of God or Allah is proclaimed.

baptism and the confession of faith in Jesus Christ as savior. Often enough there are the giving of names when one becomes a Christian or Muslim. In this way there is continuity and discontinuity between one's pre-Muslim identity and one's Muslim identity, one's pre-Christian identity and one's Christian identity.

Of course there are many different forms of Buddhism, Islam, and Christianity, each of which fashions religious identity in various ways. That point should be clear from the work of previous chapters of this book. Still, missionary religions require a shift or change in one's identity with respect to the central convictions and practices of the religious community. For instance, the *Saṅgha* is one of the Three Jewels of Buddhism, along with the Buddha and the *Dharma*. The *Saṅgha* is (i) the ideal Buddhist community including lay and ordained members but also (ii) the monastic community that varies in different strands of Buddhism. Analogously, a person makes a confession of faith in Jesus Christ and joins a Church, usually through baptism, and then lives as a disciple of Christ. This is true of infant baptism as well. But there are many kinds of Christian community. For the Muslim, identity and membership are also central, albeit with respect to Islamic practices and convictions and the worldwide Islamic community (*Ummah*). Importantly, in each of these cases there is no restriction in principle on who might become a Christian, a Buddhist, or a Muslim. And that is because these are "missionary" religions that seek to "convert" or religiously re-identify people and often morally so.

Rather than explore the details, divisions, and differences within and between missionary religions, we can now spot the point of vulnerability to a form of moral madness. Under specific social, political, and economic conditions the missionary religions *can*, but need not, become colonizing religions. Colonial expansion and conquest has taken different forms within the missionary religions at different times in history. There were Christian crusades, or military campaigns, to reclaim Jerusalem from Muslims, often mistakenly called "Mohammadans," during the Middle Ages. Pope Urban II called the First Crusade in 1095 CE. Its purpose was to restore Christian access to holy places in Jerusalem by vanquishing Muslim rule. In the modern Western world, Protestant missionaries sought converts in Korea, China, Latin America, and Africa, often with the help of colonial military and economic powers, like England and the Unites States. In Asia, the emperor Aśoka ruled the Maurya Empire from 273 to 232 BCE in India and lands beyond, seeking to spread Buddhism to other countries and also expand the power of the empire. It is also true that there were no less than five Islamic empires and four caliphates. These include the Mughal Empire (1526–1857 CE) in India and remembered today because of the Taj Mahal; the Umayyad Caliphate (661–750 CE), the Second Islamic Caliphate that established the largest Arab Muslim state in history; and the Ottoman Empire (1299–1922 CE), which was the greatest Muslim empire and also one of the longest ruling empires in history. Of course, at different times and for different reasons, the peoples brought into these empires were treated in different ways, not all of which were violent. Still, it is easy to grasp how religious convictions, practices, and institutional forms could spread in alliance with political, military, and economic powers and authorities.[25]

The complex and ambiguous history of the missionary religions and their conquests, empires, and caliphates throughout world history cannot be addressed in this book. The focus is ethical and religious on the question of the formation of peoples' moral identities. Nonmissionary religions, we noted, are vulnerable to moral madness by drawing rigid borders between the religious community and the "world" as well as imposing strict uniform markers of identity on members of the sacred community thereby denying the complexity of identities.

For missionary religions, the specter of moral madness is the conviction that other peoples' lives must be colonized and remade within the terms of the "true" religion. Historically this has been seen in the spread of Islam, the expulsion of the Jews from Spain in 1492 CE by Christians on the charge of blood libel (that is, as the supposed killers of Jesus), and many other instances throughout the ages. The root of moral madness, for Muslims, is found in the distinction between the "House of Islam" and the "House of War" (see Chapter 3). Moral madness is rooted in Christian thought and life in the idea of the "Final Judgment" of Christ's Second Coming and also the so-called "Great Commission" in Matthew 28:18–20:

> And Jesus came and said to them, "All authority in heaven and on earth has been given to me. Go therefore and make disciples of all nations, baptizing them in the name of the Father and of the Son and of the Holy Spirit, and teaching them to obey everything that I have commanded you. And remember, I am with you always, to the end of the age."

Of course, Muslims and Christians have ways to counter moral madness, say through love of enemy in Christian ethics (cf. Mt 5:38) and the special status of members of the other Abrahamic religions within the House of Islam. At this juncture it is enough to note that within the missionary religions the possibility of moral madness is lodged in the demand to convert others through coercion that overturns the responsibility to respect and enhance the integrity of others' lives.

---

25 It is beyond the scope of this book to examine new forms of politicized religion (for example, politicized Islam and politicized Christianity). Much recent attention has been paid to the Islamic State (ISIL/ISIS) and Boko Haram, but politicized and violent religion has been a prevalent throughout human history. We are aware, however, that the forms of politicized religion change with social and political cultures and historical periods, so that the kinds of communities to which religious rhetoric is directed and the political forms it takes differ based on the different target audiences and the various communities to which the wider religious tradition (in its less politicized or less violent forms) thinks it is accountable.

With the ideas of missionary and nonmissionary religions in hand as well as the threats of moral madness within those types of religion, we turn now to a deeper examination of Jewish and Christian thought as paradigmatic examples of missionary and nonmissionary religions. In doing so, we will find that the point or aim of the religious life is a profound responsibility and gratitude for life. This insight will enable us to chart the analogies between Christian and Jewish ethics even while advancing our conception of the "point of religious ethics."

Torah and the Repair of the World

What are basic ideas in Jewish moral thinking and practice? One basic idea is that traditionally Jews did not speak of ethics. That term denoted a discipline of thought arising from the Greek and Roman world. Jewish moral life focuses on obedience to God's (YHWH) commands that constitute *Torah* or "teaching" or "instruction" but sometimes called "the Law." The so-called Ten Commandments or Ten Words given to Moses on Mount Sinai are the crystallization or epitome of the Law. The Jewish life is thereby following obediently God's instruction within a community called to be a holy light to the world. There are different forms or types of *Torah*. It can refer to the *Torah*, the first five books of the Hebrew Scriptures (Pentateuch in Greek) including rabbinic commentary. *Torah* can also mean the entire scripture or even the whole of Jewish life and culture.

There are, furthermore, written, oral, and eternal forms of *Torah*. According to rabbinic teaching, the entirety of written and oral *Torah* was given by God to Moses, the greatest of the Hebrew Prophets.[26] In this way, *Torah* also denotes the covenant between God and his people, and, correlatively, the obligations and way of life enabled and required of them to be a holy people. In *Halakhah* (Jewish Law) there is special concern for the irreducible dignity of every human being. Recall that the dignity and worth of fellow human beings is captured in the Silver Rule that Rabbi Hillel said was really the whole of *Torah* (see Chapter 3). The core of Jewish moral thought is then the divine source of morality revealed in *Torah*, the dignity of human beings, and the reality of the Jewish community as the elect people of God. As Elliot Dorff has argued, "Classical Judaism defines the moral in terms of God's will as articulated in God's commandments," but also that in the Talmud "the law is not fully sufficient to define morality, that there are morals "beyond the letter of the law" (*lifnim m'shurat ha-din*).[27]

26 On the importance of Moses to the formation of the canon see Stackert, J. (2014). *A Prophet like Moses: Prophecy, Law, and Israelite Religion*. Oxford: Oxford University Press. For an examination of Rabbinic thought, see Fishbane, M. (2003). *Biblical Myth and Rabbinic Mythmaking*. Oxford: Oxford University Press.
27 Dorff, E.N. (2001). Doing the right and the good: fundamental convictions and methods in Jewish ethics. In: *Ethics in the World Religions*, (ed. J. Runzo and N.M. Martin), 90. New York: Oneworld Publications.

Within the narrative flow of the *Tanakh* is found the history of the Jews, from a creation account to their slavery in Egypt and liberation by Moses. The story is characterized in Genesis 1–11 as the great tale of human sin (Gen 3, Adam and Eve), the reality of murder (Gen 4, Cain and Abel), and God's final destruction of life through a great flood while preserving a righteous man (Noah), his family, and animals to repopulate the earth (Gen 5–9). In this story one sees the ambiguous nature of human beings, capable of great virtue and faithfulness (Noah), but also murder (Cain), temptation, and disobedience (Adam and Eve). From the perspective of religious ethics, this narrative of the people of Israel explains both the need for, and the form of God's instruction on the way to life (*Torah*).

One way that the biblical story of the Jews is crucial in Jewish morality is that it clarifies the moral standing of human beings and human moral vulnerability. Human beings are created in the image of God (*Imago Dei*) and thus have a special relation to the divine, a relation that includes the commission of Adam to name the creatures of the earth and also to "be fruitful and multiply," thereby participating in the divine act of creation.[28] Precisely which aspect of human beings reflects the divine image is debated throughout *Torah* and Jewish thought. Sometimes the divine image is related to the ability to make moral judgments, that is, to distinguish good from bad and right from wrong. It has also been found in the capacity of human beings to speak and to think and/or to love as God can love. Furthermore, God owns everything that God creates, even the human person and her or his body. This means that human beings do not have the right to govern autonomously their own lives and bodies. Because God "owns" human beings, there are rules of health, sexuality, sleep, diet, and the like important for the stewardship of the body and life by the faithful Jew. By the same logic, suicide is prohibited because we do not own ourselves. The creation of human beings by God established bodily, social, and reflective basic goods – as we have called them – that are important for living obediently to the divine will. Judaism thereby teaches that one is to enjoy human pleasures within the framework of Jewish law and thought. Of special importance is the family in which sex can bring joy and companionship as well as children. The family – as a form in which basic goods are integrated – provides for needs, is the context for offspring, is the source for early education, and supports future

---

28 On should note that the monotheistic religions take different positions on the human relation to God. Jews and Christians agree that human beings are created *in the image of God* but then differ on its meaning. Christians are especially concerned to relate the divine image to Jesus as the Christ. Muslims, conversely, adhere to the strict prohibition of making images of God (Allah) and therefore not even human beings are images of God. Human beings are understood as the "vice-regents" of God on earth. On this see, Schweiker, W., Jung, K., and Johnson, M. (2006). *Humanity Before God: Contemporary Faces of Jewish, Christian, and Islamic Ethics.* Minneapolis, MN: Fortress Augsburg Press.

generations. The family is the primary unit of Jewish life closely linked to the Jewish community.

In the creation story, human beings (Adam: literally "dust creature;" Eve: "living one" or "source of life" – and so the human is living or breathing dust) live in the Garden of Eden – a paradise – and, initially, lack self-awareness (they do not know they are "naked"). God commands them not to eat of the Tree of the Knowledge of Good and Evil, and should they do so they will die. In this well-known story of Western culture, Adam and Eve do eat of the Tree, they do become mortal, and they do become self-aware (they hide from God out of shame for their nakedness). God exiles them from Eden into a world of good and evil where the human being must always struggle to do good, but often without knowing in a specific case what one ought to do. In a word, the story relates a conception of the moral strength and weakness of human beings and the need for moral guidance, the need for *Torah*. However, just as important, the creation story indicates that human worth is not dependent on what someone does or their personal capacities. The worth of a human being is rooted in the fact that he or she is created by God. This further means that any insult or wrong doing to another human being is an affront to God. A Jew is to treat every person with respect. We return to this point below because it is the crucial idea to combat moral madness in a nonmissionary religion like Judaism.

Two key figures, Abraham and Moses, fill out, ethically speaking, the surrounding narrative important to Jewish morals.[29] "Righteousness was asleep until it was awakened by Abraham" (*Midrash Tehillim*, Psalm 110). In Abraham, God found a human being who was obedient to the divine command, even the command to leave his homeland and to sacrifice his son Isaac. Because of his fidelity, God would make Abraham the father of a great nation. Jewish morality, like other religions, conceives of morality not only in terms of actions as what are morally important, but also the inner life of consciousness – intentions, passions, attitudes, emotions, and thoughts.[30] With Abraham, according to *Midrash Tehillim* (the *Midrash* is the rabbinic exegesis of the *Tanakh*), human

---

29 In saying this we do not mean that Jewish ethics is a kind of "narrative ethics" often associated with some contemporary Christian and philosophical ethics. Additionally, sociologists like Robert Bellah note that Israelite religion was always expressed in narrative form even when articulating moral and speculative ideas, what he calls "mythospeculation," and never reached the kind of "theoretic culture" associated with the other "axial" religions. Our purpose is not to judge the adequacy of Bellah's account of the Israelite "axial moment" but to note that the use of narrative form in the Hebrew scriptures is not a version of recent "narrative ethics." Again, see Bellah, R. (2011). *Religion in Human Evolution: From the Paleolithic to the Axial Age*. Cambridge, MA: Belknap Press of Harvard University Press.

30 Some thinkers would disagree and insist that a difference between Jewish and Christian ethics is the great weight Christian thought places on interior states of the moral agent. We clearly disagree with that claim. See Green, R.M. (2001). Christian ethics: a Jewish perspective. In: *The Cambridge Companion to Christian Ethics*, (ed. R. Gill), 138–153. Cambridge University Press.

beings were awakened to the meaning of righteousness. Here the close connection between God and God's command and the Jewish conception of morals can be seen in the figure of Abraham, the symbolic father of the monotheistic religions. Righteousness is within the reach of human beings even if this entails ongoing moral struggle, as Abraham also experienced.

However, it is with Moses, the Exodus from slavery in Egypt, and the giving of the *Torah* at Sinai that the core of Jewish morality is to be found. Not only does Moses lead the people from slavery, but God speaks the Law to him in the form of Ten Words or Commandments that Moses conveys to the people. It was a people who gathered at Sinai to receive the Law, and also, ironically, to break it by worshipping idols. There is, then, century upon century of commentary by Jews on the Ten Words in the Talmud and Mishnah. The Law is the comprehensive guide for individual and communal life. Further, the Jewish community has special importance in Jewish ethics. After all, it was the community that made covenant with God for all ages. This means that personal morality and interpersonal relations are always set within the community.

There are specific features and responsibilities of the Jewish community. Jews are to be a light to the "nations" and thus a Holy People set apart in a special relation to God. This apartness is expressed in cultic rites, say, in the circumcision of male children, but also symbolized by the *minyan*, that is, a prayer quorum of 10 Jewish adult males needed for study and proper worship. In many respects the community meets the basic goods of life needed for education, religious life, justice, and medical needs. And, further, this community is for life; it is nonvoluntary and in this way the individual Jew cannot be severed from the community. The purpose of the individual Jew and the Jewish community is to know and to do the will of God. As it is stated in the passage from Deuteronomy at the head of the chapter, the Jews will be "loving the Lord your God, and holding fast to him ...." The community is to choose life in obedience to God's will.

It should be clear that Judaism manifests the various attributes of nonmissionary religions, but also, importantly, has beliefs that can be used to defuse moral madness that might under specific conditions be realized, namely, the obligation to show respect to every human being as created by God and also the mission to "repair the world." In order to further the picture of Jewish ethics, one must explore the latent threat of limiting the scope of moral responsibility to the Jews alone at the expense of the moral standing of those outside of the community. That this type of moral madness is possible within Judaism might be hard to conceive given the centuries of persecution that Jews have endured. In the face of the horrors of the Jewish Shoah, the murder of over six million Jews at the hands of German Nazis during World War II, it might seem unimaginable to claim that contemporary Judaism and even the State of Israel could be subject to moral madness. That is not our claim. We are not making judgments about the moral rectitude of this long-suffering people. In fact, the point is that in ancient Israel one finds annunciated a principle to combat moral madness in every form. In this way, Robert Bellah, a sociologist of religion, rightly noted the axial breakthrough in ancient Israel in the Hebrew Prophets' concern for the poor, the outcast, the widow, and the slave.[31]

Unlike Christians, Jews do not believe that the *messiah*, the savior lord, has already come into human history.[32] The world remains broken. Poverty, war, dreadful disease, and hatred are defining features of this broken world. Of course, only God (YHWH) can bring the messiah and repair the world. But Jews are covenant partners with God and this means that an essential mission of Judaism is to repair the world. Jews must help God bring about and make real the messianic hope of peace and justice under God's rule. From this deep conviction about what God commands, *mitzvot*, flows convictions about social justice, the dignity of every human being, and the task of healing and repairing the world. And that is the point. When the conviction about the human as made in the image of God is bound to the command to help God repair the world, no human being is outside of a Jewish conception of social justice. What is more, the Jewish community exists not as community whose identity constricts the scope of its moral responsibility. On the contrary, the Jews are to be the Holy People of God elected to be a light to the nations about the command to repair the world. The responsibility to be the covenant people of God is the grounds of Jewish identity. There is also a frank admission of human fallibility as well as the need to protect the community. Without denying human dignity, this realism about violence and even the limits of reconciliation are born, no doubt, from the centuries of persecution that the Jewish community has endured.

Although Jewish identity is rooted in the community, it nevertheless has, by a *mitzvoth* from God, to work with God to "repair the world" and this entails respect for every human being and also the struggle for social justice. As the Jewish ethicist Ronald Green has noted, "Christianity has always tried to extend its reach universally to embrace people of all backgrounds both in terms of membership and in the scope of its ethical concern. In contrast, Judaism," he argues, "has tended to focus on the experience of one continuing ethnic community."[33] And yet Jewish particularism focused on the life of the community is interwoven with an ardent commitment to moral universalism, that is, the claim that no one is outside the scope of the Jewish responsibility. This commitment is the grounds for self-criticism. The command of God and the work to repair the *world* means that Jewish distinctiveness is always oriented

---

31 Robert Bellah, *Religion in Human Evolution*, esp. ch. 6.

32 The question of Jewish messianism and the claim of some to have been the "messiah" are long disputed issues in classic and also contemporary Jewish thought. We need not explore the details of this debate in order to grasp a Jewish conception of religious self-criticism.

33 Green, R.M. (2001). Christian ethics: a Jewish perspective. In: *The Cambridge Companion to Christian Ethics*, (ed. Robin Gill), 142. Cambridge University Press.

toward an inclusive moral community while also remaining true to the defining feature of the Jewish people in their distinctive way of life. On reaching this conclusion, we turn to an example of missionary religions.

The Way and Abundant Life

This chapter seeks to establish the "point" of religious ethics and one can summarize that point in two ways, namely, how to use religious sources for guiding a responsible life, both personal and communal, and also how to combat the threat of "moral madness" that arises with religious traditions. The second point of combating moral madness necessarily involves self-criticism within a religious tradition. How might that principle of self-criticism become articulated in a missionary religion?

Christianity and Islam are no doubt the most ardent, maybe most aggressive, missionary religions. The Gospel of Luke in the New Testament of the Christian Bible along with its companion the Acts of the Apostles trace the growth of the early Christian community from its origin in the circle of disciples gathered around Jesus to what were conceived to be "the ends of the Earth." The Gospel of Matthew concludes on these words that we have also cited above (Mt 28:18–20):

> And Jesus came and said to them. "All authority in heaven and on earth has been given to me. Go therefore and make disciples of all nations, baptizing them in the name of the Father and of the Son and of the Holy Spirit, and teaching them to obey everything that I have commanded you. And remember, I am with you always, to the end of the age."

This saying is apparently part of the early Church's liturgy, or pattern of worship, because it is unlikely that the historical Jesus would have referred to baptizing in the name of the Trinity, that is, the distinctively Christian conception of God as Three-in-One, as Father, Son, and Holy Spirit, and so one God in three persons. Our task is not to rehearse or to examine the finer points of Christian ideas about the Trinity.[34] The important point is that from its beginning, Christianity has been a missionary religion, seeking to make disciples of all nations.

The moral tension and instability we isolated in nonmissionary religions was the possibility of grounding moral responsibility exclusively in communal identity and thereby to exclude those outside the sacred community from the

---

34 Ideas about the Trinity were not completed as doctrine until the fourth century CE and so hundreds of years after Jesus's historical ministry. What is more, Christians continue to debate the meaning of this idea about God. For instance, Eastern Orthodox theology is markedly different from Western Christianity, Catholic and Protestant, on understanding the relations among the "persons" of the Godhead.

scope of one's moral responsibility. We saw how Jewish morality works against this possibility and provides the means of religious self-criticism. The danger in a missionary religion is to try violently and coercively to enfold and remake the identity of others within the religious mission, a specific kind of moral madness. That seems a possibility about the passage from Matthew's just cited. Yet things are more complicated. Just as one finds within Jewish ethics a coun-terbalance to moral madness, there is some analogical counterbalance in Christianity as well. This is not to say that Christians have always lived by their most basic responsibilities! The long history of colonial conquest, crusades, and religious wars among Christians aptly show how morally difficult it is to balance religious identity and responsibility. Can Christian ethics help us indi-cate the tension found among the missionary religions?

Like Jews and Muslims, Christians did not originally call their thought about how to live in fidelity to Christ a form of "ethics." The early followers of Jesus often spoke about being in "the Way." And because Christianity arose out of Judaism, it was always occupied with the question of how to live in fidelity to God's commands as well as the teaching and example of Jesus. Furthermore, early Christians who pondered questions about the meaning of their faith for how to live did not call their reflection "theology." Theology was a term for reflection on the Roman gods of nature, the theater, and the empire, including beliefs about the divinity of the emperor.

As Christians spread throughout the Roman Empire and attracted converts who were intellectuals, Greek and Roman philosophical movements, like Stoicism, Platonism, and others, were found useful in making the new faith intelligible to the surrounding and often hostile social world. This posed the challenge of the *accommodation* of the convictions of the early followers of Jesus to later thinkers. Even St. Paul in his Letter to the Romans (Rm 13) appar-ently was willing to grant that God had established Roman rule and thus the legitimacy of the non-Christian rulers. Some early Christian teachers spoke of themselves as "philosophers," that is, lovers of wisdom that was taught and manifested in Jesus Christ. What is more, Greek and Roman "philosophy" was preoccupied with the question of how to live in order to flourish and attain "happiness" (*eudaimonia*) and the practices necessary for such a life. In that way, much of philosophy was about ethics. So although the term "ethics" did not make its way into Christian thinking for some time, from the beginning and in different forms, "ethical" issues were central to the new religious movement. This too raised the problem of accommodation. Jesus lived in a tension between a specific community of disciples believed to be the in-breaking Kingdom of God and a more universal ethical intention and responsibility.[35] Yet it was left to later thinkers to explain the extent to which Jesus' teaching about "blessedness"

---

35 This tension has been explored in great detail in Troeltsch, E. (1992). *The Social Teachings of the Christian Churches*, vol. 1–2. Louisville, KY: Westminster John Knox Press.

(see Mt 5–7) would transform or be accommodated to Greek and Roman ideas about *eudaimonia* as well as the universal intent of his commandments about love of others, the neighbor, and even the enemy.

Hidden in this question about the use of the term "ethics" to describe Christian reflection on how to live is also an indication of the break between Christianity and Judaism. For Jews the moral life was always lived in relation to God's command, law or *Torah*, and so guided by legal reasoning and judgment. The Christian focus on love, rather than traditional *Torah* teaching, signals, at points, a different morality. This is the case even though Judaism and Christianity have analogical principles for how to treat others rightly, the Golden and Silver Rules.

In this light it is hardly surprising that Christianity has been called a "religion of love." One reads in the New Testament letter 1 John 4:8 that God is love. Jesus Christ gave a new commandment to his disciples that they should love each other as he loved them (Jn 13:34). St. Paul speaks of the three basic spiritual gifts as faith, hope, and love and in his great hymn to love (I Cor 13:1–13) insists that love is the greatest of these gifts. Most radically, Jesus is attributed as teaching in the so-called Sermon on the Mount that one is to love one's enemies (Mt 5–7). The question that presents itself to Christians throughout the ages is what "love" means and how is it to be lived faithfully in the rough and tumble of daily existence, including the horrors of war. Moreover, when Greek and Roman conceptions of human happiness (*eudaimonia*) became fused with the emerging Christian faith, the question arose about the relation between love, the commands of God, and *eudaimonia*.

One can isolate the way in which Christians throughout the ages have sought to understand the ethical meaning of "love." How might it be an antidote to the kind of moral madness found in a missionary religion? Just as Jews have had to make sense of the various meanings of "Law" and their teaching for the life of the Jewish community, Christians have had to wrestle with the meaning and orientation of life in terms of the double-love command (love God and neighbor), the Golden Rule (love others as oneself), Jesus' command to his disciples, the relation of faith, hope and love, and the love of enemy.[36] They have done so by drawing on scripture, which for Christians includes the Old Testament (the Hebrew Bible) and the New Testament, as well as other sources of moral knowledge.

The commands to love God, the neighbor, and the enemy are given specific form in Christian thought through the "Law," epitomized by the Ten Commandments, but also the example of Jesus' ministry, St. Paul's understanding

---

36 It has also been long debated if love can be commanded. Some thinkers, like Immanuel Kant, do not believe love can be commanded whereas others, say, Søren Kierkegaard, insist that Christian love can be and in fact is commanded. There is also considerable debate about the relation between "Christian love" (*caritas* in the Latin; *agape* in Greek) and other forms of love, say friendship (*philia*) or erotic love (*eros*). We cannot here enter into these debates within distinctly Christian ethics.

of Christ, the work of the divine spirit, and through the reign of God in the world and in the Church. A detailed examination of these various foci for interpreting the ethical intention of love is not possible here. However, a few comments are needed in order to grasp the ways in which a missionary religion like Christianity can manifest moral madness and also lose its religious distinctiveness. One needs as well to understand how Christian love can be an antidote to moral madness.

Christian thinkers have long held that love of any form is a crucial element in understanding the distinctive human capacity for action (Chapter 5). At one level, this is obvious with respect to self-love. Human beings seem to act from some motive of self-regard or self-love. In the Golden Rule, one is bid to love others *as* one loves herself or himself. Of course, it is important to distinguish between right self-love and sheer egoism or inordinate pride. Christian thinkers have long done so.[37] In fact, the command to love the neighbor as the self is itself a test against pride and egoism because others must be considered morally equal with oneself. Further, some Christian thinkers, especially in the Catholic tradition, have seen love as a "virtue" or an excellence of character. Virtues are settled, habitual dispositions to act in certain ways, say, loving ways. Different thinkers variously enumerate and rank virtues. Aristotle, for example, examines a range of virtues like courage and justice but also generosity, friendliness, and many others as a mean between excess and deficiency of some motive to act. The courageous person must act on the "mean" between an excess of anger or its deficiency in relation to the person, some people are more "hot blooded" than others, and also the situation at hand. Recall that Augustine, contrariwise, held that all of the virtues are forms of Christian love, *caritas*, and Thomas Aquinas distinguished between cardinal virtues (prudence, temperance, fortitude, and justice) gained through human action and the theological virtues (faith, hope, and love) that are infused by God on the soul. Following St. Paul's ideas in 1 Corinthians 13:13, Thomas, like Augustine, teaches that love (*caritas*) is the greatest virtue and in fact the source of them all.[38]

It is important to see, then, that from a Catholic perspective "love" is a virtue but that Christian love is more radically the divine spirit acting in and through the human agent perfecting her or him into a likeness of the God who is love (see Chapter 5). Christian love is both the fulfillment of the Law (God's commands) and also the ultimate human good, ultimate felicity (*eudaimonia*) – the

---

37 See Weaver, D.F. (2002). *Self-Love and Christian Ethics*. Cambridge: Cambridge University Press.

38 The claim that love is the root of all the virtues or that the virtues are all forms of love leads to a claim about the unity of the virtues, that is, that a virtuous person must, per definition, poses all of the other virtues. That seems to be a difficult claim to make and has been much disputed. We cannot enter that debate in this book, but it is important to see that for theologians, the unity of the virtues is grounded in God's gracious action in the lives of believers and not a claim about human capabilities to attain virtues. For a recent criticism of the idea of the unity of the virtues, see MacIntrye, A. (1984). *After Virtue*, 2e. Notre Dame, IN: University of Notre Dame Press.

transcendent good. To love God and neighbor is, by grace, to achieve and receive happiness. This pattern of thought thereby binds together ancient Greek and Roman ideas about *eudaimonia* with the biblical conception of Law and God's commands. Orthodox theologians made a similar argument. The great Eastern Orthodox theologian Maximus the Confessor (d. 662) wrote:

> "But I say to you," the Lord says, "love your enemies, do good to those who hate you, pray for those who persecute you." Why did he command these things? So that he might free you from hatred, sadness, anger and grudges, and might grant you the greatest possession of all, perfect love, which is impossible to possess except by the one who loves all equally in imitation of God.[39]

Love is the imitation of God but also and ultimately the deification, the *theosis*, of the human being. The idea of the ultimate human good as *theosis* is central to Orthodox thought. Again, ultimate human happiness and obedience to the Divine action are united in the understanding of Christian love.

Protestant Christianity also holds that love is basic to the Christian life as in Martin Luther's famous phrase, "faith becomes active in love" (see Chapter 3). The fundamental relation a human being has to God is faith or faithlessness, and faith frees the Christian to love the neighbor. Protestants worried that making love and happiness the center of Christian conviction, as Catholics seem to do, risked making one's love for the neighbor actually a means to one's own happiness and thus no longer a radical love of the neighbor for himself or herself. This seems to miss the point of the "moral paradox" (see Chapter 3). In other words, the double-love *command* paradoxically dislodges love as the primary motive for Christian action and replaces it with freedom in faith.[40] Faith is active in the love of God, neighbor, and the enemy. Once the Christian accepts in faith God's mercy, then one is freed from seeking personal perfection and thus is enabled to love others, including the enemy.

In traditional Christian thought no matter what strand of the tradition one considers, love is always situated within what we can call "spheres of

---

39 Maximus the Confessor (1985). *Selected Writings*, ed. G.C. Berthold, 41. Mahwah, NJ: Paulist Press.

40 Some Protestant thinkers have drawn the contrast between *agape*, the Greek term for love and used almost exclusively in the New Testament, and *caritas*, the Latin translation of *agape*, to denote two different kinds of love. On this account, *agape* is a radical, self-giving love that does not consider the lovableness of the one loved but the quality of the love. *Agape*, then, is modeled on God's love for sinners. *Caritas*, on this account, is connected to *eros* (erotic love) and so the love of something because of its desirability and thus, ultimately, a kind of self-love. The claim, which is no longer widely held, is that Protestants think about love in terms of *agape* and Catholics do so through *caritas*. For the classic statement of this position, again which is no longer widely held, see Nygren, A. (1982). *Agape and Eros*. Chicago: University of Chicago Press.

responsibility" as well as basic and moral goods. Christian love is expressed in the family, in the Church to fellow believers, in the wider social and political world, and in one's relation with God. Analogous to Jewish ideas about human life, each of these spheres has its own distinctive duties and goods and they are related to the various goods we have explored in previous chapters (basic bodily, social, local, and reflective goods; the moral good; transcendent good(s)). Different Christian thinkers and communities have understood these "spheres" in various ways and the same is true of the goods and duties they entail. Some Christians, for instance, argue that the form love takes in the political arena is justice, and justice might demand, in some circumstances, engaging in a justified war, economic redistribution, or even capital punishment for the sake of social stability and peace. Others insist that Christian love forbids all forms of killing and therefore the Church must not enter into institutions of political power. The point to grasp is that Christian ideas about love and their relation to the moral life touch the deep inwardness of a person's life and also social life. One cannot truly love God, and hate the neighbor; one cannot love others and deny God's reality and will. In this way, one finds the principle to thwart moral madness from within the most central claim of Christian faith as a missionary religion.

The commands to love the neighbor and even more radically to love the enemy have been interpreted in different ways. Admittedly, at times, especially during the Middle Ages in the West, the idea of forced conversion as well as death sentences for the unfaithful were practiced, especially against Jews and Muslims. The belief was that forced conversion and even death was a way to save the "soul" of the pagan or infidel from the external punishment of Hell and damnation, and, accordingly, was in fact an act of love. Is there a principle about Christian love that can counter moral madness in this missionary religion?

In 1 John, one of the so-called "general epistles" in the New Testament, one finds a beginning of an answer to this question. As noted previously, the author writes,

> God is love (*agape*), and those who abide in love abide in God and God abides in them ... We love because he first loved us. Those who say, "I love God" and hate their brothers and sisters, are liars; for those who do not love a brother or a sister whom they have seen, cannot love God whom they have not seen. The commandment we have from him is this: those who love God must love their brothers and sisters also. (1 Jn 4:16b; 19–21)

Clearly, one's love of other Christians – the brothers and the sisters – is grounded in and modeled on God's love for oneself. Love of others is not based on one's desire for them or that they deserve and have some intrinsic right to such love. Rather, the ground and model of this love is God's command and acts of love. In other words, there is an essential link between love of God and love of others and it is a link established by God. God acts in and through the person who loves. This seems, then, to block any act of moral madness *within* the community. In fact, if one does any wrong to a fellow Christian, then one no longer abides in love and thereby no longer abides in God. Christian identity is constituted by abiding in God's love that grounds one's responsibility to others. Responsibility as love of others is the necessary condition for Christian identity.

Although the passage in 1 John provides a bulwark against moral madness *within* the Christian community, it does not seem to provide a safeguard and principle of self-criticism in terms of responsibility for anyone *not* in the community. It is this delimitation of the scope of responsibility that has, sadly, allowed Christians to draw a moral line between believers and unbelievers. Without further clarification, Christian love could be limited to fellow Christians and thereby leave unanswered the problem of moral madness against those outside the community. Perhaps one could argue, and some have, that the command to love the neighbor, especially in light of Jesus' "parable of the Good Samaritan" (Lk 10:29–37), answers this problem.[41] In this parable Jesus teaches that what defines a neighbor is not the proximity of the other to oneself or any other attribute of the other, say, their virtue. The neighbor is the one who acts as a neighbor and cares for another person, especially one in grave need. After all, in the parable it is the Samaritan and not a Jew who proves to act as a neighbor. Responsibility is thereby not delimited by religious identity but expanded to include anyone in need.

The parable moves in the direction of self-criticism because it was originally "told" by Jesus to fellow Jews. It presents in literary form the stark command of Jesus to love the enemy. That is the case because at the time of Jesus' ministry there was great bitterness and conflict among Jews and Samaritans. Jesus in essence says to his fellow Jews, "See, here is your enemy who loves the neighbor while you fail to do so." To read the parable in this way provides a safeguard against moral madness since the scope of responsibility is not delimited by identity and there is no suggestion that the Samaritan seeks to convert the man injured by robbers.

The principle of self-criticism is found in the link between the injunction in 1 John that one cannot love God and hate others and Jesus' radical claim about love of enemy and its parabolic expression in the story of the Good Samaritan. The mission of Christianity, ethically speaking, should not be defined in terms of coercively or violently converting others to the Christian faith, but, rather, to live out a form of responsibility that enacts in the world a nonexclusive love. Of course, someone might be converted to the Christian faith for any number of reasons, but that consequence is not the reason to practice Christian love. The

---

41 It is important to note that this parable is found only in the Gospel of Luke and thus has no parallel in the other "synoptic" Gospels (Mark and Matthew).

ground of Christian love is in the being and acting of God, the scope of which is understood and interpreted through the life and teaching of Jesus. Christians hold that when such action takes place in history and society there is a manifestation of the reign of God in the Church and in society. It is an event in which the prayer Jesus taught finds its focus, that is, that "God's will be done on earth as it is in heaven" (Mt 6:9–13). The mission of Christians is then not simply and solely to convert others, to remake their identities into Christian ones, but rather to serve in love within the spheres of responsibility for the sake of the integrity of life. The irony is that as a missionary religion Christians ought to give themselves away in love and acts of justice rather than in trying to remake the lives of others into members of the Church. The Christian believer hopes and has confidence that in doing so he or she will abide in God. That is the moral paradox, as we have called it. Responsible action constitutes Christian identity rather than identity being the ground and limit of responsibility.

The Integrity of Life and the Point of Religious Ethics

In this chapter we have isolated principles of self-criticism in a nonmissionary religion (Judaism) and a missionary religion (Christianity). In each case, albeit in different ways, a tradition's identity is preserved, but it is not the point or purpose of the responsible life. Understanding religious identities as expressions of the deepest principle of responsibility from within a religion betrays neither those identities nor delimits the scope of responsibility. Jewish particularism as a nonmissionary religion need not conflict with the universal responsibility to repair the world. The universal ethical intention of Christian love does not efface the distinctive personal and communal identities of Christian believers.

We can now formulate the analogy between Jewish and Christian ethics mindful of their profound differences and draw from these resources a principle of religious and moral self-criticism. Call it "The Principle of Integral Convictions" the aim of which is to respect and enhance the integrity of life.[42]

---

42 We do not want our principle to be confused with other positions, say, Alan Gewirth's "Principle of Generic Consistency," which states that "an agent must act in accordance with his or her own and every other agents' generic rights to well-being and freedom." See his *Reason and Morality*. Chicago: University of Chicago Press, 1978. Although our "Principle of Integral Convictions" is also concerned with coherence and consistency, we do not begin with generic features of action. We have adduced our principle from engaging and interpreting religious traditions rather than attempting to develop a freestanding rational foundation for an ethics. What is more, we speak of "convictions" for two reasons: (i) because a conviction is how a belief is held that orients human conduct, and (ii) moral beliefs can also "convict" one of moral misdeeds. When classical Protestant thinkers talked about "the convicting power of the Law" they meant the way in which moral and religious beliefs can also convict one of sin. Our point, then, is that deeply held moral beliefs are convictions that orient action and that can also convict one of wrongdoing.

That is, the principle aims to give direction for the responsible exercise of human power. By this principle we mean, as seen in Jewish and Christian thought, the need and obligation to integrate one's moral convictions in such a way that neither distinctive religious identities nor the wide scope of moral responsibility are elided.[43] Put somewhat abstractly, the principle denotes the fact that human life demands completion even as it is the "form" a completed life ought to take. This does not mean, let it be said and said bluntly, that everyone is to be just alike! Quite the contrary is the case. Everyone is to freely integrate and thus complete their lives, religiously and in their many relations, in whatever ways they choose as long as that choice does not entail demeaning and destroying the integrity of other people's lives.[44]

For Jews, this principle requires integrating convictions about being the chosen people of God with convictions about human beings created in God's image and also the mission to "repair the world." Responsibility is the integration of those convictions and so the form of moral action in such a way that Jewish identity is thereby also respected and enhanced. For Christians, the Principle of Integral Convictions is the integration of the various aspects of Christian love so that the love of God does not elide love of neighbor, self, or even the enemy. Responsibility is, again, the *form* of moral action under the Principle of Integral Convictions and thereby the way to manifest in action a distinctive Christian identity in ways that respect and enhance that same identity as well as the integrity of life before God.

So, under the Principle of Integral Convictions "responsibility" is the *form* one's moral and religious identity ought to take in relation to self, others, and the wider community of life.[45] Stated negatively, "moral madness" is the denial that responsibility entails the Principle of Integral Convictions wherein some basic conviction of a tradition is elided or exclusively chosen in the orientation of action. Moral madness is often driven by a notion of ridged logical consistency in the choices of how to form and live a religious identity. Our principle

---

43 Note that this position does not attempt to reduce all moral convictions or principles to one foundational norm or law, say Immanuel Kant's "categorical imperative," but is about the mutual and tensive relation between basic convictions. In the jargon of current thought, we are proposing a nonfoundational and yet coherent account of self-criticism.

44 In terms of moral theory, the book has developed a form of liberal naturalism, that is, the goods of life (basic, moral, transcendent) are linked to what kind of creatures we are but how life is integrated, completed, is a matter of moral freedom.

45 Again, note the distinctiveness of this argument. Rather than trying to reduce religious ethics to some universal moral principle, whether commanded by God or formulated philosophically, or binding, and limiting, religious ethics to the particular outlook and practices of a specific religious community, we are trying to show how the actual religions provide resources for articulating the Principle of Integral Convictions that interrelates particular identities with responsibility for the integrity of life. Again, it is, paradoxically, precisely the tensions *within* the religions that are productive for development of the meaning and method of religious ethics, a productive tension that is lost if one focuses only on universal obligations or particular identities.

focuses on the "integral" relations among the many convictions that constitute a religious identity. Thinking within religious traditions, and mindful of the analogy articulated by this principle about the form of responsibility, warrants the critical work entailed in ethical reflection and to do so in the name of a good that can sustain a human world. What might this mean for the constructive task of religious ethics?

Earlier in this chapter we noted that religious ethics assesses and prescribes how religious beliefs and practices can be lived responsibility by adherents of a specific religion, say, Judaism, but also, conceivably, how anyone might draw from various religious resources for the sake of taking responsibility for the integrity of life. In the previous section of the chapter we have shown what it would mean to think about the responsible life in terms of Judaism and Christianity. Now we can say a few words in terms of how one might use those sources to orient responsibility for the integrity of life. This requires relating the Principle of Integral Convictions to other dimensions of religious ethics explored in this book.

Religious Ethics: Meaning and Method is organized around five dimensions of reflection and each of these are structured by a specific tension or paradox. The same is true of this chapter and the Principle of Integral Convictions. That is to say, the challenge posed by the question of the "point of religious ethics" is how to endorse religious self-criticism without loss of a distinctive identity insofar as religious people find their transcendent good in the faith and practice of their communities and traditions. Put generally, how does a religious person or community simultaneously affirm the distinctive particularity of their religious identity and yet also the universal intention of their moral convictions in the choices made about how responsibly to form and live out one's religious identity? The *point* of religious ethics is to articulate this tension or perplexity about the particularity of identity and the universal intention of responsibility that, under the Principle of Integral Convictions, can define religious identity and come to expression within the lives of religious people and communities.

However, the idea is not merely about religious self-criticism and the tension between distinctive identities and the scope of responsibility. The book has tried to outline a multidimensional approach to religious ethics and thereby abide itself by the Principle of Integral Convictions. People struggle to "integrate" a range of basic goods, but the distinctive good of "moral integrity" is made possible only by acting on the interrelated obligations to respect and to enhance the integrity of life with and for others. The moral good finds its distinctly transcendent good through contact with, empowerment by, and orientation through the object of religious convictions and practices in some religious community. In other words, the Principle of Integral Convictions is the means to undertake acts of religious self-criticism because it also articulates for religious and moral reflection the responsibility to live by the integrity of life itself. More directly stated, the Principle of Integral Convictions states in terms internal to the religions why responsibility must be the grounds of religious identity rather than religious identity defining the meaning and scope of responsibility. In this way, the principle combats moral madness within the religions and also provides in shorthand form a task for religious ethics. It is to recognize that for religious people, the moral life is grounded in the call or command to respond to the transcendent good in ways that bestow on them a distinctive religious identity and moral integrity. Insofar as religious diversity is a constitutive feature of the moral space of our globalized world that allows for certain kinds of choices and limits for action, then religious ethics must provide orientation, including self-critical orientation, in that world. Isolating the Principle of Integral Convictions enables religious ethics to undertake that task.

Conclusion

If this claim for the Principle of Integral Convictions is right, and we contend that it is, then readers of this book can now retrace the argument of *Religious Ethics: Meaning and Method* to put flesh on the bones, as it were, of this principle. One can see how the highest, transcendent yet still really human good of the "integrity of life," as we have called it, is basic to the meaning and method of religious ethics and therefore to the moral and religious life as well. The Principle of Integral Convictions is nothing more than a shorthand term for the adventure of living the moral life within a distinctive religious identity. Our hunch, let it be said, is that nonreligious people also, in various ways, can and do integrate their lives through something like this principle. In that way the supposed difference between religious and philosophical ethics is overcome. That too has been the point of this book.

More specifically, the task of this volume has been to show how religious ethics can render morally productive, rather than destructive, a tension found in different kinds of religions about the responsible formation of religious identities. Religious ethics provides some means to counter the scourge of moral madness that has threatened and continues to threaten human and nonhuman life on this planet. In this light, the work of religious ethics, its task and point, is to orient religious peoples' lives so that, in gratitude and conviction, they may live with respect for and the enhancement of the integrity of life.

Glossary and Additional Concepts in the Study of Religious Ethics

The following list of figures and terms is drawn from the text in an effort to assist students who are new to the study of religious ethics and to assist quick reference to frequently used terms and often referenced figures. Much of the list is adapted from the "Glossary of Basic Terms" that appeared in *The Blackwell Companion to Religious Ethics*.[1] The remainder of the list was assembled from the following sources. For general terms in the study of religion and ethics, including dates for key figures, and concepts in the study of Buddhism, Hinduism, Islam, and Chinese religions, we consulted *The Encyclopedia of Religion*, the *Encyclopedia of Religion and Ethics*, *The HarperCollins Dictionary of Religion*, *Mirriam-Webster's Encyclopedia of World Religions*, *The Oxford Dictionary of the Christian Church*, and *The Oxford Dictionary of World Religions* along with the online *Stanford Encyclopedia of Philosophy*. For entries on the Penobscot and on Native American religions more generally, we relied on *Penobscot Man: The Life History of a Forest Tribe in Maine* and *Native American Religions: An Introduction*. For entries on the Igbo and African Traditional Religions, we relied on the *Igbo-English Dictionary: A Comprehensive Dictionary of the Igbo Language* and the *Encyclopedia of African Religion*. For additional information on Chinese religions, we also consulted the *Encyclopedia of China*. Full bibliographic information for these sources may be found in the bibliography.

> *Language abbreviations*: Arb.=Arabic, Arm.=Aramaic, Ch.=Chinese, En.=English, Gk.=Greek, Heb.=Hebrew, Ig.=Igbo, Lt.=Latin, Pa.=Pāli, Pn.=Penobscot, Skt.=Sanskrit

---

1 Clairmont, D.A. (2005). Glossary of basic terms. In: *The Blackwell Companion to Religious Ethics* (ed. W. Schweiker), 562–583. Malden, MA: Blackwell Publishing.

Religious Ethics: Meaning and Method, First Edition. William Schweiker and David A. Clairmont.
© 2020 William Schweiker and David A. Clairmont. Published 2020 by John Wiley & Sons Ltd.

A

Ācāra (Skt.) right conduct in accordance with social convention; an ācārya is one who teaches these rules of conduct, particularly as they relate to handing on religious law and ritual

Adab (Arb.) civility, etiquette, right norms of conduct; norms and customs; can indicate both laudatory personal traits as well as the disciplines necessary to inculcate these traits into personal behaviors

African Traditional Religion (ATR) (En.) designation used to refer collectively to the indigenous religions of the regions or specific tribes in Africa

Agape (Gk.) love or charity, often seen as the primary requirement and guide for conduct and character in Christian life (Mt 22:37). In traditional Catholic moral theology, infused supernatural virtue (caritas) that directs the human person (will and action) to its supernatural end (the love of God inclusive of neighbor love). In contemporary Christian ethics variously interpreted as (i) unconditional other-regard or (ii) equal regard for all human beings, including the self

Aggadah (Hb.) that portion of the Talmud containing narrative, sermons, and speculative explanations of rabbinic philosophy; often recasts biblical stories and accounts of the activities of rabbis in order to illustrate good behaviors and right thinking about problems

Aglebemu (Pn.) water monster of Penobscot mythology, defeated by the primeval hero Gluskabe to form the Penobscot River

Agu (Ig.) personal spirit that animates a physical body

Ahiṃsā (Skt.) nonviolence, not desiring injury or harm of another; an idea in Indian thought shared by Jainism, Buddhism, and Hinduism; also denotes correlative feelings for the well-being or flourishing of other people

Ahkām (Arb.) decision; in Islamic jurisprudence, divided into five kinds: farḍ (obligatory), mustaḥabb (recommended), mubāḥ (neutral), makrūh (discouraged), ḥarām (forbidden)

Ahu (Ig.) physical body

Akankwumoto (Ig.) justice

Akedah (Hb.) "binding," referring to the binding of Isaac by Abraham in Genesis 22 in the Hebrew Bible/Old Testament

Akrasia (Gk.) "weakness of will" exhibited primarily in intentional behavior that conflicts with the agent's values or principles; contrasted with enkrasia (continence; strong will)

Akuśula-mūla/akusula-mūla (Skt./Pa.) three unwholesome roots of action; enumerated in Pāli as lobha/rāga (greed), dosa (hatred), and moha (delusion)

Algonquian also Algonquin; language group of Native American tribes in the northeastern and upper midwestern United States and lower Canada, which includes the Wabanaki Confederation of tribes (Abenaki, Maliseet, Mi'kmaq, Passamaquoddy, and Penobscot)

Allah (Arb.) God or a supreme being; used specifically in relation to the belief in the single God of Islamic faith but also in reference to the generic term for a divine being

Alusi (Ig.) spirits of nature

Amamihe (Ig.) wisdom of the ancestors; right knowledge

Ana (Ig.) earth goddess

Anātman/Anattā (Skt./Pa.) not-self; according to Buddhist teaching, this is one of the three characteristics (along with impermanence [Anitya/Anicca] and unsatisfactoriness [Duḥkha/Dukkha]) that characterize all existence in human and divine realms

Anchorite (En./Gk.) solitary hermit who is not formally part of a monastic community

Anthropocentric (En.) centered on the human, often used to describe an ethical system exclusively concerned with the human good

Antony of Egypt (251–356 CE) early Christian desert anchorite; stories of Antony recorded by Athanasius of Alexandria were influential in the development of the later Christian monastic tradition

Apatheia (Gk.) lack of passion or control of the passions; central to early Stoic thought and Christian monasticism

Apocalyptic, apocalypticism (En.) a pattern of thought centering on dramatic transitions, whether from one "age" or mode of existence to another (often eschatological or soteriological in significance)

Apocrypha/apocryphal (Gk./En.) literally, "hidden things"; certain books that were written around the time of the canonical books of the Hebrew Bible but not accepted as part of the canon proper; accepted as part of the Christian biblical canon for some but not all Christian denominations

Apology (En.) a reasoned defense or recommendation of some religious or moral position or way of life

Aporia (Gk.) perplexity; a seemingly unresolvable tension resulting from evidence on both sides of an issue

Apostle/apostolic (Gk./En.) one of the original 12 followers of Jesus of Nazareth called by him to be his companion during his lifetime; also refers to those who spread the teachings of Jesus of Nazareth and the early Christian community

Aretê (Gk.) excellence or qualitative goodness, translated as "virtue"

Aristotle (384–322 BCE); Greek philosopher and student of Plato; author of the Nicomachean Ethics; influential on the development of philosophies of virtue

Ariya-aṭṭhaṅgika-magga (Pa.) Noble Eightfold Path; last of the Four Noble Truths that discusses the path to the alleviation of suffering

Arjuna Pandava hero of the Bhagavad Gītā of the Mahābhārata

Artha (Skt.) literally "goal" or "advantage"; traditionally, there are four arthas expounded in Hindu Indian thought: dharma (law and proper ordering of society), artha (material prosperity), kāma (sensual or erotic pleasure), and mokṣa (liberation from the cycle of rebirth); also the name of the particular Hindu śāstra concerned with the ends proper to one of the ruling class (kṣatriyas), namely wealth and power

Ash'arite (Arb.) related to the teaching and interpretive methods of Abu al-Hasan al-Ashari (d. 935 CE); respected the use of reason to prove the existence of God and the basic characteristics of God but acknowledged the limits of reason and were more conservative in their judgment about the extent of reason's power than the Mutazilites; also attributed to God the possibility for all human action while still maintaining the importance of human responsibility and accountability

Askesis, asceticism (Gk./En.) a system of practices of self-abnegation meant to combat vice and develop virtue

Aśoka (304–232 BCE) emperor of the Mauryan empire in India; renowned for bringing Buddhism to Sri Lanka

Āśrama (Skt.) stage of life of one who is a householder (specifically for the brahman and kṣatriya classes); as discussed in the Manusmṛti (Laws of Manu), there are four āśramas: student, householder, forest dweller, and ascetic wanderer

Aṣṭangika-mārga/aṭṭangika-magga (Skt./Pa.) in Buddhism, the Eightfold Path leading to the cessation of unsatisfactoriness; these are (i) right view, (ii) right intention, (iii) right speech, (iv) right action, (v) right livelihood, (vi) right effort, (vii) right mindfulness, (viii) right concentration

Aśvaghoṣa c. 89–c. 150 CE; Indian poet and author of the *Buddhacarita* (Life of the Buddha)

Athanasius of Alexandria (296–373 CE) central Christian theologian of the Patristic period; author of works on central Christian doctrines (e.g. incarnation) and of early Christian monasticism

Ātman (Skt.) in Indian religion, the concept of the individual self or soul that is eternal and is identical with Brahman (the single creative force in the universe)

Augustine of Hippo (354–430 CE) central Christian theologian of the Patristic period; influential in developing Christian accounts of love, virtue, and political theology

Aurelius, Marcus (121–180 CE) Roman emperor and philosopher often associated with the tradition of the Roman Stoics

Autonomy (En.) self-rule; specifically, the capacity for moral self-determination

Averroës Ibn Rushd (1126–1198 CE), Muslim philosopher and interpreter of Aristotle

Avicenna Ibn Sina (c. 980–1037), Muslim philosopher concerned with the unity of faith and reason; influential on the development of medieval philosophy in Europe

Avidyā/Avijja (Skt./Pa.) ignorance; in Indian cosmologies, that quality of the mind which prevents an individual from bring released from the cycle of death and rebirth (saṃsāra)

Axial age (800–200 BCE) terminology developed by the German philosopher Karl Jaspers (1883–1969 CE) to describe the period in which many of the great ethical ideas to influence subsequent human history were first articulated (e.g. the Golden Rule)

Axiology (En.) theory of value or the good

B

Baraka (Arb.) blessing; denotes the grace, favor, or virtue that is bestowed by Allah on people or on sacred places or objects (for instance, burial sites of holy persons)

Barth, Karl (1886–1968 CE) influential Swiss Protestant theologian, emphasizing the classic Protestant themes of the primacy of grace and the power of the Word of God to critique secular political culture; author of the multivolume *Church Dogmatics*

Beatitudes qualities of one who enjoys friendship with God; articulated in Matthew 5 (e.g. "Blessed are the poor in spirit ..."); opening of the Sermon on the Mount of Jesus of Nazareth, often taken to summarize the core elements of Christian ethical teaching

Benedict of Nursia (480–547 CE) author of an early influential monastic Rule in Western Christianity; founder of a monastery at Monte Cassino

Bentham, Jeremy (1748–1832 CE) British philosopher and jurist; founding figure of modern utilitarianism

Bernard of Clairvaux (1090–1153 CE) medieval theologian and abbot of one of the early Cistercian monastic communities in France

Bhagavad Gītā "song of the blessed one" is a part of the longer epic Mahābhārata

Bhakti (Skt.) in Indian religions, devotional practices often directed at gods but also to other persons

Bible sacred book of Christianity and Judaism; Hebrew Bible for Jews, Old Testament and New Testament for Christians

Brahmā (Skt.) Hindu deity responsible for creation; one of the three main gods of the Hindu trimurti, with Śiva (god of destruction) and Viṣṇu (god of protection)

Brahman (Skt.) in Hinduism the one supreme creative power of the universe; also the magical force underlying Vedic ritual practices. Both Brahman and Brahmana can mean the priest.

Brāhmaṇa (Skt.) also refers to the texts of the name Brahman; one of the four groups (varnas) in traditional Hindu society, based on ritual purity; the priestly class responsible for passing on religious knowledge and for performing sacrificial rituals that mediate between gods and human beings

Buddha (Skt.) "awakened one," usually used in reference to the historical figure, Siddhārtha Gautama (563–483 BCE) and also in reference to other enlightened beings in Buddhist cosmology; in Mahāyāna Buddhism, refers both to the historical figure and to the quality existing in all beings giving them the potential to achieve enlightenment (tathāgatagarbha or "Buddha Nature"); also Buddhism

Butler, Joseph (1692–1752 CE) British Protestant theologian, influential in the development of natural theology of love and virtue

C

Caliph/Khalīfa (Arb.) literally "representative"; in a general sense referring to one who participates in the good fortune enjoyed by one's ancestors; specifically referring to a legitimate successor of Muḥammad

Calvin, John (1509–1564 CE) early Protestant reformer, theologian, and jurist; founding figure of Reformed/Presbyterian Christian traditions whose writings influenced later discussions of law, divine command, and theologies of marriage

Canon/canonical (En.) officially recognized sacred texts, e.g. the complete Christian Bible, including the Hebrew Scriptures and New Testament

Caritas (Lt.) love, charity; enumerated as one of the three theological virtues (with faith and hope)

Cassian, John (360–435 CE) early Christian monastic writer; influential in bringing the lessons of the early desert monks to the new monastic communities in Europe

Casuistry (En.) the determination of the rightness or wrongness of actions by the application of general moral principles to particular situations or individual cases

Catholic (Gk./En.) literally "universal," meaning the quality of the Christian church whereby its message pertains to all people at all times; also specifically used to refer to the Roman Catholic Church

Catvāri-ārya-satyāni/Cattari-ariya-saccāni (Skt./Pa.) in Buddhism, the Four Noble Truths of the Buddha's teaching that (i) all life is unsatisfactory, (ii) that the origin of unsatisfactoriness consists in craving, (iii) that the cessation of craving is the cessation of unsatisfactoriness, and (iv) the mārga (Eightfold Path) is the way leading to the cessation of unsatisfactoriness

Cenobite monks who live together in a community (a monastery) subject to a rule of life and under the authority of an abbot; see also anchorite

Chi (Ig.) person god/divinity

Chih (Ch.) moral wisdom

Chineke (Ig.) supreme being who shares (Chukwu + na [who] + eke [to share outward])

Christianity referring to the monotheistic religion of followers of Jesus of Nazareth, who share belief in one Triune God (Father, Son, and Spirit) revealed in the Old Testament/Hebrew Bible and the New Testament

Christology (En.) the doctrine of the person and the work of Jesus Christ in Christian theology

Chukwu (Ig.) God, supreme being

Chun-tzu (Ch.) ideal man

Cicero, Marcus Tullius (106–143 BCE) Roman statesman and philosopher; central figure in philosophy of law and politics

Cirang (Ch.) yielding, deference

Clement of Alexandria (150–211/15 CE) early Christian authors whose writings influenced later Christian theologies of wealth and poverty

Cognitivism (En.) the view that moral judgments express beliefs that can be true or false and that true beliefs ("moral facts") can be apprehended by the mind

Conscience (En.) the natural human capacity for knowledge of moral norms and values necessary for moral judgment in general and particular cases

Conscientia (Lt.) translation of the Greek syneidesis, generally denotes the capacity for making specific moral judgments in particular situations; in Christian theology, that dimension of conscience most affected by error and sin

Consequentialist (En.) those moral theories that judge an action based on the desirability of the outcome or consequences

Cosmogony (En.) theory of the origin of the universe; often refers to the narratives found in religious traditions about the origins of the universe and the beginnings of human life

Cosmology (En.) theory of the order of universe and the proper activities of each kind of creature within it

Cupiditas (Lt.) cupidity or concupiscence; the inordinate love of finite or creaturely ends, usually contrasted with charity

D

Dalai Lama spiritual leader of Tibet; often referring to the current (14th) Dalai Lama (born Tenzin Gyatso, 1935)

Dar al-Amn (Arb.) house of safety; denotes a society not organized according to Islamic law but tolerant of Islamic practice

Dar al-Harb (Arb.) house of war; denotes a society that is not at peace and/ or one that is ruled by laws either opposed to Islam or at odds with basic Islamic values

Dar al-Islam (Arb.) house of peace; denotes a society organized according to Islamic law, values and principles

Dao (Ch.) literally "way" or "path"; refers to a specific tradition of teaching known as Daoism but also the way that best expresses living in harmony with the universe

Daodejing (Ch.) early third-century BCE text ["The Book of the Dao and Its Power"]

Daruriyat (Arb.) level of Shari'a directives indicating compelling interest

Daxue (Ch.) self-cultivation

De (Ch.) virtue; more specifically that power accrued by one who acts favorably to another; in the teachings of Confucius, virtue that was gained both through practices of moral formation and through the proper performance of ritual

Decalogue (En.) Ten Commandments given to Moses by YHWH at Sinai (Ex 20)

Deontological (Gk./En.) from the Greek deon meaning "duty," relates to theories of ethics holding that the basic standards for morally right action are independent of the good or evil ends produced or pursued; these standards identify duties or obligations

Dexing (Ch.) moral conduct; the means by which the Dao is brought into being

Dharma/Dhamma (Skt./Pa.) law, truth, way, morality, social convention; natural order of the world; in Indian traditions generally, the ordering of human affairs in accordance with the preexisting order of the universe; in Buddhism, refers specifically to the teachings of the Buddha

Dhawq (Arb.) aesthetic sensibility

Di (Ch.) lord; also shangdi – lord on high

Dilthey, Wilhelm (1833–1911 CE) German philosopher of science; contributed early studies to the philosophy of social science and the field of hermeneutics

Dogmatics (En.) systematic presentation and examination of all Christian doctrines, sometimes distinguished from ethics or moral theology; the precise meaning of the term depends on a theological position

Dualism views in philosophy and theology that hold two equal and opposing realities (e.g. good and evil or mind and matter)

Duns Scotus, John (1265/66–1308 CE) British Franciscan theologian and philosopher often associated with theological voluntarism, the view that prioritized God's freedom and sovereign will

Durkheim, Émile (1858–1917 CE) French social scientist and founder of the sociological study of religion

E

Ecclesial, ecclesiastical (Gk./En.) of or having to do with the Christian church

Ecumenical council (En.) in Christianity, a worldwide gathering of bishops to determine authoritatively matters of doctrine and practice

Emotivism (En.) a variety of noncognitivism in ethics that holds moral terms to be expressions of a person's emotional reactions

Encyclical (Gk./En.) a letter, or circular, sent to all Christian churches of a given area; in modern Roman Catholic usage the term is restricted to letters sent out by the Pope

Enlightenment (En.) period in the history of Western philosophy that prioritized the power of human reason to attain truth without interference from (especially religious) traditions or social institutions; in Buddhist discourse, the attainment by the Buddha of the highest level of truth/insight about the nature of reality

Epictetus (c. 55–135 CE) early Greek Stoic philosopher who advocated a view of ethics that sought rational conformation of human behaviors to the order of nature

Epicurus (341–270 BCE); early Greek philosopher who advocated a materialist conception of the world and an ethical approach the prioritized the maximization of pleasure, the minimization of pain, and the centrality of friendship; also Epicurean

Epistemology (Gk./En.) the theory of knowledge

Eri (Ig.) the cosmic ancestor of human communities; also used in dating periods of Igbo history

Eschatology (Gk./En.) teachings about the eschaton, or end of the world

Ethic/ethical (Gk./En.) originally, related to character or customary values; also, pertaining to any sort of reflection on morals or moral questions

Ethics (Gk./En.) a discipline of thought, i.e. a science of morals, found within both philosophy and theology, a kind of metareflection, a second order on the first order morality of religious people, that provides the interpretation, elaboration, assessment, and application of a community's "morality" for the sake of orienting human life, individually and socially

Eudaimonia (Gk.) human happiness or "flourishing"; in ethical theory, forms of eudaimonistic ethics include hedonism, the view that feeling good or pleasure is the essence of human well-being, and perfectionism, the view that doing well or excelling at things worth doing is the essence of human well-being

Evagrius of Pontus (345–399 CE) early Christian monastic writer whose work on the eight –logismoi (thoughts) gave rise to the Christian enumeration of the seven deadly sins

Evangelical (Gk./En.) in Christian thought of or related to the gospel or Word or the good news as the core of Christian faith

Existentialism (En.) any school of thought stressing the priority of the problem of existence (particularly, authentic individual being) over that of human essence

Ezeji (Ig.) yam king; position of respect and authority based on the ability to provide for the needs of a people

Ezi na ulo (Ig.) family; kinship network

F

Fatwā (Arb.) in Islam, a official opinion on a legal matter; a response given to a question about a matter of law about which existing interpretation seems inconclusive; an authoritative but not infallible opinion issued by a muftī

Fideism (Lt./En.) a religious view that holds the incapacity of the intellect to attain knowledge of divine matters and correspondingly puts exclusive emphasis on faith based on revelation

Fiqh (Arb.) literally "knowledge" but more generally the study of legal matters in Islam; discernment or interpretation of legal matters based on the Qur'ān (scripture), Sunna (custom or tradition), Ijmā (convergence of opinion or consistency), and Quiyas (use of analogy in reasoning about specific cases not covered in the former three sources)

Francis of Assisi (1181/2–1226 CE) medieval Christian mendicant and founder of the Order of Friars Minor (Franciscans)

Freud, Sigmund (1856–1939 CE) Austrian psychologist and founder of modern psychoanalysis; central figure in the social scientific study of religion

G

Gemara (Arm./Hb.) next layer of level of the Talmud after Mishnah; an interpretation of the Mishnah

al-Ghazālī (c. 1056–1111) Sunni Muslim philosopher who continued the exploration of Aristotelian philosophy and Islamic theology

Gluskabe (Pn.) primeval hero in Penobscot creation myths

Golden Rule (En.) name for the precept found in the Christian Bible, specifically the Sermon on the Mount and elsewhere: "All things whatsoever you would that men do unto you, do even so to them" (Mt 7:12 and parallels)

Gospel (En.) literally, "good news"; more specifically the central content of the Christian revelation, the glad tidings of redemption. It also designates a specifically Christian textual genre containing different accounts of Jesus' life and teachings; four of these texts (Matthew, Mark, Luke, and John) were chosen for inclusion in the New Testament and assigned unique authority and canonical status

Grace (En.) according to Christian faith, the gift or assistance of God in creation and salvation

Guru (Skt.) a teacher or instructor who trains one according to a particular way of life

H

Habit (En.) a disposition, innate or formed, to act in a certain way, often associated with virtues and vices

Hadith (Arb.) the deeds of the prophet Muḥammad; used specifically about a series of narratives about the Prophet and his followers and generally to denote "tradition"

Hajiyat (Arb.) level of Shari'a directives indicating the level of needs

Halakhah (Hb.) the body of Jewish religious law; consists of the commandments enumerated in the Pentateuch, the statements recorded in the prophetic writings, precedents handed down orally as authoritative interpretations of the written laws, as well as collected sayings

Hasidism (Hb.) an eighteenth-century Jewish reform movement, founded by Rabbi Israel ben Eliezer

Hedonism (En.) any school of thought that defines human happiness (see eudaimonia) in terms of pleasure, in Western ethics associated with Epicureanism, Hobbesianism, and later utilitarianism (e.g. Bentham)

Hegel, Georg Wilhelm Friedrich (1770–1831 CE) German philosopher and critic of Kant who emphasized the importance of Spirit as a force in world history and the centrality of tradition and culture to ethical life

Hellenistic (En.) having do with the ancient Greek and Roman world, their philosophy, civilization, etc.; more specifically, the period of Greek literature and learning from the death of Alexander the Great (323 BCE) to that of Cleopatra (31 BCE)

Hermeneutics (Gk./En.) the science of the methods of interpretation, especially (but not exclusively) textual interpretation; generally, the philosophy of human understanding

Heteronomy (En.) generally, rule by another; in ethics, used to specify a state of affairs where moral demands come from outside an agent's own person; e.g. theonomy (rule by God)

Hillel, Rabbi (110 BCE–10 CE) Jewish scriptural commentator and community founder, influential in later theological interpretations of the Golden Rule

Hinayāna (Skt./Pa.) literally "little vehicle"; a pejorative term used by the Mahāyāna to refer to those Buddhist traditions (most notably the Theravāda ["way of the elders"]) with a strong monastic community and taking the Pāli canonical texts (Tipiṭaka or "threefold basket") as authoritative; these communities are still vibrant in Sri Lanka, Burma/Myanmar, Cambodia, Laos, and Thailand among others

Hobbes, Thomas (1588–1679 CE) British philosopher of politics and law; defended a view of materialism and empiricism in epistemology and a view of ethics rooted in self-interest

Hume, David (1711–1776 CE) British philosopher whose work on causation influenced the thought of Kant and later work in epistemology; defended a view of basic moral sentiments as rooted in human nature

I

Ideology (En.) generally, any set of ideas associated with a particular view of social, natural, or supernatural reality; specifically, in Marxist discourse, the intellectual product of relations of production and consumption which systematically distorts and conceals those relations

Ifejioku (Ig.) yam spirit

Igbo (Ig.) indigenous people of Southeastern Nigeria

Ijmā (Arb.) legal consensus in Islam denoting convergence or consistency of opinion

Ijtihād (Arb.) literally "striving," used in in Islam to refer to the act of interpreting a law through individual effort and the consultation of proper theological sources

Ikpe (Ig.) judgment, case, decision, verdict

Ikpenkwumoto (Ig.) wisdom, prudent judgment

'Ilm (Arb.) knowledge

Imago dei (Lt.) literally "image of God"; according to the Hebrew Bible, humanity is created in the "image and likeness of God" (Gen. 1:26–27)

Imām (Arb.) the leader of a group of Muslims; among Shi'ite Muslims, an Imam have the status of a Caliph and are regarded as having a special relationship with the divine

Îmān (Arb.) faith; specifically confidence in Allah and in the truth of the message of his prophet, Muḥammad

Imitatio dei (Lt.) "imitation of God"

Imperative (En.) a statement about what ought to be done

Islam (Arb.) meaning to surrender or submit to the will of God; denotes those traditions taking the teachings of the Prophet Muḥammad

Ius gentium (Lt.) "law of the people"; the civil laws of particular societies

Ius ad bellum (Lt.) in the Christian "just war" tradition, those criteria that specify the conditions under which it is acceptable to initiate military action; these include just cause, proper authority, last resort, and reasonable likelihood of success

Ius in bello (Lt.) in the Christian "just war" tradition, those criteria that specify the proper actions of those in the midst of combat; these include, proportional response and noncombatant immunity

Ius naturale (Lt) "natural law"; the universal moral law common to all rational creatures

J

Jesus of Nazareth (En.) the Jewish teacher and itinerant preacher (c. 0–33 CE) whose life, death, and resurrection serve as the seminal events upon which Christian belief and practice are based. The one Christians worship as savior and lord, the Christ

Jñāna/ñāna (Skt./Pa.) in Indian religions, generally denotes any kind of knowledge including all forms of spiritual knowledge; specifically, it denotes that element of cognition in which a specific cognitive event occurs

Jiao (Ch.) doctrine/teaching; also xiejiao (popular religion), kongjiao (Confucius doctrine), fojiao (Buddha doctrine), and daojiao – Dao doctrine

Jihād (Arb.) a particular kind of striving against any internal or external evil (particularly striving against impulses in oneself or temptation outside oneself); strictly speaking a defense of Islam against aggression which may take the form of speech, writing, or physical conflict

Jinn (Arb.) spirits; supernatural beings

Judaism (En.) referring to the monotheistic religion of the Jewish people, having Abraham, Moses, and King David as its founding figures, and counting the *Torah* as its book of divine revelation

Junzi (Ch.) noble person

Justification (En.) (i) in Christian theology, the act whereby God makes or pronounces persons righteous and/or acquits punishment and mercifully forgives sins; also, the change in the human condition whereby persons pass from a state of sin into a state of righteousness; (ii) in moral theory, a procedure for establishing the validity of moral theories, actions, or principles

K

Kabbalah (Hb.) refers to a certain body of mystical teachings and practices in Judaism that focus on the immanent as well as the transcendent aspects of the divine that are perceived through the process of contemplation

Kant, Immanuel (1724–1804 CE) Prussian philosopher who sought to basic ethics in duty and the legislating powers of human reason; influential in later deontological approaches to ethics

Karma/Kamma (Skt./Pa.) action; more broadly it refers to the cumulative effects of good or bad moral action from which the status in future rebirths is determined

Khuluq (Arb.) character

Kierkegaard, Søren (1813–1855 CE) Danish philosopher and theologian who examined the relationship between rational and religious ethical demands and the demands of Christian discipleship

Kirk, Kenneth (1886–1954 CE) Anglican theologian and Oxford professor (and later bishop) whose work focused on casuistry and conscience

Kong Qiu (Confucius) (551–479 BCE); also Kong Fuzi ("Master Kong"); Chinese sage of the Zhou era (1045–256 BCE); author of Lunyu ("Analects"); also Confucianism

Kṛṣṇa (Skt.) incarnation of the Hindu god Viṣṇu; central character of the Bhagavad Gītā

Kṣatriya (Skt.) one of the four groups (varnas) in traditional Hindu society, based on ritual purity; the warrior, noble or ruling class

Kuhn, Thomas (1922–1996 CE) American physicist and philosopher of science whose work examined the nature of scientific method and paradigms

Kuśala/kusala (Skt./Pa.) good in the sense of skillful, beneficial, or expedient; refers both to what enables one to perform an particular kind of beneficial action and also to a teaching that is formed for the stage of advancement to the one who is receiving it; the opposite is akuśala, which indicates bad in the sense of not beneficial

L

Laozi (Ch.) seventh-sixth century BCE; mythical author of the Daodejing
Lex Talionis (Lt.) law of retaliation (e.g. "an eye for an eye" [Ex 21:23–25])
Li (Ch.) ritual; those directives for behavior that, if followed, ensure the proper functioning of human societies; in traditional Chinese thought, believed to be one aspect of knowledge passed on from one generation to the next and through which much of the ancient wisdom of the sages was codified
Liturgy from leitourgia (Gk.) meaning service or worship; denotes Christian worship, especially celebration of the Eucharist
Locke, John (1632–1704 CE) British empiricist philosopher and political theorist whose work, especially on the idea of the social contract, greatly influenced modern liberal democratic political theory
Logos (Gk.) "word" or "reason"; in Western antiquity, often associated with universal reason governing and permeating the world (cf. Stoicism); in Christian theology, often associated with the second person of the Trinity and the figure of Wisdom
Lokottara/lokuttara (Skt./Pa.) other-worldly; that aspect of Buddhist teaching that aims at a higher achievement, namely *nirvāṇa*; in contrast to lokiya (this-worldly) or what pertains to actions or knowledge pertaining to the world of ordinary interactions
Love (En.) in Christian theology, a good principle of both divine and human action, often specified as either agape (unconditional other-regard or universal equal-regard) often in distinction from eros (desire) or philia (friendship or mutual care); the term caritas, meaning charity or love, was used in classical theological ethics to denote the source of all virtues and the proper disposition toward God and neighbor
Lunyu (Ch.) Analects; written by Kong Qui (Confucius [551–479 BCE]); central text of early Confucianism
Luther, Martin (1483–1546 CE) founding figure of the Protestant Reformation whose writings emphasized the primary of the Bible, grace, and faith in the promises of Christ

M

Magisterium (Lt.) the teaching authority of the Roman Catholic Church, comprised of the College of Bishops

Mahābhārata (Skt.) one of the great ancient Indian epics (along with the Ramayana) that chronicles the incarnation of the god Viṣṇu as Kṛṣṇa and the great struggle between the Pāṇḍava and Kaurava families; the Bhagavad Gītā (or "song of the blessed one") is a part of this longer epic

Mahāyāna (Skt.) in Buddhism, the "great vehicle," which emphasizes the potential for enlightenment found in all beings; that form of Buddhism that predominates in China, Japan, Korea, and other East Asian countries

Maimonides, Moses (1135–1204 CE) medieval Jewish philosopher whose work focused on faith and reason, virtue, and law

Manusmṛti (Skt.) one of the foundation Hindu texts, Laws of Manu details many of the social and ceremonial aspects of life incumbent upon practitioners on a wide array of topics; notable is the explication of kinds of law, the dynamics of karma, and the origins of the caste system

Martyr (En.) literally witness, i.e. person who suffers death for their conviction

Marx, Karl (1818–1883 CE) German philosopher of politics, economics, and religion; argued for the importance of economic power and class struggle to understand social organization and for the interpretation of religion

Maslaha (Arb.) public interest

Melanchthon, Philip (1497–1560 CE) early German Protestant Reformer and collaborator with Martin Luther who emphasized good works as the natural outgrowth of Christian faith

Mengzi (372–281 BCE) "Mencius," Confucian philosopher of the Warring States period (480–222 BCE)

Messiah (Heb.) meaning "anointed one" (in Greek, christos); the term came to mean a royal descendent of the dynasty of David who would restore the united kingdom of Israel and Judah and usher in an age of peace, justice, and prosperity; the title "Christos" came to be applied in Christianity to Jesus of Nazareth by his followers

Messianism (En.) generally, the belief that a religio-political figure will appear at some time to lead society to justice, shared by Judaism, Christianity, and Islam

Metaethics (En.) the analysis of the meaning, nature, or ground of basic moral concepts, beliefs, or judgments; not directly concerned with particular questions of normative or applied ethics but with the form, validity, and justification of moral theory in general

Metaphysics (En.) a philosophical theory of the most fundamental constituents or the most general characteristics of reality as such

Məde'olinu/məde'olinɑs'kwe (Pn.) "man/woman of drum sounding"; religious specialists

Mətə'wəlinəwak (Pn.) "person of a spiritual group"; ancestor with special knowledge, powers, or revered qualities

Midrash (Heb.) "interpretation"; in Judaism a general term for rabbinic interpretation of Scripture, as well as for specific collections of rabbinic literature

Mīmāṁsā (Skt.) inquiry or investigation; one of the six schools of traditional Indian philosophy centered on logical argumentation about and commentary on the Vedas

Mishnah (Heb.) "teaching" or "repetition"; the Oral part of the *Torah* law (as found in the Talmud); an authorized compilation of rabbinic law, promulgated c. 210 CE

Mitzvah (Heb.) "command"; a religious commandment or religious obligation; there are 10 main ones (see Decalogue) and traditionally there are said to be 613 precepts, 365 negative ("do not do this") and 248 positive ("do this")

Mma (Ig.) goodness

Mmadu (Ig.) person

Mokṣa (Skt.) liberation, release; the final cessation of the rounds of rebirth

Monism (En.) a philosophical and theological position holding that there is a single rather than dual opposing substances of forced in the world (e.g. good and evil, matter and mind)

Monotheism (En.) religious belief in a single omnipotent, omniscient creator God; to be differentiated from polytheism (belief multiple gods), pantheism (belief in spiritual beings present in the natural world)

Montaigne, Michel de (1533–1592 CE) French philosopher and essayist whose writings reflected the indirect path to attaining truth about self and world

Moral (En.) [adj.] (i) generally, relating to any claim or statement that involves a distinction between rightness and wrongness and/or goodness and badness (of character, disposition, action, rule, principle), (ii) specifically, an approving description of something virtuous; [n.] (iii) a custom or guide for action that influences acceptable social behavior in a specific community; also, a quality or characteristic of the individual person that directs action. See also "nonmoral" and "premoral"

Moral anthropology (En.) account of the moral features of human nature or the human condition

Moral predication (En.) the task of using language to name, classify, or label the moral status of objects, persons, actions, intentions, relations, ends, consequences, etc.

Moral realism (En.) the view that moral truths are grounded in the nature of things ("objectively") rather than in subjective and variable human reactions to things or social convention

Moral sense (En.) a supposedly innate faculty (analogous to the sense of beauty) for detecting moral properties; in Western ethics, some forms of eighteenth-century intuitionism claimed that the perception of certain actions aroused distinctive feelings of pleasure (approval) and pain (disapproval) in spectators and that these feelings in turn motivated moral behavior

Moses of Scete (330–405 CE) also Moses the Ethiopian; early Christian desert monastic whose teachings were collected in the writings of John Cassian

Muḥammad (Arb.) the prophet from whose life and teachings are formed the foundations of Islam; lived c. 570–632 CE; his inspired speech is recorded in the verses of the Qur'an

Muhasaba (Arb.) self-examination

Mujahada (Arb.) ascetic practices

Muntzer, Thomas (1489–1525 CE) early German Protestant reformer who from Martin Luther on issues of authority and economic and social order of Christian society

Muslim (Arb.) "one who submits to the will of God"; more specifically, to be a Muslim, one must recite the shahadah

Mu'tazilite (Arb.) form of Shi'ite Muslim theology; holds that God can be known through the natural power of human reason

N

Nafs al-ammara (Arb.) commanding self

Nafs-e-lawwâma (Arb.) self-accusing soul

Namaku (Ig.) original maternal ancestor of the Igbo people, sent from heaven with her husband Eri by the creator god Chukwu

Native American/First Nation (En.) designation for the indigenous peoples of the Americas; First Nation is often used by the indigenous peoples of Canada when speaking collectively of the indigenous tribes of the Americas; current usage is to use individual tribal designations (e.g. Penobscot) unless speaking of a number of different tribes in which case language group (e.g. Algonquin) or regional designation is sometimes preferred

Natural law (En.) (i) in ancient Greek and Roman thought, a moral principle or rule that applies universally and is not based on custom or convention but rather on the inherent structure of reality to which rational creatures have access; (ii) in a Christian context, the law implanted in human beings by the Creator that allows them to know moral principles through the light of natural moral reason; often contrasted with the revealed law

Ndichie (Ig.) ancestors

Ndu (Ig.) life

Nhất Hanh, Thich (b. 1926) Vietnamese Zen Buddhist monk and author; founder of Plum Village monastic community in France

Nicolar, Joseph Nineteenth-century tribal leader of the Penobscot people and author of studies on early Penobscot culture

Nietzsche, Friedrich (1844–1900 CE) German philosopher who resisted Enlightenment rationalism, emphasizing instead the individual quest for meaning through an individual expression of freedom and power in light of the highest ideals of heroic culture

Nihilism (En.) a philosophical ethical position arguing for the ultimate absence of meaning and value in the world

Nikāya (Pa.) collection or group; used to indicate the principal divisions of the Pāli Canon of Buddhist writings

Nirvāṇa/Nibbāna (Skt./Pa.) literally, "extinguishing" or "blowing out" of the flame of desire; the conclusion of Buddhist practice in which all craving and attachment cease

Noahide Laws (En.) according to rabbinic interpretations, seven laws were given to Noah (see Genesis 9) and were incumbent upon all humanity (i.e. descendants of Noah); a gentile who follows the Noahide Laws is considered righteous; parallel to the idea of natural law. The Noahide laws include (i) mandate for all societies to establish courts of justice; (ii) prohibition of blasphemy; (iii) prohibition of idolatry; (iv) prohibition of killing innocent human life; (v) prohibition against sexual practices of incest, adultery, homosexuality, and bestiality; (vi) prohibition of robbery; (vii) prohibition of tearing a limb from a living animal for food

Nonmoral (En.) a term used to identify a class of values not involving ethical judgments about the human person or human action (e.g. "This is a good car"). See also "moral" and "premoral"

Nontheistic (En.) in metaethics, the view that standards of good and bad, right and wrong cannot be established on the basis of divine purpose or command

Norm/normative (En.) standard, rule, or principle

Nri (Ig.) early ancestral community of Igo, from which the Eri legend comes

O

Ockham, William (1287–1347 CE) British Franciscan philosopher; associated with nominalism in metaphysics, the position that there are no essences to things beyond the name given to the particulars by which those particulars are grouped together in like kinds (i.e. that there are no universal essences except as creations in the mind); argued a defense of the mendicant religious orders' interpretation of voluntary poverty

Ofo (Ig.) authority

Ogu (Ig.) innocence or guiltlessness

Oji (Ig.) the tree from which the kola nut, a traditional symbol of Igbo unity and hospitality, is harvested

Omenala (Ig.) "how things are done on the land"; doing things in conformity with local custom which reflects an intended order of creation

Ontology (En.) reflection in philosophy and metaphysics on what truly exists, what persists throughout time, or on what underlies appearance by way of existent reality

Orthodox (En.) (i) related to right belief, as contrasted with heterodox or heretical; also a level of strictness in belief and practice, often characterized by very close adherence to religious rules and standards; (ii) a name used to specify certain communities within Judaism and Christianity

Ottappa (Arb.) blame

P

Palaver in African religion, a council convened to address matters of concern to the community

Pañca-sīla (Pa.) five moral precepts that form the basis of Buddhist moral practice for all lay Buddhists; ordained Buddhist take up to 10 (dasa) precepts

Pāpa (Skt.) detrimental, evil; denoting both wrong moral acts and also destructive natural occurrences which affect human beings negatively

Papacy/Papal/Pope (En.) the office of the head of the Roman Catholic Church; traditionally understood to be the successor of Peter, one of the original 12 apostles of Jesus

Pāramitā (Skt.) in Mahayana Buddhism, the perfections or virtues developed by a Bodhisattva

Pariah (Skt./En.) lowest group in the Indian social hierarchy; currently known as Dalit ("broken") formerly called "untouchable" or "outcast"

Parliament of the World's Religions (1893, 1993) international meeting of representatives of the major world religions, first held in conjunction with the Chicago World's Columbian exposition in 1893; continued to the present day as an international gathering of religious leaders and scholars

Patristic (En.) of or related to the so-called Christian Church "Fathers," i.e. those Christian writers between the end of the first century CE. and the close of the eighth century CE. (a more limited dating closes the Patristic period at 500 CE)

Paul of Tarsus (Saul/St. Paul) early Christian apostle, author of letters included in the New Testament

Páwəhikan (Pn.) animal helpers who respond to the needs of people and have a strong connection to the spirit world and ancestors

Penance (En.) literally, "punishment"; (i) an act performed to show sorrow for sin, to atone for the sin by one's own act, and to avert punishment remaining after remission; (ii) in Christian practice the sacrament consisting of such acts, including repentance, confession, satisfaction, and absolution

Penobscot (Pn.) Native American tribe of northeastern United States in what is now the state of Maine, one of the tribes of the Wabanaki Confederation and the Algonquian language group

Pentateuch (Gk.) Greek designation of the first "five books" of the Hebrew Bible/Old Testament (Genesis, Exodus, Leviticus, Numbers, Deuteronomy)

Phronesis (Gk.) "prudence"; practical wisdom, or knowledge of the proper ends of life; (i) distinguished by Aristotle from theoretical knowledge and mere means–end reasoning, or craft, and itself a necessary and sufficient condition of virtue (see practical reason); (ii) for Christian ethics, the first principles of practical reason (commandments, natural law) are seen as analogous to the first principles of speculative reason (see synteresis)

Piety (En.) generally, the affective or experiential dimension of religious faith

Plato (429–347 BCE) Greek philosopher who recorded the dialogues of the sage Socrates; wrote on the nature of the nature of the good, the life of virtue, and political organization

Pneumatology (En.) Christian doctrine of the Holy Spirit or thought and discourse about the Holy Spirit

Polytheism (En.) belief in multiple gods

Practical reason (En.) reasoning that justifies action, either in the pragmatic sense that if one desires x and performing action y is the means to x, then one should do y; or in the moral sense that if x ought to be done, then one ought to do x whatever one's desires. Greek philosophers called practical reasoning phronesis

Prajñā/paññā (Skt./Pa.) wisdom; the highest knowledge that leads to liberation; also the final stage and culmination of Buddhist practice

Pratītyasamutpāda/patticcasamuppāda (Skt./Pa.) dependent co-arising; the central Buddhist doctrine of the interrelated nature of all causal phenomena, enumerated in 12 steps (ignorance, mental formations, consciousness, mind and body, six sense bases, contact, feeling, craving, grasping, becoming, birth, old age and death)

Premoral (En.) term used to differentiate prima facie values or disvalues (e.g. self-preservation, food, shelter, etc.) relevant to or significant for the moral life. See also "nonmoral" and "moral"

Prescriptivism (En.) in metaethics the view that moral judgements have the form of prescriptions rather than some connection to natural properties

Proairesis (Gk.) "choice" or "deliberative desire"; a decision issuing from desiring in accordance with rational deliberation

Proportionalism (En.) generally, a view in Roman Catholic moral theology that the moral judgment of a human act must consider the proportionality of the means to achieve its final end as well as the intention of the act; in contemporary Christian ethics, it is often discussed as a form of consequentialism that seeks to bring about greater benefits than harms

Protestant (En.) the word describing those Christian communities whose theological orientation derives from the Protestant Reformation that sought to purify the Christian Church from excessive reliance on institutional authority and attempts at self-justification through the performance of works, emphasizing instead the centrality of Scripture and the primacy of faith

Pūjā (Skt./Pa.) reverence, devotion, an offering of respect

Purāṇas (Skt.) those texts of traditional Hindu belief that give mythological accounts of early communities; central devotional texts for certain kinds of Hinduism

Q

Qab'hi (Arb.) evil

Qadar (Arb.) "destiny"; in Islam, the individual's fate, which is largely dependent upon free individual choices the human agent makes between good and evil; God determines the outcomes of events on a universal level

Qadi (Arb.) jurist

Qi (Ch.) energy or vital principle; what animates and motivates all things; the subject of defined breathing exercises intended to bring the human body back into balance in itself and with its surrounding environment

Qiyās (Arb.) analogical reasoning about specific cases; one of the traditional four sources of Islamic law (along with the Qurʾan, Sunna, and Ijmā)

Qiyamah (Arb.) resurrection; also the name of Surah 75 on this topic

Qurʾān (Arb.) "recitation"; the holy book of Islam, which Muslims believe is a divinely revealed scripture sent to Muḥammad from God through the Angel Gabriel in the Arabic language

R

Rabbi/Rabbinic (Hb./En.) an elder and/or teacher in the Jewish tradition

Ramaḍan (Arb.) in Islam, the month devoted to commemorating God's revelation to the Prophet Muḥammad observe through prayer and fasting

Rāmāyaṇa (Skt.) one of the great ancient Indian epics (along with the Mahābhārata); it chronicles the incarnation of the god Viṣṇu as the hero Rāma

Reformed (En.) (i) of or related to the teachings of John Calvin and later Calvinism (compare to "Reformation," which describes the teachings and traditions of Protestantism in general, as well as the historical event through which various Protestant communities were differentiated); (ii) in the Jewish tradition, a level of strictness in belief and practice, often characterized by an openness to change and modernity

Religion/religious (En.) from the Latin word "religio" meaning to tie or bind; the practice of belief in and worship of a divine being or beings; a way of life characterized by belief in or practicing worship of divine beings or some ultimate center or source of value (see Chapter 1)

Ren (Ch.) benevolence, humaneness; ethics

Renyi (Ch.) righteous conduct

S

Saint (En.) one who is revered for their moral rectitude or holiness; one who is close to God and an exemplar for others in the commute; also a seer or wise person

Samādhi (Skt./Pa.) concentration, meditation; that form of meditation centered on calming and focusing the mind (in distinction from vipassanā, which aims at insight); also the second stage of Buddhist practice

Samsāra (Pa.) the cycle or round of rebirth

Saṃskāras (Skt.) Rites of passage of the life cycle such as birth and marriage ceremonies

Saṃgha/saṅgha (Skt./Pa.) the Buddhist monastic community

Sānsana (Pa.) tradition; teaching; by extension, a religion

Sapientia (Lt.) wisdom

Sastra (Skt.) genre of Indian literature collecting teachings on particular topic of morality and learning

Sattva (Skt.) goodness, purity, brightness, intelligence, being

Schleiermacher, Friedrich (1768–1834 CE) German theologian and philosopher, emphasized the importance of religious experience understood as a sense of absolute dependence

Scientia (Lt.) knowledge of the world in its totality and in its various expressions; accepted methods by which reality can be investigated and known to the human mind

Sermon on the Mount (En.) a portion of the Gospel of Matthew in the New Testament (Matthew 5–7) that summarizes the central ethical teaching of Jesus of Nazareth especially in the Beatitude; also Sermon on the Plain (Lk 6:17–49)

Shahādah (Arb.) "act of bearing witness"; the declaration of faith that there is no deity except God and Muḥammad is his messenger; one of the Five

Pillars of Islam that also include Salah (prayer), Sawm (fasting), Zakāt (almsgiving), and Hajj (pilgrimage)

Shaman in Native American and other cultures, a sage or healer understood to have a special connection with the spiritual plane through the performance of rituals

Shan (Ch.) goodness

Shari'a (Ar.) Islamic law, a complex code of life grounded in divine revelation; the sources of Shari'a are both revealed and nonrevealed, including the Qur'ān, the Sunna, and independent juristic reasoning (ijtihād) that takes a variety of forms including analogical reasoning (qiyas), juristic preference (istihsan), considerations of public interest (istislah), and general consensus (ijma) of the learned

Shengren (Ch.) sages; teachers of past memory in whom abided the best expression of right conduct

Shifei (Ch.) right and wrong

Shi'ite (Arb.) one of the main traditions within Islam, taking Ali, cousin to the Prophet Muḥammad, as the Prophet's intended successor, and rejecting other caliphs and Sunni legal institutions are proper authorities

Siddhartha Gautama (Skt.) the historical prince of the Sakya clan in India (490–410 BCE/566–486 BCE) whose reflection on his enlightenment experience and his subsequent teaching became the basis of Buddhism

Śīla/sīla (Skt./Pa.) virtue, morality; in Buddhism, those behaviors that express good action and are the foundation and prerequisite for the practice of meditation

Silver Rule (En.) reformulation of the Golden Rule that emphasizes refraining from actions that are harmful to others; "Do not do unto others as you would not have them do unto you."

Simul iustus et peccator (Lt.) "simultaneously justified and a sinner," central teaching of Luther's theology that became central to the Protestant Reformation's understanding of justification

Sinai (Hb.) according to the Hebrew Bible, the mountain on which Moses was given the Ten Commandments tat would guide the moral life Israelites

Śiva (Skt.) Hindu god of destruction; one of the three main gods in Hinduism along with Brahma (creator) and Viṣṇu (protector)

Skandhas/khandhas (Skt./Pa.) aggregates; basic components of phenomenal reality, further divided into components (dhammas)

Socrates (469–399 BCE) ancient Greek sage and social critic whose dialogues about the good life were the subject of Plato's writings

Soteriology (Gk./En.) that branch of theology focused on the meaning of and conditions for salvation

Spinoza, Baruch (1632–1677 CE) Jewish philosopher who argued for the grounding of ethics in a monistic metaphysics

Stoicism (En.) ancient Greek and Roman philosophy that focused on understanding the order of the natural world and conforming one's behavior to make a fitting response to the reality one encounter

Suddha (Skt.) purity

Śūdra (Skt.) one of the four groups in traditional Hindu society, representing the servant class; not normally enumerated based on the distinction of ritual purity because this class was considered to be impure

Sufi (Arb.) Islamic tradition and communities of ascetic/spiritual practices

Summum bonum (Lt.) "highest good"

Sunnah (Arb.) the paradigm of behavior every Muslim must follow; the concept of the sunnah is based on the belief that the Prophet Muḥammad is a role model for all Muslims; sunnah is based on the teachings of the Qur'ān and supplemented by the corpus of hadith, the recorded sayings and doings of Muḥammad explaining and demonstrating how the teachings of the Qur'ān are put into effect; thus, Muḥammad acts as both exemplar and legislator for the Muslim community

Sunni (Arb.) one of the main traditions within Islam, holding the first four caliphs to succeed the Prophet Muḥammad as the authoritative interpreters of the Prophet's teaching

Śūnyatā/suññatā (Skt.) emptiness; a central teaching of Mahāyāna Buddhism that states that all phenomenon are empty of a substantial nature

Supererogatory (En.) those acts considered to be above and beyond what is required by morality

Sūtra/sutta (Skt.) lit. "thread" refers to a discourse of the Buddha; also a division of the Buddhist scriptural canon

Syllogism, practical (En.) a logical form in which the major premise states a general rule for conduct, the minor premise specifies the salient features of a particular situation, and the conclusion is a judgment that results in action about what ought to be done

Syneidesis (Gk.) "conscience," see "conscientia"

Synteresis (En./Gk.) technical term used in classical Western moral thought to denote human knowledge of the first principles of moral action; the term originated due to a scribal error in Jerome's "Commentary on Ezekiel" as a corruption of the New Testament Greek term syneidesis

T

Tahsinat (Arb.) level of Shari'a directives indicating the level of improvements

Talmud (Hb.) "study" or "learning"; the basic compendium of Jewish law, thought, and biblical commentary; a compilation of Jewish Oral *Torah* made between the second and fifth centuries. Rabbinic Judaism produced two Talmuds: (i) the "Babylonian" Talmud, or Talmud Bavli, the edition developed in Babylonia, and edited at end of the fifth century CE.; and (ii) the "Palestinian" or "Jerusalem" Talmud, or Talmud Yerushalmi, the edition compiled in the land of Israel at end of the fourth century CE. Both Talmuds include the Mishnah and Gemara

Tamas (Skt.) darkness, inertia, gloom, ignorance

Tanakh (Hb.) authoritative collection of Hebrew biblical text, including the *Torah* (law), Nevi'im (prophets), Ketuvim (writings)

Trṣṇā/taṇhā (Skt./Pa.) thirst, craving; in Buddhism, considered to be the root of attachment

Teleological (En.) generally, end-seeking; specifically, of any system of thought that focuses on the ends proper to particular beings and their activity in seeking those ends

Tetragrammaton (En.) the letters of Hebrew name for God, rendered in English as YHWH

Theocentric (En.) centered on God, often used to describe an ethical system that is mainly concerned about divine agency, divine purposes, and the human relationship to the divine

Theonomy (En.) rule by God or the gods

Theosis (Gk.) divinization; to make God-like

Theravāda (Pa.) one branch of so-called Hinayāna Buddhism known as the "way of the elders"; emphasizing a strong monastic community and taking Pāli canonical texts (Tipiṭaka or "threefold basket") as authoritative; these communities are still vibrant in the countries of Sri Lanka, Burma/Myanmar, Cambodia, Laos, and Thailand among others

Thomas Aquinas (1225–1274 CE) Italian Dominican theologian; central figure in the later development of Catholic virtue ethics and the natural law tradition

Tianming (Ch.) mandate of heaven; central to the justification of Chinese emperors who held power

Torah (Hb.) the law, teaching, or wisdom handed down in both written and oral form to Moses on Sinai; identified in written form with the Pentateuch; the first five books of the Hebrew and Christian bibles

Trilakṣaṇa/tilakkhaṇa (Skt./Pa.) three characteristic of all phenomenal reality (anātman/anattā, dhuḥkha/dukkha, and anicca)

Trinity (En.) in Christianity, referring to three distinct persons (Father, Son, and Holy Spirit) in a single divine being

Tripiṭaka/tipiṭaka (Skt./Pa.) three "baskets" of Buddhist writings (Sūtra/sutta, vinaya, and abhidharma/abhidhamma)

Triratna/tiratana (Skt./Pa.) three jewels, denoting the basic elements of Buddhist tradition (Buddha, Dhamma, Sangha)

U

'Ulamā (Arb.) scholarly community of specialist interpreters of Islamic theology and law

Ummah (Arb.) the worldwide community of Muslims

Umunna/e (Ig.) local patrilineage/matrilineage

Universalism (En.) in moral theory, the status of truths or rules that apply at all times in all places, regardless of social and historical context

Upaniṣad (Skt.) genre of ancient Indian (Hindu) literature of stories, prayers, and speculative investigation into the nature of the self (ātman) and its unity with the creative power of the universe (brahman)

Utilitarianism (En.) a moral theory according to which an action is right if and only if its performance will be more productive of pleasure or happiness, or more preventive of pain or unhappiness for the greatest number of relevant beings, than any alternative

V

Vaiśyas (Skt.) one of the four groups (varṇas) in traditional Hindu society, based on ritual purity; the merchant class

Vajrayāna (Skt.) in Buddhism, the "thunderbolt" or "diamond vehicle"; often called esoteric or tantric Buddhism; refers to the many schools of Tibetan Buddhism

Value (En.) the quality of being good, important, or of human concern, or an entity that possesses this quality

Varṇas (Skt.) the four social classes in ancient Indian society

Veda (Skt.) Originally oral hymns and chants, these became the primary texts of early Vedic Indian religion; includes the Ṛg Veda, the Yajur Veda, the Sāma Veda, and the Atharva Veda

Vedānta (Skt.) the tradition of theological and philosophical thought stemming from commentary on the Upaniṣads; among the different schools are found Advaita (nondual), Viśiṣṭādvaita (qualified nondual), and Dvaita (dual)

Venial sin (En.) in Roman Catholic moral theology a sin that, unlike mortal sin, does not wholly remove the soul from sanctifying grace

Vimutti (Pa.) release from suffering; freedom

Virtue (En.) generally, an excellence or good quality; a good quality inhering in a human disposition to act

Viṣṇu (Skt.) Hindu protector God; one of the three main gods in Hindu cosmology along with Brahmā (creator) and Śiva (destroyer)

Vocation (En.) calling; referring either to one's professional calling or, in some Christian denominations (e.g. Roman Catholicism) the sense of calling to a particular way of life such as marriage or priesthood

Voluntarism (En.) in theological ethics, the view that the standard of good and evil/right and wrong is ultimately based on the freedom and will of God rather than on an a rationally established moral order; also the prioritization of will rather reason in making moral decisions

W

Wabanaki (Pn.) "people of the dawn"

Wali (Arb.) saint, friend, patron

Weber, Max (1864–1920 CE) German sociologist who examined the impact of religion and culture on social organization, economic life, and the rise of modernity

Wesley, John (1703–1791 CE) British Protestant theologian and social reformer; founder of the modern Methodist traditions

X

Xiao (Ch.) filial piety

Xin (Ch.) trustworthiness (also the individual human mind)

Xing (Ch.) original nature (of human beings or of all things)

Xiuchi (Ch.) shame

Xue (Ch.) learning

Xunzi (Ch.) Xun Kuang (310–230 BCE), Confucian philosopher of the Warring States period (480–222 BCE)

Y

Yajña (Skt.) sacrifice; refers in particular to the early Vedic fire sacrifice but is used broadly in Indian religion to refer to acts of sacrifice more generally

Yawm ad-Dīn (Arb.) day of judgment

Yi (Ch.) moral sense; righteousness; more specifically, fulfilling one's obligations

Yoga (Skt.) literally, "work"; self-discipline or practices of self-mastery

Yogin/Yogini (Skt.) practitioner

Z

Zeno of Citium (344–262 BCE) was a Greek philosopher and the founder of Stocism

Zhen (Ch.) truth

Zheng-ming (Ch.) rectification of names

Zhi (Ch.) wisdom; also the aims or goals (usually in reference to the ancient sages)

Zhong yong (Ch.) doctrine of the mean

Zhuangzi (Ch.) Daoist text, written by Zhuang Zhou, fourth–third century BCE

Zongjiao (Ch.) religion; school of religion/doctrine

Zwingli, Huldrych (1484–1531 CE) Swiss Protestant reformer whose views of reason and revelation and the nature of the sacraments differed somewhat from his contemporary Martin Luther

Bibliography

Achebe, C. (1992 [1958]). *Things Fall Apart*, with an introduction by K.A. Appiah. New York and London: Alfred A. Knopf.

Afigbo, A.E. (1981). *Ropes of Sand: Studies in Igbo History and Culture*. Ibadan: Published for University Press in association with Oxford University Press.

Agozino, B. and Anyanike, I. (2007). Imu Ahia: traditional Igbo business school and global commerce culture. *Dialectical Anthropology* 31: 233–252.

Alexander, C. (2009). *The War that Killed Achilles: The True Story of Homer's Iliad and the Trojan War*. New York: Penguin.

Anastas, P. (1973). *Glooskop's Children: Encounters with the Penobscot Indians of Maine*. Boston: Beacon Press.

Antonaccio, M. (2005). Moral truth. In: *The Blackwell Companion to Religious Ethics* (ed. W. Schweiker), 27–35. Malden, MA: Blackwell Publishing.

Antonaccio, M. (2012). *A Philosophy to Live By: Engaging Iris Murdoch*. Oxford: Oxford University Press.

Appleyard, J.A. (1971). How does a sacrament 'cause by signifying. *Science et Esprit* 23 (2): 167–200.

Aquinas, Thomas. (1981 [1948]). *Summa Theologiae* 5 vols, (trans. Fathers of the English Dominican Province). Lexington, KY: Westminster John Knox Press Christian Classics.

Armstrong, R.J., Hellman, J.W., and Short, W. (eds.) (1999). *Francis of Assisi: Early Documents, vol. I: The Saint*. New York: New City Press.

Asante, M.K. and Mazama, A. (eds.) (2008). *Encyclopedia of African Religion*, 2 vols. Thousand Oaks and London: SAGE Publications.

Aśvaghoṣa (2008). *Life of the Buddha* (trans. P. Olivelle). New York: New York University/JJC Foundation.

Athanasius (1980). *The Life of Antony and the Letter to Marcellinus* (trans. R.C. Gregg). Mahwah, NJ: Paulist Press.

Augustine of Hippo (1892). "Letter 189" to Boniface (412 CE). In: *Nicene and Post-Nicene Fathers*, Vol. I (ed. P. Schaff), 1171–1174. New York: Christian Literature Company.

Religious Ethics: Meaning and Method, First Edition. William Schweiker and David A. Clairmont.
© 2020 William Schweiker and David A. Clairmont. Published 2020 by John Wiley & Sons Ltd.

Augustine of Hippo (1965). *The Catholic and Manichaen Ways of Life (De Moribus Ecclesiae Catholicae et, De Moribus Manichaeorum)* (trans. D.A. Gallagher and I.A. Gallagher). Washington, DC: Catholic University of America Press.

Augustine of Hippo (1984). *Concerning The City of God Against the Pagans* (trans. H. Bettenson and intro. J. O'Meara). New York: Penguin Books.

Augustine of Hippo (1994). "On the Grace of Christ and on Original Sin" and "On Marriage and Concupiscence". In: *Anti-Pelagian Writings*, Nicene and Post-Nicene Fathers, first series, Vol. 5, (ed. P. Schaff and trans. P. Holmes, R.E. Wallis, and B.B. Warfield), 635–804. Peabody, MA: Hendrickson Publishers.

Augustine of Hippo (2010). *On the Free Choice of the Will, On Grace and Free Choice, and Other Writings* (ed. P. King). Cambridge: Cambridge University Press.

Augustine of Hippo (2012). *The Trinity (De Trinitate)*, 2e, (ed. John E. Rotelle, O.S.A. and trans. Edmund Hill, O.P.). Hyde Park, NY: New City Press.

Aurelius, Marcus. (1964). *Meditations* (trans. M. Staniforth). New York: Penguin.

Baggini, J. (2015). *Freedom Regained: The Possibility of Free Will.* Chicago: University of Chicago Press.

Bakewell, S. (2010). *How to Live or A Life of Montaigne: In One Question and Twenty Attempts to Answer It.* New York: Other Press.

Bellah, R. (2011). *Religion in Human Evolution: From the Paleolithic to the Axial Age.* Cambridge, MA: Belknap Harvard University Press.

Benedict of Nursia (1982). *The Rule of St. Benedict in English* (ed. T. Fry). Collegeville: Liturgical Press.

Bernard of Clairvaux (1976). *Five Books on Consideration: Advice to a Pope* (trans. J.D. Anderson and E.T. Kennan). Kalamazoo: Cistercian Publications.

Betz, H.D. (1995). *The Sermon on the Mount: A Commentary on the Sermon on the Mount, including the Sermon on the Plain (Matthew 5:3-7:27 and Luke 6:20-49)* Hermeneia: A Critical and Historical Commentary. Philadelphia: Fortress Press.

Bodhi, Bhikkhu, (ed.) (1999). *Abhidhammattha Sangaha*. BPS Pariyatti: Onalaska.

Bodhi, Bhikkhu, (1999). "The Noble Eightfold Path: The Way to End Suffering," Access to Insight (Legacy Edition), http://www.accesstoinsight.org/lib/authors/bodhi/waytoend.html (accessed 23 June 2019).

Bowker, J. (ed.) (1997). *The Oxford Dictionary of World Religions.* New York: Oxford University Press.

Brockinton, J. (2003). The Sanskrit epics. In: *The Blackwell Companion to Hinduism* (ed. G. Flood), 116–128. Malden, MA: Blackwell Publishing.

Bruchac, J. (1985). *The Wind Eagle and Other Abenaki Stories.* Greenfield Center: Bowman Books.

Bucar, E.M. (2008). Methodological invention as a constructive project: exploring the production of ethical knowledge through the interaction of discursive logics. *Journal of Religious Ethics* 36 (3): 355–373.

Bucar, E.M. (2011). *Creative Conformity: The Feminist Politics of U.S. Catholic and Iranian Shi'a Women*. Washington, DC: Georgetown University Press.

Bucar, E.M. and Barnett, B. (eds.) (2005). *Does Human Rights Need God?* Grand Rapids, MI: Eerdmans.

Buitendag, J. (2007). Marriage in the theology of Martin Luther – worldly yet sacred: an option between secularism and clericalism. *Hervormde Teologiese Studies* 63 (2): 445–461.

Bujo, B. (2005). Differentiations in African ethics. In: *The Blackwell Companion to Religious Ethics* (ed. W. Schweiker), 423–437. Malden and Oxford: Blackwell Publishing.

Cahill, L.S. (1996). *Sex, Gender, and Christian Ethics*. Cambridge: Cambridge University Press.

Calvin, J. (1960 [1536]). *Institutes of the Christian Religion* (ed. J.T. McNeill). Philadelphia: Westminster Press.

Candlish, S. (2007). *The Russell/Bradley Dispute and Its Significance for Twentieth-century Philosophy*. New York: Palgrave Macmillan.

Carmody, D.L. and Carmody, J.T. (1993). *Native American Religions: An Introduction*. New York and Mahwah: Paulist Press.

Carter, J.R. (2005). Buddhist ethics? In: *The Blackwell Companion to Religious Ethics* (ed. W. Schweiker), 278–285. Malden, MA: Blackwell Publishing.

Carter, J.R. and Palihawadana, M. (trans.) (1987). *The Dhammapada*. New York and Oxford: Oxford University Press.

Cassian, J. (1985). *Conferences* (trans. C. Luibheid). Mahwah, NJ: Paulist Press.

Chan, W.-T. (1963). The humanism of Confucius. In: *A Source Book in Chinese Philosophy*, 14–48. Princeton: Princeton University Press.

Chen, S. and Choi, C.J. (2005). A social exchange perspective on business ethics: an application to knowledge exchange. *Journal of Business Ethics* 62: 1–11.

Chidume, C.G. (2014). The symbolism of the Kolanut in Igbo cosmology: a re-examination. *European Scientific Journal* 2: 547–552.

Cholij, R. (n.d.). "Priestly celibacy in patristics and in the history of the Church" http://www.vatican.va/roman_curia/congregations/cclergy/documents/rc_con_cclergy_doc_01011993_chisto_en.html (accessed 23 June 2019).

Chryssavgis, J. (1986). The spiritual father as embodiment of tradition. *Phronema* 1: 19–31.

Clairmont, D.A. (2010). Theravada Buddhist Abhidhamma and moral development: lists and narratives in the practice of religious ethics. *Journal of the Society of Christian Ethics* 30 (2, Fall/Winter): 171–193.

Clairmont, D.A. (2011). *Moral Struggle and Religious Ethics: On the Person as Classic in Comparative Theological Contexts*. Oxford: Wiley Blackwell.

Clairmont, D.A. (2011). Why does the Buddha close in eyes in my eden: a buddhist ecological challenge and invitation to Christians. In: *Green Discipleship: Catholic Theological Ethics and the Environment* (ed. T. Winright), 340–358. Winona, MN: Anselm Academic.

Clairmont, D.A. (2013). Medieval consideration and moral pace: Thomas Aquinas and Bernard of Clairvaux on the temporal aspects of virtue. *Journal of Religious Ethics* 41 (1): 79–111.

Clement of Alexandria (1919). *Exhortation to the Greeks/The Rich Man's Salvation/ To the Newly Baptized*, Loeb Classical Library 92, (ed. J. Henderson and trans. G.W. Butterworth). Cambridge, MA and London: Harvard University Press.

Clooney, F.X., S.J. (2003). Pain but not harm: some classical resources toward a Hindu just war theory. In: *Just War in Comparative Perspective* (ed. P. Robinson), 109–125. Ashgate: Hampshire and Burlington.

Clooney, F.X., S.J. (2005). Practices. In: *The Blackwell Companion to Religious Ethics* (ed. W. Schweiker), 78–85. Malden, MA: Blackwell.

Cogan, M. (1992). Chronology-old testament. In: *The Anchor Bible Dictionary*, vol. 1 A-C (ed. D.N. Freedman), 1002–1022. New York: Doubleday.

Collins, J.J. (2004). The Psalms and the song of songs. In: *Introduction to the Hebrew Bible*, 313–326. Minneapolis: Fortress Press.

Confucius (1998). *The Analects* (trans. D. Hinton). New York: Counterpoint.

Coogan, M.D., Brettler, M.Z., Newsom, C.A., and Perkins, P. (eds.) (2001). *The New Oxford Annotated Bible, with the Apocrypha*, 3e, New Revised Standard Version. New York and Oxford: Oxford University Press.

Cross, F.L. and Livingstone, E.A. (eds.) (2005). *The Oxford Dictionary of the Christian Church*, 3e. New York and Oxford: Oxford University Press.

Csikszentmihalyi, M. (2005). Differentiations in Chinese ethics. In: *The Blackwell Companion to Religious Ethics* (ed. W. Schweiker), 381–394. Malden, MA: Blackwell Publishing.

Dalai Lama, The Fourteenth (June 2016). Why I'm hopeful about the world's future. *The Washington Post*, Opinions: 13.

Darlington, S.M. (1998). The ordination of a tree: the Buddhist ecology movement in Thailand. *Ethnology* 37 (1): 1–15.

Darlington, S.M. (2012). *The Ordination of a Tree: The Thai Buddhist Environmental Movement*. Albany: SUNY Press.

Day, G.M. (1995 [1996]). *Western Abenaki Dictionary. Vol. 1: Abenaki-English; Vol. 2: English-Abenaki*, Canadian Ethnology Service Paper No. 128-9. Hull, Quebec: Canadian Museum of Civilization.

de Silva, P. (1991). Buddhist ethics. In: *A Companion to Ethics* (ed. P. Singer), 58–68. Oxford: Blackwell.

Deloria, V. Jr. (2005). Indigenous peoples. In: *The Blackwell Companion to Religious Ethics* (ed. W. Schweiker), 552–559. Malden, MA: Blackwell.

Descartes, R. (1984). *The Philosophical Writings of Descartes*, 3 vols, (trans. J. Cottingham, R. Stoothoff, D. Murdoch, and A. Kenny). Cambridge: Cambridge University Press –1991.

Dilthey, W. (1976). The development of hermeneutics. In: *Selected Writings* (ed. and trans. H.P. Rickman), 247–263. Cambridge: Cambridge University Press.

Doniger, W. (1998). *The Implied Spider: Politics and Theology in Myth*. New York: Columbia University Press.

Doniger, W. (ed.) (1999). *Mirriam-Webster's Encyclopedia of World Religions*. Springfield, MA.

Doniger, W. (2009). *The Hindus: An Alternate History*. New York: Penguin Press.

Dorff, E.N. (2001). Doing the right and the good: fundamental convictions and methods in Jewish ethics. In: *Ethics in the World Religions* (eds. J. Runzo and N.M. Martin), 89–114. New York: Oneworld Publications.

Dupus, J.-P. (2013). *The Mark of the Sacred* (trans. M.B. Debevoise). Stanford, CA: Stanford University Press.

Durkheim, E. (1995). *The Elementary Forms of Religious Life* (trans. K.E. Fields). New York: Free Press.

Ebben, B. (1972). Church marriage versus traditional marriage. *African Ecclesiastical Review* 14 (3): 213–226.

Echeruo, M.J.C. (1998). *Igbo-English Dictionary: A Comprehensive Dictionary of the Igbo Language, with an English-Igbo Index*. New Haven and London: Yale University Press.

Ejizu, C.I. (1987). The taxonomy, provenance, and functions of ọfọ: a dominant Igbo ritual and political symbol. *Anthropos* 82: 457–467.

Ejizu, C.I. (2002). *Ofo: Igbo Ritual Symbol*. Enugu: Fourth Dimension Publishing.

Eliade, M. (ed.), editor in chief (1987). *The Encyclopedia of Religion*, vol. 16. New York: Macmillan.

Elshtain, J.B. (1995). *Augustine and the Limits of Politics*. Notre Dame, IN: University of Notre Dame Press.

Elshtain, J.B. (2001). Bonhoeffer on modernity: Sic et Non. *Journal of Religious Ethics* 29 (3): 345–366.

Ezeanokwasa, J.O. (2011). *The Legal Inequality of Muslim and Christian Marriages in Nigeria: Constitutionally Established Judicial Discrimination*. Lewiston, NY: Edwin Mellen Press.

Fasching, D.J., de Chant, D., and Lantigua, D.M. (2011). *Comparative Religious Ethics: A Narrative Approach to Global Ethics*, 2e. Oxford: Wiley.

Fishbane, M. (2003). *Biblical Myth and Rabbinic Mythmaking*. Oxford: Oxford University Press.

Flood, G. (1996). *An Introduction to Hinduism*. Cambridge: Cambridge University Press.

Flood, G. and Martin, C. (2012). *The Bhagavad Gita: A New Translation*. New York: W.W. Norton and Company.

Frankena, W. (1988). *Ethics*, 2e. Upper Saddle River, NJ: Prentice Hall.

Frankfurt, H. (1988). *The Importance of What We Care About*. Cambridge: Cambridge University Press.

French, W. (2005). Ecology. In: *The Blackwell Companion to Religious Ethics* (ed. W. Schweiker), 469–476. Malden and Oxford: Blackwell Publishing.

Gabriel, M. (2015). *Why the World Does Not Exist* (trans. G.S. Moss). Cambridge: Polity Press.

Gadamer, H.-G. (1975). *Truth and Method.* New York: Continuum.

Geertz, C. (1966). Religion as a cultural system. In: *Anthropological Approaches to the Study of Religion,* vol. 3 (ed. Michael Banton ASA Monographs), 1–46. London: Tavistock Publications.

Gethin, R. (1998). *The Foundations of Buddhism.* Oxford: Oxford University Press.

Gethin, R.M.L. (2001). *The Buddhist Path to Awakening.* Oxford: Oneworld.

Geuss, R. (1981). *The Idea of Critical Theory: Habermas and the Frankfurt School.* Cambridge: Cambridge University Press.

Gewirth, A. (1978). *Reason and Morality.* Chicago: University of Chicago Press.

Girard, R. (1977). *Violence and the Sacred* (trans. P. Gregory). Baltimore, MD: Johns Hopkins University Press.

Glanzberg, Michael, "Truth", In *The Stanford Encyclopedia of Philosophy* (Fall 2014 Edition), (ed. E.N. Zalta). http://plato.stanford.edu/archives/fall2014/entries/truth (accessed 23 June 2019).

Glassé, C. (2008). *The New Encyclopedia of Islam,* 3e. Lanham, MD: Rowman and Littlefield.

Green, R.M. (1978). *Religious Reason: The Rational and Moral Basis of Religious Belief.* Oxford and London: Oxford University Press.

Green, R.M. (2001). Christian ethics: a Jewish perspective. In: *The Cambridge Companion to Christian Ethics* (ed. R. Gill), 138–153. Cambridge: Cambridge University Press.

Gustafson, J.M. (1996). *Intersections: Science, Theology, and Ethics.* Cleveland, OH: Pilgrim Press.

Guyer, Paul and Rolf-Peter Horstmann, "Idealism", In *The Stanford Encyclopedia of Philosophy* (Fall 2015 Edition), (ed. E.N. Zalta), http://plato.stanford.edu/archives/fall2015/entries/idealism (accessed 23 June 2019).

Hallisey, C. (1996). Ethical particularism in Theravāda Buddhism. *Journal of Buddhist Ethics* 3: 32–43.

Hallisey, C. (2005). Buddhist ethics: trajectories. In: *The Blackwell Companion to Religious Ethics* (ed. W. Schweiker), 312–322. Malden, MA: Blackwell Publishing.

Hansen, S.D., Alge, B.J., Brown, M.E. et al. (2013). Ethical leadership: assessing the value of a multifoci social exchange perspective. *Journal of Business Ethics* 115: 435–439.

Harris, I. (1995). Buddhist environmental ethics and detraditionalization: the case of EcoBuddhism. *Religion* 25: 199–211.

Harvey, P. (2000). *An Introduction to Buddhist Ethics.* Cambridge: Cambridge University Press.

Hastings, J. (ed.) (1926 [1908]). *Encyclopedia of Religion and Ethics,* vol. 13. New York: Charles Scribner's Sons.

Hays, C.M. (2009). Hating wealth and wives? An examination of discipleship ethics in the third gospel. *Tyndale Bulletin* 60 (1): 47–68.

Hume, D. (2004 [1777]). *An Enquiry Concerning the Principles of Morals*. Amherst, NY: Prometheus Books.

Huntington, S. (1997). *The Clash of Civilizations and the Remaking of World Order*. New York: Touchstone.

Hylton, P. (1990). *Russell, Idealism, and the Emergence of Analytic Philosophy*. Oxford: Clarendon Press.

Ikenga-Metuh, E. (1985). The paradox of transcendence and immanence of God in African religions. *Religion* 15: 373–385.

Isichei, E. (1976). *A History of the Igbo People*. New York: St. Martin's Press.

Ivanhoe, P.J. (2005). Origins of Chinese ethics. In: *The Blackwell Companion to Religious Ethics* (ed. W. Schweiker), 374–380. Malden, MA: Blackwell Publishing.

Janowski, B. and Welker, M. (2000). *Opfer: Theologische und kulturellen Kontexte*. Frankfurt: Suhrkamp.

Jaspers, K. (1962). *Socrates, Buddha, Confucius, Jesus: The Paradigmatic Individuals* (ed. H. Arendt and trans. R. Mannheim). New York: Harvest/HBJ Book.

Jayatilleke, K.N. (2011). *Facets of Buddhist Thought: Collected Essays*. Kandy: Buddhist Publication Society.

Jell-Bahlsen, S. (2014). The dialectics of Igbo and Christian religion in contemporary Nigeria. In: *Interface Between Igbo Theology and Christianity* (eds. A.-K. Njoku and E. Uzukwu), 51–65. Newcastle: Cambridge Scholars Publishing.

Joas, H. (2013). *The Sacredness of the Person: A New Genealogy of Human Rights*. Washington, DC: Georgetown University Press.

Jones, L. (ed.) (2005). *Encyclopedia of Religion*, 2e, 15 vols. Detroit: Macmillan.

Jonsen, A.R. and Toulmin, S. (1988). *The Abuse of Casuistry: A History of Moral Reasoning*. Berkeley: University of California Press.

Joyce, Richard, "Moral anti-realism", In *The Stanford Encyclopedia of Philosophy* (Fall 2015 Edition), (ed. E.N. Zalta), http://plato.stanford.edu/archives/fall2015/entries/moral-anti-realism (accessed 23 June 2019).

Kalupahana, D. (1976). *Buddhist Philosophy: A Historical Analysis*. Honolulu: University Press of Hawaii.

Kant, I. (1956 [1788]). *Critique of Practical Reason* (trans. L.W. Beck). Indianapolis, IN: Bobbs-Merrill.

Kant, I. (1977 [1788]). *Critique of Practical Reason* (trans. M. Gregor and intro. A. Reath)., Cambridge Texts in the History of Philosophy. Cambridge: Cambridge University Press.

Kant, I. (1997 [1785]). *Groundwork of the Metaphysics of Morals* (ed. M. Gregor and intro. C.M. Korsgaard). Cambridge: Cambridge University Press.

Kass, L. (2004). *Life, Liberty and the Defense of Dignity*. San Francisco: Encounter Books.

Kasulis, T.P. (2005). Cultural differentiation in Buddhist ethics. In: *The Blackwell Companion to Religious Ethics* (ed. W. Schweiker), 297–311. Malden, MA: Blackwell Publishing.

Kelsey, J. (2010). Response to paper for 'ethnography, anthropology, and comparative religious ethics' focus. *Journal of Religious Ethics* 38 (3): 485–493.

Kelty, M., (O.C.S.O.) (1994). Flute solo. In: *My Song is of Mercy: Writings of Matthew Kelty, Monk of Gethsemani* (ed. M. Downey), 2–72. Lanham, MD: Rowman & Littlefield.

Keown, D. (1992). *The Nature of Buddhist Ethics*. New York: Palgrave.

Keown, D. (1996). Karma, character, and consequentialism. *Journal of Religious Ethics* 24: 329–350.

Keown, D. (2005). Origins of Buddhist ethics. In: *The Blackwell Companion to Religious Ethics* (ed. W. Schweiker), 286–296. Malden, MA: Blackwell Publishing.

Kierkegaard, S. (1983). *Fear and Trembling/Repetition: Kierkegaard's Writings*, vol. 6, Rev. Ed., (ed. and trans. H.V. Hong and E.H. Hong). Princeton: Princeton University Press.

Kirk, K.E. (1934). *The Vision of God: The Christian Doctrine of the Summum Bonum*, Abr. Ed. London: Longmans, Green and Co.

Klemm, D.E. and Schweiker, W. (2008). *Religion and the Human Future: An Essay on Theological Humanism*. Oxford: Wiley Blackwell.

Korieh, C.J. (2006). African ethnicity as mirage? Historicizing the essence of the Igbo in Africa and the Atlantic diaspora. *Dialectical Anthropology* 30 (1/2): 91–118.

Korieh, C.J. (2007). Yam is king! But cassava is the mother of all crops: farming, culture, and identity in Igbo agrarian economy. *Dialectical Anthropology* 31 (1/3): 221–232.

Korsgaard, C.M. (2018). *Fellow Creatures: Our Obligations to Other Animals*. Oxford: Oxford University Press.

Kripal, J.J. (2007). *Esalen: America and the Religion of No Religion*. Chicago: University of Chicago Press.

Kuhn, T.S. (1970). *The Structure of Scientific Revolutions*, 2e. Chicago and London: University of Chicago Press.

Ladd, J. (1957). *The Structure of a Moral Code: Navaho Ethics*. Cambridge: Harvard University Press.

Laksana, A.B. (2010). Comparative theology: between identity and alterity. In: *The New Comparative Theology: Interreligious Insights from the Next Generation* (ed. F.X. Clooney, S.J.), 1–20. New York: Continuum.

Lear, J. (2008). *Radical Hope: Ethics in the Face of Cultural Devastation*. Cambridge, MA: Harvard University Press.

Leese, D. (ed.) (2009). *Brill's Encyclopedia of China*. Leiden and Boston: Brill.

Levinas, E. (1969). *Totality and Infinity: An Essay on Exteriority* (trans. A. Lingis). Pittsburgh, PA: Duquesne University Press.

Little, D. and Twiss, S.B. (1978). *Comparative Religious Ethics: A New Method.* New York: Harper and Row.

Long, C.H. (1964). The West African high god: history and religious experience. *History of Religions* 3 (2): 332–336.

Luther, M. (1961). *Martin Luther: Selections from His Writing* (ed. with Intro. J. Dillenberger). Garden City, NY: Anchor Books.

Luther, M. (1962). The estate of marriage. In: *The Christian in Society II, Luther's Works,* vol. 45 (trans. W. Brandt), 17–49. Philadelphia: Muhlenberg Press.

MacDougall, P. (2004). *The Penobscot Dance of Resistance: Tradition in the History of a People.* Durham: University of New Hampshire Press.

MacIntyre, A. (1984). *After Virtue,* 2e. Notre Dame, IN: University of Notre Dame Press.

MacIntyre, A. (1999). *Dependent Rational Animals: Why Human Beings Need the Virtues.* Peru, IL: Open Court Publishing.

Macy, J. (1990). The greening of the self. In: *Dharma Gaia: A Harvest of Essays in Buddhism and Ecology* (ed. A.H. Badiner), 53–63. Berkeley: Parallax Press.

Maddox, R.L. (1990). The recovery of theology as a practical discipline. *Theological Studies* 51: 650–672.

Magesa, L. (1997). *African Religion: Moral Traditions of Abundant Life.* Maryknoll, NY: Orbis Books.

Mahoney, J. (1989). *The Making of Moral Theology: A Study of the Roman Catholic Tradition.* Oxford: Clarendon Press.

Maimonides, M. (1963). *The Guide of the Perplexed,* vol. 1 (trans. S. Pines). Chicago and London: University of Chicago Press.

Mann, K. (2007). *Slavery and the Birth of an African City: Lagos, 1760–1900.* Bloomington: Indiana University Press.

Marty, M.E. (2005). *When Faiths Collide.* Oxford: Blackwell.

Marx, K. and Engels, F. (1978). *The Marx-Engels Reader,* 2nd rev ed. (ed. R.C. Tucker). New York: W. W. Norton & Co.

Matthews, G.B. (1997). Perplexity in Plato, Aristotle, and Tarski. *Philosophical Studies: An International Journal for Philosophy in the Analytic Tradition* 85 (2/3): 213–228.

Matthews, G.B. (1999). *Socratic Perplexity and the Nature of Philosophy.* New York and Oxford: Oxford University Press.

Mauss, M. (1922). *The Gift: Form and Function of Exchange in Archaic Societies.* London: Routledge.

Maximus the Confessor (1985). *Selected Writings* (ed. G.C. Berthold). Mahwah, NJ: Paulist Press.

McBride, B. (1999). *Women of the Dawn.* Lincoln, NE: University of Nebraska Press.

McGrath, A.E. (1990). *Understanding the Trinity.* Grand Rapids, MI: Zondervan.

McKenny, G.P. (2005). Technology. In: *The Blackwell Companion to Religious Ethics* (ed. W. Schweiker), 461–462. Malden, MA: Blackwell.

McNeill, J.T. and Gamer, H. (1990). *Medieval Handbooks of Penance: A Translation of the Principal Libri Poenitentiales*. New York: Columbia University Press.

Melville, G. (2016). *The World of Medieval Monasticism: It History and Forms of Life* (trans. J.D. Mixson). Collegeville, MN: Liturgical Press.

Midgley, M. (1993). *Can't We Make Moral Judgments?* London: Palgrave Macmillan.

Miller, R.B. (1991). *Interpretations of Conflict: Ethics, Pacifism, and the Just-War Tradition*. Chicago: University of Chicago Press.

Miller, R.B. (2016). *Friends and Other Strangers: Studies in Religion, Ethics, and Culture*. New York: Columbia University Press.

Montaigne, M.d. (1958). *The Complete Essays of Montaigne* (trans. D.M. Frame). Palo Alto: Stanford University Press.

Müller, F.M. (1894). *Buddhacarita*. In: *Sacred Books of the East*, vol. 49, 137–147. Oxford: Clarendon Press.

Murdoch, I. (1992). *Metaphysics as a Guide to Morals*. New York: Allen Lane/ Penguin Press.

Narain, A.K. (1993). Review of the dating of the historical Buddha. Die Datientng des Historischen Buddha, Part I (Symposien Zur Buddhismus Forschung, IV. I), Edited by Heinz Bechert. Gottingen: Vandenhoek & Ruprecht, 1991. *The Journal of the International Association of Buddhist Studies* 16 (1): 187–201.

Nasr, S.H., Dagli, C.K., Dakake, M.M. et al. (eds.) (2015). *The Study Quran: A New Translation and Commentary*. New York: HarperCollins.

Neiman, S. (2002). *Evil in Modern Thought: An Alternate History of Philosophy*. Princeton: Princeton University Press.

Neusner, J. (1993). Judaism. In: *Our Religions* (ed. A. Sharma), 291–356. New York: HarperCollins.

Nicolar, J. (2007). *The Life and Traditions of the Red Man* (ed. A. Kolodny). Durham: Duke University Press.

Niebuhr, H.R. (1999). *The Responsible Self: An Essay on Christian Moral Philosophy*. Louisville, KY: Westminster John Knox Press.

Niebuhr, R. (1979). *An Interpretation of Christian Ethics*. New York: Seabury Press.

Nietzsche, F. (1967). *On the Genealogy of Morals and Ecce Homo*, Reissue Ed., (ed. and trans. W. Kaufmann). New York: Random House.

Njoku, T.A.-K. (2014). Motifs from Igbo Sacred texts as primary indicators of Igbo theology and religion. In: *Interface Between Igbo Theology and Christianity* (eds. A.-K. Njoku and E. Uzukwu), 66–84. Newcastle: Cambridge Scholars Publishing.

Nmehielle, V.O. (2004). Sharia law in the northern states of Nigeria: to implement or not to implement, the constitutionality is the question. *Human Rights Quarterly* 26 (3): 730–759.

Nygren, A. (1982). *Agape and Eros*. Chicago: University of Chicago Press.

Obadare, E. (2012). A sacred duty to resist tyranny? Rethinking the role of the Catholic Church in Nigeria's struggle for democracy. *Journal of Church and State* 55 (1): 92–112.

Ogden, S. (1988). *On Theology*. New York: Harper & Row.

Olivelle, P. (2005). *Manu's Code of Law: A Critical Edition and Translation of the Mānava-Dharmaśāstra*, 103. New York: Oxford University Press.

Onwurah, E. (1989). Kinship and marriage among the Igbo of Nigeria. *Sevartham* 14 (1): 3–12.

Oraegbunam, I.K.E. (2009). The principles and practice of justice in traditional Igbo jurisprudence. *Ogirisi: A New Journal of African Studies* 6: 53–85.

Pals, D.L. (2014). *Nine Theories of Religion*, 3e. Oxford: Oxford University Press.

Payutto, P.P. (1995). *Buddhadhamma: Natural Laws and Values for Life* (trans. G.A. Olson). Albany, NY: SUNY Press.

Peters, F.E. (2005). *The Children of Abraham: Judaism, Christianity, Islam*, New Edition. Princeton, NJ: Princeton University Press.

Pinckaers, S. (1995). *The Sources of Christian Ethics* (trans. Sr. Mary Thomas Noble, O.P.). Washington, DC: Catholic University of American Press.

Plato (1952). *Gorgias* (trans. and intro. W.C. Helmbold). New York: The Library of Liberal Arts.

Plato (1984). Euthyphro. In: *The Dialogues of Plato*, vol. 1 (trans. R.E. Allen). New Haven: Yale University Press.

Plattig, M. and Baeumer, R. (1998). The desert fathers and spiritual direction. *Phronema* 13: 27–40.

Porter, J. (2005). Trajectories in Christian ethics. In: *The Blackwell Companion to Religious Ethics* (ed. W. Schweiker), 227–236. Malden, MA: Blackwell.

Porter, J. (2016). *Justice as a Virtue: A Thomistic Perspective*. Grand Rapids, MI: Wm. B. Eerdmans.

Queen, C., Prebish, C.S., and Keown, D. (eds.) (2003). *Action Dharma: New Studies in Engaged Buddhism*. London: Routledge Curzon.

Queen, C.S. and King, S.B. (eds.) (1996). *Engaged Buddhism: Buddhist Liberation Movements in Asia*. Albany: SUNY Press.

Rachels, J. and Rachels, S. (2014). *The Elements of Moral Philosophy*, 8e. New York: McGraw Hill.

Rahman, F. (1979). *Islam*, 2e. Chicago: University of Chicago Press.

Rahman, F. (1986). Islam: an overview. In: *The Encyclopedia of Religion*, vol. 7 (ed. M. Eliade), 303–322. New York: Macmillan.

Rao, A. (2009). *The Caste Question: Dalits and the Politics of Modern India*. Berkeley: University of California Press.

Rawls, J. (2005). *Political Liberalism*, 2e. New York: Columbia University Press.

Reeder, J.P. Jr. (1998). What is a religious ethic? *Journal of Religious Ethics* 25 (3): 157–181.

Ricoeur, P. (1967). *The Symbolism of Evil*. New York: Harper & Row.

Ricoeur, P. (1981). *Hermeneutics and the Human Sciences* (ed. and trans. J.B. Thompson). Cambridge: Cambridge University Press.

Ricoeur, P. (1995). *Figuring the Sacred: Religion, Narrative, and Imagination* (ed. M.I. Wallace). Minneapolis, MN: Fortress Press.

Riesebrodt, M. (2010). *The Promise of Salvation: A Theory of Religion* (trans. S. Randall). Chicago: University of Chicago Press.

Rubenstein, R.E. (2004). *Aristotle's Children: How Christians, Muslims, and Jews Rediscovered Ancient Wisdom and Illuminated the Middle Ages*. New York: Houghton, Mifflin, and Harcourt.

Rufai, S.A. (2012). A foreign faith in a Christian domain: Islam among the Igbos of Southeastern Nigeria. *Journal of Muslim Minority Affairs* 32 (3): 372–383.

Sacks, J. (2002). *The Dignity of Difference: How to Avoids the Clash of Civilizations*. New York: Continuum.

Sahlins, M. (1972). *Stone Age Economics*. Chicago: Aldine-Atherton.

Sahlins, M. (2008). *The Western Illusion of Human Nature*. Chicago: Prickly Paradigm Press.

Scheid, D.P. (2011). Saint Thomas Aquinas, the thomistic tradition, and the cosmic common good. In: *Green Discipleship: Catholic Theological Ethics and the Environment* (ed. T. Winright), 129–147. Winona, MN: Anselm Academic.

Scheid, D.P. (2016). *The Cosmic Common Good: Religious Grounds for Ecological Ethics*. Oxford and New York: Oxford University Press.

Schilbrack, K. (2013). What isn't religion? *Journal of Religion* 93 (3): 291–318.

Schleiermacher, F. (1988 [1799]). *On Religion: Speeches to Its Cultured Despisers* (trans. R. Crouter). Cambridge: Cambridge University Press.

Schmithausen, L. (1997). The early Buddhist tradition and ecological ethics. *Journal of Buddhist Ethics* 4: 1–74.

Schopenhauer, A. (2005). *The Basis of Morality*, 2e (trans. A.B. Bullock). Mineola, NY: Dover.

Schweiker, W. (1990). *Mimetic Reflections: A Study in Hermeneutics, Theology, and Ethics*. New York: Fordham University Press.

Schweiker, W. (1992). The drama of interpretation and the philosophy of religions: an essay on understanding in comparative religious ethics. In: *Discourse and Practice* (eds. F. Reynolds and D. Tracy), 263–294. Albany: SUNY Press.

Schweiker, W. (1995). *Responsibility and Christian Ethics*. Cambridge: Cambridge University Press.

Schweiker, W. (1998). *Power, Value, and Conviction: Theological Ethics in the Postmodern Age*. Cleveland, OH: Pilgrim Press.

Schweiker, W. (2004). *Theological Ethics and Global Dynamics: In the Time of Many Worlds*. Oxford: Blackwell.

Schweiker, W. (2005). On religious ethics. In: *The Blackwell Companion to Religious Ethics* (ed. W. Schweiker), 1–16. Malden, MA: Blackwell Publishing.

Schweiker, W. (ed.) (2005). *The Blackwell Companion to Religious Ethics*. Malden, MA: Blackwell.

Schweiker, W. (2006). *Humanity Before God: Contemporary Faces of Jewish, Christian, and Islamic Ethics* (eds. K. Jung and M. Johnson). Minneapolis, MN: Fortress Augsburg Press.

Schweiker, W. (2010). *Dust that Breathes: Christian Faith and the New Humanism*. Malden and Oxford: Wiley Blackwell.

Schweitzer, A. (1987). *The Philosophy of Civilization* (trans. C.T. Campion). Buffalo, NY: Prometheus Books.

Sen, A. (2006). *Identity and Violence: The Illusion of Destiny.* New York: Norton.

Sharma, A. (2012). *Problematizing Religious Freedom.* London: Springer.

Siderits, M. (2007). *Buddhism as Philosophy: An Introduction.* Indianapolis and Cambridge: Hackett Publishing.

Sidgwick, H. (1966). *The Methods of Ethics*, 7e. New York: Dover Books.

Singer, P. (2001). *Unsanctifying Human Life: Essays on Ethics* (ed. H. Kuhse). Oxford: Blackwell.

Smith, J.Z. (ed.), general ed. (1995). *The HarperCollins Dictionary of Religion.* San Francisco, CA: Harper San Francisco.

Soroush, A. (2000). *Reason, Freedom, and Democracy in Islam: The Essential Writings of Abdolkarim Soroush* (ed. and trans. M. Sadri and A. Sadri). Oxford: Oxford University Press.

Speck, F.G. (1919). Penobscot shamanism. *Memoirs of the American Anthropological Association* 6: 28, 239–283.

Speck, F.G. (1935). Penobscot tales and religious beliefs. *Journal of American Folklore* 48 (187): 1–107.

Speck, F.G. (1997 [1940]). *Penobscot Man: The Life History of a Forest Tribe in Maine.* Orono: University of Maine Press.

Spohn, W.C. (2007). *Go and Do Likewise: Jesus and Ethics.* New York: Continuum.

Spotted Elk, M. (2003). *Katahdin: Wigwam Tales of the Abnaki Tribe.* Orono: Maine Folklife Center.

Stackert, J. (2014). *A Prophet Like Moses: Prophecy, Law, and Israelite Religion.* Oxford: Oxford University Press.

Stout, J. (2004). *Democracy and Tradition.* Princeton and Oxford: Princeton University Press.

Subedi, S.P. (2003). The concept in Hinduism of 'just war. *Journal of Conflict & Security Law* 8 (2): 339–361.

Swan, L. (2001). *The Forgotten Desert Mothers: Sayings, Lives, and Stories of Early Christian Women.* Mahwah, NJ: Paulist Press.

Taylor, C. (1982). Responsibility for self. In: *Free Will* (ed. G. Watson), 11–26. Oxford: Oxford University Press.

Taylor, C. (2004). *Modern Social Imaginaries.* Durham, NC: Duke University Press.

Thanissaro, B., (1999). "Introduction" to "The Four Noble Truths." Access to Insight Library. http://www.accesstoinsight.org/lib/study/truths.html (accessed 23 June 2019).

Tierney, B. (1997). *The Idea of Natural Rights: Natural Rights, Natural Law and Church Law, 1150-1625.* Atlanta: Scholars Press.

Tierney, B. (1997). *Origins of Papal Infallibility, 1150-1350: A Study on the Concepts of Infallibility, Sovereignty, and Tradition in the Middle Ages.* Leiden: Brill.

Tillich, P. (1995). *Morality and Beyond* (foreword W. Schweiker). Louisville, KY: Westminster/John Knox Press.

Tracy, D. (1981). *The Analogical Imagination: Christian Theology and the Culture of Pluralism*. New York: Crossroad.

Tracy, D. (1996 [1975]). *Blessed Rage for Order: The New Pluralism in Theology*. Chicago: University of Chicago Press.

Troeltsch, E. (1992). *The Social Teachings of the Christian Churches*, 2 vols. Louisville, KY: Westminster John Knox Press.

Uchendu, V.C. (1965). *The Igbo of Southeast Nigeria*. New York: Holt, Rinehart and Winston.

Uchendu, V.C. (2007). Ezi Na Ulo: the extended family in Igbo civilization. *Dialectical Anthropology* 31 (1/3): 167–219.

Udoye, E.A. (2011). *Resolving the Prevailing Conflicts Between Christianity and African (Igbo) Traditional Religion Through Inculturation*. Münster: LIT Verlag.

Ufearoh, A. (2010). Ezi-Na-Ulo and Umunna: in search of democratic ideals in traditional Igbo family. *Ogirisi: A New Journal of African Studies* 9: 94–105.

Uzukwu, E.E. (1982). Igbo world and ultimate meaning and reality. *Ultimate Meaning and Reality* 5 (3): 188–209.

van Buitenen, J.A.B. (ed.) (trans.) (1978). *The Mahābārata. 4. The Book of Virāṭa 5. The Book of the Effort*. Chicago and London: University of Chicago Press.

Van Norden, B. (2012). *Virtue Ethics and Consequentialism in Early Chinese Philosophy*. Cambridge: Cambridge University Press.

van Roojen, M. (2015). *Metaethics: A Contemporary Introduction*. New York and London: Routledge.

Vaughan-Lee, L. (ed.) (2013). *Spiritual Ecology: The Cry of the Earth*. Point Reyes, CA: Golden Sufi Center.

Vroom, H. (2008). Law, Muslim majority and the implementation of Sharia in Northern Nigeria. *International Journal of Public Theology* 2: 484–500.

Walshe, M. (trans.) (1995). *The Long Discourses of the Buddha: A Translation of the Dīgha Nikāya*. Boston: Wisdom Publications.

Ward, V. and Sherlock, R. (eds.) (2017). *Religion and Terrorism: The Use of Violence in Abrahamic Monotheism*. Lanham, MD: Lexington Books.

Ware, K. (1974). The spiritual father in orthodox Christianity. *Cross Currents* (Summer/Fall): 296–313.

Warner, K.D., O.F.M. (2011). Retrieving Saint Francis: tradition and innovation for our ecological vocation. In: *Green Discipleship: Catholic Theological Ethics and the Environment* (ed. T. Winright), 122–123. Winona, MN: Anselm Academic.

Watson, G. (1986). Free agency. In: *Moral Responsibility* (ed. J.M. Fischer), 81–96. Ithaca, NY: Cornell University Press.

Weaver, D.F. (2002). *Self-Love and Christian Ethics*. Cambridge: Cambridge University Press.

Weber, M. (1949). *The Methodology of the Social Sciences* (eds. E.A. Shils and H.A. Finch). New York: Free Press.

Weimann, G.J. (2009). Divine law and local custom in Northern Nigerian zinā trials. *Die Welt des Islams* 49: 429–465.

Weithman, P. (2016). *Rawls, Political Liberalism, and Reasonable Faith.* Cambridge: Cambridge University Press.

Welton, D.M. (1897). The old testament wisdom (Chokma). *The Biblical World* 10 (3): 183–189.

Willemen, C. (trans.) (2009). *Buddhacarita: In Praise of Buddha's Acts.* Berkeley: Numata Center for Buddhist Translation and Research.

Witte, J. Jr. (1997). *From Sacrament to Contract: Marriage, Religion, and Law in the Western Tradition.* Louisville, KY: Westminster John Knox.

Wolterstorff, N. (2008). *Justice: Rights and Wrongs.* Princeton, NJ: Princeton University Press.

Yearley, L.H. (1990). *Mencius and Aquinas: Theories of Virtue and Conceptions of Courage.* Albany, NY: SUNY Press.

Zalta, Edward N. (ed.) (2014, 2015). *The Stanford Encyclopedia of Philosophy,* https://plato.stanford.edu (accessed 23 June 2019).

Index

Religious Ethics: Meaning and Method, First Edition. William Schweiker and David A. Clairmont.
© 2020 William Schweiker and David A. Clairmont. Published 2020 by John Wiley & Sons Ltd.